DEAD
RINGERS

THE **SUNY** SERIES

CULTURAL STUDIES IN CINEMA/VIDEO

WHEELER WINSTON DIXON | EDITOR

DEAD RINGERS

The Remake in Theory and Practice

edited by

JENNIFER FORREST
AND
LEONARD R. KOOS

STATE UNIVERSITY OF NEW YORK PRESS

Published by
State University of New York Press, Albany

For information, address State University of New York Press,
90 State Street, Suite 700, Albany, NY 12207

Production by Marilyn P. Semerad
Marketing by Patrick Durocher

Library of Congress Cataloging-in-Publication Data

Dead ringers : the remake in theory and practice / edited by Jennifer Forrest and Leonard
R. Koos.
   p. cm.
  Includes index.
  ISBN 0-7914-5169-0 (alk. paper) — ISBN 0-7914-5170-4 (pbk. : alk. paper)
   1. Motion picture remakes—History and criticism. I. Forrest, Jennifer, 1958– II. Koos,
Leonard R., 1958–

PN1995.9.R45 D43 2001
791.43'75—dc21
                                        2001020010

10 9 8 7 6 5 4 3 2 1

CONTENTS

ILLUSTRATIONS

ACKNOWLEDGMENTS

We would like to thank Helena Robinson and Terry Geesken of the Museum of Modern Art for their enthusiastic extra efforts in matching as closely as possible remake publicity stills with their originals, Kristine Krueger of the Academy of Motion Picture Arts and Sciences, and Rosemary C. Hanes of the Library of Congress for their help in locating rare stills for this volume's cover, and Lou Ellen Kramer of U.C.L.A.'s Film and Television Archive for all her help in organizing marathon viewings of original films and their remakes. Special thanks go to a good friend, Douglas Bell, for making possible the interview with Norman Corwin, and to Norman Corwin for allowing us into his home and onto his rather full dance card. Dudley Andrew deserves much credit for his generous encouragement of the evolution of this volume, even though the editors were unknown to him. Very warm thanks go out to James Peltz at SUNY Press for his assistance (and great sense of humor) in the earlier stages of the editing process. We would also like to recognize the editors of the University Press of New England for permission to reprint a chapter from Carolyn Ann Durham's *Double Takes: Culture and Gender in French Films and Their American Remakes* (1998), *Literature/Film Quarterly* for allowing us to publish an expanded version of Thomas Leitch's seminal 1990 essay, *Discourse* for the right to reissue Marty Roth's article from the fall 2000 edition, *Cinema Journal* for Tricia Welsch's spring 2000 essay, and *Camera Obscura* for Laura Grindstaff's spring 2001 essay.

CHAPTER ONE

Reviewing Remakes: An Introduction

JENNIFER FORREST AND LEONARD R. KOOS

> Great films are not made. They are remade!
>
> —*Stand-In* (Garnett, 1937)

In *Stand-In* (Garnett, 1937), Atterbury Dodd/Leslie Howard, the representative of the East Coast bankers who own Colossal Pictures, is sent to correct the financial mismanagement of the studio. He enters Mrs. Mack's boarding house inhabited by stand-ins, has-beens, stuntmen, and bit players and meets "Abe Lincoln" at the door. While waiting downstairs, Dodd overhears the actor wearing the familiar top hat, beard, and coat tails of the sixteenth president of the United States tell a fellow boarder, herself reduced from silent star to talkie extra, that he has been waiting for seven years for the remake of *The Battle of Gettysburg*[1] to make his comeback. That there will be a remake, he is convinced. That he uses the term "remake" locates the practice as standard in current studio production. "Abe Lincoln's" assurance that Hollywood will always return to themes of cultural, historical, and mythological importance to Americans links the remake to standard production formulas, from genre pictures to series

1

and sequels, to star vehicles that capitalize on a performer's established persona, and to imitations of others studios' successes.

Stand-In's "Abe Lincoln" could just as easily have answered the door as a cowboy, waiting for the lull in the production of Westerns to end, and determined to be prepared for when opportunity knocks. But his preparation is limited to the visual portrayal. The boarding-house scene in *Stand-In* deftly plays on the irony of an actor having assumed his role to the point of iconographically becoming Abe Lincoln, and yet who is utterly unable to remember the words to the Gettysburg Address, needing unexpected prompting from the very British Dodd. Although the viewer knows that this down-on-his-luck bit player's screen life is over, it is not only because he has forgotten his lines, nor that he is a has-been like many of the silent stars that didn't successfully make the transition to the talkies, nor even that he is no longer marketable like Lester Plum's child actress who Hollywood didn't want anymore once she grew up, but because the studios simply aren't making Civil War movies or biographies of the life of Abraham Lincoln at this time. After all, one can hardly predict when a picture will be remade. Some remakes appear within a few years of an original (*Pépé le Moko* [Duvivier, 1936] was remade two years later as *Algiers* [Cromwell, 1938]), some fifty years later as in *Down and Out in Beverly Hills* (Mazursky, 1986), the remake of *Boudu sauvé des eaux* (Renoir, 1932). "Abe Lincoln" has made the colossal error of becoming a type with very narrowly circumscribed market value. He would have done better to be a cowboy, since the Western was a very successful genre during the 1930s, and thereby lessen the margin of error in specializing in a type. However limited "Abe Lincoln" is as a type, he serves as a living symbol of the recyclable nature of film material.[2] What is clear from "Abe's" presence is that there will always be remakes, if not of *The Battle of Gettysburg*, then of some other film. His comment above all shows how much the remake was an institutionalized element of Hollywood production, and this long before the thirties.

While genre films, cycles, series, and sequels, and star persona vehicles have found their legitimate place in film theory and criticism, the same cannot be said for the remake, which, at least since the fifties, has been treated as a less than respectable Hollywood commercial practice. Remaking is far from being a uniquely American phenomenon, but because American film production has dominated world cinema since the late teens, Hollywood receives the lion's share of critical attention. The perception of Hollywood as exclusively a commercial enterprise makes its recourse to the remake reflect the worst in Western capitalist production, a type of production where catering to the tastes of a mass public entails forfeiting on film substance. Or does it?

In *Stand-In*, the caricatured foreign Hollywood director Kodolfski explains to Atterbury Dodd that the studio viewing of the "finished" but terribly flawed film *Sex and Satan* (a subgenre jungle picture) does not mean that it cannot be doctored up before release. He cries out prophetically, "Great films are not made. They are remade!"[3] Although Kodolfski is not referring to the remake per se, i.e., a new version of an older film that was commercially exhibited, he is not altogether off the mark. Some of the cinema's most important films are remakes. *The Maltese Falcon* (Huston, 1941), considered by many to be a masterpiece of the nascent *noir* mode, was the third "adaptation"[4] of the Dashiell Hammett story: *The Maltese Falcon* (Del Ruth, 1931) and *Satan Met a Lady* (Dieterle, 1936). Fritz Lang's *Scarlet Street*, his 1945 version of both Jean Renoir's *La Chienne* (1931) and his own 1944 *Woman in the Window*, can hardly be described as a bland imitation of the original. While many remakes are indeed uninspired copies of their originals—probably in proportion to the amount of uninspired "original" films produced annually—the existence of many critically acclaimed remakes hinders us from adopting as a general rule the widely accepted notion that all remakes are parasitical and not worth any critical consideration outside a political and economic evaluation of Hollywood's commercial filmmaking practices. The remake is a significant part of filmmaking both as an economic measure designed to keep production costs down *and* as an art form. Because many remakes qualify for this double status, *Dead Ringers* proposes to remove the phenomenon from the purgatory of casual reference and the summary dismissal and place it within the purview of serious film criticism.

Not all remakes are of the same order. They reflect the different historical, economic, social, political, and aesthetic conditions that make them possible. Most early cinematic remakes from 1896 to 1906 were generally indistinguishable from dupes (duplicated positive prints), others were remakings of successful films whose negatives were exhausted. The former were instrumental in the construction of cinematic norms from narrative structure to cinematic techniques, both for viewers and filmmakers. The influence of technological innovations—some would say advances—such as sound, color film, special effects (especially as concerns some genre films like the Western, the musical, and the horror film), and computer digitalization, are often the reason behind testing new (and often expensive) ground with pretested stories and storyboard breakdown. Recourse to the remake sought to counter losses incurred during the Depression. The remake helped keep some independent and Poverty Row film companies solvent during the 1930s (Taves 334). Recycling old material equally served to feed the "maw of exhibition" resulting from the major studios' block-booking. More recently, the remake reflects the competition posed to blockbuster studio productions by very successful and critically praised independent films. The remake has reappeared whenever audience attendance has been low or threatened because of the advent of rival technologies like radio, television, and video. Hollywood has always had recourse to canned projects that promised to ensure stable audience attendance more than new and riskier projects. Equally important was the major studios' investment in story properties and the desire to maximize their returns.[5] Studios owning the options for dramatization rights to a novel or play often remade a film several times. Good examples of this in-studio practice are Paramount's *Accent on Youth* (Ruggles, 1935), which it remade twice (*Mr Music* [Haydn, 1950] and *But Not for Me* [Lang, 1959]), and M-G-M's *The Last of Mrs. Cheyney* (Franklin, 1929) which was remade twice by the same studio, first under the same title in 1937 (Richard Boleslawski), and subsequently as *The Law and the Lady* (Knoph, 1951). The remake sometimes reflects a director's desire to revisit or rework themes because of what has been called "generic evolution," or because of newly available technology, or because of budgetary restrictions on the original. It can serve to fulfill the aspirations of a star who is given the opportunity to chose a project. For example, Frank Sinatra "had always been intrigued with [John] Garfield's role in *Four Daughters* [Curtiz, 1938] and indicated to the studio head [at Warner Brothers] that he'd be willing to remake that story—as a semimusical" (Druxman 59). The switch in genres, as in the shift from melodrama of *Sadie Thompson* (Walsh, 1928) and *Rain* (Milestone, 1932) to the semimusical *Miss Sadie Thompson* (Bernhardt, 1953), or from the *noir* thriller *The Asphalt Jungle* (Huston, 1950) to the Western *The Badlanders* (Daves, 1958), often reflects an effort not only to mask the source material by hiding it in another genre, but also to tap the talents of the stars carrying the vehicle: Rita Hayworth's singing voice and dancing for *Miss Sadie Thompson*, Alan Ladd's box-office draw as a cowboy for his performances in *Shane* (Stevens, 1953) and other Westerns. Whatever the case, while some remakes are demonstrably failures, others are undeniably superb, and almost all interesting for what they reveal, either about different cultures, about different directorial styles and aesthetic orientations, about class or gender perceptions, about different social-historical periods and changing audience expectations, about the dynamics of the genre film, or simply about the evolution of economic practices in the industry.

Not all remakes are even recognizable as such. Disney's animated *Beauty and the Beast* (Trousdale, 1991) resembles remarkably the conceptualization of the characters and the mise-en-scène of Jean Cocteau's 1946 film of the same name, yet we have found no reference in the press or film literature to the former being a remake of the latter. So too with the animated *The Hunchback of Notre Dame* (Trousdale, 1996), which seems to draw less from Victor Hugo's novel than from the William Dieterle 1939 version starring Charles Laughton. And the animated *Aladdin's* (Musker, 1992) direct antecedent is neither Sir Richard Burton's, nor Edward Lane's, nor John Payne's translations of *The Arabian Nights*, but *The Thief of Bagdad* (Berger, Whelan, and Powell, 1940). Some critics (and probably some copyright lawyers) would say that an animated film cannot qualify as a remake because the medium is not the same as photographic film. Indeed, we would not say that a screen version of a successful Broadway play, even when it recreates much of the play's staging, is a remake, because these are two distinct mediums. Both Cocteau and Trousdale's versions of *Beauty and the Beast*, however, are films that draw upon the same tradition of cinematic narrative construction (camera movement, editing and shot length, shot distance, etc.), and are exhibited in the same venues, significantly bridging the distance between animation and photographic film. Finally, the reformulation of these original films into an animated context further complicates matters by their generic shift to the musical format.

Remakes often do not credit their sources. Robert Ray claims that *Flying Tigers* (Miller, 1942) is "actually a remake of *Only Angels Have Wings* [Hawks, 1939], with no credit given to Hawks" (119). Indeed, he contends that Hawks "should have sued for plagiarism."[6] Ray adds that *Flying Tigers* was not alone in this full-scale lifting from Hawks; "All of the major combat films were, in effect, remakes of *Only Angels Have Wings*" (120). If we consider *Flying Tigers* alone in its chronological relation to *Only Angels Have Wings*, it is undoubtedly a remake. But in relation to other World War II combat films using Hawks's blueprint—*Destination Tokyo* (Daves, 1943), *Thirty Seconds Over Tokyo* (LeRoy, 1944), and *The Purple Heart* (Milestone, 1944), etc.—*Flying Tigers* loses its remake status and becomes the first of many actualizations of the combat film subgenre, of which *Only Angels Have Wings* serves to activate the American myth at the heart of all genre films. According to Robert Ray, the myth that structures all genre films is that of an illusory but reassuring resolution, with the viewer liberated from the necessity to choose between conflicting modes of behavior, as in the individual versus the group/community (56–57). The remake and the genre film may share precisely the ability to dramatize this familiar American paradigm, with the difference that the remake can jump from genre to genre (as in Warner's B-movie producer Bryan Foy and his ten remakes of *Tiger Shark* [Hawks, 1932]), adapting its formulaic structure to the genre at hand.

And yet, not all American remakes take their cues from typically American scenarios. In the late 1980s, Hollywood appeared to step up vigorously its remaking activity, especially of foreign films (among which French films figure prominently), and as a consequence, the accusations relating Hollywood's seemingly shameless and dishonorable commercialism to cultural piracy and political imperialism escalated. Critics jumped to reveal, if not the political agenda of the remake, then its political repercussions. While little issue is made of domestic remakes, with reviewers limiting themselves to remarks on whether the new version is better or worse than the original, remakes of foreign films are a sore spot of contention. Reviewers from both sides of the Atlantic cried out in disgust against the practice, denouncing Hollywood's rapaciousness, its plundering of ready-made foreign products in the bankruptcy of its own creative reserves. Sharon Waxman echoes many of these critiques in her summary of the average American moviemaker's viewpoint:

> For Hollywood, American moviemakers say, remakes are a way of investing in a concept that has already proved itself with an audience, in a business where millions are at stake with each movie deal. And why release a foreign original, they figure, when they can make much more money remaking it with American stars and to American tastes? (C1+)

Vincent Canby, too, points an accusing finger at the American film industry of the new Hollywood, which is actively pursuing this business tactic, and in the process "swallowing up other countries' movies with a desperation unknown in the past, and never before to such muddled effect" (2: 1+). Terrence Rafferty predicts the short-lived nature of this trend, taking for granted a general critical and popular consensus regarding his unflattering review of *Diabolique* (Chechik, 1996), the remake of Henri-Georges Clouzot's *Les Diaboliques* (1955), hoping that because *Diabolique* is "unlikely to repeat the success of 'Twelve Monkeys' and 'The Birdcage,'" it "may slightly dampen Hollywood's enthusiasm for Franco-American hybridization experiments" (102). For Rafferty, experiments in "hybridization" illustrate that such efforts can and will only end in failure, because cultural difference is the ultimate obstacle to the homogenizing culture of Hollywood. Ginette Vincendeau, for example, locates the very failure of American screenwriters to adapt *Mon Père ce héros* (Lauzier, 1991)[7] in the uniqueness of the French "family narrative," which, "far from being universal, [is] deeply rooted in cultural difference" (23). She makes the case for the untranslatability of certain "cultural" aspects of French films, aspects which their American versions brazenly assume can be made universal, citing their disappearance in the remade versions. *Point of No Return* (Badham, 1993), in her argument, replaces the "symbolic father-daughter dyad [which] is deeply rooted in both French cinema and culture," here making "Bob" and Maggie closer in age, thereby orchestrating the introduction of sexual rivalry between "Bob" and Maggie's young man. And *Sommersby* (Amiel, 1993), the remake of *Le Retour de Martin Guerre* (Vigne, 1982), "removes the fundamental point of the French film, the unknowability of an individual" (23), reconceptualizing the hero in terms of the recognizable thematic paradigm of the Western's loner. Once again, the American remake reveals its affinities with American culture as articulated in film genres. It would be safe to assume, however, that French remakes of French originals reproduce those generic qualities peculiar to the French mythical imagination found in their films, as would German remakes of German films, and so on.

   Point of No Return did not need to be reworked to fit into a familiar generic narrative, because, as Vincendeau points out, the original was already an "Americanized" French film, whose "cultural references" were those belonging to "supposedly international generic codes" (25).[8] The film's international success, she adds, should have ultimately precluded any need for a remake. On the other hand, *Le Retour de Martin Guerre*— a generic period drama, yet hardly an "Americanized" film—had remaking potential precisely because of its adaptability to the generic norms of American frontier mythology. The dynamics of the original were altered precisely in those areas that did not correspond to the norms of the American generic formula.

In her recent discussion of American remakes, Vincendeau distinguishes between American and French cinematic traditions, asserting that the former privileges "clear-cut motivation, both of causality (no loose ends) and character (good *or* evil)," whereas the principle of the latter is "ambiguity" (23). The American remake of a French/European film[9] serves to reveal this difference primarily through film endings, with the former providing a comforting resolution altogether absent in their European counterparts. The incompatibility of the two cinemas emerges equally in the dissimilar relations the remake establishes with its characters; American cinema deals in black-and-white oppositions with the neat elimination of all the grays. In this sense, the remake functions as the ideal point of cultural comparison between the two cinemas with one intended ostensibly for the supposedly naive, childlike American, the other for the ironic, adult European.

While the sociology of the original versus the remake makes for rich findings regarding the fundamental cultural differences between, for example, the French and the Americans, it compensates little for the often successful domestic and international distribution of the remake of a foreign film at the expense of the original. In his 1952 "Remade in USA," André Bazin deplores the practice of remaking that has absolutely nothing to do with the updating of an old picture and everything to do with geography (56). He cites as examples the remakes of *Pépé le Moko* (Duvivier, 1937)/*Algiers* (Cromwell, 1938), *Le Jour se lève* (Carné, 1939)/*The Long Night* (Litvak, 1947), and *Le Corbeau* (Clouzot, 1943)/*The Thirteenth Letter* (Preminger, 1951), of which only the first truly corresponds to the temporally immediate "geographic" category, the remakes of the Carné and Clouzot films appearing eight years later, and with World War II serving as the generally acknowledged demarcation, not only between two cinemas, but between two worldviews as well. For Bazin, this is clearly a case of plagiarism and economic terrorism, easily remedied by adequate distribution, a tactic that Hollywood, he adds, seems loathe to perform. He summarizes the American producers' attitude as indicative of an aggressive ideological conspiracy arising from the conclusion that the lack of success of, for example, *Le Jour se lève* in foreign markets has less to do with inadequate distribution and more to do with its divergence from American filmmaking styles. With the rights purchased, the film is then remade in Hollywood studios in the signature Hollywood style, and "throw[n] back on the market with a U.S.A. countermark" ("Remade" 56–57).[10] What Bazin finds particularly irritating is the way American producers copy the images rather than work merely from the basic storyline, as did Duvivier in his lifting of certain gangster film elements, most notably those established by Hawks's *Scarface* (1932). From the "American social mythology" of the gangster genre, Duvivier only retained universally accessible aspects of a "certain tragic romanticism of the bandit in the city" ("Remade" 57). Everything else, Bazin contends, is recast in a French sociologically specific context, that of the French imaginary of colonial North Africa. Duvivier's adoption of George Raft's coin-tossing becomes citation, while Cromwell's decision to keep the Algerian context, and his almost identical recreation of the decor are plagiarism. But truthfully, it becomes difficult to distinguish between the two practices, since one could say just as easily that *Sommersby* "rethinks" or reconceptualizes *Le Retour de Martin Guerre* in the American frontier context. And if Cromwell's remake of *Pépé le Moko* kept the French cultural bagage, it is precisely because that context corresponded to the transposition of familiar generic locales (the city for the gangster film, the frontier for the Western) to other, often exotic sites.[11] What did change in remaking *Pépé le Moko*, however, was its genre; Duvivier's pseudo-gangster film was refashioned as a romance, which in its later incarnation, *Casbah* (Berry, 1948) became a musical.

There are, of course, important considerations that Bazin has not entertained in the carbon-copying of the visuals of 1930s foreign products. First, Hollywood had become during the Classic period an international cinematic community with the arrival of foreign artists and technicians to southern California. Indeed, with the failure of multilanguage film production,[12] Hollywood invited many of these artists to come and virtually recreate their successes for the American screen. While Duvivier did not direct the American version of *Pépé le Moko*, he did direct *Lydia* (1937), his adaptation/remake of *Un Carnet de bal* (1938). Anatole Litvak directed *The Woman I Love* (1937), which is a remake of his French film *L'Equipage* (1935). And if Fritz Lang directed the remake of *La Chienne*, it is only because Jean Renoir refused. "Geographic," image-duplication remaking during the 1930s, therefore, must also be considered as both a residual practice inherited from the perspective of multilanguage film distribution as well as a realistic effort to maintain stylistic consistency in the domestic and international distribution of what was essentially a commercial film product. Robert Ray observes that the continuity system of the Classical Hollywood film aimed to efface the visible traces of style, a system that broke down considerably with the postwar introduction of style and the way it drew attention to its artificial nature (153). Foreign films prior to 1945 very often did not meet the level of craftsmanship (sound, lighting, eye-line continuity, reverse-angle shots, etc.) required of Hollywood's standardized "invisible" narrative form, nor did they conform to the ideology of what Ray calls the tension between the outlaw hero and the official hero (individual versus the social/communal code, adventure versus domesticity, the frontier versus the settlement), in which films attempt to resolve the contradictions between the two codes, ultimately favoring the outlaw over the official. Ray contends that we must recognize the role Hollywood played during the ascendancy of the Classic cinema in establishing American cinematic norms as the international standard:

> By also dominating the international market, the American Cinema insured that for the vast majority of the audience, both here and abroad, Hollywood's Classic Period films would establish the definition of the medium itself. Henceforth, different ways of making movies would appear as aberrations from some "intrinsic essence of cinema" rather than simply as alternatives to a particular form that had resulted from a unique coincidence of historical accidents—aesthetic, economic, technological, political, cultural, and even geographic. Given the economics of the medium, such a perception had immense consequences: because departures from the American Cinema's dominant paradigms risked not only commercial disaster but critical incomprehension, one form of cinema threatened to drive out all others. (26)

While Bazin complains about the image lifting that takes place in much of Hollywood's remaking of French films, and Vincendeau refers to how Hollywood remakes "streamline their source material" (23), it is not only a question of Hollywood appropriating as much from the original as possible while expending the least amount of energy and expense possible. This equally points to the formal structure of Hollywood movies themselves and the way in which Hollywood creates the seamless quality of its films, first by the "systematic subordination of every cinematic element to the interests of a movie's narrative," and second, by the effacement of conscious style in order to "establish the cinema's illusion of reality and to encourage audience identification with the characters on the screen" (Ray 32, 34). Operating on the principle that consumers buy what looks familiar, Hollywood affixes its stylistic signature in the remaking of a foreign film in order to ensure the success of its international and domestic reception. It would seem, therefore, that Hollywood in the 1930s and 1940s did not noticeably alter the visual construction of a foreign film because it was effective. It did, however, "correct" the foreign film's sub-Hollywood craftsmanship and its deviations from the familiar and highly marketable Hollywood narrative.

But this is only a partial picture. It can be inferred from Bazin and Vincendeau's critiques that audiences, special interest groups, and governments in other countries don't have any say in the types of films that are exhibited in their movie theaters, as well as not having any influence in the types of films that are made. But there is no historical or economic foundation to this claim. For example, we know that in the pre–World War II period, Germany imported only those films that were "'German' in character" (Balio 35). And while the "moral" concerns at the root of the foundation of the Hollywood Production Code are generally assumed to come exclusively from American puritanical prudishness, they actually reflect both American *and* foreign demands. For example, as Richard Maltby points out, "Hollywood's married movie stars slept in single beds [in films] to meet a requirement of the British Board of Censors," and not those of the Production Code (38). Lest sleeping arrangements seem like an insignificant modification, consider that the British Board of Censors would equally not approve any film with the slightest hint that a character was insane, a condition that radically determines the shape an entire film can take (Maltby 37). Maltby goes on to note that, in the 1930s, "More than 60 percent of domestic sales, together with virtually the entire foreign market, were made in territories under 'political censorship'" (72), circumstances which affected exhibition first, but eventually production as well, as the creation of the Production Code confirms. The same holds for today's Hollywood. Foreign censors as well as American reformers then and today look at the American films distributed worldwide as entertainment, hence as business, not as art. And as articles of popular entertainment aiming to appeal to the largest possible audience, they are held to different, stiffer moral standards than art, so as to ruffle the least amount of feathers. While American commercial films promote a distinctly American ideology, the audience helping to mold the form that ideology takes is decidedly international.

Bazin understands the dynamics of the market, acknowledging that, because half the world is accustomed to consuming films that possess a certain American flavor, America must make films that bear the made-in-the-USA label. Nevertheless, he finds that "Americanization" takes on a more menacing aspect in the misguided American industrial mentality that anything can be reproduced. According to Bazin, Hollywood producers approach foreign films according to a naive logic that presupposes that the original's success lies solely in its visual form and that the retracing of those images will undoubtedly and inevitably reproduce that success in a different market. Still, Bazin does not hold these producers entirely responsible for this strategy, acknowledging that they too are the passive representatives of the larger economic and sociological phenomenon of Americanization ("Remade" 56).

Bazin operates under the assumption that remaking is a purely American practice, his rhetoric implying that this practice is a product of the standardization of filmmaking practices and the monopolization of the world market by the American cinema during the Classic Hollywood period (1930–1945). His historical orientation is manipulated to reflect the Classic Hollywood cinema as a political apparatus, which it was and is, but willfully ignoring that remaking has taken place on both sides of the Atlantic, dating back to the birth of the cinema in 1895. European remakes escape from the pejorative judgment against remaking practices as an example of the predatory nature of capitalism when juxtaposed to the sheer quantity and scope of the international distribution of American films.[13] Because European films cannot compete or are financially and politically blocked from competing with the huge American film distribution machine, they assume a noncommercial aura. Those who cooperate with this machine by agreeing to have their films remade are seemingly forced to compromise their artistic status for the sake of staying alive in the business. Vincendeau notes that French filmmakers who coproduce in the American remake of an original French film realize that they can make more on a coproduction than they can on the original. The danger, however, is that, while they may have no other recourse than to collaborate with Hollywood in order to reap full financial benefits from their product, they may be doing an even greater disservice to their national cinema: they diminish even further the already paltry foreign distribution of French films through increasing the dominance and reception of the Hollywood narrative as the only acceptable model (24).

Most recent critiques of American remakes spring from such political considerations, primarily from the French fight to keep its national and cultural identity during negotiations for the General Agreements on Tariffs and Trade (GATT), with France trying to control the influx of

American films and their "ideology/propaganda" into its borders. Roger Cohen describes this backlash against America as the European defense against a "marauding commercialism from [a] Hollywood intent on standardizing the world's tastes at the level of 'Jurassic Park' or the techno-thrills of Sylvester Stallone in 'Cliffhanger.'" Marin Karmitz, a French film producer interviewed by Mr. Cohen states that,

> Of course the U.S. movie industry is a big business, . . . but behind the industrial aspect, there is also an ideological one. Sound and pictures have always been used for propaganda, and the real battle at the moment is over who is going to be allowed to control the world's images, and so sell a certain life style, a certain culture, certain products and certain ideas. (2: 1+)

Indeed, so great is the threat that "the conviction is clearly growing in Europe that, as the French writer Mr. [Regis] Débray puts it, 'an American monoculture would inflict a sad future on the world, one in which the planet is converted to a global supermarket where people have to choose between the local ayatollah and Coca-Cola.'" He paints the portrait of a France ideologically and economically pressured from both sides either by an extremist fundamentalism or by the tyranny of American uniformity. Such options would certainly make national and cultural integrity of primary importance to any country.

By the end of World War I, the rules for what constituted a film—film length, narrative structure, camera and lighting techniques, film speed, shot length/editing—came for the most part from the American filmmakers, who implemented the technology and the techniques that, in turn, had a tendency to make all other national cinemas seem less advanced and their product consequently less accomplished or effective in their "reproduction" of reality. Alexander Walker points out that at the end of the silent era, the American movie industry furnished "eighty-two per cent of the world's film entertainment. The foreign circulation of American-made features accounted for forty per cent of the films' total gross" (45). Although silent films had a greater capacity for communicating internationally than the new talkies, the impressive figures for the international distribution of made-in-Hollywood images supports Ray's contention that American cinema possessed a capacity for seeming more "real" than other national industries (365). Even in the United States during the early years of transition from silence to sound, the illusion of reality to which audiences were accustomed was ruptured, and audiences soon tired of technically inferior sound production. The temperamental microphone cut down on camera and actor movement, making all the more evident to audiences what they felt was the superiority of the seemingly seamless or visually superior production quality of the silents.

However, the representation of Hollywood as a rogue King Kong, bombarding the world with a certain American ideology, squeezing out weaker cinematic voices with the overwhelming output of its film product begs to be modified by a consideration of the historical factors that allowed the American cinema to get such a considerable lead on its European competitors. During the post–World War I period, while it is true that American studios controlled exhibition in the United States—they owned a significant number of first-run theaters and, thereby, controlled the networks of distribution—it is equally true that "Europeans devoted their limited capital and purchasing power to rebuilding their shattered economies; little was left to rehabilitate their home film industries" (Balio 32). And during the first decade of talking films, although America virtually lost its European market on the continent due to political disruptions, its domestic market was large enough and commercial activity relatively unfettered for the American cinema to maintain its status as the major film industry in the world.

Nevertheless, one cannot deny the depth of America's ethnocentrism and chauvinism. In the 1928 discussions by film production personnel regarding the move from silence to sound, director William C. de Mille struck a positive note and countered the doomsayers—producers, directors, actors/actresses, and technicians who feared that they would lose the royalties accruing from overseas sales—with a pep talk based on the international appeal of American products in general:

> In as much as the introduction of American films into Europe has resulted in Europeans wearing American hats and shoes and almost everything else, so we may be sure that in a couple of generations from now, all Europeans will be speaking English so that they may continue to see and understand American films. (Walker 66)

Walker adds that, "Hollywood's role as 'America's overseas empire' has seldom been as confidently stated before or since" (66). Any number of contemporary critics would undoubtedly agree.

If it is generally assumed that recent remakes of foreign films participate in American global colonization, is there any way for a remake to respect both a country's cultural integrity and a director's authenticity? Literary translation provides an interesting parallel to the problem of cultural translation to which Vincendeau refers. Literary translation falls into two different practices which the cinematic remake can be said to follow; on the one hand, *literal* translation remains faithful to the letter of the text, but loses the style intrinsic to its source text; on the other, *free* translation remains generally faithful to the spirit of a source text while adapting it to the aesthetic, moral, and cultural concerns of a target culture. While imitation of model texts from antiquity and the later classical periods was encouraged up to the end of the eighteenth century until the invention of "originality," translation has always been looked upon as a necessary but often unfortunate fact of international and intercultural communication. Free translation is especially pernicious in that it either has the capacity or actively strives to replace the original. For example, during the French Romantic period, "translation was presented not as a source but as an example: it was to function as a full-fledged original work in the target language. This was how [Alfred de] Vigny's translation [of *Othello*] was in fact received" (Woodsworth 77). In addition, there exist ideological complications in the translation from a colonized culture into the language of a colonizer in the effort to erase the cultural and linguistic differences of the other, which is more or less the critique that has been lodged against Hollywood's "imperialistic" habit of appropriating foreign films and adapting them to the Hollywood "thematic paradigm."[14] According to this paradigm, the ambiguity of Martin Guerre's identity which is central to *Le Retour de Martin Guerre*, is displaced in the remake onto the familiar image of the outlaw hero who already has a strong identity upon his arrival in the community to which he restores harmony, and then leaves (or in the case of *Sommersby*, is hung), his own code and identity intact. This version is then distributed worldwide, indoctrinating the world's imagination into American ideology. From this perspective, resistance is not only in the national/cultural "narrative patterns" to which Vincendeau refers, but as well in a Hollywood ideology that acts as a censor to values that challenge its own. Cultural difference serves as irreconcilable proof both of the indelible nature of national/cultural identity and of the vulnerability of that same identity to effacement, the first argument suiting the needs of romantic ideology, the second those of a Marxist one.

The capacity of American cinema to "colonize" through its control of the image makes the struggle between the two cultures quite imbalanced. Historically, however, industries that have been squeezed out of competition in one sector of the market normally react with a reconceptualization of their market, as in a shift from mass production to that of quality. The resistance of French narrative patterns to translation of which Vincendeau speaks ultimately calls upon the quality/quantity dichotomy, which in turn invokes the superiority of the original versus the inferiority of the copy opposition. Indeed, Terrence Rafferty makes a cultural distinction between highbrow and lowbrow viewers, between cultured and popular, between literate and illiterate, between the filmgoers of yesterday ("of the fifties") who were the "genteel subtitle readers" of Clouzot's *Les Diaboliques*, and those of today's *Diabolique* who "demand more stimulation" (102). In this scenario, not only are mainstream filmmakers predatory capitalists, but their audiences are decidedly vulgar, endowed with the short attention span of a 4-year-old child and the overactive libido of a 17-year-old boy (for whom the bodies of the film's female stars are fetishized).

The high versus low culture bias emerges characteristically in the separation of French and American moviemaking into two categories, the art film and the commercial film. France makes quality films, it is said. America is concerned with the quantity of films it produces in order to dominate and glut the market. Daniel Toscan du Plantier, the president of Unifrance, defines the two systems according to their relation to profit: "The United States is a market that reasons in terms of profit. We in France are aware of profit but not obsessed by it. We are driven by intangible values. That difference is clear in the movies we make" (Cohen B1+). Roger Cohen elaborates this position; "The French, in other words, see cinema as an art, a vehicle for the poignant exploration of emotion and ideas, passion and existential dilemmas. Hollywood, they argue, generally reduces movies to crass assemblages of gags and thrills built around a star" (B1+). Needless to say, as Pamela Falkenberg points out, publicizing a film's "art" status is in itself a form of marketing that attempts to hide its strategies, for "under capitalism, art is precisely that commodity whose exchange value depends upon its denial of its status as a commodity" (44). Indeed, the art cinema as we know it has not been a staple of European cinema from the medium's beginnings, but is a product of the postwar "fragmentation of the mass audience" into, on the one hand, the small art-house filmgoers and, on the other, the "old-fashioned, entertainment-seeking-moviegoers" (Ray 138). Richard Schickel notes that, prior to 1945, "A Renoir, a Chaplin, an Eisenstein, or a Griffith aimed for the largest possible number of viewers, at a kind of universal communication. There was no great temptation to appeal to a small group of cognoscenti" (162). The American audience may have subsequently split, but the viewers going to see European art films were not such a minority to have no influence on American cinematic trends. On the contrary, Ray observes, "in the early 1960s . . . more and more foreign movies worked their way to the top of the box-office lists" (269) forcing American filmmakers to adopt and adapt some of the European art film's visual style, most notably that of the French New Wave–like *cinéma vérité* (jump-cutting, handheld cameras, long tracking shots, rapid editing, and so forth). Ray notes, however, that this influence soon metamorphosed into empty stylization in the hands of Hollywood filmmakers.

Part of the distinction between the two cinemas—the art and the commercial—is, as Vincendeau notes, that Classical Hollywood cinematic structure is determined to a significant degree, first, by the use of stars, and second, by recourse to generic notions of story (23). French cinema, it is claimed, is less inclined to find vehicles tailored for the star, and French "art" films create the illusion that they are genre-free. In other words, Hollywood markets products that will sell, which means that persuasive packaging—reworking familiar generic formulas, providing spectacular special effects, the presence of a star (i.e., the persona such a star brings from other films)—is everything. French/European cinema, on the other hand, seemingly operates in the market only indirectly and unwillingly, its primary concern being the creation of a quality work of art whose seriousness, willingness to "realistically" address contemporary (or historical) issues, and whose open ending and stylistic discontinuity challenge the complacency and passivity of the spectator. The audience at an art film does not get a mimetic image of itself. Instead, audience members are made uncomfortable by the film's refusal to fall into familiar and reassuring patterns, ones that in genre deceptively strive to reconcile collective and personal moral contradictions. The commercial cinema is one of masks, the art cinema one of truth.

This ideological stance can be directly linked to the *Cahiers du cinéma*'s "politique des auteurs" of the early 1950s, which served to establish the art cinema in opposition to France's own Hollywood, the tradition of quality, an attack orchestrated strangely enough from references to American directors, some iconoclastic like Orson Welles, others ballplayers like John Ford, but all with distinctive cinematic signatures. According to Ray, the "politique des auteurs" of the *Cahiers du cinéma* critics was less the cause for the separation into two cinemas than a response to the already existing "gap between popular and critical tastes that originated in the fifties" (141). While the 1950s were indeed the heyday of the *ciné-club* phenomenon in France, the concept of offering specialized screenings to an informed audience originated in the 1920s in the writings of the French film theorist Louis Delluc, and with the early examples of Le Ciné-Club de France (founded in 1924 by Germaine Dulac, Jacques Feyder, and Léon Moussinac) and La Tribune Libre du Cinéma (founded in 1924 by Charles Léger). At the same time, specialized cinemas like the Studio des Ursulines, the Studio 28, L'Oeil de Paris, and the Studio des Agriculteurs began to appear in Paris, whose programs featured noncommercial, avant-garde fare, as well as, particularly in the case of the Ciné-Latin, revivals of previously released films. This tendency continued through the 1930s and, following World War II, developed extensively, such that by 1946, eighty-three Parisian *ciné-clubs* could boast membership of over 50,000 subscribers. In the late 1940s and early 1950s, the conventional *ciné-club* format of a screening followed by discussion and debate fulfilled an important goal of the process of "educat[ing] the viewer" (Pinel 41). These screenings, of course, were dominated by old films deemed worthy of multiple viewings. For Bazin in the 1950s, *ciné-clubs* were instrumental in the creation and development of a cinematic canon in which film was no longer a disposable consumer object, but rather a temporally resistant cultural product comparable to the other arts ("Reprises" 53). Although claims for the artistic status of films dates back to the early silent cinema, it is in the 1950s, at the moment that *cinéphiles* and institutionalized cinema critics emerge, that one finds oneself referring to and studying film as a mode of artistic expression.[15]

In his 1951 article, "A propos des reprises," to support his argument that film had finally come into its own, Bazin compares the relation of filmgoers of the Classic periods to the films they viewed with that of the postwar era. Unlike literature whose imaginary realm materializes in the minds of its readers, and unlike theater where old plays can be, and are very often, updated in meaningful ways through direction and set design in order to facilitate greater spectator accessibility, films are fixed, sometimes embarrassingly so, in their own social context, conventions, and outmoded technology. These factors constituted a significant impediment to a film's box-office longevity beyond its initial runs. Bazin notes that great directors responded to the dated nature of their works, reissuing some of their films by adding sound to silents (as D. W. Griffith did with *Birth of a Nation*), or by cutting or adding footage (as Abel Gance did with his *Napoléon vu par Abel Gance*), so as to make them conform to the "latest fashion," such that the relative obsolescence of its formal techniques and mise-en-scène cease to inhibit the spectator's ability to access its more essential aspects ("Reprises" 53).[16] Bazin recognizes, however, that these modernized versions were quite different fish than the earlier ones. He notes, for instance, that when Chaplin updated a film, he withdrew the original from circulation so that the two would not be in financial competition with each other. But with the emergence of the *ciné-club* audience—a critically sophisticated and realistically minded group, he suggests—such factors would no longer be an obstacle.

Bazin complains in his 1952 "Remade in USA," about the short span of time between the runs of an original French film and its American remake, joining this article ideologically together with the earlier, "A propos des reprises." Simply put, if there exists an audience for old and foreign films, then there is no need to remake. If remaking occurs, there can be no other explanation than the ruthlessness and greed of Hollywood industry executives. Bazin assumes either that the art-house group is representative of the entire cinema-going public, or that all French filmgoers belong to that group. Whatever the case, he leaves out of his assessment the "old-fashioned, entertainment-seeking moviegoer" for whom the "aging" would continue to be a barrier to the amusement experience. We should not forget that most of French film production equally falls into the latter category. As Daniel Toscan du Plantier admits, "only about 20 of the 150 French films made a year are worth watching," which probably means that only 20 can qualify for the art-film classification, the rest falling into the mainstream commercial group (Cohen 2: 1+).

The issue of financial competition, along with that of the datedness of films from prior years, reminds us that the cinema, more visibly so than any other medium, is an industry whose product's style is often made more modern in order to maintain mass-market appeal. Bazin contends that the attraction of new film releases is the way in which they avail themselves of the latest technology in order to create an even greater illusion of reality. Two recent remakings/updatings illustrate the important role played by an evolving illusion of reality. The filmmakers of the recent re-release of the *Star Wars* trilogy addressed the issue of the originals' outdated technology by beefing them up to meet the exacting tastes of the 1990s viewer, who has already been on a steady diet of sophisticated computer digitalization. And John Carpenter's *Escape from L.A.* (1996) takes the same story structure, even much the same character breakdown of *Escape from New York* (1981), and transposes them to Los Angeles, compensating for the original's modest budget and less advanced technology to bring it up to 1990s standards. Are these new films remakes or simply updatings along the lines of Chaplin's addition of sound and René Clair's and Gance's addition of new or restored footage to old films? Most would agree that the new *Star Wars* is an updating because the structure of the original is only minimally modified. *Escape from L.A.* is a remake because it is a new production, with a different cast and location, and a modified story line. Or it is a sequel? Or is it both?

Bazin subscribes to an evolutionary model of the cinema, and comments that old films, even ones from the not too distant past, draw attention to the premature obsolescence of film technology and style, thus asserting the regular if not constant mobility of cinematic conceptions of reality and, thereby, filmic aesthetics of realism. He modifies this model, however, pointing to the artificial nature of its construction. While Bazin identifies the filmgoers desire for greater and greater cinematic realism as an operative aspect of the cinema's success, he underlines the conventional, and ultimately artificial nature of what each successive period accepts for realism in the technology and the stylistic techniques currently at the industry's disposal. So in terms of the commercial cinema, if a film's story continues to have a market potential that is only unrealized because of its "technical infirmities" ("Reprises" 54), updating/remaking appears justified. But in the eyes of the art cinema audience, remaking violates the sanctity of an original work. As noted earlier, Bazin decries "stupid" Hollywood producers who desecrate the code of imitation by reproducing an original film's images, when they should be reworking the story and endowing it with a director's personal style ("Remade" 57). As a film critic with a great appreciation for the filmic art, Bazin cannot reconcile the economics of film production with the romantic notion of the inviolability of the original, a notion which most art-house patrons aggressively embrace, and this contradiction forces him, as well other critics, to make distinctions between true and false remakes, distinctions which are made to conform to a general auteurist critique.

The "true," and censurable, remake, therefore, is the film that copies the way that the original's images are presented on the screen. The "false" remake is not a remake at all but an adaptation. In a special *Ciné-mAction* edition dedicated to the study of the remake, *Le Remake et l'adaptation*,[17] Daniel Protopopoff and Michel Serceau state, for example, that Luchino Visconti, undeniably an auteur, understood while making his *Ossessione* (1942),[18] that "every remake is a new reading, a readaptation, or a reinterpretation" ("Faux remakes" 40–41). Indeed, they conclude that "everything depends in the final analysis on the stature of the director, not to mention on his/her will to be an *auteur*" (41). If a producer is behind a remake with the sole goal of capitalizing on the success of an original, they suggest, then you can be sure that the director is not an auteur, and that the result will be a plagiarized version. Fritz Lang's *Scarlet Street* (1945), a remake of Jean Renoir's *La Chienne* (1931) is an original film; John Cromwell's *Algiers* (1938), a remake of Julien Duvivier's *Pépé le Moko* (1937), however, plagiarizes shamelessly. Both, it is worth noting, make liberal use of the visual structure of the originals upon which they are based.

There exists a second type of "true" remake for the French critics. Bazin's general assessment of the legitimate modification and reissue of a film by its original author echoes the *CinémAction* contributors' acceptance of what they call the "autoremake," or the reworking by a director of his or her own material, as in Alfred Hitchcock's *The Man Who Knew Too Much* (1956) (his remake of the 1934 film of the same name), Howard Hawks's *A Song is Born* (1948) (his musical remake of the 1941 *Ball of Fire*), Leo McCarey's *An Affair to Remember* (1957) (his remake of the 1938 *Love Affair*), and Abel Gance's 1937 remake of his 1919 *J'accuse*, to name a few. According to Daniel Protopopoff, Raoul Walsh's remake of *High Sierra* (1941) with *Colorado Territory* (1949) is a legitimate remake because "he used one of his films as a starting point for an entirely separate creation, in another Hollywood style possessing its own conventions and stereotypes," such that because the backdrop of the remake is different, "no work has anything to begrudge the other" ("Panoramique" 128). As for Leo McCarey's *An Affair to Remember*, while there is neither shifting from one generic landscape to another nor substantial variation to the general story, there is nevertheless evidence of the generic evolution of what the French call the "American comedy," which can be seen in the "confrontation of the two variants" (129). Protopopoff concludes that "the autoremake is not a plagiarism, it is a legitimate remake, the best way not to betray the spirit of a film" (131). For Michel Serceau, the autoremake fits into the signature themes and "visual and narrative schemes" of an auteur such as Hitchcock: "To say that a great director always remakes the same film is yet another truism. The formula saves on the analysis of the process. A great director doesn't always remake the same film. He seeks, from different subjects and scenarios, the right fit between thematics and form, the form through which the thematics can be inscribed and expressed" ("Hitchcock" 139). In the works of another auteur, Howard Hawks, Daniel Serceau locates his signature in a repetition, defined by "a need for perfectionism, itself inseparable from a practice of innovation and the unremitting examination of events" (*"El Dorado"* 144). These examples show that a master's revisiting of old material falls into established art and literary world practices, with the latest edition welcoming comparison not only with the earlier effort, but with the artist's entire oeuvre. While the new work asserts its own identity in distinction to a first version, both old and new garner new meaning by their very intertextuality.

The same is not true, however, for the "false" remake or the literal translation because it truly enters into competition with an original, particularly in the case of remakes of foreign films. Bazin hoped back in the early 1950s that the rise of the *ciné-club* would necessitate a redefinition of the context and practice of remaking films, potentially calling for the demise of the remake that updates. With the establishment of film archives like the Cinémathèque Française (founded in 1936 by Henri Langlois and Georges Franju) and the development of the *ciné-clubs* in the late 1940s and early 1950s, an informed if not elite audience emerged, which asserted its preference for the original over the remake, ultimately demanding a kind of permanent distribution of the former while rendering unnecessary the latter ("Remade" 56). Indeed, there would be no need to remake any further, since great original films would be available for reviewing. Although Bazin's article predates television's entrance into the screenings of old films, this, too, would soon provide another avenue for the reviewing of great classics. Why would Hollywood want to remake a film that has earned recognition both for its artistic and/or commercial value, especially if it is available for rescreening?

It would seem that Bazin fairly accurately predicted the future of the remake in America, at least for the 1960s through the 1970s, because Hollywood remaking of domestic and foreign films did indeed drop off considerably during the early art cinema house and television movie years. But these were also the transitional years from the old Hollywood to the new, in which the conditions of film production and marketing underwent some restructuring to accommodate a new, younger audience. Ray notes how the 1960s and 1970s were the stage for an unprecedented re-releasing of old films such as *Gone With the Wind* (1939, re-released in 1967–68) and *The Sound of Music* (1965, re-released in 1973); where Hollywood would normally have remade, it reissued. In addition, from 1966 to 1977, Hollywood was engaged in the greatest production of sequels ever, a practice that, like early cinematic serials, have strong family ties to the remake, and in some instances are linked together as a phenomenon (262). He comments that, whereas Classic Hollywood had "relegated outright sequels to the B-movie ranks, preferring to build on major hits by casting the same performers as similar, but different, characters (1942's *Casablanca* became 1944's *Passage to Marseille*, 1944's *To Have and Have Not* became 1946's *The Big Sleep*), the New Hollywood appeared far less flexible, depending to an extraordinary extent on 'continuations' of successful films," such that "one-third of the 220 leading money-makers were either sequels themselves or films that prompted sequels" (262). Furthermore, American cinema underwent a change in guard from the directors of the old to the new Hollywood, as well as the end of the old studio system (Ray 266–67). Finally, influenced by the success of the French New Wave's stylistic innovations, Hollywood was engaged in meeting the needs of the "fragmented" postwar audience, making the creation of new versions of old films inadequate to the task at hand. In one sense one could say that the New Wave had already tested the waters near which Hollywood itself would never have ventured alone.

As mentioned earlier, since the mid-1980s, we have been experiencing a resurgence of remaking activity. In his study of the transition years from silent to sound cinema, Alexander Walker comments that, "At the best of times Hollywood is not really a creative place: it is an imitative industry in which only a few creative people are tolerated at any one time. What is imitated is the last big success; and in these jittery times [the transition period from silence to sound], one man's success the night before could be another man's imitation the morning after" (139). The "jittery times" that presently worry the major studios result from competition coming from the critically and often financially successful independent film, as well as the astronomical costs needed for producing, marketing, and distributing a film. It is no wonder that Hollywood's battle tactic has been to resort to the plundering of ready-made foreign projects. For Vincendeau and many others, such business practices reflect Hollywood's eternal quest for production efficiency: why build a project from its unstable conceptual stages when one can eliminate costly product development by starting with pretested material (24)?

Vincendeau's reference to greedy executives who are "too busy to read scripts" is perhaps too facile an explanation, reflecting an ideological preoccupation with the way films are made in the United States, without consideration for the box-office voting power of the filmgoing audience in the production of a certain kind of film. For Bazin and other foreign critics, American audiences are the passive consumers of the "Americanization" phenomenon, incapable of desiring anything except that which Hollywood has trained them to crave—the "seamless" Hollywood film— a seamlessness whose violation begins only with the foreign film's language barrier.

One solution to remaking that has been proposed from many quarters is to dub foreign pictures entering the United States, so as to allow them to compete on similar turf. Europe was introduced to the dubbed film during the 1930s. American producers discovered that dubbing was a significantly cheaper alternative to the foreign-language version, as well as having the benefit of retaining the "commercial value of the Hollywood stars" (Balio 33–34). While French/European audiences adapted remarkably well to dubbing, the contrary has certainly been true for Americans. American resistance to dubbing has been ridiculed as just one more sign of the American filmgoer's lack of sophistication, especially when compared to the European's purported culturally superior approach to foreign subjects. Following this line of thought, the emergence of an America receptive to dubbing would therefore point to a movement away from American small town isolation toward a more cosmopolitan attitude. In Roger Cohen's discussion of the remake dilemma, he quotes David Seale, president of American Multi-Cinema, as believing that dubbing's time has finally arrived in America: "the great American suburban middle class has been changed by wider travel and extensive immigration and could now take to dubbed French movies en masse" (B1+).[19] According to this reasoning, all that has been holding back Americans from embracing the dubbed film is their lack of exposure to other cultures. But American audiences may be too much the pawns of the Hollywood technical illusion of reality to ever accept dubbing as an alternative to remaking, primarily because of the way dubbing draws attention to the artificial nature of the film, impeding the seamless illusion of reality provided by the cinematic experience. Thomas Elsaesser isolates the problem of the dubbed film:

Sound, whether musical or verbal, acts first of all to give the illusion of depth to the moving image, and by helping to create the third dimension of the spectacle, dialogue becomes a scenic element, along with more directly visual means of the mise-en-scène. Anyone who has ever had the bad luck of watching a Hollywood movie dubbed into French or German will know how important diction is to the emotional resonance and dramatic continuity. Dubbing makes the best picture seem visually flat and dramatically out of sync: it destroys the flow on which the coherence of the illusionist spectacle is built. (359–60)

Indeed, anyone who has seen a Hollywood film dubbed into French will remark how the flat sound unveils the illusory harmonious marriage of cinematic image and sound that the filmmakers are at such pains to hide. Ray notes that, in contradistinction to the identification with characters that the theater demands of its patrons, the Classic Hollywood cinema demanded much more: "Hollywood cinema's illusion of reality depended on a far more substantial identification with the film's whole diegesis, that non-existent, fictional space fabricated out of temporal and spatial fragments, which came to seem more rich, interesting, and fully constituted than the actual, material space of the audience's own lives" (38). The new Hollywood continues this tradition, and dubbing works only to fragment irreparably the "rich, interesting, and fully constituted" cinematic space. Lest the reader be tempted to concur with European critics that, because America refuses to embrace the dubbed film, the American filmgoer is either a shameless collaborator in Hollywood's colonization of the world, or a hopelessly passive rube incapable of adapting to the "self-conscious" film, it must not be forgotten that dubbing has no relation whatsoever to the "self-conscious" film's construction. Rather, dubbing belongs to postproduction practices linked with distribution and exhibition. Since European audiences have been accustomed to the dubbed film since the era of the early talkies, dubbing merely constitutes yet another convention of film viewing, one that creates for the European an acceptable illusion of reality.

Given the nature of the beast, the scope of this study of the remake is necessarily limited. *Dead Ringers* responds immediately to the historical contextualization of the phenomenon as it took form during the late 1980s and the 1990s. Critics painted the portrait of Hollywood as cultural predator. But as Robert A. and Gwendalyn Wright Nowlan's reference work *Cinema Sequels and Remakes* (1989) demonstrates, every national cinema remakes its own and other nations' films. And every national cinema has cultural and historical traditions that engender their own generic conventions and expectations. The recent phenomenon of the Hong Kong cinematic remake, for example, is a rich field meriting fuller critical attention, especially, as Patricia Aufderheide notes in "Made in Hong Kong: Translation and Transmutation," part of Hong Kong's "cultural uniqueness" is that its "national cinema has always been commercially successful" not only locally, but internationally as well (192). Conversely, while like most foreign cultures it has been influenced by the all-pervasive American film, whose narratives it borrows (as in Samo Hung's disguised political critique of communism in *Eastern Condors* [1986], for example) and often parodies, Hong Kong cinema will imitate any international success, American or otherwise, as well as plumb the well of its own cinematic traditions. From a different cultural perspective, Andrew Horton shows how Emir Kusturica's "remaking" of Francis Ford Coppola's *Godfather* and *Godfather II* (as representative of the dominant cinema) with *Time of the Gypsies* (1989), along with his references to film traditions from his own nation, from Classical Hollywood, and world cinema serves to legitimize Yugoslavian cinema, to certify it as a "member of a club that includes not only Hollywood but world cinema itself" (179, 181). The remake is an underexplored subject warranting a more systematic treatment in terms of individual national, cultural, and cross-cultural traditions, as well as their relation to an international commercial cinema dominated by Hollywood productions.

Dead Ringers is heavily weighted toward an examination of American remakes, particularly those of French films. As previously noted in this introduction, film criticism of the past ten years has taken Hollywood to task for what has been identified as American cinema's rapacious remaking frenzy. At no other time in cinema history, it has been argued, has Hollywood revealed so clearly its lack of commitment to developing fresh creative products than in its pursuit of the ready-made film package. In their attack on Hollywood's marketing strategies, European and American critics alike have treated the practice exclusively in terms of the Euro-American circuit: when Hollywood isn't remaking films from its own archives, it is looking toward Europe, in particular France. Vincent

Canby's "Movies Lost in Translation" (1989), Sharon Waxman's "A Matter of Deja View: French Cry Faux Over U.S. Film Remakes" (1993), Michael Williams and Christian Mork's "Remake Stakes Are Up: H[olly]wood Hastens Pursuit of French Pic[ture] Properties" (1993), Roger Cohen's "Aux Armes! France Rallies to Battle Sly and T. Rex" (1994), and Josh Young's "The Best French Films You'll Never See" (1994) are not a country-specific sampling of the articles on remakes appearing in the popular press: they are almost without exception the only types of popular press articles critiquing the remake. This France/Hollywood exchange indicates a narrow debate that initially reflects many of the concerns touched upon during the GATT negotiations of the last decade (with France once again playing a preponderantly large role in the talks). Equally at play are the dynamics of the polarity America, worldwide representative of popular culture, and France, age-old representative of high culture. America does new versions of old films, France does new adaptations of classic novels, because, for the French, "from remake to plagiarism, the distance is not great, and the plagiarist is discredited in a society like ours which idolizes innovation and banishes imitation" (Mouren 90). Ironically, while American films cite a remake's origins in a written not a filmic text because of the Copyright Statute, French films do the same, but so as to invite comparison, not with previous adaptations, but with the "book itself which everyone knows." If forced to do remakes, notes Yannick Mouren, French auteur directors will only make a film adaptation of a work of literature (93). Finally, if America remakes more French films than films from any other nation, it is most assuredly because not only does France produce the greatest number of films in Europe, it is second to the United States in film production in the West. While occasionally an American director will decide to remake a classic or influential French film (e.g., William Friedkin's *Sorcerer* [1977], the remake of Henri-Georges Clouzot's *Le Salaire de la peur* [1953], and Jim McBride's *Breathless* [1983], his remake of Jean-Luc Godard's *A Bout de Souffle* [1959]), the large majority of remakes are of popular comedies whose writer/directors do not possess elite auteur membership, Francis Veber being the most notable example (*Le Grand Blond avec une chaussure noire* [1972]/ *The Man With One Red Shoe* [Dragoti, 1985], *La Chèvre* [1981]/*Pure Luck* [Tass, 1991], *Les Compères* [1983]/*Fathers' Day* [Reitman, 1997]), *Les Fugitifs* [1986]/*Three Fugitives* [Veber, 1989]). In *Double Takes: Culture and Gender in French Films and Their American Remakes* Carolyn A. Durham rejects the standard theories explaining the American penchant for remaking French films and proposes that Hollywood is "attracted to foreign films precisely to the extent that they resist foreignness and represent concerns and interests fully consistent with the cultural climate of the United States" (200). Those culturally specific elements that are foreign to the American cultural experience usually disappear in the remake. What remains are those parts that are perceived by their makers as "universal" and "transcultural" (Durham 23). The question arises, Is the ethnocentrism of American remakers so deep as to confuse American cultural specificity with universal concerns? Perhaps, and yet such a generalization is problematic when one considers the foreign markets which make Hollywood films the unchallenged leader in international distribution. Foreign censorship is not just a memory from the 1930s, when, for example, the Japanese "eliminated all scenes of kissing, and the British cut references to the Deity and religious sacrements, as well as scenes judged to depict cruelty to animals," while others cut parts deemed politically seditious (Sklar 224–25).

Haranguing Hollywood along purely ideological lines of industrial-commercial imperialism only serves to hide the pervasiveness of remaking as a general cinematic practice, regardless of country of origin. Without the benefits of the larger picture, this view can be nothing but limited and therefore distorting. While the politics of the remake do contribute immeasurably to an understanding of the practice, a political dimension alone hinders a systematic evaluation, for example, of the prominent historical and aesthetic role of the remake from the cinema's beginnings to Classic Hollywood cinema—perhaps the richest period in both original and remade productions—to the 1950s' remake of 1930s' Classic films, to the recent rash of remakes—this too taking place during a period particularly rich in the successfully competitive production of independent films. Equally lost in this criticism of Hollywood's ideological contamination are the constantly evolving relationship and the fruitful exchange between the remake and other films, not to mention film genres. As Jacqueline Nacache argues, the relationship between remakes and originals is "neither their resemblance nor their dissimilarity, but an intense *circulation* of images, of ideas, of words . . . in a *system of exchange* which leaves aside aesthetic evaluations, cultural classifications, and critical nostalgia, and brings to light . . . this system of *communicating vases* which characterize so intimately Hollywoodian narrative and aesthetics" (80). But the "system of exchange" is hardly restricted to the relationship between remakes and their originals, for as Claire Vassé notes, all remakes participate in that quality which all works of art share: the "intertextual dimension" (85). Vassé, like Nacache and Durham, recommends that one abandon "value judgments" in order to let both remake and original unveil the mutual "enrichment" that only emerges from a juxtaposition of the two (89). While the spectator is far from obligated to compare the two works, much less know of the other film's existence, his or her experience is nevertheless fullest in the discovery of those seemingly insignificant elements that one film can highlight about the other and vice versa.

Finally, while it is very convincing to discuss the American remake of foreign films in terms of the theft of the integrity of other national identities, as well as in terms of Hollywood's effort to standardize, Coca-Cola-ize the world, this position facilitates the convenient omission of other cultures from such "reprehensible" practices. We are led to believe that European films adapt, readapt, cite, pay homage to, parody, but do not remake, the former activities being linked to artistic and literary traditions of high culture, the latter being representative of American films and their ties to commerce and commercial interests. And yet Werner Herzog's claim that his *Nosferatu the Vampyre* (1979) is not a remake of F. W. Murnau's *Nosferatu* (1922) "in the American sense of the word" prompts Raphaël Millet to query sarcastically, "Would there be a European sense of the word 'remake'? A noble version?" (98). Millet counters incredulously Herzog's assertion, stating for the record that the film is "a step by step, shot for shot remake of Murnau's *Nosferatu*," in the American sense of the word (97). The cry against remaking is loudest when the original film falls into the art category. How, critics wonder, could a producer even think of remaking great films like *Les Diaboliques* (Clouzot, 1955)[20] or *Red Dust* (Fleming, 1932)? And yet, the made-for-television movie *Reflections of Murder* (Badham, 1973) is considered a first-rate version of *Les Diaboliques*, as is John Ford's remake of *Red Dust* with *Mogambo* (1953). The outrage at the American remaking of foreign films especially leads one to assume that foreign pictures automatically merit art status, feeding off the art cinema's ability to pass itself off as a noncommodity. The truth, however, is that every national cinema in the West, and probably in the East as well, remakes both its own films and those of other countries; every national cinema is both a business *and* a producer of art. The remake is integral to an understanding of the relation between the two positions.

The timeliness of a serious study of the remake cannot be denied, since, as has been shown, it has been the subject of many articles in the press for the last nine years. And not surprisingly, since the manuscript for this book was finished, two books devoted to the remake have appeared, Carolyn A. Durham's *Double Takes: Culture and Gender in French Films and Their American Remakes* (1998), a modified chapter of which is reprinted in this volume, and Andrew Horton and Stuart McDougal's *Play It Again Sam: Retakes on Remakes* (1998). The former treats exclusively American remakes and their French originals, while the latter embraces the phenomenon in the broadest use of the term: American remakes of American films, cross-cultural remakes, cultural myths in film and comic books, citation, allusion, and homage, the television to screen transition, as well as screen to radio. As well, the editors of the French journal *Positif* devoted their May and June 1999 issues to an exploration of the remake, almost a follow-up a decade later to the *Ciné-mAction* (1989) issue on the same theme. Contrary to the 1989 effort, *Positif*'s June issue calls almost unanimously for an appraisal of the aesthetics and poetics of the remake as a legitimate artistic practice; the May issue, however, reheats and re-serves the same anti-American/Hollywood hash. In addition, there are several reference works which anticipated and facilitated the recent scholarly treatments of the topic: Michael B. Druxman's *Make It Again, Sam: A Survey of Movie Remakes* (1975), James L. Limbacher's *Haven't I Seen You Somewhere Before? Remakes, Sequels, and Series in Motion Pictures and Television, 1896–1978*, and Robert A. and Gwendolyn Wright Nowlan's *Cinema Sequels and Remakes, 1903–1987* (1989).

While a number of critics and reviewers pray regularly for the death of the lowly remake, the history of the practice points to its centrality and longevity in filmmaking, not to mention that a significant number of the cinema's most important films have been remakes. The remake highlights more than any other type of film the double nature of the cinema—movie studios manufacture commercial products destined for an "innocent" mass public, as well as create moving works of art destined for a more discerning and sophisticated public, often in the same package. The remake also forces us, both audience and critics, to confront our ambivalence toward its reflexivity, toward its ability to unmask its commercial underpinnings *and* to reveal its links to either traditional or postmodern art practices by inviting comparison with a work's earlier incarnations.

NOTES

1. *The Battle of Gettysburg* was directed by Thomas Ince in 1913. We have found no reference to remakes of that particular film. *Stand-In's* reference to seven years since an original film could technically apply to the United Artist's production *Abraham Lincoln* (1930). "Abe Lincoln" might be alluding less to a remake of a particular film per se than to the Civil War genre films of the early teens. World War I provided a new source of film subjects such that the Civil War film was replaced with the more generic war film (Koszarski 186).

2. Although credited remakes of a film rarely go beyond two or three versions, there are some notable exceptions. A truly successful plot formula can have seemingly limitless recycling potential. Kenneth Macgowan states that "producer Bryan Foy boasts that he used the plot of *Tiger Shark* (1932) successfully in ten other films by changing the title, the locale of the story, and the names of the characters" (344). Indeed, in *1997 Movie & Video Guide*, Leonard Maltin et al. note that the plot of Hawks's original was "reused several times (*Slim, Manpower,* etc.)." In instances of repeatedly used plot formulas such as this, such similarities in theme are constitutive of subgenres.

3. This statement is supported by actual production practice. Tino Balio points out that "[Irving] Thalberg treated the finished film as raw material. Thalberg was noted for testing audience reaction to his films before they were released. If audiences did not like something or failed to respond in the appropriate way, he did not hesitate to have parts of the picture reshot" (75). Ernst Lubitsch, too, used a similar approach during his tenure as production chief at Paramount (Balio 79).

4. Leonard Maltin's *1997 Movie & Video Guide* invariably uses the term "remake" for less than satisfying, if not disappointing, films. He and his editorial staff, however, speak of adaptations and versions for the better variety of remakes; they state in passing that *Scarlet Street* was "filmed earlier by Renoir," or that *Miss Sadie Thompson* was "previously made as" *Sadie Thompson* and *Dirty Gertie From Harlem.* But *Point of No Return* is an "awful, slicked-up Hollywoodization" and a "pointless rehash" of *La Femme Nikita,* and Blake Edwards's *The Man Who Loved Women* (1983) is a "lackluster, snail's pace remake" of the François Truffaut film of the same name. The quality of the "good" remake lets the film assume title to authenticity and originality. The "bad" remake is just more proof of the repetition that mars the Hollywood commercial film.

5. Studios did not generally reuse properties that were the most expensive because "they were by definition easily recognizable by many people and therefore were likely to make audiences feel cheated if reused." Instead, recycled subjects

belonged primarily to the B movies, the originals being B films that were not great box-office successes, and therefore did not risk being remembered by a great number of the viewing patrons (Balio 100).

6. *Flight From Glory* (Landers, 1937) tells a strikingly similar tale to *Only Angels Have Wings*, making it potentially the "original" for Hawks's later film, thereby seriously undermining Ray's argument about its role as a prototype for WWII combat films. Hawks was not unfamiliar with the territory, having remade *The Front Page* (Milestone, 1931) with *His Girl Friday* (1940), and *Ball of Fire* (1941) with *A Song is Born* (1948).

7. *My Father, the Hero* (Miner, 1994) was made and released after Vincendeau's article.

8. Vincendeau equates international generic codes with the American commercial cinema, drawing attention to the dominance of American cinema in the international arena.

9. Hollywood in 1980s and 1990s seems to predominantly remake French films. Whether this has to do with the content of French films, the perception of an inherent quality, or the quantity of French films produced as compared to the rest of Europe has yet to be determined.

10. All translations from the French are the authors'.

11. Hollywood films have frequently taken the Middle East and North Africa as locales. *Morocco* (Von Sternberg, 1930), *Cairo* (W.S. Van Dyke II, 1942), *Background to Danger* (Walsh, 1943), and *Sirocco* (Bernhardt, 1951) are just some examples of the scope and general appeal of the exoticism of Middle Eastern and North African cultures to American audiences.

12. During the golden years of silent film production, America outproduced all other national cinemas, putting out roughly 700 films per year (Sklar 217). Understandably, sound films threatened the American hold on the international film market. In response, some studios conceived of multiple-language films, in which "complete foreign casts were assembled to make duplicate performances of American features, taking over the sets as soon as the English-language players were finished with them" (222). Paramount's multiple-language film studio was located in Paris, and in 1930, it produced "sixty-six features in twelve different languages." The venture failed because of the Depression. Interestingly, Otto Preminger revived the multiple-language film in 1953 with *The Moon is Blue*, which was filmed simultaneously in German.

13. Proportionally, however, their remaking activities may be just about the same. Statistical analysis of the production of remakes on both sides of the Atlantic warrants further attention.

14. We are using the term introduced by Robert B. Ray in *A Certain Tendency of the Hollywood Cinema, 1930–1980.*

15. The terminological association of art and cinema in France would seem to originate with André Calmettes's 1908 film *L'Assassinat du Duc de Guise* featuring the famous Comédie Française actor Charles Le Bargy. Although christened a "film d'art," this term before the 1920s often meant little more than the participation of renowned actors from the legitimate stage in the film production. In 1911, the Italian poet, Ricciotto Canudo, published in France his "Manifeste des sept arts," identifying cinema as the seventh art, an appellation that would become synonymous with the medium during the 1920s.

16. In the transition from silence to sound, talkies suddenly made silent films seem technologically ancient, and many Hollywood studios responded by "pulling some silent films out of exhibition to give them the new wonder ingredient" (Walker 91).

17. There exists an earlier body of work on the remake in a special edition of *Segnocinema* number 15 (November 1984).

18. This was the second of four treatments of James M. Cain's *The Postman Always Rings Twice*: *Le Dernier Tournant* (Chenal, 1939), *The Postman Always Rings Twice* (Garnett, 1946), and *The Postman Always Rings Twice* (Rafelson, 1981).

19. Janet Maslin reviews *Jungle 2 Jungle* (Pasquin, 1997), the American remake of *Un Indien dans la ville/Little Indian, Big City* (Palud, 1994), and notes how the French original was distributed in the United States by Disney in a dubbed version. It is difficult to ascertain whether the film's lack of success in the United States is because it was "badly dubbed" or whether because the film, although it enjoyed a phenomenal success in France, is in reality a "dismal French comedy" (B3).

20. *Les Diaboliques* has been remade three times: twice for television, *Reflections of Murder* (Badham, 1973) and *House of Secrets* (Leder, 1993), once for the cinema, *Diabolique* (Chechik, 1996).

WORKS CITED

Aufderheide, Patricia. "Made in Hong Kong: Translation and Transmutation." Horton and McDougal 191–99.

Balio, Tino, ed. *Grand Design: Hollywood as a Modern Business Enterprise, 1930–1939.* Berkeley: U of California P, 1993. Vol. 5 of *History of the American Cinema.* 6 vols. 1990–99.

Bazin, André. "A propos des reprises." *Cahiers du cinéma* 1.5 (September 1951): 52–56.

———. "Remade in USA." *Cahiers du cinéma* 2.11 (April 1952): 54–59.

Canby, Vincent. "Movies Lost in Translation." *New York Times* 12 Feb. 1989: B1+.

Cohen, Roger. "Aux Armes! France Rallies to Battle Sly and T. Rex." *New York Times* 2 Jan. 1994: B1+.

Delisle, Jean and Judith Woodsworth. *Translators Through History.* Amsterdam: John Benjamins, 1995.

Druxman, Michael B. *Make It Again, Sam: A Survey of Movie Remakes.* South Brunswick: A. S. Barnes, 1975.

Durham, Carolyn A. *Double Takes: Culture and Gender in French Films and Their American Remakes.* Hanover: UP of New England, 1998.

Elsaesser, Thomas. "Tales of Sound and Fury: Observations on the Family Melodrama." Grant 350–80.

Falkenberg, Pamela. "'Hollywood' and the 'Art Cinema' as a Bipolar Modeling System." *Wide Angle* 7.3 (1985): 44–53.

Grant, Barry Keith, ed. *Film Genre Reader II.* Austin: U of Texas P, 1995.

Hirsch, Foster. *The Dark Side of the Screen: Film Noir.* New York: Da Capo, 1981.

Horton, Andrew. "Cinematic Makeovers and Cultural Border Crossings: Kusturica's *Time of the Gypsies* and Coppola's *Godfather* and *Godfather II.*" Horton and McDougal 172–90.

Horton, Andrew, and Stuart Y. McDougal, eds. *Play It Again, Sam: Retakes on Remakes.* Berkeley: U of California P, 1998.

Koszarski, Richard. *An Evening's Entertainment: The Age of the Silent Feature Picture, 1915–1928.* Berkeley: U of California P, 1990. Vol. 3 of *History of the American Cinema.* 6 vols. 1990–99.

Macgowan, Kenneth. *Behind the Screen: The History and Techniques of the Motion Picture.* New York: Dell, 1965.

Maltby, Richard. "The Production Code and the Hays Office." Balio 37–72.

Maslin, Janet. "Dad and Son Become Bonding Buddies." *New York Times* 7 March 1997: B3.

Millet, Raphaël. "Non, Nosferatu n'est pas mort: Toujours à trainer dans les courants d'air. . . ." *Positif* 460 (June 1999): 97–99.

Mouren, Yannick. "Remake Made in France." *Positif* 460 (June 1999): 90–94.

Nacache, Jacqueline. "Comment penser les remakes américains?" *Positif* 460 (June 1999): 76–80.

Pinel, Vincent. *Introduction au ciné-club: Histoire, théorie, pratique du ciné-club en France.* Paris: Les Editions Ouvrières, 1964.

Protopopoff, Daniel. "Panoramique sur le phénomène." Serceau and Protopopoff 127–31.

Protopopoff, Daniel, and Michel Serceau. "Faux remakes et vraies adaptations." Serceau and Protopopoff 37–45.

Rafferty, Terrence. "Sisters and Brothers: 'Diabolique' redux, and 'A Family Thing.'" *New Yorker* 1 April 1996: 102–03.

Ray, Robert B. *A Certain Tendency of the Hollywood Cinema, 1930–1980.* Princeton: Princeton UP, 1985.

Schickel, Richard. *Movies: The History of an Art and an Institution.* New York: Basic Books, 1964.

Serceau, Michel. "Alfred Hitchcock: L'Image à la rencontre de l'idée." Serceau and Protopopoff 133–39.

———. "*El Dorado* est-il un autoremake de *Rio Bravo*?" Serceau and Protopopoff 141–47.

Serceau, Michel, and Daniel Protopopoff, eds. *Le Remake et l'adaptation.* Paris: CinémAction, 1989.

Taves, Brian. "The B Film: Hollywood's Other Half." Balio 313–50.

Vassé, Claire. "L'Art de la bigamie." *Positif* 460 (June 1999): 85–9.

Vincendeau, Ginette. "Hijacked." *Sight and Sound* 23.7 (July 1993): 23–25.

Walker, Alexander. *The Shattered Silents: How the Talkies Came to Stay.* New York: William Morrow, 1979.

Waxman, Sharon. "A Matter of Deja View: French Cry Faux Over U.S. Film Remakes." *Washington Post* 15 July 1993: C1+.

Weinraub, Bernard. "Studios Smarting From Oscars Snub of Hollywood Fare." *New York Times* 17 February 1997: A1+.

Williams, Michael, and Christian Mork. "Remake Stakes Are Up: Hollywood Hastens Pursuit of French Pic Properties." *Daily Variety* 19 April 1993: 5+.

Woodsworth, Judith et al. "Translators and the Emergence of National Literatures." Delisle and Woodsworth 67–98.

Young, Josh. "The Best French Films You'll Never See." *New York Times* 30 October 1994: H17+.

CHAPTER TWO

Twice-Told Tales: Disavowal and the Rhetoric of the Remake

THOMAS LEITCH

At first glance movie remakes—new versions of old movies—may seem no different from other film adaptations of earlier material. But the peculiar nature of the relationships they establish with their earlier models and with their audience makes them unique among Hollywood films, and indeed among all the different kinds of narrative. Short stories and novels are often adapted for stage or screen; ballets are sometimes recreated or rechoreographed; comic strips are occasionally revived by new artists; plays are reinterpreted by each new set of performers; but only movies are remade. The film industry does not have a logical monopoly on remakes, since a given story, for instance, can inspire two or more dramatic adaptations, but the industry's, and especially Hollywood's, voracious appetite for material has produced a series of utterly characteristic twice-told tales with no close analogue in or outside the movies. Only remakes are remakes.

The theoretical problems raised by remakes have seldom been remarked. In the standard survey of Hollywood remakes, *Make It Again, Sam*, Michael B. Druxman gives no attention to the peculiar textual and intertextual status of the pairs of films he is considering. Nor does his emphasis on Hollywood remakes of earlier Hollywood films allow him to consider a phenomenon that has become far more frequent since he wrote: the explosion of American remakes of foreign films, usually European (largely French) films repackaged for American audiences, who are presumably attracted by the aura of these films—the favorable critical reception they may have received, their intellectual cachet, their prestige value—but who are more inclined to sit through a version with familiar stars speaking a familiar language. Despite the continued appearance of what we might call archival remakes—*Stella* (Erman, 1990), *The Last of the Mohicans* (Mann, 1992), *Little Women* (Armstrong, 1994), *Sabrina* (Pollack, 1995)—Hollywood recyclers have turned their attention in recent years more and more insistently abroad. Although the political issues raised by Hollywood remakes of Hollywood originals and by American remakes of foreign films are very different, I want to focus in this essay on the textuality of archival remakes because I believe the rhetoric of these films can profitably be used to illustrate the rhetorical problems all remakes set themselves, to construct an elementary taxonomy of remakes, to consider the trope of disavowal in the textual status of all remakes, and to explore the importance of this disavowal for a general theory of intertextuality.

The uniqueness of the film remake, a movie based on another movie, or competing with another movie based on the same property, is indicated by the word *property*. Every film adaptation is defined by its legally sanctioned use of material from an earlier model, whose adaptation rights the producers have customarily purchased. Adaptation rights are something the producers of the original work are held to have a right to sell, with the understanding either that their sale will not impair the economic potential of the original property (a film-rights sale may actually increase the number of copies of a novel printed and sold) or that the price of purchasing adaptation rights reflects the probable loss of the original property's appeal (as in the case of musicals, whose runs are normally killed by the appearance of a film version). But of all the different types of adaptations, only remakes compete directly and often without legal or economic compensation with other versions of the same property.

It is clear that remakes necessarily entail adaptation to a new medium, for a remake in the same medium would risk charges of plagiarism.[1] How could a lyric poem be remade by another poet? Either the effect of particular words and images would have to be sacrificed, in which case the remake would be so loose as to be unrecognizable, or the new poem would have to follow its model so closely as to be actionable. But adaptations to a new medium do not encounter these problems because of a legal distinction between the original work itself and its status as property. Once Warner Brothers had acquired the adaptation rights to *The Maltese Falcon*, they were entitled to borrow anything they liked from the novel—characters, settings, scenes, even dialogue, in addition to the plot—on the theory that the rights to this material were properly disposable as subsidiary rights, though not to be identified with the novel itself.[2] Even such a close adaptation as John Huston's 1941 film, Warners' third adaptation of the novel, was clearly distinct from the novel, a distinction clear to anyone who could tell the difference between a book and a movie.

But remakes differ from other adaptations to a new medium and translations to a new language because of the triangular relationship they establish among themselves, the original film they remake, and the property on which both films are based. The nature of this triangle is most clearly indicated by the fact that the producers of a remake typically pay no adaptation fees to the makers of the original film, but rather purchase adaptation rights from the authors of the property on which that film was based, even though the remake is competing much more directly with the original film than with the story or play or novel on which both of them are based. Although we might describe any story as parasitic on its models, remakes are parasitic on their original films in a uniquely legalistic way. Since most remakes attempt to supersede their originals for all but a marginal audience watching them for their historical value, remakes typically threaten the economic viability of their originals without compensating the producers of the original in any way.

This emphasis on competition may seem misplaced, since remakes by the same filmmakers seem intended not so much as competition with their original films as revisions of them. Producer/directors like Alfred Hitchcock, Frank Capra, and Howard Hawks could return to their earlier successes in their later years, with the goal of improving on the original film (Hitchcock's *The Man Who Knew Too Much* [1934/1956]), scoring another success with popular material (Capra's *Pocketful of Miracles* [1961], a remake of his *Lady for a Day* [1933]), reworking a successful story to accommodate a new star (Hawks's *Ball of Fire* [1941] and *A Song Is Born* [1948]), or continuing a meditation on a beloved story, situation, or star (Hawks's *Rio Bravo* [1959], *El Dorado* [1967], and *Rio Lobo*

[1970]). But such examples are rare compared to the great majority of remakes, in which the revisionary impulse is subordinated to the goal of increasing the audience by marginalizing the original film, reducing it to the status of the unseen classic.

The competition between remakes and their originals has not always been so acute because for a long time studios thought of their films as having strictly current value; this year's films no more competed with last year's than today's newspaper with yesterday's. A budget-minded studio like Warners could not only recycle *The Maltese Falcon* three times but could also release dozens of unofficial remakes of its own films (e.g., the circus film *The Wagons Roll at Night*, based on the boxing film *Kid Galahad*) and those of other studios (e.g., *Torrid Zone*, loosely based on Columbia's *His Girl Friday*, itself a remake). The parasitism of the remake becomes clearest when re-releasing becomes a likely possibility, when the old film is available alongside the new for video rental, or when both films are in release in the same market at the same time, generally because the remake is a foreign-language version of the original film specifically designed to appeal to a foreign audience more likely to see it than the original on which it is based.[3]

The triangular relationship among the remake, its original film, and the source for both films defines two leading problems in the rhetoric of the remake, the relation it establishes with an audience that allows it to be understood and enjoyed on the terms it prescribes. The first of these problems concerns the rhetoric of exposition—the way a remake arouses the audience's pleasurable anticipation by the way it sets forth its premises. The audience for any remake is several audiences, each one of which the remake sets out to please even though their expectations are different and often apparently contradictory. Of course, the audience for any film is actually a collection of many different viewers with different desires, and film genres of any sort operate by appealing to a broad spectrum of common desires (for vicarious adventure and romance, for example, or the fulfillment of common fantasies). But a remake's very status as a remake presupposes audiences who come to it with broadly incompatible backgrounds which encourage different wishes and expectations. The remake aims to please each of these audiences: the audience that has never heard of the original film it is based on, the audience that has heard of the film but not seen it, the audience that has seen it but does not remember it, the audience that has seen it but liked it little enough to hope for an improvement, and the audience that has seen it and enjoyed it. For some of these audiences the existence of the original film will not even be an issue; for others it will provide a benchmark against which to measure every scene in the remake. But even though these different audiences will have very different expectations of the remake, most remakes do their best to satisfy them all.

This attempt begins with the film's opening shots. Most remakes try to be readily intelligible to an audience that has never even heard of their originals, but ideally they provide additional enjoyment to audiences who recognize their borrowings from their sources; at the very least, they try not to make knowledge of the earlier film a liability by allowing that knowledge to spoil the audience's suspense. The resulting problems mark an important distinction between remakes and their cousins, film sequels, which continue the story of an earlier film by bringing a new set of characters to a familiar setting (*Friday the 13th*) or inventing new adventures for characters established by an earlier film (*Police Academy*). Since sequels are nearly always produced by the same company, and often by many of the same people that produced their originals, and since they are designed to capitalize on the success of the originals by tapping the appetites the earlier films aroused, their exposition usually makes pointed reference to the earlier films they are designed in large measure to advertise. In their exposition, sequels can draw freely from the films whose stories they are continuing without disappointing either the audience who has seen the original film (and who presumably will already be interested in the characters made familiar by the earlier films) or the audience who has not (and who therefore requires some sort of background information in order to follow the new story). In fact, since sequels are rarely separated by more than a few years from their originals, a primary function of their exposition, especially in the age of the VCR, is to create an appetite for the original film, as every Sherlock Holmes or Mike Hammer story is an advertisement for every other.

Remakes also seek to please both audiences who have seen the films on which they are based and audiences who have not, but their task is complicated by the fact that instead of advertising the original films, they are competing with them, and so cannot risk invoking memories of the earlier film too fervently even though they are limited in the kinds of novelty they can introduce, since they are telling the same story again rather than developing a familiar story in a new direction. Remakes most often address this problem by adding a twist to their exposition, teasing knowing audiences as they bring new audiences up to their level of background

knowledge. Kurt Neumann's original version of *The Fly* (1958) was structured as a mystery (why did Helene Delambre kill her husband François,
whom she obviously adored, by crushing his head and arm under an
industrial press? why did she bring down the press twice? why does she
confess to the killing but refuse to explain her motive? why is she obsessed
with finding a housefly with a white head?) to which the melding of man
and fly is the answer. But since such a structure would be less effective for
the remake of a well-known story, David Cronenberg's 1986 version of
the film employs a much more linear structure. This is not to say that
remakes must avoid mystery altogether. In John Carpenter's 1982 remake
of *The Thing*, the coffin-shaped excavation the Americans discover in the
ice reminds the audience of the block of ice (here unseen) in which the
Thing was encased in Christian Nyby's 1951 version without telling them
where the Thing is now; and the opening sequence of Brian De Palma's
1980 *Dressed to Kill* alludes overtly though elliptically to the shower
sequence in Alfred Hitchcock's 1960 *Psycho* and establishes a thematic
relation between sex and violence (and showers) for audiences who have
never seen *Psycho*, while withholding until the final sequence the specific
point of the association. Such expository strategies help make different
audiences with different expectations into a single, more unified audience, giving the new audience a crash course enabling them to have the
same kind of informed expectations as the audience who has seen the
original film, but implying at the same time that familiarity with the original film will provide an additional teasing intimacy with this one. In
either case, the audience knows just enough to form definite expectations
about what kinds of things will happen, but not enough to know exactly
what will happen.

When remakes offer special rewards for viewers who remember the
original film, they are most likely to take the form of throwaway jokes
whose point is not necessary to the film's continuity and which therefore
provide an optional bonus of pleasure to those in the know. When Ted
Kotcheff's *Switching Channels* (1987) first shows us the corrupt District
Attorney Roy Ridnitz (Ned Beatty), he is shouting, "All right, he can be
City Sealer!"—a reference to the office Billy Gilbert's Joe Pettibone is
offered by the corrupt Mayor in Hawks's *His Girl Friday* (1940). The
school the young hero of Tobe Hooper's *Invaders from Mars* (1986)
attends is Menzies Elementary, presumably named after William
Cameron Menzies, who directed the first *Invaders from Mars* (1953). Even
the main title of a remake can involve an in-joke. The film identified as

"John Carpenter's *The Thing*" (1982) in its opening and closing credits never explicitly mentions the film on which it is based anywhere in the credits, reproducing instead the earlier film's credit "Based on the story 'Who Goes There?' by John W. Campbell, Jr." But the main title uses exactly the same design—the words "The Thing," in an identically stylized script, seem to come up in flames, filling the entire screen—as that of Nyby's film.

The process by which remakes prepare a position for their different audiences is complex not only because these audiences are not assumed all to be approaching the remake from the same perspective but because remakes invoke their models in order to get audiences into the theater in the first place only to deny them once (or even before) the credits have run. The success of a remake depends either on its providing different pleasures to audiences who have different kinds of knowledge and interest in the original film, or more often on its establishing some common ground from which audiences of different interests can assimilate it in the same way. Remakes like *The Thing*, *The Fly*, and *King Kong* (1976) not only position the audience by setting forth their stories in a way that provides audiences familiar with earlier versions of the story with a teasing intimacy that still does not spoil their anticipation of later developments; they are typically advertised in a way that gives the audience unfamiliar with earlier versions of the story enough background information to appreciate its potential appeal while encouraging the audience for the original film to be dissatisfied with its artifices or omissions or compromises and so to accept the remake as the definitive version of a story for which they had already had an appetite. John Guillermin's Kong is more humanized than Merian C. Cooper's and Ernest B. Schoedsack's original Kong, for example; he climbs a taller building; and his climb is more psychologically motivated—the twin towers of the World Trade Center remind him of a landmark formation on his primitive island. The assumption throughout is that even an audience attracted by the aura of a mythically inflated monster story like the 1933 *King Kong* would still prefer an avowedly demythicized, psychologically naturalized version of the story.

The problem of making its story intelligible to a new audience without making it boring to an audience familiar with the original film is therefore closely linked to the second, more general rhetorical problem characteristic of the remake: the problem of intertextuality, of establishing a normative relation to its original film. The exposition of a remake determines the way its audience defines their initial attitude toward the film; its intertextual stance, the general attitude it adopts toward its original, helps define the way the audience makes sense of their experience of the film as a whole.

Although remakes by definition base an important part of their appeal on the demonstrated ability of a preexisting story to attract an audience, they are often competing with the very films they invoke, even if those films have been out of release for many years. As soon as a new version of *Unfaithfully Yours* or *To Be or Not to Be* is announced, its title invokes the memory of the earlier film, a memory the producers assume to have positive associations even for audiences who have never seen the original. In fact, remakes typically invoke the aura of their originals rather than their memory.[4] Conventional wisdom assumes that the original film was outstanding—otherwise why bother to remake it at all?—yet the remake is better still—otherwise why not simply watch the original, or watch it again? The audience for a remake is responding to the paradoxical promise that the film will be just like the original, only better. The fundamental rhetorical problem of remakes is to mediate between two apparently irreconcilable claims: that the remake is *just like* its model, and that it's *better*.

In this respect, again, remakes differ sharply from film sequels. Even though some sequels, like *Friday the 13th, Parts 4–6*, gravitate toward remakes, and occasional remakes, like *Invasion of the Body Snatchers* (Kaufman, 1978), contain elements of sequels, the rhetorical stance of the two genres reflects their fundamentally different appeal. The audience for sequels wants to find out more, to spend more time with characters they are interested in and to find out what happened to them after their story was over. The audience for remakes does not expect to find out anything new in this sense: they want the same story again, though not exactly the same. And except for film scholars and other purists and diehard reactionaries who sit through remakes more or less expecting that the remake will not be as good as the original, the audience for remakes hopes they will be better than the originals; if they didn't, they'd be watching the originals instead. So an essential distinction between sequels and remakes is that the sequels are packaged and consumed on the basis of a promise that even though they tell a different story, they're just as good as the original, whereas remakes are committed to a more paradoxical promise: that they'll follow the original more closely than a sequel would, but that they'll differ more from the original, because they'll be better.

Remakes seek to mediate between the contradictory claims of being just like their originals only better in several different ways. A given remake can seek to define itself either with primary reference to the film it remakes or to the material on which both films are based; and whether it poses as a new version of an older film or of a story predating either film, it can take as its goal fidelity to the conception of the original story or a revisionary attitude toward that story. Hence there are four possible stances a remake can adopt, each with its own characteristic means of resolving its contradictory intertextual claims.

The simplest of these stances is that of the *readaptation* of a well-known literary work whose earlier cinematic adaptations the remake ignores or treats as inconsequential. The goal of the readaptation, like that of the literary translation, is fidelity (however defined) to the original text, which it undertakes to translate as scrupulously as possible (presumably more scrupulously than earlier versions) into the film medium. Film versions of Shakespeare's plays or Dickens's novels typically establish a clear hierarchy of textuality by treating their source material as a classic text to be preserved and dismissing the textual claims of earlier film versions of these stories. The implication of this stance is that although everything may be a text, some texts (e.g., Alexandre Dumas's *La Dame aux camélias*) are more authoritative, more textual than others (any of the dozen film versions of *Camille*), which can be ignored in the interests of the original text, however fervently they may have invoked that text themselves. The effect is to subordinate the competition between the remake and any earlier film version to the competition between the remake and the original property, so that Tony Richardson's and Franco Zeferelli's film versions of *Hamlet* (1969, 1991) try to avoid comparison with Laurence Olivier's 1948 *Hamlet* by invoking Shakespeare's play rather than the earlier film.[5] Readaptations can present themselves as just like their models only better because they pose as original translations of the models to a new medium rather than remakes of earlier movies.

But not all film versions of classic literary texts take fidelity to the original text as their goal. Frank Kermode's study *The Classic*, which deals with institutional attempts to come to terms with literary classics like Virgil by reconsidering their relation to later generations of readers, makes a useful distinction between two general attitudes toward classic texts. Kermode's concept of intertextuality is based on an imperialistic analogy. Contending that "the Empire is the paradigm of the classic: a perpetuity, a transcendent entity, however remote its provinces, however extraordinary its temporal vicissitudes," Kermode shows the application of the Aristotelian distinction between an entity's unchanging essence and its mutable disposition to the cultural belief in the power of the literary classic, which "retains its identity without refusing to subject itself to change" (28, 45). In narrative theory this distinction between essence and disposition is translated into a distinction between story and discourse, the core of meaningful events which remains constant in different versions of the same story and the changing ways in which those events are inscribed or enacted. When authors sell rights to their work, they are selling the right to adapt the story to a new discursive mode—film—and remakes are adaptations of a given story to a new discursive incarnation within the same mode of representation. Most audiences make a rough distinction of some kind between story and discourse, as when they refer to the original way a Western like *Unforgiven* handles its familiar revenge story, but remakes depend on an unusually sharp institutional distinction between their story (which links them to some other film) and their discourse (which sets them apart from a re-release of that film).

Audiences for literary classics, according to Kermode, have traditionally confirmed their status as classics in one of two ways. Some audiences have adopted a historical approach, asking what *The Aeneid* meant to its original readers and then considering the application of that meaning to their own modern situation. From this historical or archeological perspective, which he links to the survival of ideals of empire, Kermode derives the critical tradition of hermeneutics, the attempt to fix a determinate meaning for every text by adducing its creator's authority. This respect for the historical authority of the original text is clearly behind readaptations that emphasize their dependence on earlier classic (that is, noncinematic) texts. But other readers have adopted a contrary approach that Kermode calls accommodation, insuring the survival of the classic by making it responsive to a more peremptory demand for contemporary relevance, typically through allegory, figuration, and prophecy (so that instead of asking what Virgil's Fourth Eclogue meant to its original audience, Christian audiences considered how it could be read as a prophecy of the nativity). From this revisionary perspective Kermode traces the rise of those contemporary modes of criticism which value change, plurality, and indeterminacy in interpretation as they interrogate classic texts not in order to establish their true meaning but in order to ask what they can say directly to a modern audience. When this attitude is focused on the literary source behind a film remake, the resulting film is an *update* rather than a readaptation.

Updates are characterized by their overtly revisionary stance toward an original text they treat as classic, even though they transform it in some obvious way, usually by transposing it to a new setting, inverting its system of values, or adopting standards of realism that implicitly criticize the original as dated, outmoded, or irrelevant. Such films often signal their ambivalent attitude toward their original sources in their titles (e.g., *Boccaccio 70*, *Camille 2000*, *Joe Macbeth*, *Lt. Robin Crusoe, U.S.N.*) or adopt a tone that can verge on parody (as in at least three different versions of *The Three Musketeers*: Allen Dwan's 1939 production with Don Ameche and the Ritz Brothers, George Sidney's 1948 version with Gene Kelly and Lana Turner, and Richard Lester's two films, *The Three Musketeers* [1973] and *The Four Musketeers* [1974]). As Orson Welles's Shakespearean films, unlike Olivier's, pose as newly realized works rather than film versions of classic plays, updates in general are not content to occupy a subordinate position to the literary classics they adapt but compete directly with those classics by accommodating them to what are assumed to be the audience's changed desires.

Like remakes that seek to direct the audience's attention to their literary sources, remakes that focus on their cinematic sources can either accept the original text's authority on its own terms, by attempting to disclose and valorize those terms, or seek to redefine the earlier film's authority by appealing more directly to the desires of a contemporary audience through accommodation. The first of these strategies produces the *homage*—an appropriately foreign term for what has until recently been an exclusively foreign phenomenon. An homage is a remake like Werner Herzog's *Nosferatu the Vampyre* (1982) whose primary purpose is to pay tribute to an earlier film rather than usurp its place of honor. Like readaptations, homages situate themselves as secondary texts whose value depends on their relation to the primary texts they gloss; the difference is that the hallmark of readaptations is fidelity in transcription, whereas a faithful homage would be a contradiction in terms (the most faithful homage would be a re-release). Homages therefore present themselves as valorizations of earlier films which are in danger of being ignored or forgotten.

Although they have long been common in Europe, homages have been slow to appear in Hollywood because of the difference between the status of the literary classic and the film classic in American culture. A literary classic like *The Aeneid* has an imperial authority rooted in the institutions of literary culture and occupies a central position in that culture no matter how many times it is reinterpreted (by Christian apologists for Virgil) or rewritten (by Dante and Milton). It continues to represent an aesthetic, and to a great extent an ethical, ideal, exerting a lasting influence on future audiences' conventions and standards of behavior because of its privileged position in the pedagogical canon: generations of English schoolboys who detested *The Aeneid* still knew passages of it by heart and adopted its ethical system as their own. But film classics occupy a much more marginal status in American culture because film itself, although it is acknowledged to wield a prodigious influence over its audience's thoughts and actions, is commonly discounted as an ethically and aesthetically suspect medium, so that the concept "film classic" has a much narrower meaning in America than in France. The New Wave films of Jean-Luc Godard, François Truffaut, and Claude Chabrol took the time to pay homage to American genre films even as they were most fiercely declaring their originality because their directors took American films more seriously than most Americans; and Alfred Hitchcock's artistic reputation was consolidated in France ten years earlier than in America, where the impulse behind homages, to celebrate the films on which they are based, first informed the compilation films of Robert Youngson (*The Golden Age of Comedy* [1958], *When Comedy Was King* [1959], etc.), which take silent comedy seriously in an archival sense by resurrecting classic sequences for an audience that would otherwise have no access to them.

Youngson's films are more notable as a fan's valentine to earlier films than as films in their own right; it is only with the entrance of film into the curriculum of American universities that the ideal of the homage emerges full-blown in Peter Bogdanovich's *Targets* (1968), produced the same year as Truffaut's Hitchcockian homage *The Bride Wore Black*. *Targets* begins deceptively by presenting Boris Karloff as still another Karloffian monster in a film-within-a-film, proceeds to deplore the entrapment of Karloff in so many one-dimensional and interchangeable roles, but finally holds him—and what Leo Braudy has called his "virtually benevolent gothic horror" (207)—as a heroic value which judges and defeats the shocking banality of the deranged young sniper (Tim O'Kelly). Though its pre-title credits[6] pose it as an investigation into the reasons for epidemic violence in America, *Targets* offers no satisfactory answers to the questions these credits raise, for it is really something quite different: a meditation on the past, an elegiac lament for the present, and a celebration of the mythic power of such classic films as *The Criminal Code*

(1931), which Karloff's young director (played by Bogdanovich) screens with the pointed remark that they don't make them like that anymore. The two most celebrated recent American series of homages illustrate the range of attitudes possible within the homage. Woody Allen's homages to Ingmar Bergman (*Interiors* [1978], *A Midsummer Night's Sex Comedy* [1981], and *Another Woman* [1988]), Federico Fellini (*Stardust Memories* [1980]), and German expressionist cinema (*Shadows and Fog* [1991]) show the impulse toward tribute and celebration at its purest, for Allen never gives a sense of wanting to transcend his masters. By contrast, Brian de Palma's fantasias on themes from Hitchcock's *Vertigo* and *Psycho* (*Sisters* [1974], *Obsession* [1975], *Dressed to Kill* [1980], *Body Double* [1986], *Raising Cain* [1992]) and Howard Hawks's *Scarface* (1983) show the celebratory impulse increasingly complicated by an impulse to develop, to elaborate, and (in *Body Double*) to combine motifs from the original films in a way that marks the frontiers of the homage.

Homages deal with the contradictory claims of remakes—that they are just like their originals, only better—by renouncing any claim to be better. The contradiction is clearest in the final variety of remake, the *true remake*, which combines a focus on a cinematic original with an accommodating stance which seeks to make the original relevant by updating it. "True remake" may sound like a feeble term, but it aptly emphasizes the way this fourth variety of remake depends more directly, albeit ambivalently, than the other three on the triangular relationship among the remake and its two sources (the film credits and pays the authors of a preexisting, typically literary, source while borrowing more directly from an unacknowledged cinematic original) and is more temperate than such labels as "plagiarism" or "ripoff." Calling these films "true remakes" also offers a reminder that each of the other types of remake—the readaptation, the update of a literary original, the homage—marks a deviation from a norm: the film whose primary model is an earlier film it seeks to displace. The status of the true remake is so paradoxical that Kermode's analysis of the survival of the literary classic through accommodation offers only limited help as a model. The modern classics Kermode analyzes—*The House of the Seven Gables* and *Wuthering Heights*—respond to the tradition of earlier classics, classics of empire, by "evasions of narrative authority" (107), acknowledging the authority of their models by refusing to imitate it directly and instead calling attention to their own artifice and the active role of their audience in shaping multiple meanings which are encouraged by the modern classic's "failure to give a definitive account of itself" (114). Kermode's modern classic, in other words, severed from the ideal of an essentially immutable empire which moored earlier classics to a single array of meanings and tolerated a limited amount of accommodation to revisionary interpretations, emphasizes the problematic, contingent nature of its own meanings.

This is a very precise account of what happens in the production of film homages, which take seriously the classic status of their originals and the idea of film classics generally. But nothing remotely like this happens in the production of film remakes because most classic films which are remade—and the whole notion of the classic film—do not exert anything like the imperialistic force Kermode ascribes to the literary classic. Since mainstream films are designed as products to be consumed rather than as visions of empire, their successors compete with them much more openly and radically than revisionary classics compete with earlier classics. In Kermode's view, what is at stake in the competition between Virgil and Emily Brontë is a set of moral values and an attitude toward the production of meanings. But the competition between movie remakes and their originals represents a far more complex version of the operation of imperialistic power.

In true remakes, the notion of empire is essentially economic rather than philosophical, since the producers of the remake wish not only to accommodate the original story to a new discourse and a new audience but to annihilate the model they are honoring—to eliminate any need or desire to see the film they seek to replace. The exemplary case is that of Thorold Dickinson's *Gaslight* (1939), which M-G-M remade in 1944 under George Cukor's direction after purchasing and destroying the negative of the British film. The true remake admires its original so much it wants to annihilate it.[7]

The contradictions implicit in all remakes but most pointed in true remakes surface with particular clarity in two 1981 films based on novels by James M. Cain: Bob Rafelson's *The Postman Always Rings Twice* and Lawrence Kasdan's *Body Heat*. Rafelson's film resolves the problem of its contradictory status as an updated classic by distinguishing between positive and negative textual markers—richness, originality, and the imperial power of the classic, on the one hand, and artifice, datedness, and repression of important material on the other—and ascribing them, respectively, to the two different texts that stand behind it. In this way the remake is able to valorize Cain's original text, toward which it adopts an attitude of hushed reverence, while ascribing any dated qualities in need of revision to Tay Garnett's 1946 film version. David Mamet's screenplay presents the notorious sex scenes in Cain's novel the earlier film had omitted, makes Jack Nicholson's Frank Chambers considerably more ambivalent than John Garfield's trapped innocent, and restores Cain's emphasis on the insurance scam the lawyer Katz (Smith in the Garnett film) uses to exonerate Frank and his lover Cora Papadakis (Lana Turner/Jessica Lange) for killing Cora's husband Nick. By presenting itself as a more authentic version of Cain's story than the earlier film, the remake is able not only to finesse around its own departures from Cain (for example, its slow pace as opposed to the rapid pace of Cain's novel, and the fact that it ends with Frank grieving over Cora's death in a car accident rather than with Frank's impending execution, technically unjust but morally right, for Cora's murder—so that Rafelson's postman doesn't even ring twice) but to circumscribe its own textuality by invoking exactly two earlier texts: Cain's novel, which is the source of all its value, and Garnett's film, which represents all the errors the remake avoids.

The rhetorical strategies of *Body Heat* are even more economical, for although the film is a loose remake of Billy Wilder's *Double Indemnity* (1944), based in turn on Cain's 1936 novel, it manages to make the same distinction between beneficial and baneful textual markers without explicitly invoking either model. In both films, a weak man (Fred MacMurray in the earlier film, William Hurt in the second) falls in love with an alluring woman (Barbara Stanwyck/Kathleen Turner) who encourages him to kill her husband so that they can be free and wealthy. After planning and carrying out an ingenious murder scheme, each man realizes that the woman has played him along from the beginning and wants to be rid of him. When this scheme unravels, each man tries to take revenge on his lover, but both are caught by the police. Despite the differences in the two films—and there are many—the later film implicitly invokes the earlier at any number of points. Hurt and Turner first meet outside a bandshell to the accompaniment of forties swing music; throughout the film she wears retro-forties clothing; her one gift to him is an anachronistic fedora. Kasdan's screenplay often recalls Chandler's stylized dialogue. Turner comes on to Hurt by spilling cherry ice on her white dress and asking if he doesn't want to lick it off, echoing the moment when Stanwyck tells MacMurray that he's driving ninety in a forty-five-mile-per-hour zone. Hurt, for his part, tells Turner, "You shouldn't wear that body," recalling Stanwyck's question to MacMurray: "Do I have my face on straight?" and its accompanying implication, common to *film noir*, that one's public face is only a mask that hides the emotions within. Even Richard Kline's color cinematography repeatedly invokes the *noir* look of *Double Indemnity* in its generally desaturated compositions, alternating between the overexposed whites and neutrals of the daytime settings—courtrooms, law offices, an overlit diner—and the black-and-monochromatic nighttime scenes, in which red or green is usually the only strong color.

At the same time, *Body Heat* takes pains to deny any explicit borrowing from *Double Indemnity*. Its title, setting, and characters' names and professions are all new; its leading pattern of images (a heat wave which encourages and represents the loss of inhibitions and the breakdown of moral scruples, leading to steamy sex and murderous explosions) is set against *Double Indemnity*'s repeated images of entrapment or enslavement by sexual passion; even its publicity refers to the original film only in general terms, as when it promises that "*Body Heat . . .* echoes the powerful impact of '40s *film noir* melodramas like *Double Indemnity* and *The Postman Always Rings Twice*—but with energy, irony and passion that could only flare out of the '80s."[8] The credits announce simply that the film is "written and directed by Lawrence Kasdan."[9] The net effect of this dance of invocation and denial is not only to make the characteristic promise of the remake—that it's just like the earlier film, only better—but to indicate the ways in which a copy can be better than the original. The remake updates the older film, restoring its repressed material ("passion that could only flare out of the '80s"), erasing any dated references that may have tied the film to a particular period (MacMurray's remark that the Dietrichsons' house "must have cost about six thousand dollars" is replaced by Hurt's facetious "just like my house"—an ascription of extravagance designed not to become outdated because it is not tied to a particular number of dollars), while in this case invoking the period of the original film even though the remake is set in a later period. The remake, to emphasize its enabling paradox, takes what is presented as a classic, timeless story and updates it—partly by the paradoxical attempt to remove all markers of any historical period whatever.

The economy with which *Body Heat* manages to invoke a timeless earlier text as the source of its power even as it simultaneously ascribes its limitations and shortcomings to the particular historical circumstances that mark that earlier text suggests a more precise and comprehensive account of intertextuality than the imperial power of Kermode's classic. Kermode's distinction between essence and disposition suggests that remakes could be described as old stories incarnated in a new discourse. Such a description accords well with Kermode's account of the modern classic, which emphasizes its discursive status, its lack of access to simple and direct meanings, at every turn. But true remakes, unlike Kermode's revisionary modern classics, are not exhibited and consumed as new discursive presentations of familiar stories. They are presented as the stories themselves, shorn of the discursive accidents that disfigured their originals.[10] *Body Heat* is not offered as merely a new version of a familiar story; it is the definitive version that renders its model obsolete, like a new Buick just arrived in the showroom. Just as Rafelson's *Postman Always Rings Twice* presents its own discourse as timeless in its fidelity to Cain's classic text by impugning the discourse of the earlier film as less "modern" than that of the novel, *Body Heat* does not, on its own accounting, add new material to an old story but liberates values that were present in the story all along but were obscured by the circumstances of its earlier incarnation. Whatever discursive value the remake has is simply ascribed either to the text of the original novel or, more economically, to the original (presumably untextualized) story, while the discursive markers of the original film are denigrated. The specific markers of *Body Heat*'s own discourse—the stylized dialogue, the retro clothing, the monochromatic visuals—are intended to call attention to the discourse of the original film, not the remake. The true remake is pretending, in effect, that it has no discourse of its own to become outdated; it is completely congruent with a story whose original discursive manifestation it disavows.

The notion of disavowal has had some currency in theories of cinematic representation ever since Christian Metz adopted the formula of theatrical disavowal ("I know very well, but all the same . . .") whereby Octave Mannoni had characterized the audience's attitude toward the illusions of theatrical representation.[11] But disavowal—that is, the combination of acknowledgment and repudiation in a single ambivalent gesture—is apt in far more specific ways to the remake's model of intertextuality, since remakes by definition establish their value by invoking earlier texts whose potency they simultaneously valorize and deny through a series of rhetorical maneuvers designed at once to reflect their intimacy with these earlier texts and to distance themselves from their flaws. Readaptations deal with the resulting contradictions by distinguishing between two source-texts, one of which is acknowledged and the other repudiated. Updates distinguish between the valuable story of the earlier text and its flawed discourse, which is in need of redaction.

Homages subordinate their own textual claims to those of their originals. Each variety of remake defines itself by the way it distinguishes the textual markers that it wishes to claim as the source of its value from those it wishes to efface or deny. The true remake differs from other kinds of remakes by disavowing its own textuality along with its intertextuality. More radically than readaptations, updates, and homages, which only acknowledge one earlier text, whether literary in the first two cases or cinematic in the third, true remakes depend on a triangular notion of intertextuality, since their rhetorical strategy depends on ascribing their value to a classic earlier text and protecting that value by invoking a second earlier text as betraying it. *The Postman Always Rings Twice*, like readaptations, accomplishes this goal by distinguishing between two earlier texts, *Body Heat* by disavowing its implication in the very notions of textuality it invokes.

Readaptations, updates, homages, true remakes: given the remake's dependence on a triangular model of intertextuality, these four possibilities form an exhaustive, albeit severely simplified, taxonomy of the remake. They do not, of course, exhaust the range of stances filmmakers have claimed for their remakes. When William Friedkin remarks of *Sorcerer* (1977), his remake of Henri-Georges Clouzot's *Le Salaire de la peur* (1953), that "there are remakes, and there are transformations. *Sorcerer* is a transformation which I want to stand up as the perfect example of the genre,"[12] his claim to stand outside this taxonomy—there are remakes that somehow are not transformations, presumably because they simply replicate the original without changing anything, but *Sorcerer* is not one of those replications—simply reinscribes the remake's dependence on disavowal for its own definition. In fact, *Sorcerer*—which, despite its obligatory credit acknowledging its literary source (the novel by George Arnaud)—invokes Clouzot's original film precisely in order to mark its distance from that original, is a textbook example of the true remake, however its director may prefer to describe it.

Kermode's model of intertextuality does not adequately describe the rhetoric of the true remake because it overlooks the way remakes, unlike Kermode's modern classics, seek to impugn their originals' discursiveness, their textuality, in order to disavow their own. In Kermode's account of the relation between modern classics and their imperial models, the later work incarnates the timeless essence of the earlier but enshrines it within a new discourse whose adequacy becomes a more and more urgent issue, as modern classics establish their rhetorical authority by deliberately and repeatedly undermining their claims to the unquestioning thematic authority they impute to the classic of empire. Again, this analysis applies to homages but not to true remakes, for they establish their rhetorical authority by attributing all discursive problems to their models. Each new remake, no matter how many or complex its borrowings from earlier versions, presents itself as less problematic than they are. Kermode's model of intertextuality cannot account for the disavowal characteristic of true remakes because it reserves imperialistic power to the original classic, the vision of imperial empire, whereas recent theorists of empire have recognized that precursor texts can be colonized as well as colonizers—a point that can be better appreciated if we turn briefly from the intertextuality of archival remakes to that of contemporary remakes which undertake to translate their originals from one culture to another.

It might seem that the archival remake's triangular model of disavowal does little to illuminate the intertextuality of recent remakes of foreign films like *The Man Who Loved Women* (Edwards, 1983) or *Three Men and a Baby* (Nimoy, 1987) or *Cousins* (Schumacher, 1989) or *Sommersby* (Amiel, 1993) or *Point of No Return* (Badham, 1993) or *The Vanishing* (Sluizer, 1993), since these films tend to emphasize their dependence on their cinematic predecessors rather than their (often obscure) common literary sources. But the triangular structure of disavowal remains as crucial in these remakes as in *Body Heat* because all of them divide their predecessor films into two sources, one of which is acknowledged and advertised as the source of the remake's currency, the other of which is repudiated as the source of the textual impurities it is the business of the remake to exorcise. This ambivalent relationship emphasizes an aspect of textuality Kermode does not consider: the mutually colonizing potential of both the original property and its remake, a potential which can best be approached through a pair of analogies. When the popular series of children's books starring Nancy Drew and the Hardy Boys were revised beginning in 1960, one aim of the revisions was to erase the earlier stories' racism by eliminating racial and ethnic slurs and stereotypes. The success of this sort of melioristic revision is to define assimilationist American culture's evolution by measuring its progress over itself, the earlier American culture in which the stereotypes were acceptable. The sign of this progress is the later texts' colonization of their predecessors, which they aim to efface from currency, from memory, and ideally, by physically outlasting them, from existence. In Douglas Sirk's celebrated Universal remakes (*Magnificent Obsession* [1954] and *Imitation of Life*

[1959]), by contrast, the point of Sirk's notorious stylistic parody is not only the 1930s culture that took such soapy melodramas seriously but also the contemporary culture that wants another disavowing peep at them even while measuring its progressive distance, for example, from the obvious racism of John M. Stahl's 1934 *Imitation of Life*.[13] Although Sirk's films obviously establish a triangular relationship among themselves, their valorized predecessor texts (proven melodramas that are both timeless and timely), and their disavowed predecessor texts (dated movies whose textuality is betrayed by their unfashionable social mores), a more subtle, but more salient, triangular relationship operates between the films and the audience which both enjoys them as parody and consumes them as family romance. Sirk's films thus mark their own culture's *différance*, its distance from itself: their disavowal is fetishistic in Freud's clinical sense of the term,[14] since their ostensible goal—to recreate for a new filmgoing generation the timeless domestic dramas of an earlier era—is complicated to the point of negation by a critique of those very domestic dramas and, indeed, of the audience and the filmmaking apparatus themselves. In Nancy Drew and the Hardy Boys, the laundered later text takes the place of the earlier in the hope of driving it from consciousness; the point of Sirk's parodies is precisely the self-critique enabled by multiple layers of self-consciousness. Kermode's theory of intertextuality does not account for either of these cases. The Nancy Drew revisions exercise an imperialistic force over their originals that is exactly the opposite of the power Kermode ascribes to the originals; Sirk's Universal melodramas, though their ambivalent textual claims resemble those of both *The House of the Seven Gables* and *Wuthering Heights*, illustrate the limits of an intertextual theory which locates the colonizing impulse in only one of a pair of texts on which the other is clearly parasitic.[15]

When Hollywood filmmakers remake contemporary foreign films, the situation is imperialistic, but not in the sense to which Kermode refers when he speaks of the imperial power of the classic text which must be reckoned with by later generations. Instead, it is the filmmakers, not Virgil, who are the colonizers. The goal of the contemporary remake is to translate not a language but a culture, appealing to the aura of their originals as European, serious, complex, adult, art-house films while domesticating exactly the elements that created that aura in the first place. Hence Jim McBride's 1983 remake of *Breathless*, while carefully preserving Jean-Luc Godard's unlikely international romance, avoids the technical innovations—the jump-cutting, handheld camera movements, and capriciously understated narrative and psychological connections—that had made the original film so disturbing and distinctive. And George Sluizer's 1993 American remake of his own dark thriller *The Vanishing* (1988) corrects the error that made the earlier film so bleak and unsettling by providing a happy ending for American audiences and Kiefer Sutherland, a star in whose welfare they could be expected to have a residual investment. More generally, the mark of such films' colonization of their foreign originals is the insistence on textualizing not only the predecessor films but the foreign culture itself, which is divided along textual lines into a positive culture to be acknowledged as romantic, exotic, dangerously unregulated, and a negative culture to be repudiated as uncompromising, difficult, and ultimately unresponsive to the demands of American consumers.

There is, of course, nothing unusual in the phenomenon of a powerful culture coming to terms with the productions of a foreign culture by domesticating them. Colonizing the other by effacing its otherness is a trope that has so dominated modern writers from Joseph Conrad to Edward W. Said that it has become a founding move in the discipline of cultural studies. The disavowal of the remake offers a textual, generic model for analyzing the discourses of colonialism while avoiding the current impasse in postcolonial studies: the problem of how, in Gayatri Spivak's terms, the colonized voice can speak without denying or betraying its otherness by adopting the language of imperialistic oppression or facing an annihilating silence.[16] Remakes pose this problem as a problem of disavowal, the pivotal activity of all generic transformation—ultimately, of textuality in general. The disavowal of the remake, that is, is paradigmatic of all generic intertextuality, from formulaic genres like the Western and the musical to the discourses of colonialism. Jane Feuer and Rick Altman, for instance, have pointed out many ways in which self-reflexive musicals demythicize the artifice of their conventions only to remythicize themselves by ascribing their artifice to some other inferior version of the musical myth. And Christian Metz has gone so far as to claim that all movies are carefully wrought discourses masquerading as artless stories. The rhetorical trope of disavowal could stand as a model of the intertextuality of commercial cinema, whose effect depends on constantly denying its implication in the representational codes on which it depends by preinterpreting itself so as to foreground some questions about its interpretation while suppressing others. But such preinterpretation is no more common to Hollywood movies than to any formulaic genre, from Harlequin romances to epic poems, for it is the nature of every genre to foreground some thematic issues and representational problems while repressing others, as Kermode's modern classic emphasizes questions of textual authority and the remoteness of the past—problems of knowledge—at the expense of questions concerning, for example, the "fine awareness of the nature of human relations and the problem of maturity"[17]—problems of action. Hollywood movies are no more purely or simply generic than any other works, for all discourse, as E. D. Hirsch and Alastair Fowler have argued, is understood with reference to its place within a genre.

The remake's model of intertextuality, in other words, is a model which can be extrapolated to cover every genre and, by implication, every text or utterance whose rhetorical efficacy depends on decentering itself by dissimulating its own discursive or intertextual operations. In the economy of remakes, William Friedkin's generic transformation accompanied by disavowal is business as usual, the immutable process of intertextuality whether or not self-evident lines of "culture" or "colony" or "difference" are being marked as crossed.

Remakes always present themselves as remakes, films to be watched with reference to the classic films they replace, but insist at the same time that they are not merely remakes by presenting their models, like the Fourth Eclogue, as forerunners instead of true originals. In the same way, every genre film, however modest its aims—and that includes the simplest Hopalong Cassidy programmer—encourages its audience to expect the conventions of the genre but then withholds any explicit acknowledgment that it is borrowing those conventions, either by ignoring their conventionality, by transforming them, or by ascribing them ironically to some earlier film. Remakes simply provide an unusually clear example of the operations of every genre, showing in particular the way films in every genre inevitably compete with earlier films by valorizing some aspects of their presentation (the convention that heterosexual opposites attract, or that the decisive moments in public history are based on private decisions informed by the principals' personal freedom) as timeless and imputing others (the convention that good guys wear white hats, or that the thing to do with a bunch of raw young performing talent is to put on a show) to earlier films marked by a dated discourse. This ritual disavowal of discursive features is, in fact, the characteristic move in the establishment of any genre—or any empire.

Only remakes are remakes; the peculiar rhetoric of disavowal in films like *Body Heat* and *Point of No Return* sets them apart from all other stories. But this rhetoric can serve as a model for the intertextual operations of a much wider range of films, genres, and stories, and for the textual calculus of imperial power, by recasting them all, in ways they never acknowledge, as twice-told tales.

NOTES

This chapter is a reprint, with revisions, of "Twice-Told Tales: The Rhetoric of the Remake," originally published in *Literature/Film Quarterly* 18 (1990–91): 138–49.

1. An exception could be made, of course, for the many dramatic versions, ancient and modern, of the stories of Oedipus, Faust, Don Juan, Salome, and the house of Atreus, whose stories are too venerable, and in many cases untraceable to their origins, to warrant fears of plagiarism suits. Jean Giraudoux went so far as to title his comedy *Amphitryon 38*, in recognition of the thirty-seven fictional treatments of the story of Amphitryon he found preceding it, without incurring any threat of legal action from earlier Amphitryons or their authors. But these stories, like those based on the "matter" of Araby or King Arthur in medieval Britain, are not remakes in the technical sense of reworking a single fixed and specific progenitor text.

2. Compare the status of the translation of a written text to a new language, which seeks to overcome precisely this distinction between property rights and the work itself in its attempt to recapture as much of the work itself as possible without fear of transgressing the licensed boundaries of property rights.

3. It might be argued that remakes of foreign films, since their originals inhabit a different section of video rental outlets, do not compete directly with the originals, since audiences browsing the shelves will have made a preliminary decision whether they want to see a foreign film before choosing an individual title. But however they are catalogued and whatever browsing strategies their consumers adopt, remakes compete in a more general sense with their foreign originals for the power to construct the technical and cultural basis on which a given story is to be packaged as entertainment. An exception to this rule might well be made, however, for foreign-language films prepared simultaneously by the original production companies—for example, *Mary*, Hitchcock's German-language version of *Murder!* (1930), or Josef von Sternberg's German- and English-language versions of *The Blue Angel* (1930)—on the grounds that these versions were specifically designed not to compete with each other but to be released to nonoverlapping markets.

4. Mention should be made here of what Michael B. Druxman calls the "*non*remake," the film promoted on the basis of its supposed similarity to an earlier film it only incidentally resembles. See Druxman's account of Michael Curtiz's *The Sea Hawk* (1940) for Warners (173–74).

5. In the same way, recent film versions of historical events like Columbus's journey to the western hemisphere and the gunfight at the O.K. Corral invariably pose as more faithful to history itself, treated as a master text, than to the earlier versions like David MacDonald's *Christopher Columbus* (1949) and John Ford's *My Darling Clementine* (1946) that have allegedly censored or distorted the historical record. Such films commonly advertise themselves as revisionist histories rather than remakes, even when they are clearly trading on the aura of their distinguished cinematic predecessors.

6. The film begins with three questions fading in on the screen:

Why did a lunatic sniper kill or maim 11 innocent victims in Texas on June 3, 1966?

Why were over 7,000 Americans slain or wounded by gunfire in 1967?

Why in 1968, after assassinations and thousands of [*sic*] more murders, has our country no effective gun control law?

The second screen announces: "This motion picture tells a story that sheds a little light on a very dark and very deep topic."

7. Such oedipal language recalls the intertextual theories of Harold Bloom, and indeed true remakes, though not precisely described by any of Bloom's revisionary ratios, have a good deal in common with several of Bloom's dialectical moments, particularly the one associated with daemonization.

8. The quoted passages appear on the box in which Warners released the videotape of *Body Heat*.

9. The reluctance to acknowledge a film's direct debt to earlier films in the credits is common to many remakes, so that *Switching Channels*, a surprisingly close remake of *His Girl Friday*, is billed as "based on the play *The Front Page*," and *Unfaithfully Yours* (1982) is "based on a story by Preston Sturges." Credit sequences prefer to emphasize the film's roots in a story or novel or play (even a screenplay) rather than an earlier film, even if it follows the film much more closely. One reason Michael Mann may have been willing to break this rule in citing Philip Dunne's screenplay for the 1936 *Last of the Mohicans* in the credits of Mann's own 1992 version of the story is that the earlier film, unlike most remakes, was no longer a competitive threat in either an economic or an aesthetic sense, since it had lapsed into greater obscurity than the Fenimore Cooper novel on which both versions were distantly based.

10. It is in this regard that the rhetoric of the remake differs most sharply from that of any of Bloom's examples.

11. See Mannoni, "L'Illusion comique ou le théâtre du point de vue de l'imaginaire," in *Clefs pour l'imaginaire ou l'autre scène*, quoted by Metz (76).

12. I am grateful to Nicole Minnick for bringing Friedkin's remark to my attention.

13. The baroque visual hysteria of *Imitation of Life*, for example, simultaneously reflects and ridicules Universal's casting of Lana Turner, whose daughter Cheryl Crane had just stabbed Turner's lover Johnny Stompanato to death, as the mother who competes with her daughter Sandra Dee for the romantic favors of John Gavin.

14. Freud's links fetishistic disavowal, which he reserves to infants and adult males, first through castration anxiety to psychosis, then, in his later work, to neurosis. See "The Loss of Reality in Neurosis and Psychosis" (1924), "Fetishism" (1927), *An Outline of Psycho-analysis* (1940), and "Splitting of the Ego in the Process of Defence" (1940), in *Standard Edition* 19: 183–90; 21: 149–58; 23: 141–207, 271–78.

15. Compare J. Hillis Miller's analysis of the reciprocal relation between ostensible parasites and hosts in "The Critic as Host" (Bloom et al. 217–53).

16. Spivak's way of addressing this problem, tellingly, is by incessantly exposing the subject position of her own discourse, distinguishing herself from herself through a disavowing critique of the positioning that makes discourse possible. See for example "Strategy, Identity, Writing," and "Questions of Multiculturalism" (43, 45, 60).

17. Kermode (132), quoting Q. D. Leavis (135), with whom he is in sharp and interesting disagreement.

WORKS CITED

Altman, Rick. *The American Film Musical.* Bloomington: Indiana UP, 1987.

Bloom, Harold. *Poetry and Repression: Revisionism from Blake to Stevens.* New Haven: Yale UP, 1976.

Bloom, Harold et al. *Deconstruction and Criticism.* New York: Seabury, 1979.

Braudy, Leo. *The World in a Frame: What We See in Films.* Garden City: Doubleday, 1976.

Druxman, Michael B. *Make It Again, Sam: A Survey of Movie Remakes.* South Brunswick: Barnes, 1975.

Feuer, Jane. "The Self-Reflexive Musical and the Myth of Entertainment." *Quarterly Review of Film Studies* 2.3 (1977): 313–26.

Fowler, Alastair. *Kinds of Literature: An Introduction to the Theory of Genres and Modes.* Cambridge: Harvard UP, 1982.

Freud, Sigmund. *The Standard Edition of the Complete Psychological Works.* 23 vols. Trans. James Strachey et al. London: Hogarth, 1961.

Hirsch, E. D., Jr. *Validity in Interpretation.* New Haven: Yale UP, 1967.

Kermode, Frank. *The Classic: Literary Images of Permanence and Change.* Corrected ed. Cambridge: Harvard UP, 1983.

Leavis, Q. D. "A Fresh Approach to *Wuthering Heights.*" *Lectures in America.* Ed. F. R. Leavis and Q. D. Leavis. New York: Pantheon, 1969.

Mannoni, Octave. *Clefs pour l'imaginaire ou l'autre scène.* Paris: Seuil, 1969.

Metz, Christian. "A Note on Story/Discourse." *The Imaginary Signifier.* Trans. Celia Britton et al. Bloomington: Indiana UP, 1982.

Spivak, Gayatri Chakravorty. *The Post-Colonial Critic: Interviews, Strategies, Dialogues.* Ed. Sarah Harasym. New York: Routledge: 1990.

CHAPTER THREE

Economy and Aesthetics in American Remakes of French Films

MICHAEL HARNEY

What is a cinematic remake? To answer that question one must first deal with the aesthetic diglossia that pervades film criticism. "Serious" critics expressing themselves in the idiom of the intellectual elite tend to deplore the remake as a pointless and inherently second-rate product. Thus, John Simon, typifying the aesthetic coterie (and dismissing, be it noted, both the original and the remake) characterizes the American version of *La Femme Nikita* ("a trashy but effective piece of goods") as typical of "supererogatory Hollywood remakes of European movies," although, of course, the remake is "trashier and less effective." Joe Chidley praises with fainter damnation: "*Point of No Return*," he allows, "is more than a cheap ripoff of a French movie—it is a well-acted, slickly produced ripoff." In his review of *Sommersby*, the remake of *Le Retour de Martin Guerre*, Simon scolds the film industry for its "perennial obsession with updating stories." The author of an original story, a "true artist" who can "transport us to his time," is contrasted with "less gifted interpreters" who "drag [us] to a time and place [the original artist] did not envisage." Generally concurring with this antiremake sentiment, Stanley Kauffmann ("*Point of No Return*!") affirms that the results of the remaking trend "may be grim," and that "offhand" he can recall "only one truly memorable remake,"

Some Like It Hot by Billy Wilder and I.A.L. Diamond, a "great film" that makes us forget earlier French and German versions. Dismissive of *Point of No Return*, he generalizes concerning the movie industry's remaking penchant: "Hollywood keeps thinking that if it buys a plot, it buys a film." Stanley Klawans likewise assumes a categorically scornful approach to remakes when he dismisses *Sommersby* as "the clearest evidence to date of how feebly the American studios now grip the world market, even while seeming to throttle it."

Vernacular reviewers working for publications aimed at the broader mass market either positively endorse the remake as a concept (at least tacitly) or reveal a certain inconsistency in their attitude toward this category of film production. *Time* dismisses *Point of No Return* as perhaps having "no point." It would appear that a remake of "an unimprovably stylish, very entertaining thriller" is a gratuitous entreprise from the outset. The same magazine's Richard Corliss, while faintly disparaging the "cunning Hollywood script doctors" who refashion *Sommersby* from *Le Retour de Martin Guerre*, points out the "austere business" done by the original French "art-house hit." The American version, transformed, inevitably, into a "fervid romance swathed in star quality," its glib protagonist a "Southern cousin to *The Music Man*'s Professor Harold Hill," remains nonetheless "a seductive entertainment," in fact the "cleanest, ripest version of the tale" and a "robust Hollywood fantasy." While admitting that *True Lies* is an "odd action film," Corliss classifies the director, James Cameron, as one of the truly interesting "ambitious artists," "Hollywood's most daring and extravagant auteur," an "artist-brigand" whose films are more interesting, even as failures, than the more modest successes of lesser figures. While labeling *True Lies* "an abrasive essay in gung-ho gigantism," "a loud misfire," Corliss barely mentions that it is a remake of Claude Zidi's *La Totale!* (1992); nothing is made of the fact of Cameron's $100 million (or more) endorsement of the remaking fashion.

The occasionally inconsistent posture with regard to remakes could be attributed to a given publication's affiliation to this or that corporate network. Pauline Kael, an aesthete, has frequently enunciated just such a theory of conflict of interest as the motivation for the majority of reviewers' opinions, positive and negative, in the popular press and magazines. It is, however, no great revelation to allege conflict of interest as a factor, conscious or unconscious, in the formulation of cinematic opinion in commercial publications. Any salaried journalist might understandably hesitate to condemn a film produced by his or her own corporation or conglomerate. However, neither wholehearted advocacy nor erratic condemnation of remakes may be unequivocally imputed to a critic's niche in the conglomerate ecology.

The remake is an old phenomenon in the movie industry. Examples, going back to the earliest decades of the industry, are too numerous to inventory here (see Nowlan and Nowlan, "Introduction" xi–xii; Eberwein 28–30). To mention only one celebrated property among many examples from the first several decades of film, one could point to *The Maltese Falcon*, versions of which were made in 1931, 1936 (as *Satan Met a Lady*), and 1941. Scripted and directed by John Huston, the latter version is generally regarded as definitive. This confutes any notion of remaking as aesthetically pernicious in and of itself. We could adduce many other examples of remakes' improving over originals (including *Some Like It Hot*, mentioned by Kauffmann). John Huston's first film is, in fact, a specimen of a very common breed of film, namely, that of remakes of literary properties. Rex Beach's *The Spoilers* (1914, 1923, 1930, 1942, 1955) exemplifies the remaking of a script that is itself based on another medium. Directors, in addition, have been known to remake their own work (e.g., Hitchcock's two versions of *The Man Who Knew Too Much*; Raoul Walsh's *High Sierra* and *Colorado Territory*). Remakes of fondly regarded modern works (such as Jim Thompson's *The Getaway*, Garson Kanin's *Born Yesterday*) and of venerable classics (such as the recent *Last of the Mohicans*, *Bram Stoker's Dracula*, *Mary Shelley's Frankenstein*, *Little Women*) conform to the same appropriative principle as adaptations of best-sellers (e.g., *Gone with the Wind*, *Valley of the Dolls*, and *Presumed Innocent*).

The fact that the Motion Picture Academy assigns a category to screenplays based on another medium reflects the fact that remaking, whether as movie from text or movie from movie, is a procedure necessarily hardwired into the filmmaking mentality. Alain Masson conjectures that the ongoing mania for remakes reflects the film industry's urge to renovate and update. Remakes have the same function, in the ongoing campaign of commodification and market expansion, as the introduction of sound or color or the development of special effects (77).

Remaking and readapting have been done throughout the history of film, given that the medium, the most capitalized of narrative forms, must be an opportunistic exploiter of raw materials, including previously market-tested products. Each film, viewed as a locus of investment and as an intensive utilizer of labor, equipment, and supplies, must presell itself as a project before it can sell itself as a product. The search for preexisting properties—entities with antecedent market sectors—is thus a natural supplement to cinematic fund raising. In this process, novels, plays, short stories, and TV shows adapted into screenplays do not differ importantly from scripts, domestic or foreign, remade into other scripts.

Past literary and dramatic traditions offer parallels to the current trend in remaking foreign films. Stanley Kauffmann points out that throughout the nineteenth century the British and American popular theater "fed on remakes," as "busy scribblers . . . adapted French and German plays—from tragedy to farce—for the maw of the hungry theater" (rev. of *Point of No Return*). Looking still further back, Stuart Klawans reminds us that "Producers have been borrowing (or, even better, stealing) plots across international borders since well before the cinema began" (rev. of *Sommersby*). He situates the cinematic borrower in the same tradition as the Elizabethan theatrical producer who sought to please the crowd by reworking such foreign (in this case, Italian) properties as *The Merry Wives of Windsor*. This historical perspective, however, does not, Klawans asserts, exculpate the contemporary cinematic remake of its peculiar aesthetic infirmity, born of a corporate opportunism that is at once parasitical and symbiotic. *Sommersby*, he demonstrates, is really not an American film at all, but an international collaboration of Warner Brothers, Le Studio Canal +, Regency Enterprises, and other interests. A "new strain of international co-production" seeks the "lucrative appearance of coming from Hollywood," while conveying time and setting in "semaphoric" (i.e., minimally stereotypic) terms. The world of such international productions is vanilla, "a generalized past, prettified by . . . cinematography and adjusted toward modern sensibilities." It is, in short, consumable by the broadest range of cultures. The corporate internationalism described by Klawans logically expedites remaking from the opposite direction as well, as is pointed out in a recent note concerning a possible French version of *Thelma and Louise* (Bellafante, "The Girls of GATT").

When such exploitation of existing works occurs, updating, revision, and cultural adjusting will be inevitable. It is a post-Romantic emphasis on originality and creativity—themselves concepts formed in reaction to capitalistic commercialization and commodification—that explains, in large measure, the high-culture critics' categorical aesthetic prejudice against the remake and their steadfast predilection for the *sui generis* as opposed to the generic. This cultural-elitist prejudice against cinema that is too flagrantly mass-oriented was itself critiqued by Walter

Benjamin, who observed that it is "a commonplace," expressing "the same ancient lament that the masses seek distraction whereas art demands concentration from the spectator" (239).

At the same time, there can be no question, in the reality of film production, of any real partition between the dimensions of the popular and the generic on the one hand, the elitist and the personal on the other. Paul Coates, while recognizing a cultural schism among both filmmakers and audiences, suggests a synergetic relationship between genericism and individualism. The former without the latter inclines toward the predictable and the formulaic; the latter without the former is predisposed to an "intensifying hermeticism." While "genre is an implicit critique of individualism," artistic individuality "irrigates the desert of the merely generic." His treatment of the problem is Aristotelian: "Form needs matter, and high culture ascends by standing on the shoulders of the low" (ix).

To understand cinematic production, one must, affirms Coates, transcend "Romanticism's Promethean transvaluation of values" and such facile categorizations as the kitsch/art division. One must come to grips with the concept of entertainment. The latter phenomenon is "the antiart of a world with no time for art." It is the diversion offered by the world to "those it has rendered incapable . . . of the aspiration to art" (2). Entertainment, a "perennial" element of cultural history, is a "transhistorical presence" that is best understood not in terms of the fleeting transgression of carnival but rather the recurrent intermission "incorporated into regimes of exploitation" (3). Art, even bad art, is that work which strives to reveal human beings, to hold up "a fearsome mirror to our selves and social orders." Entertainment is, by contrast, both a "mode of address to the most superficial levels of the personality" and a denial of the very existence of social and psychological depth. Entertainment "disperses between the sub- and the superhuman." It purveys "dreams of redemption [that are] cynically aware of their own unreality" (3).

The roots of the present conflict between entertainment and art grow far back into the period before the invention of film. Entertainment, arising as an extreme form of appropriated discourse, is, in a sense, carnival suborned and prostituted. Art is its equal but opposite reaction—a self-declared contravention of distributive commodification. It is in light of this emerging divide, and in terms of period, nationality, and ideal-typical genres, that the Marxist critic Robert Weimann assesses styles of appropriation and representation. He discusses how a decline in "discursive representativeness" in nineteenth-century France exemplified by

Baudelaire, Verlaine, Mallarmé, and Rimbaud, and characterized by a "deep gulf between the verbal representations and the social representativity of the poet"—is countered, during the same era, by a more "democratic," "optimistic" American literature (typified by Melville and Twain), which remained ready "to shoulder the burden of representation on the levels of both textual signification and social function" (36).

Weimann, be it noted, discusses only canonical authors—that is, authors who were already required reading in a culture which he supports by his own appropriation of them as objects fit for analysis. Flaubert's work, epitomized by the incomplete *Bouvard et Pécuchet*, expresses, for him, a "crisis in discursive appropriation" (34–35). Henry James and Thomas Mann produce literature which defines itself as the representation of "the erosion of representativeness itself" (37). Moving toward a conclusion which discusses "Modernism and the New Economy of the Signifier," Weimann postulates a societal transformation marked by a metamorphosis in literary production. Symptomatic of the latter process are "the emerging forms of narrative immediacy, the repudiation of omniscience, the stylized modes of point of view" (40). Exalting such authors as Flaubert (as well as, in addition to James and Mann, Ernest Hemingway), Weimann speaks of the idiosyncratic in terms of its generic significance. However, to accept authors and texts literally prescribed by the official culture which Weimann endorses by his reading choices contradicts the fact of modern capitalist literary production as a collective marketing enterprise. Markets are always specialty markets first, then mass markets. One might even say that the term *mass market* is a pleonasm. A limited readership (or viewership) is an audience; a mass distribution and consumption, whether through textual circulation, filmic projection, or televised broadcasting, is a market. Mass education has insured, by its assigned readings of literary texts, that the individual approximate the generic in the generality of its consumption. The high school and the university are to literature, we might say, as the multiplex is to cinema.

While implementing a useful conceptual apparatus centered on the concept of authorial appropriation as the principal mechanism of literary representation as production, Weimann compares styles of representation in terms of periodic contrasts. Thus, he assumes, we can "compare representation in modern fiction" with "heroic and courtly epic up to and including Chrétien de Troyes, Hartmann von Aue, Wolfram von Eschenbach, Gottfried von Strassburg, and, even, late borderline cases like Sir Thomas Malory" (32). Epic poets, he contends, are defined by the limited capacity for proprietary authorial engagement. Between the "act and the product of representation" there is, in the assumed feudal mode of literary production, scant possibility for "self-projection or alienation." The artist relates to means and modes of production "communally, as some unquestionably given, shared property" (32). He summarizes Marx's understanding of modes of appropriation as they articulate with modes of production: "the act of assimilation constitutes itself on the basis of the givenness of what is to be assimilated" (32–33).

Periodic discontinuities arise, in Weimann's view, from evolving circumstances of appropriation that both affect and constitute "changeful modes and functions of representation." Where divisions between appropriator and properties are minimal, representation is of minor consequence. The divide, he points out, is that between the premodern and "romantic and realistic" modes of representation. The latter imply deliberate "self-projection," interacting with an "intellectual assimilation of the world." The ubiquity of this assimilation came to heighten the "expression of individuality" in the self-projection. The latter process remained limited as long as—to paraphrase Marx in the *Grundrisse*—appropriation defined itself as "'the reproduction of presupposed relations.'" (qtd. in Weimann 33).

In the modern period, affirms Weimann, literary appropriation (*Aneignung*) is less and less determined by "the given state of communal property." In contrast to the availability of "cultural materials, literary conventions, and traditions" of the earlier environment, a set of conditions emerges which increasingly obliges authors themselves to appropriate "the means and forms of literary production." Alienated from the means of production, which are no longer an indisputable part of their "social and self-fashioned intellectual selves," distanced from the means and modes of literary production that were once the shared property of the community, both writer and reader come to emphasize the former's idiosyncratic perspective as a crucial ingredient of literary art.

Two objections may be made to Weimann's schema. First, that appropriative modes, as he defines them, can be discovered in other periods than those he uses to demarcate as modern and premodern. Second, that what he defines as premodern—the communal appropriation, the relative absence of self-projection, and alienation in authorial representation—exists throughout historical time, and is probably the dominant mode at all times. Again, to privilege a specific kind of text as the only text, ignoring all other forms, is to practice a kind of communal appropriation of another kind. It is to buy, lock stock and barrel, the conceptual apparatus of canonical practice. Precapitalist narrative production, regardless of subsequently imposed legal or aesthetic categories, is primordially designed for local, communal consumption. What defines capitalism is a selective and opportunistic slicing out of the communal text pie for purposes of commodification and distribution. Like any other elitist critic, Weimann privileges the select population of canonical texts and forms of text, ignoring the vast array of products which are not deemed worthy of study by the critical elite.

By contrast, that outgrowth of capitalism which Adorno calls the culture industry is more ecumenical in its opportunism and cares mainly about market potential. As a hedge against risks, it seeks prognosticative indicators of the likelihood of a project's success. These preferred indicators are of three principal types: (1) the folkloric, which could include all manner of themes, motifs, tales, and other ready-made materials in the public domain; (2) the historiographic, which would include "true stories," such as historical incidents, biographies, and episodes from current events; (3) the literary, which would include classics, bestsellers, and previously produced scripts (i.e., films inviting a remake).

The movie industry, of which the Disney corporation is the most prominent and successful example, prefers the first of these prognosticative criteria. Folkloric narrative, whether conveyed in short or long forms, is inherently formulaic. It endlessly remakes the same stories, employing, with superficial variations in setting and costume, the same motifs, themes, stereotyped characters, and plots. The intertextuality of the folkloric is vastly expanded by the film industry, which converts regionally and ethnically specific folk narrative into global and generic popular narrative. One might say that folkloric production and circulation are the cottage industry of which film is the industrialized rationalization. Film is like folklore, only more so, in its predilection for the formulaic. This is precisely what most annoys Adorno about mass entertainment, especially movies, whose plots consist of "ready-made clichés to be slotted in anywhere; they never do anything more than fulfill the purpose alloted them in the overall plan" (Horkheimer and Adorno 125).

Adorno's pejorative characterization can be read as an inadvertent paraphrase of Vladimir Propp's "law of transference," which insures that "components of one tale can, without any alteration whatsoever, be transferred to another" (7). The history of the cinematic remake is sustained by a pragmatic observance of this principle of thematic and structural transference. As Michel Ciment argues, it is the appeal to favorite themes (e.g., in the case of Raoul Walsh's Western remake of his own *High Sierra*, those of pastoral and anarchic individualism), and the near-identity of properties, that attracts writers and directors to remaking (86).

The concept of distance from means and modes of production must be examined more closely in the light of these formulaic considerations. Weimann and other Marxist critics emphasize this point to varying degrees and in various ways. It is a crucial tenet of the Marxian schema. The axiom overlooks, on the one hand, the fact that in preliterate societies literary artistry routinely does without any material means of production. Neither pen and paper, nor their analogues, are a necessary part of the well-documented dynamics of oral-folkloric literary composition (Lord 124–37, 140–57; Ong 140–55). This technique and its analogues produce the vast pool of texts that constitute both officially "preliterate" literature (epics, ballads, folk tales), and that unclassified population of texts (broadly definable as coherent segments of utterance) too transient, too trivial, too unclassifiable to attract critical or scholarly notice. When such performative texts find written form, there is every reason to believe that the act of copying them derives from an aesthetic or intellectual regime separate from that of their creators. The cleric or the folklorist or the courtier or the ethnographer transcribes the performance of the jongleur, the storyteller, the singer, the street comedian. By contrast, the critic, whether scholar or journalist, goes after big game. The small-scale, the occasional, the improvisational, the merely verbal—these make, in their polyglot, polymorphous aggregate, for a textual vermin beneath the notice of critical law.

Weimann misses the point by postulating as a feature of modernity a restricted access to means of production. In terms of basic narrative, any would-be author has the requisite means in his possession: the human vocal apparatus. Whether the product circulates and is consumed, always depends on the local level, upon the idiosyncratic engagement of artist with audience. This relationship hinges upon intangible factors such as the talent and personality of the artist, the interests and tastes of a given public at a given moment in a given community. At the same time, this environment of face-to-face immediacy, of improvisational and traditional orality—ubiquitous even in the midst of rampant capitalism, state-centralized social stratification, and increasingly diversified technologies—always lies handy to anyone who wishes to dip into the vast and ever-growing common pool of accreted stock materials that knows no

copyright, nor any other preemptive individualist or proprietary imped-
iments to access. The dimension of orality is the small-scale, open
marketplace, which, in its myriad regional and local instantiations, is
omnipresent and enduring. The dimension of literacy, that provides
Weimann and like-minded elistist critics with their own predefined
stock of materials for study, is the realm of state-supported capitalism,
which is that of mass markets, including that of mass literacy and its
textual canons.

The oral-folkloric method of production—in which means and
method are one—finds its autonomous analogue in current day technology, which in point of fact permits present-day authors, through access to
internet distribution, word processing, desktop publishing, video equipment, and laser printing, to become the independent producers and distributors of their own written or visual texts. Analogous distributive
potential, and relative cheapness and accesibility of productive means, are
to be found in the areas of film, television, music, and painting.

This technological capacity does not thereby reduce the alienation
of the artist from what, in late capitalism, constitutes the principal barrier
between artist and audience: the distribution of the goods within the market system. Authors of today find themselves more and more in a position
similar to that of the independent filmmaker who can indeed produce the
film, with aesthetic control and even at a high level of technological quality. There remains, however, the problem of distribution and access to the
broader markets. This access is largely controlled by networks of distributors and sellers/exhibitors. The pattern, in its basic outlines, was, as
Fredric Jameson points out, predicted by Marx in terms of a transmutation of "production . . . into consumption and distribution" (269). Where
the "displacement from production to circulation" is the principal consideration in artistic endeavor (Jameson 272), we have a tributary economy, characterized by brokering, localized patronage, and cliental net-
working. This is another aspect of the culture industry, especially
moviemaking, that vexed Adorno. Industrial-cultural production, he
believes, is characterized by "distribution and mechanical reproduction,"
and therefore "lives parasitically from the extra-artistic technique of the
material production of goods," thus showing no regard for "the laws of
form demanded by aesthetic autonomy" (14).

The commercial transactions and mercantile negotiation at the
heart of movie remaking exasperate many critics because the remake
forcibly reminds one that movies, as performative products only fully real-

ized through consumption, are situated in the market. The small cinematic success of the art-house or independent film so preferred by individualist critics is viewed by the impresario as a marketing test hinting at possibly broader reception in the game of distribution and access, which is the global cinematic mart. This is perhaps even more the case of those foreign films (such as *La Femme Nikita*) which are intended to imitate glossy Hollywood product and conventional narrative themes but find an art-house distribution in the United States merely because they are foreign productions. To play the game of remaking pretested merchandise requires big money for both production (if the film is going to be a vigorous player) and distribution (if the maximum number of venues is to be attained). This results in an inevitable amalgamation of the aesthetic and the pecuniary. David Denby recognizes the inescapable nature of the problem while deploring its hybrid results. Critics and movies, he laments, are necessarily "at odds" when it comes to the bigger productions, especially of the prime summer season, whose output can only be described as "industrial products." The typical big summer movie is like

> a theme park, a trade show . . . a multifunctional marketing vehicle. It sells itself, it sells toys, it sells food, it sells books and music. You can say it's zero as art, but you haven't said much of anything, since art was far from the minds of the people making it. (rev. of *True Lies*)

Even the cheapest movie costs a lot of money, compared with such other media as literature's word processor and paper or painting's canvas and paint. Even art movies are conceived and made in the expectation of profit. To "remake" a film is to shoot a re-rendering, a reworking, a paraphrasing of the original's script—in effect, to Americanize, in the case of French originals, a Renault or a Citroën into a Ford or a Chevy. One does this to sell the resultant product, for profit, to the greatest number of customers, domestic and foreign. To retrofit foreign films, French or otherwise, American producers tend to deploy various high-toning or upgrading strategies. The outcome of the upgrading—the resultant look of sets, costumes, production design—does not differ from the spit and polish of sets and costumes in, say, the Fred Astaire-Ginger Rogers films, the Busby Berkeley musicals, and other glamour pictures of decades past. Hollywood producers have always felt that escapist films should be shot in escapist fashion: that the big markets are made up of people who want to be visually, thematically, narratively taken away from it all. So it should be no surprise, for example, that the French *Trois hommes et un couffin*'s working bachelors (airline pilot, etc.) living in a modest Parisian flat are converted into *Three Men and a Baby*'s upscale professionals (architect, actor, etc.), residing in a palatial New York City penthouse. The art-house film, consumed by the cultural elite in this country, is often characterized, paradoxically, by earthy or eccentric characters, marginal settings, and countercultural subject matter. The paradox of remaking for a broader audience resides in Hollywood's ornamental overhaul of these folksy individualizing elements. Richard Corliss describes this renovative Hollywoodization in terms of product enhancement and expanded markets:

> Cunning Hollywood script doctors [have] to approach the European originals not as finished portraits but as sketches in need of coherence, heart, pizazz. It's what rewriters do: refashion a boutique item so it will jump off the shelves at the mall. (rev. of *Sommersby*)

Hollywoodization is analogous to architectural gentrification. But it is not merely an entrepreneurial conversion of charmingly dilapidated brownstones or picturesquely rundown Victorians into higher-priced townhouses and condominiums. Cinematic reconditioning is actually like buying up blocks of quaint old fixer-uppers and using their design as the blueprint for whole housing tracts.

Application of this analogy, to be sure, presupposes a stipulation. The upgrading of backdrop that inevitably accompanies "boutique-to-mall" transformations does not necessarily imply elegance of costume or decor as the sole renovative criterion. The constant in remaking is the money spent on sets, costumes, and locations. The rule is not really to ameliorate, but to amplify—to produce something that is the same, only more so. While this "Disneylandization" of originals, particularly French originals, may or may not represent a plundering and endangerment of the donor culture's "aesthetic patrimony" (Durham 5), outlandish embellishment is an unmistakable symptom of the adaptive process. Thus, like their Gallic counterparts, the bachelor fathers of the American *Three Men* are engagingly hassled by workaday problems. The complications of their daily lives are simply more extravagant, the disruptions more vertiginous, than analogous elements in the original. In the French *Trois Hommes*, diaper-changing implies being late for work; in the American version, it entails the loss of a million-dollar contract. In Hollywood films, the stakes are higher, the ante always upped. That is why it is a mistake to categorize American remaking as merely the expression of a bourgeois sensibility. French originals tend to accept the everyday, the normal, the modest. The inhabitants of this socioeconomic middle ground would have to be called a bourgeoisie—a middle class. American movies, by contrast, generally see things in terms of rags or riches, and nothing in between. A French comedy will tend to portray ordinary fellows (*Le Sucre* comes to mind) frantically trying to minimize their losses. American comedies are predisposed to focus on ordinary folks' frenzied efforts to become extraordinary (recall *Rain Man*'s Las Vegas digression). It is going for broke, aiming at jackpots rather than modest winnings, that obsesses Hollywood moviemaking.

The remake of *Le Salaire de la peur* (1953) as *Sorcerer* (1977) provides an instructive variation on the amplificatory pattern. Henri-Georges Clouzot's *Le Salaire* is about dead-broke drifters and expatriates, desperate to get out of a South American backwater. Their poverty is abject but nondescript, the details of their backgrounds inexplicit because immaterial to the elemental nature of their penury. William Friedkin's *Sorcerer*, by contrast, augments the résumés of the hirelings, converting them into glamorous fugitives from the worlds of high finance, international terrorism, and organized crime. It places them in a South American hellhole that is not just poverty stricken, but colossally dismal, filthy, and sordid. In its wallowing amid mud and shanties, in its personages' slumming with the wretched of the earth, *Sorcerer* is the dystopic counterpart to the sanitary utopia of upscale films. Not that appalling slums and miserable backwaters do not exist in the real world; only that when Hollywood represents such environments, it does so not from documentary fervor but from a desire to induce escape through overstatement. Whether by opulence or squalor, transcendence of the mundane is the objective.

Historical antecedents of the expedient recasting of elements that characterizes the cross-cultural cinematic remake also reveal a market-oriented deflection of original materials. The thematic shift in question generally responds to factional or ideological agendas. Peter Stallybrass discusses, for example, the strategic marginalization or appropriation of the Robin Hood tale (another frequent subject of film remakes) by interest groups that are the supporters, subverters, or surrogates of the state. Variously interpreted in ballad, chapbook, pageant, or masque, the most famous bandit of them all provided the nucleus of a "symbolic system" which amalgamated carnival practices and "forms of popular protest and action" ("Drunk" 62). Not surprisingly, this "symbolic system" came to be manipulated by the very order it had concurrently emerged to confront, as Robin Hood came to be domesticated by his "reinscription . . . within the ideological enclosure of the nation-state" (66; see also Georgakas 74–76).

From a broader historical perspective, Stallybrass and Allon White consider the repression of carnival in terms of a "phobic alienation" of carnivalesque elements by the "bourgeois unconscious" (171). This alienation from the indigenous European carnival tradition over several centuries culminated in the characteristic "compensatory plundering" of ethnographic materials garnered from colonized, non-European cultures (172). The absence of socially sanctioned, collective carnivalesque practices is accompanied, in modern psychological clinical case studies, by a tendency toward individualized, hysterical "pastiche and parody" of carnival practices and forms (174). Repression of carnival encompasses a "gradual, relentless attack on the 'grotesque body' of carnival by the emergent middle and professional classes from the Renaissance onwards." This class response took the form of an ever-increasing "demonization and . . . exclusion of the carnivalesque." Bourgeois convention and discourse "reinflected" the primordially collective practices and languages of carnival into a "negative, individualist framework" (176). Carnivalesque behavior becomes an idiosyncratic, neurotic enactment of "desperate ritual fragments salvaged from a festive tradition, *the self-exclusion from which* had been one of the identifying features of [the bourgeois] . . . class" (176). Abjuring and suppressing "calendric festive practices" through personal restraint and legislative decree, bourgeois culture succumbs, from the seventeenth through the nineteenth centuries, to a neurotic need to appropriate the elements of carnivalesque ritual: "feasting, violence, drinking, processions, fairs, wakes, rowdy spectacle and outrageous clamour" (176).

In the modern context, entertainment, the precipitate of repressive appropriation in the realm of media, is the correlative of hysterical sublimation in the psychic domain. Two basic exploitative tendencies present themselves. On the repressive side, thematic looting such as the pseudo-ethnographic adaptations mentioned by Stallybrass and White— of materials deemed germane to specific ideological agendas of the moment—promotes such extravagances as the neopastoral modification of the image of North American peoples in such films as *Little Big Man, Dances with Wolves,* and *Geronimo: An American Legend.* On the hysterical side, the carnivalesque catalogue just cited could be taken as a repertoire of standard transgressive themes in escapist narrative genres. The outrageous sexuality, obstreperous nihilism, and outright anarchism so characteristic of the Western, action, fantasy, thriller, and science-fiction genres may be taken as examples of the kind of reinscription and cooptation described by Stallybrass. The subversion often expressed (as in the ferociously anticorporate stance of the *Alien* and *Robocop* movies) corresponds to the allowable subversion typified by domesticated versions of Robin Hood. At the same time, these disorderly, often apparently insurgent elements in the more popular genres could be viewed as the industrialized manifestation of carnival's "escape-valve" aspect, according to which stylized protests against the social order are, paradoxically, "contributions to that order." The upper classes traditionally permitted, even encouraged the topsy-turvy of carnival as "a means for the subordinates to purge their resentments and to compensate for their frustrations" (Burke 201).

The process of appropriation and reinscription, particularly of texts experienced as escapist—i.e., carnivalesque—replicates the tendency in earlier traditions to adapt preexisting texts. Medieval European literary production, in fact, distinguished itself as an almost exclusively appropriative regime, in that most of medieval literature that came to be regarded as canonical remade earlier texts. In the popular (i.e., nonwritten) culture, this process was enacted through the practices and techniques of the minstrel as adaptor/performer of traditional works. In the literate culture, textual production was regulated at both the macro level (i.e., that of the work) and the micro level (i.e., that of style) by the global conception of *auctoritas*, and by such rhetorical conventions as *amplificatio*, a highly formulaic system of *topoi*, and so on (Curtius chaps. 3–5, 14–16). Such remaking, as prominently exemplified by medieval versions of such late-classical texts as the *Alexander Romance* and the *Book of Apollonius of Tyre*, invariably involved extensive "medievalization" of characters, setting, and ideology (Fraker 55–6, 59–61; Michael 29–73, 88–140; Kortekaas 3–9). Frequently condemned typical attributes of television and movie production, such as the propensity for sequels and "prequels" (e.g., the numerous installments of James Bond films; the TV series devoted to the exploits of the youthful Indiana Jones) were staples of medieval literary practice (e.g., numerous continuations of late-medieval chivalric romances like *Amadís of Gaul*; late-medieval epics on the *Youthful Deeds of the Cid*, dating from at least a century and a half after the primary epic work devoted to the hero's adult exploits).

The medieval remake of a previously existing text was not a capitalizing appropriation but rather a deferential adoption. Nonetheless, the predisposition to utilize preexisting texts as the basis for production manifests a common impulse in both medieval and modern contexts. What the capitalist remake of cinema and the precapitalist remake of medieval literature have in common is a concept of precedent. It is the textual precedent that justifies the remake in both cases. On the one hand, we may ask: what were the medieval correlatives of the modern era's ostensible imperatives of profitability? On the other: what are the modern analogues of medieval doctrinal criteria? To say that modern remakes originate in the profit motive does not fully explain the phenomenon, any more than the medieval penchant for amplifying existing texts derives simply from the gnomic imperatives of medieval Christianity. In the same way that not every classical work was adapted by medieval writers, not all successful foreign films are remade. In both the medieval and the modern cases, only a small percentage of works are assessed as properties suitable for reworking. In the medieval context, what we would call market potential was perceived in terms of demographic prospects in service of didactic imperatives. A plot was chosen (as in the case of the *Alexander Romance*) following the same criteria as in the selection of topics for sermons. The transaction whose proliferation was sought was not monetary but doctrinal. Consumption underwrote dogma. In the cinematic remake, the relationship is reversed: dogma underwrites consumption. The ideas whose circulation is promoted function as a currency.

Taking for granted the commercial factor—that only those projects are produced that can attract capital by virtue of potential audience or audiences—some critics postulate ideological or political elements as the rationale for reworking a previously filmed plot. Michael A. Katovich and Patrick T. Kinkade explain the remake as a response to a given historical conjuncture—as an expression, in other words, of the political and social concerns of filmmakers and audiences (620–21). The "image-making" of the 1950s (post–World War II, McCarthy era, Cold War) supports "mediated realities and fantasies" of a different order from the "post-Vietnam, post-Watergate, post-AIDS eras" (621). In contrast to the findings of public opinion polls of the 1950s, that reveal such collective apprehensions as the need for military preparedness, and such social fixations as xenophobia, the post-Vietnam era is revealed as both less assertive and less optimistic. Characterized by "loneliness, anomie, isolation, alienation, self-obsession, and self-hatred," it experienced the individual as "decentered" and "unconnected to history" (624). Where the 1951 version of *The Thing* idealizes a synthesis of the soldier's rational pragmatism and the scientist's utilitarian erudition, the 1982 version, by contrast, dramatizes a "pathological integration of science, medicine, and the military" (626). The 1951 version's idealistic scientist, dauntlessly eager to communicate with the alien, is isolated from his colleagues because of his misguided underestimation of the danger posed by the intruder organism. The prophetic scientist in the 1982 version is incarcerated because his colleagues perceive his frenzied warnings as a paranoic overestimation of danger. In the earlier version, the group is vindicated in its apprehensions, the individual marginalized for his quixoticism. In the later, the raving individual is a Cassandra, oracular in the precision of his deadly foreknowledge, while the group is complacently dilatory in its response to the common peril. Katovitch and Kinkade see in the latter film's pessimism a postmodern personification of madness as a "realism which cannot be placed properly in the rational/bureaucratic framework" (627). Remakes of science-fiction and horror films of the 1950s are overwhelmed by such themes as "doom, terror, loss of agency, ineffectual resistance to threats, information without practical application, and failure to distinguish nature from copy" (627). Recent film, whether as remake or original, reveals a "societal transformation" in the form of a subversion of myths of "group solidarity, ingenuity and invincibility" (633).

While there may have arisen a demonstrable societal transformation toward the subversive and the nihilistic, which finds expression in the ideological intention of films, we must not forget contemporary capitalism's limitless capacity to assimilate all themes, all genres, including those of rabid anticapitalism. Where the escape-valve carnivalesque once was a factor tolerated, even fomented, by a predominant elite aiming at social control, modern capitalism, symbiotically ensconced at the core of political and economic power, seeks mainly to augment its profits. We must not, therefore, mistake ideological shifts detected in films for any real ideological shift among the members of the ruling directorate. Any ideology serves as fodder for the machine. Thus, the opposite of the subversive ideologies detected by Katovitch and Kinkade underlies the plots of films such as 1982's *The Thing*. This film's finale actually shows men sacrificing their lives for humanity. In some plots, heroic altruism may be reduced to an elemental dyadic amity, either the reciprocal loyalty of friendship (as in the *The Getaway*, whose symbolic escape to Mexico is reiterated in *The Shawshank Redemption*) or the primeval solidarity of kinship (as in the two recent remakes of the Wyatt Earp legend). The system, the polity, may be irredeemably rotten, but a primordial individual goodness remains salvageable. Thus, *Le Salaire/ Sorcerer, Nikita/ No Return, Martin Guerre/Sommersby, La Totale!/True Lies*, all repudiate the system, while vindicating its personnel. Whether polity is residually endorsed or not, person-to-person amity materializes as the fundamental unit of social performance.

Sommersby's anachronisms and incongruities, stemming from indiscriminate transposition of historical and cultural particulars, have been astutely catalogued by John Simon. Nineteenth-century photography, written records, and handwriting analysis are only some of the real-world elements whose circumvention undermines the verisimilitude of the tale as retold. At the same time, notes Simon, justifying "the broad outlines of the old story" required introducing "complicated and confusing additions." In the French version, Gérard Depardieu's impersonator is a sometimes ambivalent but generally enterprising opportunist who looks to take advantage of a good thing and strives with desperate ingenuity to escape punishment. He inhabits a rural world of the past recreated through understated depiction of detail. Where the country domain of then and now are the same, the film lets the similarity speak for itself, allows it to construct the setting; where different, the contrast is indicated with discreet intensity (e.g., the legality of fraudulent appropriation of another's estate, a capital offense in the kin-ordered world of the sixteenth century). Richard Gere's charlatan is both more opportunistic and more contradictory than his French counterpart. The estate he appropriates is bigger; the social issues he personifies (liberation of women; social assimilation of ex-slaves; overthrow of the feudal and repressive South by the capitalist and liberal North; participation in world markets) are of overtly greater consequence; his love affair is more intense; his fall more precipitous and more pitiful (his execution stems not from violation of property law but from his shouldering of the real Sommersby's guilt in a murder). The drive for legitimacy is overwhelming—the character gives up his life in order to die a propertied and respected man.

Perhaps most obvious in their treatment of the relationship between the individual and the nation-state, markets, and national cultures, with all their affinities and disharmonies, are the pairs *La Femme Nikita/ Point of No Return* and *La Totale!/ True Lies*. The transmutation/Americanization of these pairs emphasizes what might be called the *mise-en-état*—i.e., the placement of the narrative setting and its personages in symbiotic contiguity with the state and its mercantile surrogations and abettors. The dates of originals and adaptations, among the four pairs studied here, suggest a pattern. The oldest film of the cluster, *Le Salaire de la peur*, waited twenty-five years for its remake; between *Le Retour de Martin Guerre* and *Sommersby*, ten years elapsed. By contrast, *Nikita* (1990) and *La Totale!* (1992) were being rewritten and remade within a year or so of their release.

Not that we can generalize about any transformation in the economy or culture of France—only that the ready-made, "off-the-shelf" nature of *Nikita* derives from both its American look in terms of production values and its American outlook in terms of theme. The look is glossy, action-filled; the theme is market-oriented, "state-crafty." The deliberately American gloss of *Nikita's* production values and photography preconditions the quickness of its adaptation. The French film's portrayal of an intimately transgressive, callously obtrusive bureaucracy betrays, of course, not only a certain geopolitical hyperrealism but also the very fact of the film's actual corporate antecedents. Its heroine's status as the feminized avatar of James Bond partakes of the venerable cinematic tradition of the lavishly spending state—a paradise for the community of high-tech vendors—underwriting a regime of surveillance and assassination, a program implemented in a fantasy land of fortuitously subversive victims at home, of serendipitously nasty quarry abroad.

It is no accident, perhaps, that remakes are often of texts whose plot involves a remaking of personages, in the form of reeducation, imposture, shape-shifting, metamorphosis, rebirth, role-playing, etc. (recall recent remakes of *Born Yesterday* and *Invasion of the Body Snatchers*). The originals/remakes discussed in this chapter often dramatize the recruitment and indoctrination of outsiders by ongoing enterprises and regimes. Being already narratives devoted to a remaking (we might say, an incorporation) of personages in benefit of voracious collectivities, the French originals lend themselves to the fabrication of remakes that frame the remaking of their protagonists. There is, as Michel Chion points out, an affinity between the theme of "replaced people" and the principle of remaking. The cinematic character is, in a sense, "'bodysnatched'" by the actor; the body of the actor/character is "the site of a rift" between actor and role (100, my translation). The assimilative theme, moreover, is mimetic of the very commercial transaction executed by the producers of remakes. Thus, in *Le Salaire/ Sorcerer*, the desperate adventurers are reshaped by the superintendent corporation into proficient haulers of explosives; in *Martin Guerre/ Sommersby*, the despondent and lonely wife seeks a surrogate husband, while the friendless humbug pursues a legitimizing spouse; in *Nikita/ No Return*, the mysteriously autonomous agency recasts and retrains a derelict for the role of sophisticated operative. As John Simon points out with regard to *No Return*, the "remodeling" of the "murderous guttersnipe" is effected apparently through "teaching her good manners and good English." The actual training in language and manners is discharged by a personage Stanley Kauffman calls a "social-graces teacher." But the suspense of the *Nikita/ No Return* plot, as Chidley points out, largely derives from the protagonist's submission to the tutelage of the cryptic personage known as Bob. Although, as Chidley puts it, "[*Point of No Return*] is no *My Fair Lady*," Bob is the chief educator, the functionary Pygmalion to the slovenly Galatea. We might say that just as the American film is a clone of the French, the character Nikita/Maggie is a clone of her tutor. *Adam's Rib*, both as filmic precedent and mythic reference, is thus also a pertinent analogue.

The interpenetration of story and storytelling, of personages and producers, is pointedly insinuated by Richard Corliss in his appraisal of *True Lies*. The latter film's protagonist is a spy masquerading in his daily life as a nerdy computer salesman and ordinary family man. His wife "is Penelope, unaware that she's married to Ulysses." Like the other films discussed in the present essay, the metamorphic masquerade at the heart of *True Lies* involves a recruitment. *La Totale!/ True Lies* shows a wife converting her husband into a more sensitive and at the same time more adventurous mate, a husband transfiguring his wife into a more alluring partner who is also a fellow agent. The story necessarily entails, argues Corliss, a "double resonance" of "domestic and cinematic" lies. He quotes James Cameron, the director of *True Lies*, on the "'comedy potential of the lies, the façades, the allegory of relationships.'" The "'unknowability of people'" that emerges, for Cameron, as the story's cardinal theme, derives in large measure from the "'strange, dialectic world'" of the film's star, Arnold Schwarzenegger: "'On the one hand, he's a family man; on the other, he's a superstar, which means that so much is expected of him.'" Doubling and redoubling, identity crisis and mistaken identity are at the heart of *True Lies*. Stanley Kauffmann observes of the dime-store Don Juan and phony spy who tries to seduce the Schwarzenegger character's wife: "this would-be seducer is pretending to be exactly the sort of man she doesn't know her husband is." *True Lies* thus contains both the material it "exploits and subverts" and the parody of that material.

Another aspect to the "upscaling" factor mentioned earlier is the relationship between the degree of marginality of the recruited personages and the degree of officiality of the regime fortified. *Martin Guerre*'s humble peasant grange is infiltrated by an essentially common Everyman seeking a haven from indigence. *Sommersby*—"an imposture of a Hollywood film, about a man who's an impostor" (Stuart Klawans)—makes of its impersonator-hero a visionary picaroon who, while representing the liberal nation-state and modern capitalism, paradoxically impersonates both the sexual liberator of his landowner wife and the Great White Savior of the newly freed black folk of the region. The nondescript oil company in *Le Salaire* conscripts mostly ordinary drifters whose antecedents are barely hinted at. Its remake both augments the magnitude of the company and the importance of the political machine that colludes with it (while, as noted earlier, enhancing the men's life history). The cultural trajectory of the more recent remakes is as short as the chronological lapse between the originals and their American versions. *Nikita*'s preposterously trashy, drug-addicted protagonist is transformed, by the pitilessly efficient agency of an omnipresent government, into an outlandishly elegant, ravishingly efficient hit woman. The American film, save for a barely perceptible embellishment of sets and hardware, tells a virtually identical tale. The streamlined metamorphosis highlights by its conspicuous hyperbole the underlying thematic opportunism of what Joe Chidley calls "the Europe-to-Hollywood pipeline." Despite the basic story's "tedious love story and dime-store psychologizing," argues Chidley, *Point of No Return* is "naughtily entertaining," largely due to its retention of "the feel and smart-aleck attitude of a . . . French film." Indeed, the American version, "except for the actors, the locations and the lack of subtitles . . . *is* a . . . French film." The remake shares with the original its "plot, characters and even, at times, individual shots." The problem of identity, in other words, now encompasses the actual formal distinction between original and remake.

WORKS CITED

Adorno, Theodor W. "Culture Industry Reconsidered." *New German Critique* 6 (1975): 12–19.

Ansen, David. Rev. of *Point of No Return*. *Newsweek* 29 March 1993: 65.

——— . Rev. of *True Lies*. *Newsweek* 18 July 1994: 58.

Arroyo, Jose. "Cameron and the Comic." Rev. of *True Lies. Sight and Sound* 4.9 (1994): 26–28.

Bartholomew, David. *Cinema Sequels and Remakes, 1903–1987.* Book review. *Library Journal* 1 Feb. 1989: 62.

Bellafante, Ginia. "The Girls of GATT. (French actresses Juliette Binoche and Isabelle Adjani may star in French remake of 'Thelma and Louise')." *Time* 17 Jan. 1994: 67.

Benjamin, Walter. "The Work of Art in the Age of Mechanical Reproduction." *Illuminations.* Ed. Hannah Arendt. Trans. Harry Zohn. New York: Schocken, 1969. 217–51.

Bowman, James. Rev. of *Sommersby. American Spectator* April 1993: 56–57.

Burke, Peter. *Popular Culture in Early Modern Europe.* New York: Harper Torchbooks, 1978.

Canby, Vincent. Rev. of *Sommersby. New York Times* 5 Feb. 1993: B1+.

Chidley, Joe. Rev. of *Point of No Return. Maclean's* 29 March 1993: 46.

———. Rev. of *True Lies. Maclean's* 25 July 1994: 58–59.

Chion, Michel. "Les Enfants du remake: Sur deux versions des 'Bodysnatchers.'" *Positif* 459 (1999): 100–03.

Ciment, Michel. "De la Sierra au Colorado: Sur deux films de Raoul Walsh." *Positif* 459 (1999): 85–88.

Coates, Paul. *Film at the Intersection of High and Mass Culture.* Cambridge: Cambridge UP, 1994.

Corliss, Richard. Rev. of *Sommersby. Time* 22 Feb. 1993: 69.

———. Rev. of *True Lies. Time* 18 July 1994: 55–56.

Curtius, Ernst Robert. *European Literature and the Latin Middle Ages.* Trans. Willard R. Trask. New York: Harper and Row, 1953.

Denby, David. Rev. of *True Lies. New York* 25 July 1994: 46–47.

Drake, Jason. Rev. of *Sommersby. Sight and Sound* 3.5 (1993): 56–57.

Durham, Carolyn A. *Double Takes: Culture and Gender in French Films and Their American Remakes.* Hanover: UP of New England, 1998.

Eberwein, Robert. "Remakes and Cultural Studies." Horton and McDougal 15–33.

Fraker, Charles F. *The Libro de Alexandre: Medieval Epic and Silver Latin*. North Carolina Studies in the Romance Languages and Literatures, 245. Chapel Hill: U.N.C., Dept. of Romance Languages, 1993.

Georgakas, Dan. "Robin Hood: From Roosevelt to Reagan." Horton and McDougal 70–79.

Horkheimer, Max and Theodor Adorno. *Dialectic of Enlightenment*. Trans. John Cumming. 2nd ed. London: Verso, 1986.

Horton, Andrew, and Stuart Y. McDougal, eds. *Play It Again, Sam: Retakes on Remakes*. Berkeley: U of California P, 1998.

Jameson, Fredric. *Postmodernism, or the Cultural Logic of Late Capitalism*. Durham: Duke UP, 1991.

Katovich, Michael A., and Patrick T. Kinkade. "The Stories Told in Science Fiction and Social Science: Reading *The Thing* and Other Remakes from Two Eras." *Sociological Quarterly* 34.4 (1993): 619–37.

Kauffmann, Stanley. Rev. of *Sommersby*. *New Republic* 8 March 1993: 28.

——— . Rev. of *Point of No Return*. *New Republic* 19 April 1993: 28–29.

——— . Rev. of *True Lies*. *New Republic* 5 Sept. 1994: 34–35.

Klawans, Stuart. Rev. of *Sommersby*. *Nation* 8 March 1993: 316–19.

——— . Rev. of *True Lies*. *Nation* 5 Sept. 1994: 249–51.

Kortekaas, G.A.A. *Historia Apollonii Regis Tyri: Prolegomena, Text Edition of the Two Principal Latin Recensions, Bibliography, Indices and Appendices*. Groningen: Bouma's Boekhuis, 1984.

Lane, Anthony. Rev. of *True Lies*. *New Yorker* 25 July 1994: 77–79.

Leitch, Thomas M. "Twice-Told Tales: the Rhetoric of the Remake." *Literature/Film Quarterly* 18.3 (1990): 138–50.

Lord, Albert B. *The Singer of Tales*. Cambridge: Harvard UP, 1960.

Lowry, Brian. Rev. of *True Lies*. *Variety* 11 July 1994: 41.

Maslin, Janet. Rev. of *Point of No Return*. *New York Times* 19 March 1993: B:4.

——— . Rev. of *True Lies*. *New York Times* 15 July 1994: B1+.

Marx, Karl. *Grundrisse*. Trans. Martin Nicolaus. New York: Random House, 1973.

Masson, Alain. "Améremake." *Positif* 459 (1999): 76–81.

McCarthy, Todd. Rev. of *Point of No Return*. *Variety* 22 March 1993: 50.

Michael, Ian. *The Treatment of Classical Material in the "Libro de Alexandre."* Manchester: Manchester UP, 1970.

Natale, Richard. Rev. of *Sommersby*. *Variety* 1 Feb. 1993: 96.

Nowlan, Robert. A., and Gwendolyn Wright Nowlan. *Cinema Sequels and Remakes, 1903–1987*. Jefferson: McFarland, 1989.

Ong, Walter J. *Orality and Literacy*. London: Methuen, 1982.

Pauly, Rebecca M. *The Transparent Illusion: Image and Ideology in French Text and Film*. New York: 1993.

Rev. of *Point of No Return*. *Time* 29 March 1993: 67.

Propp, Vladimir. *Morphology of the Folk Tale*. Trans. Lawrence Scott. 2nd rev. ed. Austin: U of Texas P, 1986.

Rettig, James. Rev. of *Cinema Sequels and Remakes, 1903–1987*. Book review. *Wilson Library Bulletin* 63.9 (1989): 138.

Romney, Jonathan. Rev. of *True Lies*. *New Statesman and Society* 12 August 1994: 33.

Schatz, Thomas. *Hollywood Genres: Formulas, Filmmaking, and the Studio System*. New York: Random House, 1981.

Sharman, Leslie Felperin. Rev. of *True Lies*. *Sight and Sound* 4.9 (1994): 49–50.

Simon, John. Rev. of *Sommersby*. *National Review* 29 March 1993: 69–70.

———. Rev. of *Point of No Return*. *National Review* 10 May 1993: 53.

———. Rev. of *True Lies*. *National Review* 29 Aug. 1994: 63–64.

Stallybrass, Peter. "'Drunk with the Cup of Liberty.' Robin Hood, the Carnivalesque, and the Rhetoric of Violence in Early Modern England." *The Violence of Representation: Literature and the History of Violence*. Ed. Nancy Armstrong and Leonard Tennenhouse. London: Routledge, 1989. 45–76.

Stallybrass, Peter, and Allon White. *The Politics and Poetics of Transgression*. Ithaca: Cornell UP, 1986.

Travers, Peter. Rev. of *Point of No Return*. *Rolling Stone* 18 Feb. 1993: 69–70.

———. Rev. of *Sommersby*. *Rolling Stone* 18 Feb. 1993: 65–66.

———. Rev. of *True Lies*. 25 Aug. 1994: 96.

Vincendeau, Ginette. "Hijacked." *Sight and Sound* 3.7 (1993): 23–25.

Weimann, Robert. "Text, Author-Function, and Appropriation in Modern Narrative: Toward a Sociology of Representation." *Literature and Social Practice*. Ed. Philippe Desan, Priscilla Parkhurst Ferguson, and Wendy Griswold. Chicago: U of Chicago P, 1989. 29–45.

Williams, Michael, and Christian Mork. "Remake Stakes Are Up; H[olly]wood Hastens Pursuit of French Pic[ture] Properties." *Variety* 19 April 1993: 5+.

Young, Josh. "The Best French Films You'll Never See; Hollywood Is Scooping Up Remake Rights. But the Genuine Article Is Seldom Seen in the United States." *New York Times* 30 Oct. 1994: B1+.

CHAPTER FOUR

The "Personal" Touch:
The Original, the Remake,
and the Dupe in Early Cinema

JENNIFER FORREST

The newness of the medium notwithstanding, the remake figured prominently in the cinematic experience from 1896 to 1906. From the Lumière brothers' first programs in the Salon Indien of the Grand Café issued the rush to imitate its subjects. Edison's *Clark's Thread Mill* is considered by many a remake of *La Sortie des usines*; Biograph's *Empire State Express* (1896) and Edison's *The Black Diamond Express* (1896)[1] are both remakes of *Arrivée d'un train*; and Biograph's *Sausage Machine* (1897) is a remake of *Charcuterie mécanique*. But although Americans may have been the most enthusiastic remakers on the international scene—circumstances facilitated by America's nonparticipation in international copyright—the remake was hardly a peculiar American phenomenon.[2] On the contrary, even George Méliès's earliest efforts imitated Lumière subjects; his *L'Arroseur* (1896) is taken from *L'Arroseur arrosé*, and *Arrivée d'un train* (1896) and *Les Forgerons* (1896) from Lumière subjects of the same name (Deslandes 417; Sadoul 155). Charles Pathé broke into filmmaking with a train arriving from Vincennes (Sadoul 64). Britain's Robert William Paul also did his versions of Lumière realism with waves at the seaside and the arrival of the Epsom Derby (Sadoul 64), while the Swede, Ernest Florman, "plagiarized" an even earlier film made for the Edison kinetoscope, *The Barbershop* (1894) (Deslandes 267). Film producers even remade their own works; according to Alan Williams, the earliest "remake" ever was of the Lumières' *Sortie des usines* because the negative was so worn from making copies that a new version, as faithful to the original as possible, had to be shot (159). And Pathé had a habit of recycling some of its successful films roughly every five years, a gesture that reflected changes in film structure.[3] On the one hand, the practitioners of the new medium imitated each other in their quest for subjects that would show off their marvelous machines, continuing a nineteenth-century tradition which appealed to the imagination through a variety of machines from photographic cameras, to x-rays, and phonographs (Gunning 58).[4] As Tom Gunning points out, it was the "Cinématographe, the Biograph, or the Vitascope that were advertised on the variety bills in which they premiered, not *Le Déjeuner de bébé* or *The Black Diamond Express*" (58). The Lumière brothers' early withdrawal from film production to concentrate on the manufacture of equipment and raw film reflects this privileging of the machine over film, whose usefulness was limited to that of publicity (Sadoul 52). On the other hand, the practice of large-scale piracy reveals much about the early cinema's popular beginnings[5] and the widespread conviction—however much motivated by commercial concerns—that the product the new machine produced belonged to the public domain. In this sense, the early remake differs radically from its later incarnations, in which permission to remake must be obtained and sources acknowledged both financially and legally. It is essential, therefore, to distinguish between the pre- and post-1906[6] definitions of the remake, locating their point of intersection at the moment when film emerged from the veil of public domain to enter into the legal realm of the Copyright Statute.

From 1902 to 1911, the courts were called upon to determine the nature of film authorship, but they were only the finalizing—but no less instrumental and legitimizing—element in bestowing on cinema a belated notion of originality and origin. Suing rival companies for copyright infringement occurred only after a series of important events took place in the industry; first, patent infringement litigation turned against Edison, making the company lose its economic edge in equipment and film sales, and forcing it to "play catch-up" with its more successful competitors (Levy 211); second, economic and organizational changes within the industry itself gradually shifted focus from equipment to film production, forcing manufacturers to reassess their position on the secondary status of films; third, the increasing length and narrative complexity of films, as well as the cinema's courting of a middle-class audience (Jeanne Thomas Allen 177),[7] deemphasized the photographic nature of the medium and promoted its written sources in the adaptation from literature or the theater, or in the original screenplay. Once the courts located a film's written component as its point of origin, crediting became *de rigueur*.

A final consideration in an assessment of the early cinematic remake as distinguished from its later form is its role in the creation of the first film genres, from the bad boy, trick, fire, chase, and rescue films, to the féeries, the actualities, the travelogue, the comedies, and so on. Although the imitation of competitors' subjects and techniques was linked to the film commodity's ability to sell equipment, one cannot underestimate the significance of the remake in establishing the conventions of a cinematic experience that by 1903 was already severing its ties with its popular amusement beginnings. The pre-1906 cinema drew upon the expectations of an audience accustomed to the conventions of an attractions format, and yet, after ten years of going to the movies, audiences were already educated in cinematic norms. One important link between pre- and post-1906 remaking emerges here: remaking from the outset foregrounded repetition as an operating principle of cinema. In his discussion of genre, Joseph W. Reed notes, "Movies come from movies, and any given movie repeats things from hundreds of others" (8). Repetition creates genre, and although cinema prior to 1906 repeated tricks and acts from noncinematic mediums, the rush to imitate other cinematic successes initiated from the outset an exchange unique to cinema that resulted in the creation of film genres.

Far from being merely a dirty, deceitful exercise, the remake wove itself into the very fabric of the new medium. But while it has always been part of the cinematic experience, it has not always played the same role. This study should not only contribute to an understanding of remaking practices prior to 1906 but suggest as well that the remake is not just one phenomenon but many, and that it means something radically different when considered according to other cinematic contexts—e.g., the remake after the reorganization of the moving-picture industry, the Classic Hollywood remake, and the post-1960s remake—thereby underscoring the active role the remake continues to play to this day in cinematic production.

The early remake's partner in crime was the dupe,[8] which did not outlive its early cinematic currency for reasons linked to the vertical and horizontal integration and standardization of film as an industry, to the ability of the new medium to reach a mass public through film exhibition, to the legal inclusion of film in notions of proprietorship and authorship, and to the general recognition of the film product not only as a market commodity, but as a work of art as well. The remake and the dupe—and the variations with which they were associated[9]—worked the same territory during the first ten years of cinema. Indeed, however much the remake and the dupe seem distinct entities to present-day thinking, they functioned in strikingly similar ways in the early cinema's market for film product, a market fundamentally different from that of the post-1906 period, as we shall see. If they differed, it was merely in modes of duplication. In 1902, for example, in the interest of cutting production costs to a bare minimum, the Edison Company duped European fiction films (Musser, *Emergence* 322).[10] The duping of foreign fiction films also made it possible for American companies to respond to the pronounced preference audiences had for such subjects (Musser, *Emergence* 331). But if a rival company's films had been registered for copyright, as in the case of Biograph films as of 1902, then the only viable alternative to duping was remaking. The intention, however, was the same. According to Charles Musser, Edison's remakes were the "ethical equivalent" of duping, because they kept costs below those of an original studio production (389). Given the short length of film subjects, the ressemblance of the remake to the dupe becomes even more evident; there is little room or time for great variation. Without being technically dupes, some of the Edison Company's remakes merited the title just the same; *Skirmish Between Russian and Japanese Advance Guards* (1904) (a remake of Biograph's *The Battle of the Yalu* [1904]) resembled so closely the original as to be "virtually identical" to it (Musser, *Emergence* 359). As for the charge that duping was a dishonest commercial practice, the market in dupes was at least partially legitimized by foreign companies whose works were pirated. For example, Biograph was fairly open about its duping, dealing directly with the original producers of foreign films, sometimes proposing to serve as an exchange for "prints made from the original negative (for fifteen cents a foot) or duplicates made from prints (twelve cents a foot)" (Musser, *Emergence* 365). And finally, in the formation of the Motion Picture Patents Company, Edison's negotiations with Pathé involved putting an end to duping through the licensing of

Edison as the distributor for Pathé originals; whether the company was duping or distributing, Edison would obviously make a percentage from the sales. The ambition, therefore, was to reach the most cost-effective way to achieve the maximum financial returns.

It was only with the *American Mutoscope & Biograph Co. v. Edison Mfg. Co.*[11] (1905) copyright infringement case that the courts legally distinguished the two practices. Initially, Judge Lanning does not distinguish between different forms of copying; repeating Biograph's allegations against Edison, he says that, "the allegation of the bill is that the defendant has published and sold, and is now publishing and offering for sale, *copies* of the complainant's copyrighted photograph, to which *copies* it has given the title above quoted" (265, emphasis added). With the judge deferring to an earlier case involving dupes as a precedent (*Edison v. Lubin* [1903]),[12] the reader first assumes that the copies in question are dupes;[13] Edison's film, *How a French Nobleman Got a Wife Through the New York "Herald" Personal Columns* (1904), is in fact a remarkably close remake of Biograph's *Personal* (1904). The judge, however, put the burden of proving the degree of copying involved on Biograph. A viewer today would need no further evidence to see that Edison's film was an unauthorized imitation of *Personal*, but given early film's connections to largely unprotected vaudeville and fairground attractions where performers' acts were routinely stolen outright, it was far from certain that a moving picture's way of telling a story warranted protection.

As with Edison previously, Biograph had been copyrighting its films as photographs.[14] Unlike patent protection, the only way to test the validity of copyright protection was through the courts.[15] Because moving pictures were a new medium not yet included in the Copyright Statute, what was at stake in *Biograph v. Edison* was not only whether films could be copyrighted, but also if the Copyright Statute should officially recognize the industry's new brand of films in a category separate from photographs. The case hinged on whether Biograph had used proper procedure—a procedure for which there was no legal precedent—for registering a discontinuous, multishot moving picture for copyright protection as a single-shot film.[16] With the precedent of *Edison v. Lubin*, it had become increasingly clear by 1905 that film property qualified for some protection. But with the upheaval provoked by the transition from continuity to discontinuity, from single-shot to multiple-shot film construction, the margin for copyright error was large. As it is customary in piracy trials for defendants to "establish a defense of uncopyrightable material, fair comment, or fair use"

(Spring 218), it was logical for the Edison Company to pursue this line of defense. If improperly registered, Biograph's *Personal* would fall into the public domain (Spring 123).[17] In the earlier case, *Edison v. Lubin*, it was in Lubin's interest to attempt to invalidate Edison's copyright and place the latter company's work in the public domain. In the later case, *Biograph v. Edison*, Edison followed the same course of action and first tried unsuccessfully to find Biograph's copyright registration in error. Failing that, Edison's only recourse was to have the court legally address the difference between the dupe and the remake, between a literal copy and a treatment copy. Edison, therefore, strongly denied having copied—which here means the same thing as duped—"any part of the complainant's photograph" (267). By doing so, Edison had implicitly identified its film as a treatment copy, forcing Judge Lanning to address recourse to the difficult "process of exclusion or elimination of similarities of material" involved in treatment copying (Spring 218). Edwin S. Porter's deposition emphasizes the differences between the two films stating that he had made an original negative, and citing the techniques and methods involved in making his film:

> The negative prepared by me did not and does not contain a single copy of any of the pictures of complainant's films. Each impression is a photograph of a pantomime arranged by me, and enacted for me at the expense of the owner of the film which I produced. My photograph is not a copy, but an original. It carries out my own idea or conception of how the characters, especially the French nobleman, should appear as to costume, expression, figure, bearing, posing, gestures, postures, and action. (*Biograph v. Edison* 267)

On the surface, he seems to be speaking about the degree of personal expression[18] he brought to the film; if the two films resemble each other in ideas or storyline, he suggests, they are nevertheless dissimilar in the means by which the story is told. But examining his words in the context of the trial, it soon becomes clear that the differences of which he speaks refer specifically to the mechanical reproduction involved in a dupe; in other words, the print from which Edison exhibition copies were made was an original master print, not a duped print; the different actors, "costume, expression, figure, bearing, posing, gestures, postures, and action," are incontrovertible proof that *French Nobleman* is not a dupe. Judge Lanning's decision reflects this distinction, as he merely limited the purview of the case to its charges; Biograph did indeed hold a valid copyright, and

Edison's film was not a duped copy. He left the question of the remake's infringement on the Biograph original to be decided at a later date.

As André Gaudreault points out in his discussion of the latter case, the Edison Company "wanted to win their case," since this would allow it to continue profiting from other Biograph remakes from the same year, and give them license to continue to do so in the future ("Infringement" 120).[19] Although film sales could be lucrative,[20] film companies up until the creation of rental exchanges and of the Motion Picture Patents Company seemed to expect greater profits in the marketing of equipment (Staiger 192). There is no question that the early film companies' business acumen with respect to their inventions/equipment prevailed in their dealings with each other and their markets. John Izod stresses the "promptness with which most of the successful inventors patented their discoveries, and scrutinized each others' patents for possible loopholes," loopholes from which every possible advantage would be made (1). Film companies had also always "scrutinized" each others' film subjects, treating them, not like other people's property but, as with Louis Lumière, like publicity for their equipment (Sadoul 52); the targeted market was not the spectator but the exhibitor. Much like loopholes in patents, rival companies intended to profit from faulty copyrights, no copyrights, or from a relatively litigation-free atmosphere where one cited a competitor for patent infringement, not for copyright violation. In his deposition, Porter's, and by extension Edison's, valorization of the mechanical print over a film's expressive or artistic integrity dealt with film in its very materiality. And this emphasis on film's material nature was supported by general industry practices where, although film production costs multiplied with increasing complexity in film structure (single-shot to multiple-shot films, single-reel to multiple-reel films, simple attraction format to rich theatrical production values), films continued to be sold by the foot, with no distinction made between films of greater or lesser artistic quality, production expense, or talent (Staiger 198).

Beyond the company's concern for immediate profit, one must also consider the cameraperson's appropriation of new techniques and subject ideas in terms of the cultural context in which massive borrowing took place. John Fell notes that "Few early filmmakers had much, if any background in the arts" ("Cellulose" 42), so art conventions could not determine the choice and treatment of early cinematic subjects. In addition, there were obviously no film schools imparting general trade knowledge. Camerapersons had to keep up-to-date in their trade, regardless of how short-lived an amusement it was predicted the cinema would be (Musser, *Emergence* 298). New methods often corresponded to the changing nature of film subjects. Camerapersons mastered new techniques in the interest of maintaining their own market value, while also satisfying both a quest for more specialized knowledge of their field, and a desire to find subjects appropriate for the abilities of the new medium. Paul Spehr notes that Billy Bitzer and other cameramen who worked for Biograph, "admired the effects achieved by Méliès and tried, often without success, to copy them." Because Biograph was concerned about production costs, it did nothing to promote such experimentation. So, Bitzer often tried them out on his own time with bits and pieces of unused film, a professional curiosity from which Biograph benefitted financially, just as other companies reaped advantage from their own employees' inquisitive natures ("Influences" 108). The experimentation had an end greater than the mere sales potential of the techniques; early cinematic imitation/copying/repetition, from the allusion to the outright remake, worked to create a tradition in which audiences were educated, and upon which filmmakers could expand.

For some camerapersons, mastery often assumed the characteristics of authorship, a situation that had much to do with what Porter's deposition identified as the mechanical production of an original negative. For film manufacturers, authorship involved a financial transaction; it could be bought or appropriated. For example, Edison even "copyrighted films it did not make" (Musser, *Emergence* 514n9).[21] In addition, films functioned less like novels in a bookstore than like new vaudeville acts or fairground attractions, with manufacturers stealing ideas from their rivals and trying to reproduce them. In the latter instance, the easiest and most cost-efficient route was, of course, duping; Edison and Biograph both purchased French films and sold them with their own, passing off the French works, especially those of Georges Méliès,[22] as their own.[23] Authorship or company of provenance only became an issue when a manufacturer's profits were affected. For example, Lubin often duped or remade, and then undersold versions of successful Edison films; *Uncle Tom's Cabin* (1903), which Edison offered for $165, was remade by Lubin and sold for $77. According to Charles Musser, the Lubin version was "shot at fewer frames per second and eliminated a cakewalk dance but was remarkably similar in other respects," a compromise over which few economically minded exhibitors would shed many tears (*Emergence* 361). But camerapersons sometimes passed off techniques taken from elsewhere as their own. Jacques Deslandes tells us that the Englishman George Albert

Smith, a friend of Georges Méliès, wanted to copyright the tricks he used in his films, tricks that were being performed on film by Méliès not only at the same time, but with a "complexity [that] greatly surpassed those of the photographer from Brighton" (354). The modern day critic would be inclined to view this appropriation as duplicitous, but such a categorical dismissal would reveal nothing about the context of Smith's behavior. By way of parallel, if we consider the degree of accomplishment involved in filming tricks along with the popular origins of such tricks (Biograph's *The Vanishing Lady* was based on an attraction trick as well as on Méliès's film of the same name [Musser, *Emergence* 231]), Smith may have felt that he had just as much right to authorship as Méliès.

Imitation often not only involved reproduction of the new technique, but also appropriation of the context in which it was used, as in Edison's remake of Biograph's *Personal.* David Levy assesses Porter's role with the Edison Company as that of an "employee whose job it was to follow instructions," and that, if he was "assigned the task of helping them play catch-up," he really couldn't be held accountable for the remakes he made (211). But Porter did have immense talent and did influence the mise-en-scène of his films, both remakes and originals. If he made an almost identical remake of *Personal,* as he did of other Biograph films, one could, of course, cite the company's concerns for keeping production costs to a minimum. One could also refer to the nineteenth century's more relaxed view toward the integrity of a wide variety of artistic works and the way in which they were made available to the general public.[24] There is more here than just the brazen plundering of the public domain. Early camerapersons bring to mind Medieval and Renaissance poets who were "essentially translators, writing at a time when translation, imitation and creation were inextricably bound" (Nama 36). The emerging medium required appropriate subjects; people like W. K. L. Dickson turned to New York's popular amusements for material; others like Louis Lumière looked to salon painting and to photography (Deslandes and Richard 262, 268–69).[25] As in Medieval and Renaissance translation from a rich source language to a "poorer" target language, liberal borrowing served to enrich immeasurably the latter. Like these poets, many camerapersons/filmmakers may have truly believed that through *imitatio*—a Medieval and Renaissance notion that heartily embraces plagiarism—a new creation emerged.

But in the copying of other film subjects not directly related to noncinematic source mediums, the relation between a copy and an original may spring less from "translation" than from generic considerations. After all, films were so short that the normal repertoire of a genre's constituent parts and the variations such parts made possible within a particular genre were so limited as to make imitation the equivalent of copying. A notable example of the generic limitations of the earliest cinema would be all the documentary realist films made of arriving trains or of crashing waves. Like most historians, Jacques Deslandes notes that the greater part of early cinematic productions "prolonged the traditional genres of the fairground attraction" (162), but the cinema from its inception had already started reconceptualizing the attraction in very cinematic terms, not so much in the interest of "prolonging" the attraction, as in enriching its own language by means of the greater generic sophistication of other mediums; tricks that would be difficult if not impossible to perform on the stage, were feasible with film. In fact, Joseph Reed proposes that "the proper metaphor for genre is not formula but language" (92). Story is not the stuff, he claims, upon which audience recognition is built (91–92). The myriad arriving trains, crashing waves, and regimental reviews produced the recognition necessary for the creation of a cinematic language. The presence of a cinematic language is nowhere more visible than in the Edison remake (*Uncle Josh at the Moving Picture Show* [1902]) of Robert Paul's *The Countryman's First Sight of the Animated Pictures* (1901). Miriam Hansen notes that the Edison remake contains "clips from earlier Edison films (the major departure from the British source)," which draws upon a variety of early cinematic genres: "a dance film, a scenic view showing a train (rushing toward the camera at an oblique angle, as in the well-known Lumière film or Biograph's *Empire State Express* [1896]), and a sexually suggestive knockabout comedy" (25). Except for the clips projected on a screen-within-the-screen, the Edison version is a faithful remake of the British original. But their insertion, while testimony to the economics of recycling, also points to an appeal to the spectator to recognize the various genres as the clips appear on the screen-within-the-screen.[26] Recycling as an economically sound practice only partially accounts for the presence of these films-within-the-film; more important is the recognition factor which accounts for the choice of subjects projected on the screen viewed by Uncle Josh. The identification of the genres displayed in the films-within-the-film is a joyful confirmation of the existence of cinematic norms. Repetition of rival companies' film subjects, even at this early stage, was indistinguishable from the remake, and was, despite all the negative press, essential to the dynamics of generic recognition. Whether making a genre film or writing a translation, no matter how faithful the imitation, the filmmaker/translator always adds a new dimension to the "original"; the result is at the same time similar to, yet different from, the model upon which the work draws. The imitator's style, like the translator's and the original artist's, leaves traces of its "personal character" (Shiff 40). In this light, despite its role in the Edison Company's concerted effort to "win their case," Porter's defense of the originality of his work in *Biograph v. Edison* may indeed have been genuine, especially if one abandons the approach of distinguishing the imitation from an original. The opposition imitation vs. original is an application better suited to other periods in film history and to other artistic mediums that had made such disinctions meaningful.

But unlike well-known Medieval poets, imitation and mastery did nothing to confer titles of authorship on their creators. Indeed, in *Biograph v. Edison*, while Biograph identifies Wallace McCutcheon and Frank J. Marion as *Personal*'s "authors," Edison refers to Porter only as the *French Nobleman*'s "photographer" (263, 267). When Spehr says that rampant imitation, without acknowledging authors, took place because "Copyrights and the laws defining property were not well defined" ("Influences" 109), he is only painting part of the picture. It was not at all clear whether moving pictures qualified as property for which rules needed to be defined and authors credited, especially when one considered the company they kept—vaudeville and fairgrounds, whose acts were not protected. The general indifference of the manufacturing companies to duping and remaking did nothing to clarify the situation: no company pursued a rival company's dupe or remake for copyright infringement until 1903. And although *Moving Picture World* published three editorials in 1907 decrying the increase in piracy, from 1896 to 1909, there were only three copyright infringement cases involving films, the last having to do, not with duping or remaking, but with an unauthorized adaptation from a novel.

The first *Moving Picture World* editorial on the subject (July 6, 1907) describes remake and dupe pirates as immoral and criminal:

> The question of morals involved in the piracy of films is a nice one, but how to bring it home is another. The man who for the sake of dollars becomes a film pirate has no sense of morals; it is impossible to appeal to his honor—that's gone. His conscience? Well, he has put that in his pocketbook. His sense of justice, of doing to others as he would that others should do to him? Oh, that's a fable, all

exploded, nothing doing, but if his employee steals a $5 bill he goes
for his pound of flesh and demands justice for the thief. Where is
the difference? There is none. Both are thieves. ("Who is Pirating
Films" 275)

The anti-Semitic tone of the editor's indictment seems to implicate a particular group of filmmakers, but in reality piracy was practiced by all. If
the film world abominated remakes and dupes, one wonders why the
manufacturing companies did not pursue infringement litigation more
aggressively both before and after 1903. Only Edison and Biograph, however, were financially in a position to litigate in a protracted fashion, with
Edison being by far the more economically stable of the two in the first
ten years of cinema.[27] Litigation was costly, particularly patent infringement cases, and not just in the courtroom battle. For example, Biograph
could not distribute films for commercial projection for a period of time
until the Edison patent infringement suit against them, *Edison v. American Mutoscope Co.* (March 10, 1902), was decided in their favor, after
which they proceeded to make "massive copyright registrations for previously produced subjects" (Levy 210; Spehr, "Film Making" 416). Not so
with copyright infringement cases, where defendants could continue selling their pirated goods up to the moment of the court's decision.[28] For
example, in the 1905 *Biograph v. Edison* case, Edison had more to gain
than just the profits from their version of Biograph's *Personal*; between
1904 and 1905, Edison had remade three other Biograph films and stood
to continue to profit from their sales. Indeed, if Biograph had won its suit
against Edison, it could have proceeded to prosecute Edison for copyright
infringement of other remade Biograph properties.

But there are other considerations in the blind eye turned to early
cinematic piracy. In the next installment of *Moving Picture World* (July
13, 1907) the editor states that domestic manufacturing firms were
informed of the piracy problem "on numerous occasions, and evidence
has been offered, but silently rejected, because they see nothing before
them at the present time but the almighty $" ("Who is Pirating Films"
291). Even though the *Moving Picture World* editor attempts to shame
even those "firms of good repute"—which may be merely the larger and
more economically stable firms—"who certainly ought, to say the least, to
know better and have more regard for their reputation," the problem was
that everyone, reputable and disreputable firms alike, did exactly unto
others as they would others not do unto them; they duped and remade

each others' films (September 21, 1907, 451; Gaudreault, "Infringement" 115). Only when it became clear that film sales would continue to out-strip equipment sales did film manufacturers realize that remaking and duping seriously threatened the commercial run of what was increasingly assuming the form of valuable properties.[29] The *Moving Picture World* edi-tor's moral scolding reflects less indignation over a long-used and much abused practice, than a response to the changes taking place both within the industry and in film structure itself, and the way these changes threat-ened the continued viability of the dupe and the remake.

The third reason why the manufacturing firms didn't sue aggres-sively can perhaps be found in *Biograph v. Edison*. Although Judge Lan-ning reconfirmed the appellate court's ruling on *Edison v. Lubin* in agree-ing that the Biograph film did indeed hold a valid copyright, he did not know, however, if the Edison film infringed upon the Biograph copyright (268). The judge recognized that "The two photographs possess many similar and many dissimilar features"; both films take place at Grant's Tomb and surrounding areas; both contain scenes from the New Jersey countryside; both are composed of seven to eight scenes; both refer to the same characters—a French nobleman in search of a wealthy American wife and a group of female suitors; both tell the same story in much the same way. But he adds that, "The defendant's pictures were taken at times different from those of the complainant, and by securing a different set of actors, dressed in different costumes" (267). The judge defines dissimi-larity in very literal terms, partially because he merely distinguishes the Edison film from a dupe. But this literal approach can also be partially attributed to the generic categories characteristic of the nascent medium. The film spectator who regularly patronized the cinema would respond with familiarity to short film subjects (e.g., arriving train, crashing wave, regimental review films) much like we do today to Westerns, melodramas, and musicals, as well as recognize the subtle, but nevertheless evident, unfamiliar elements in a filmmaker's contribution to a particular "genre." In an atmosphere where exhibitors featured Lumière, Méliès, Biograph, Edison, Paul, and others, scenes of arriving trains and crashing waves, dif-ference for the spectator emerges in the smallest of details. In accepting such seeming trifles as different time of shooting, "different set of actors," and "different costumes," the judge in *Biograph v. Edison* interprets dif-ference in a much looser sense than we would today, and accordingly, he put the burden of proof on Biograph to show that more than just an idea was reproduced in Edison's film. Biograph would have to prove that the film's *expression*, its particular way of telling the story, was appropriated by the Edison film. On the surface, either the dupe was the criterion for the determination of copying (literal copy), or such factors as different time of day, costume, and actors constituted sufficient signs of difference in a treatment copy, or both.[30]

Having outruled literal copying, Judge Lanning turns to treatment copying, stating that, "As the proofs now stand, there is doubt upon the question of its [Biograph's] right to any relief whatever" (268). All while respecting the letter of the law, the judge betrays deeper misgivings regarding the medium, ones that reflect the cultural marginalization of the cinema when compared with the primacy of art institutions such as the literature, painting, and music of recognized masters. He expresses doubt twice in his decision, once regarding whether a "photograph of a building or any other object, which is a mere mechanical reproduction of the physical features or outlines of the object" can be cited for "originality or novelty on the part of him who takes it." The second time, as cited above, he wonders whether the Edison remake is a plagiarized version of Biograph's film. His doubts recall the period's "cultural exclusion of photography," a result of the general sacralization of culture, which began in the mid-nineteenth century, but which became most pronounced at the turn of the century (Levine 149). Because notions of "originality and novelty" spring up in a society concerned with the integrity of an individual artist's creation, their application to a medium such as photography—for films were registered for copyright as photographs—would be considered by many inappropriate. As Lawrence Levine points out, it was felt that the photographer merely reproduced external reality, that a "mechanical process stood between the creator and the product, whereas the artist created something from within him/herself" (163).

As for Judge Lanning, while he neither denies the expressive capacity of the medium nor that of the photographer who arranges the scenes before the camera, he stops short of granting creative abilities of a culturally significant kind to a medium that mechanically reproduces those arrangements. Contrary to the sensibility reigning up until the early nineteenth century, moving pictures, like photography (however much recognized by copyright law), recreated a reality that appeared indistinguishable from servile imitation. Only creations of a different order—those linked to established modes like literature, painting, and sculpture, as we shall see—would permit the cinema to aspire for *inventio* in its modern application. In this sense, the potential mechanical reproducibility of any subject would invalidate any of the new medium's claims to "originality and novelty."[31]

It can also be inferred that Judge Lanning in *Biograph v. Edison* would have concluded that, however much a discontinuous, multi-shot moving picture tells a story that resembles the unfolding of a written narrative (266), the story/idea of Biograph's *Personal* drew from the same common pool of public entertainment traditions and, therefore, did not qualify for copyright protection.[32] Cinema also may not have been significantly highbrow to warrant such protection, given nineteenth-century entertainment practices in which versions, adaptations, and translations of masters like Mozart and Shakespeare flourished on both the American and European stage in the first half of the century. What Lawrence Levine notes regarding music is easily applicable to other art forms; the attitude prevalent in the first half of the nineteenth century reflected an "ethos that did not consider opera—or most forms of music, for that matter—to be finished, inalterable works of art" (95). Neither were films "finished, inalterable works of art" during the first ten years of cinema, a situation which shows that straightforward notions of public domain may have played a much smaller role than sales and exhibition practices in undermining recognition by film manufacturers and the courts of the authority of an original film. Manufacturing companies did business based on the incomplete nature of their product. This would change when editorial responsibility shifted from the film exhibitor to the manufacturer.

Early film productions were sold as complete films or as separate shots or tableaux; the exhibitor could purchase the length of film s/he desired. The exhibitor was usually the projectionist, as well as editor, and lecturer, providing the narrative foundation for the visual accompaniment. S/he often "completed" films; out of economic necessity separate scenes or tableaux were purchased, leaving the narrational sequencing and evolution to the exhibitor to decide. In addition, because many if not most early film subjects drew upon popular amusements or from a "well-known story or event, viewers brought this special knowledge to bear on the film." But this "special knowledge" was not always enough, and the spectator had to rely upon the exhibitor to contextualize a film's meaning (monstration, to use Gaudreault's term, i.e., a narrator external to the story itself), as well as to "clarify" its meaning, through a "live narration and other sounds (music, effects, even dialogue added by actors from behind the screen)" (Musser, *Emergence* 2). As Charles Musser notes, this intervention on the part of the exhibitor involved his or her creative, as well as interpretative abilities, bringing to the fore his or her "authorial vision" (*Emergence* 2, 219, 223). Because color added to the film product's attraction, some exhibitors even hand-painted the films they purchased (Deslandes and Richard 203–204).[33] In addition, in shows such as those of the exhibitor Edwin J. Hadley, "the emphasis was placed on the exhibitor himself and on the skill with which he was able to accomplish the illusion of the moving images. It was the projectionist, like Hadley, who, *by actually operating the almost magical equipment*, represented to his rural audiences those electrical wizards who had created the motion picture" (Lowry 142, emphasis added). So long as the exhibitor exerted such authorial control over the completion of the film product, the latter's origins could not be readily and easily identified. On the contrary, each individual exhibition worked to erase all traces of an ideal original print; each exhibition version, authorized by the very sales practices that made such multiple versions possible, became just one more early cinematic remake. In this light, Biograph's suit against Edison in 1905 reflects less concern for the artistic integrity of the master print than for the loss in sales and distribution profits the remake represented.[34]

As films became longer, more complexly constructed, and more focused on fiction subjects, filmmakers began to draw increasingly on literature and the theater, another factor which worked to legitimize the film director's creative vision. While for a time, lecturers, whose presence had declined considerably from 1904 to 1907, found themselves called upon to eliminate either the "total illegibility" of or the difficulties presented by many of the narratively dense films, they were soon replaced by intertitles. Intertitles provided the cinema with classical modes of narration in which the narratives became "self-explanatory" and "self-contained"; the narrator was no longer an external element to film exhibition, but was incorporated into the very fabric of the film (Hansen 79). In other words, the film narrator moved from outside to inside the film itself, reducing the editor/lecturer to the role of projectionist (Gaudreault, "Showing and Telling" 278–79). As Gaudreault notes, the use of intertitles put an end to the myriad versions/remakes of a particular film that the exhibitor/lecturer system facilitated by creating narrational "uniformity"; every copy of an authorized print was the same and could not be altered, at least not as easily as in the old system. Intertitles also isolated control of the film product in the hands of the film producer (Gaudreault, "Showing and Telling" 279). The disappearance of the lecturer, as well as the shift from sales to film rentals, reflects the general reorganization and growth of the film industry, resulting in the "concentration of meaning within the film as product and commodity," which in turn increased films' "independence [and that of the producers] from the sphere of exhibition" (Hansen 98). Finally, positioning the narrative voice within the film itself also worked to redefine the previous collective nature of film exhibition and to increasingly isolate a film's expressive qualities as being the creation of one artist.

But during the first ten years of the cinema the remake enjoyed great mobility before it actually infringed a copyright. Testimony to the lenient attitude toward the remake was the Edison Company's registration of the *French Nobleman* for copyright protection. One could say that this action serves as a public demonstration of and claim for the originality of the film, and yet, it was hardly extraordinary, especially when one considers that Edison sometimes copyrighted films it didn't even make (Musser, *Emergence* 514n9). The company was confident that its version was not a dupe, and as such qualified for a protection that would guarantee it the exclusive right to the film's profits. Indeed, the Edison company applied for copyright protection with the same aggressiveness it sought patent priority; the purpose was to keep its hold on the commercial market. But ironically, whatever its economic motivations, the Edison Company's harassment of smaller companies through patent infringement suits and spying[35] (Balshofer and Miller 17–19, 36–41), and its deposition of prints for copyright registration—in short everything that calls to mind the power of the Edison name, its financial resources and clout—contributed significantly to the cultural legitimization of the film product as artistic creation, destining it for authorship status.

The contribution of the industrialization of the cinema in earning the protection of the integrity of the film product can hardly be underestimated, especially when compared to the preindustrial nature of its sister entertainments that were unable to obtain comprehensive copyright protection. For while the early cinema shared audiences, exhibition sites, and acts/subjects with its popular precursors and competitors, it would succeed where the latter would fail.[36] Vaudeville acts, for example, registered for copyright as dramatic compositions but did not have a notational system which would enable the courts to isolate and identify the nature of an act's originality (Jeanne Thomas Allen 182). Film, on the other hand, was copyrighted as photographs, not as performance (J. T. Allen 185).[37] In addition, although they could "present a single act for as many as twenty years," performers from vaudeville and other popular amusements from the period operated as individuals (J. T. Allen 181); they bargained for protection of their intellectual property from weakness in numbers and financial backing.[38] General restructuring of the film industry (shift from sales to rentals, shift of editorial responsibility from exhibitor to producer, etc. [Musser, *Emergence* 7]), however, allowed companies to have greater control over the destinies of their products. Finally, films had an infinitely greater capacity for mass production and distribution; one vaudeville stage performance could be viewed by only one audience, whereas one film could be exhibited simultaneously across the country (as well as in foreign countries) before countless audiences (J. T. Allen 178).[39] The size, scope, and growing power of the film industry obliged Congress to amend the Copyright Statute in 1912 with the inclusion of moving pictures as its own category, distinct from that of photographs.

Another important consideration in the legitmization of the cinema was its promotion to the status of art as a by-product of the creation of the Motion Picture Patents Company (MPPC) in 1908; its patent pool reflected not only a business strategy geared primarily toward market domination but also how that strategy's foundation in patent proprietorship and the right to benefit financially from one's inventions also indirectly benefitted qualifying film authorship as artistic expression. First, in the formation of the MPPC, all parties agreed to "prohibit duped films" (Staiger 193). Second, in the U.S. Government's antitrust suit against the MPPC (1914), the defendants resorted to many plausible defenses, including one in which they distinguished between commodities and works of art, with the latter being exempt from interstate trade regulations. They argued that films are "not articles of commerce like lumber, cheese, beef or turpentine." They insisted that films are creations possessing a "literary and dramatic essence" (Staiger 200). Duping was increasingly viewed as a risky venture because of the greater vertical and horizontal organization and policing of the moving picture industry.[40] Greater industry consolidation resulted in the emergence of film product as the preferred commodity, not the hardware which filmed, developed, and projected it. And paradoxically, at the same time that film replaced equipment as the budding industry's focus, acquiring the status as commodity, it was also elevated to a work of art. In addition, there are other factors in the changing status of the film product, such as meeting audience expectations. Michael Chanan notes that film-makers began to develop greater sensitivity towards the expressive possibilities of the new medium; audiences then began to demonstrate preferences which pointed the film-makers in certain directions, reinforcing certain tendencies; and then dealers began to realise the consequences of these developments—to realise, in other words, that for aesthetic reasons too—though that is not a word they would have used—the film was no ordinary commodity. (184)

The influence of the spectator on the kinds of films produced can, of course, be attributed at least partially to manufacturers' and exhibitors' appeal to the middle class. As a result, the cinema began to share less and less with vaudeville and amusement parks and more and more with the legitimate theater. Films became more literary, borrowing many of their stories from the theater (Gaudreault, "Showing" 278), while film producers courted actors from the stage for their productions. The transformation of the film product's legal and economic standing also enhanced, therefore, its aesthetic value.

Changes in internal film structure as early as 1904 also contributed to the legal and cultural legitimization of moving pictures. Gaudreault and Gunning distinguish between two different cinematic practices (monstration and narration, the "cinema of attractions" and narrative cinema, respectively), the first belonging to the pre-1906 period, the second to the post-1906 period. Biograph's novel hybridization of these two modes (monstration and narration) in *Personal* makes it the model for a new kind of film: the chase film" (Gunning 60). In *Personal*, a French nobleman who has placed a personal advertisement for an American wife is aggressively pursued by a group of female suitors; the chase itself provides the "causality and linearity" of narrative technique; the focus on the difficulties the women encounter in their pursuit constitute the visual spectacle (Gunning 60). Biograph's film was not only remade by Edison, but also by Lubin (*A New Version of "Personal"/Meet Me at the Fountain*, 1904), and finally by Pathé (*Dix femmes pour un mari*, 1905)[41] (60), making it exemplary in other important ways. It also came to represent the introduction of a new kind of generic model which other filmmakers then proceeded to emulate. Although not all films subsequent to *Personal* were chase films, after 1906, narrative concerns and the mixing of genres, both resulting in lengthier films, increasingly dominated film structure, a transition that made it necessary for the film industry to look for its subjects elsewhere than in popular amusements.

Harper Bros. et al. v. Kalem Co. et al. (1909) provides a historical account of this transition. The Kalem Company had made a film version of General Lew Wallace's popular novel *Ben Hur* without obtaining the author's permission. Harper Brothers possessed the sole right to dramatize the book, and Klaw and Erlanger were the licensees of a play based on the novel. Although the case involved neither a remake nor a dupe, it was historically instrumental in implicitly defining the remake in terms of a dramatization referring back to an original play/novel/photoplay, and not to other dramatizations from the same medium. In this case, written expression and the copyrighted author's right to license any dramatic adaptation of his or her material addressed the question of sources in a meaningful way for the courts. The decision of this copyright infringement case and its 1911 appeal, *Kalem Co. v. Harper Bros.* shifted attention away from the mechanico-photographic nature of the medium—the focus of the first two cases discussed in this chapter—by locating cinematic origins in an original written work, or in this particular case, in a novel, evidence in itself that the nature of the film product had radically changed. In the 1911 appeal, the judge is particularly insistent that a moving picture is not a "copy" of a novel—and he means "copy" in the most literal interpretation of the word. Akin to Judge Lanning's use of it in *Biograph v. Edison*, he states, "To transcribe a musical composition by making a record upon a phonograph blank, or by perforating a sheet of paper, requires neither creative [n]or artistic power, but merely the common skill of the artisan. Yet, to make such record is not to copy the composition, as has been held in every reported case that has come to our special knowlege" (149). A copy would be an object that is virtually indistinguishable from another by virtue of the means of expression used to create it. The Kalem Company's filmed version of General Lew Wallace's novel *Ben Hur* was not, therefore, a "copy"; it was recognizable to the public as related to the novel, and was titled accordingly, but by virtue of dissimilar means of expression—words are not moving pictures—Kalem did not infringe General Wallace and his estate's copyright to the novel (149). But because, according to the 1891 revised Statutes, "authors have the exclusive right to dramatize any of their works," here there was infringement (152). Justice Holmes in the 1911 *Kalem Co. v. Harper Bros.* case, therefore, upheld the earlier decision by Judge Ward. In France between 1906 and 1908, similar terminology was used by the courts, who conferred priority on a written source and emphasized the author's right to control and receive royalty fees from any dramatizations of his or her works (Abel 28). As in *Kalem Co. v. Harper Bros.* the French courts protected first "literary authors against unauthorized film versions of *their* work as intellectual property," and only by extension did they provide protection to films that were "authorized adaptations." From hereon in, each adaptation, including the remake, qualified as a new dramatization of a written source, not as a copy of another film.

The issue of an adaptation's competition with a precursor—although here not in the same medium—arose in 1916 with *Harper Bros. et al. v. Klaw et al.*, when it had become clear that the cinema was capable of rendering great drama as effectively as the theater. In the earlier *Harper Bros. et al. v. Kalem Co. et al.* (1909) both Harper Brothers *and* Klaw and Erlanger had brought suit against the Kalem Company. As stated earlier, Harper Bros. possessed the sole right to dramatize the book, and Klaw & Erlanger were the licensees of a play based on the novel; the play had been duly authorized with the stipulation that Klaw and Erlanger could not make any changes to the body of the text in its dramatizations. In the 1916 case, the copyright holder to the play wanted to prevent the licensee from making a movie of the play and vice versa. Judge Hough decreed in favor of both plaintiff and defendant in the suit and countersuit. He recognized that the status of film in 1916 was much different from that of its beginnings; "When this contract was made [1899] the moving picture art was (in the trite phrase) in its infancy. There were moving pictures, but it was then completely beyond the known possibilities of the art to produce a series of pictures representing such and so spectacular and elaborate a play or performance as in the Ben Hur of Klaw & Erlanger" (162). In his statements, it is clear that he feels that moving pictures in 1916 were quite up to the job—after all, D. W. Griffith's epic *Birth of a Nation* and his lavish *Intolerance* date from 1915 and 1916, respectively. Where the judges in *Kalem Co. v. Harper Bros.* (1911) state that a film dramatization is not the same as a stage performance, it is assumed that the filmed version would not enter into direct competition with the successful play. With the 1916 *Harper Bros. v. Klaw*, however, Judge Hough recognizes the destructive effect that the film could have on the future life of the play

> In my opinion there is implied a negative covenant on the part of the plaintiffs (the grantors of defendants' restricted license) not to use the ungranted portion of the copyright estate to the detriment, if not destruction, of the licensees' estate. Admittedly, if Harper

Bros. (or Klaw & Erlanger, for the matter of that) permitted photo-plays of Ben Hur to infest the country, the market for the spoken play would be greatly impaired, if not destroyed. (165–66)

It is clear from the protection accorded both the author and/or copyright owner of a written source, along with any licensee for its dramatization, that they are duly secured against the profit losses that would most certainly be incurred if an unauthorized version put itself in direct competition with another dramatic adaptation.

Only when films became significantly profitable, longer, and denser and started borrowing their narratives more heavily from literature and theater, could the remake come into its own, in that legally it had only to answer to a written source and not to the film with which it came into competition. Until *Edison v. Lubin* (1903), no systematic discussion had taken place to determine what the proper procedure for copyright registration was. Even though Edison was the only company to register film before 1902, a court's findings could easily have invalidated those registrations as faulty.[42] Indeed, as Charles Musser notes, "The legality of Edison's method of copyrighting film had not been established by the courts. This would happen in 1903 and only then on appeal to a higher court" ("American Vitagraph" 38n47). Not long afterward, Edison's registration practices were invalidated with the creation of the multishot film. But first classifying film as a series of photographs to be registered as a single photograph (*Edison v. Lubin*), and then as a series of noncontinuous photographs telling a single story to be registered as a single photograph (*Biograph v. Edison*) represent the first steps toward establishing not only the narrator, as Gaudreault points out, but authorship and proprietorship as well. Literature and its moving-picture equivalent, the photoplay, took it even further; in controlling the right to all dramatizations, the novel or written material always has the last word. Because of the priority of the written source, therefore, all remakes subsequent to film's inclusion in copyright law are, in essence, adaptations.

The early cinematic remake and dupe most often did not have, nor were they legally bound to identify written or other sources; they competed directly and openly with their precursors. Both sought to faithfully replicate and capitalize on the successes of rival films, whether through scene-by-scene recreations or through the making of a negative of a positive print. Both sought to benefit financially from their originals, but not, as in later remake versus original scenarios, to upset the authority of the original so much as to pass themselves off as legitimate positive copies of an original (this applies to both the dupe and the remake). Edwin S. Porter's remake of Biograph's *Personal* at first carried the same title as the original (Gaudreault 117). And Lubin's remake of the same Biograph film went so far as to incorporate the Biograph title into its own: "A New Version of 'Personal,'" counting on exhibitor and audience familiarity with *Personal.* According to David Levy, the Lubin film was a "straight dupe," neither a remake nor a new version at all. If this is true, then the copresence of both remake and dupe in this group of *Personal* films would indeed blur the distinction between the two practices during this period (217). Adding to the identity crisis would be the literal remaking of a film with the complete exhaustion of its negative's use. The Lumières' *Sortie des usines* was one such remake (Williams 159), as was also Cecil Hepworth's *Rescued by Rover* (1905), which "required two remakes of the film because the negative wore out in the printing" (Chanan 185).

The mechanical nature of the medium coupled with its ability to visually reproduce "physical features or outlines of objects" such as those of a "building or any other object," left Judge Lanning of *Biograph v. Edison* wondering if the cameraperson displayed any "originality or novelty" in taking such photographs, or whether they were merely skilled artisans (265). Photography had always suffered from the misconception that the camera merely reproduces "reality." Elizabeth Ann McCauley notes that, in mid-nineteenth-century France, if a photographer took public property as his or her subject (as Biograph did in using Grant's Tomb for *Personal*), "the issue hinged on whether the photographer's work was a servile imitation (and therefore in no way the photographer's own property protected by copyright) or an original creation" (31). Judge Lanning's query is no different concerning the cinema. His remarks reflect the difficulty the legal branches had in dealing with the inventions that offered the illusion of identical reproduction. If moving-picture cameras all performed exactly in the same way in the earliest years of cinema—and, in a sense they did— then no film deserved copyright protection in terms of its expression; the photo and film, like the objects they photographed, would belong in the public domain. But in the *Edison v. Lubin* appeal, the judge decided that a moving-picture photograph does exhibit expression through the "study of lights, shadows, general surroundings, and a vantage point adapted to securing the entire effect" (242), and Judge Lanning in *Biograph v. Edison* decided that photographs and moving pictures do not just mechanically reproduce, but that both were "an expression of an idea, or thought, or conception" of the person who takes them (265). With *Kalem v. Harper Bros.* in 1911 and *Harper Bros. v. Klaw* in 1916, it had become increasingly clear that moving pictures belonged more to creative than to reproductive methods by virtue of their narrative structure.

The increasing narrative complexity and length of films, while contributing to pushing the moving-picture industry toward vertical and horizontal organization, also put an end to the practice of duping and stripped the remake of its link to mechanical replication, replacing the notion of reproduction that had previously defined it with that of adaptation. A survey of a series of copyright infringement cases involving dramatization rights to literary works in the latter half of the 1910s demonstrate that a definite shift had taken place from an emphasis on the photographic expressivity of a film to its written component.[43]

Buster Keaton's *Seven Chances* (1925) illustrates this shift to perfection in that the first half of the film credits and dramatizes the written source of the title,[44] while the last half reenacts the narrative and the spectacle of a purely cinematic source, without, however, acknowledging it. The latter half's chase sequence, however much modified, updated, and expanded, is unmistakably a remake of Biograph's *Personal*. The story concerns James Shannon/Buster Keaton, who lacks the courage to propose to his girl/Ruth Dwyer. One day a lawyer representing a deceased relative arrives to tell him that he stands to inherit $7 million if he marries by 7:00 P.M. on his birthday. Needless to say, this day is none other than his birthday, and he begins the mad rush to get married. After the refusal of his girl (due to a misunderstanding that will be rectified at the end of the film), Shannon/Keaton proceeds to propose to seven women who belong to his club, and by whom he is turned down one by one in the most humiliating fashion. At this point the film abandons the narrative motivation of the "seven chances" of the title—a thread that will be picked up again only in the happy finale when Shannon is reunited and married to his beloved at the stroke of seven—and enters into the sensational chase sequence.

The second section of *Seven Chances* reprises *Personal*'s basic components: while Shannon is proposing marriage and being turned down, the lawyer and Shannon's partner put an announcement in the local newspaper inviting any and all interested women to show up at the chapel at five o'clock that afternoon. The narrative of the first half of the film builds up to the stunt-filled, spectacular sequence in which Keaton shows off his acrobatic and comedic talents as the group of women who have gathered at the church start to chase his character through the streets and the hills. *Personal*'s small group of women become five hundred in Keaton's film; the humorous, but minor obstacles encountered by the women in the earlier film are transferred to Shannon/Keaton and the dangers the French nobleman meets with in the chase are magnified ten-fold (e.g., the avalanching boulders); the short chase sequence of *Personal* is drawn out in *Seven Chances* for maximum comic effect. Keaton's chase sequence does not mechanically reproduce *Personal* within his own film like Edison did with *Uncle Josh at the Moving Picture Show*, nor does it seek to imitate *Personal* as faithfully as Edison did with *French Nobleman*. Yet, however much the film recalls the generic chase spectacle—a category to which *Personal*, too, belongs[45]—that figures at the end of a number of Keaton's other films (*Our Hospitality* [1923], *Go West* [1925]), no film-goer familiar with *Personal* can mistake its presence in *Seven Chances*. But while Tom Gunning identifies the presence of narrative "causality and linearity" in the chase sequence in *Personal* (60), the narrative authority of that sequence within *Seven Chances* is powerless to constitute anything more than a reference, a citation, and an elaboration on and a recycling of the model. No feature film—a definition that does not pertain to *Personal*—can visually reproduce a narrative sequence without invoking its written source.[46] Therefore, it is not because *Personal* had no written source that Keaton was not obliged to acknowledge *Personal*, but because it was not narratively complex enough to constitute infringement. And perhaps more important in this consideration of the use *Seven Chances* makes of *Personal*, no one filed copyright infringement against the former's filmmakers.

NOTES

1. Edison's version may, in fact, be a remake of a remake. Charles Musser notes that Edison camerapersons, White and Heise, made *The Black Diamond Express*, and that it was "an imitation of Biograph's popular *Empire State Express*" (*Emergence* 164). Musser refers to "antecedents" rather than to remakes with respect to film subjects having popular amusement origins. For example, he notes that Biograph's *The Vanishing Lady* was "modeled on a well-known magic trick,

though an earlier Méliès subject served as a more direct antecedent" (*Emergence* 231). He refers to Vitagraph's 1898 film of the same name as a "version," not identified either with Méliès's or Biograph's films.

2. Although I agree to a limited degree with Paul Spehr's statement that remaking was "a valid way of learning and was probably essential for the transformation of the films, from a rudimentary to a sophisticated form of distrubtion," I disagree with his contention that Americans have a compulsion to remake because "the entire [American] culture was founded on borrowed or adapted ideas," and that they "had little difficulty using others' ideas" ("Influences" 109). Everyone remade, regardless of nationality. The remake is as instrumental to cinematic processes as the imitation, version, and adaptation are to literary ones. Also, on the one hand, Georges Sadoul notes the Lumières' documentary, *Pompiers* (1896), had "a rather far-reaching and long influence, since this subject will often find itself taken up again by the earliest French and English cinemas, finally leading in 1902 to [*The*] *Life of an American Fireman*, to this life of an American fireman, with which Edwin S. Porter prepared his famous *Vol du Grand Rapide* (*The Great Train Robbery*, 1903) and opened the road to dramatic cinema in the United States" (43). On the other hand, Deslandes sees the film rooted in a purely American exploitation of the theme predating the cinema (376). All translations from the French are mine.

3. For example, Pathé remade the following films: *Ali Baba et les quarantes voleurs/Ali Baba and the Forty Thieves* (1902 and 1907); *La Fée des roches noires/The Fairy of the Black Rock* (1902 and 1907); *La Fée printemps/The Fairy of Spring* (1902 and 1907); *Par le Trou de la serrure/Peeping Tom* (1901 and 1905).

4. At the 1900 Exposition Universelle in Paris, x-rays and moving-picture cameras fell into the same peripheral group as photography (Toulet 180).

5. In America, the size of Edison's Kinetograph, as well as the construction of the Black Maria Studio and shooting in a studio rather than outdoors reflects the influence of these amusements in the conceptualization and implementation of cinema (Allen, "Vitascope" 150). But the link even predates film projected on a screen. John Fell notes that W.K.L. Dickson, who was expected to find subjects for the Edison "peep-show kinetoscopes," "turned to New York music halls, burlesque, traveling shows, and vaudeville to supply bits of self-contained performance" ("Cellulose" 39; Musser, *Emergence* 78).

6. Designating 1906 as the division between one form of remake and the beginning of another is somewhat arbitrary, especially since unhampered, yet dwindling, duping and remaking of the pre-1906 variety continued into the early teens. But most historians of early cinema recognize pre-1906 film as grounded in "the act of showing and exhibition," and post-1906 film as privileging narra-

tional practices (Gunning 56–57). André Gaudreault sees the 1905 *Biograph v. Edison* copyright infringement case as evidence of the emergence of the "pluripunctual" film, in which a narrator is incorporated into the fabric of the film itself through editing so as to connect the discontinuous shots of the multi-shot film ("Infringement" 119–20). This cutoff date is valid even for France: "The last months of 1906 mark an important stage in the evolution of the seventh art: one ceases to consider it simply as an attraction, bestowing on it the dignity of spectacle in a class all its own" (Deslandes 491).

7. Roberta Pearson notes that the effort to upgrade the audiences attending films required, first, that cinemas move from the "narrow, crowded, and unsanitary storefront shows in bad neighborhoods" to picture palaces; second, that the film subjects be upgraded (124). This meant switching from an emphasis on the arbitrary action marking the nickelodeon cinema to the psychological exploration of characters, which would in turn result in a change of acting styles (126). The histrionic would be replaced with the "verisimilar" (122).

8. The definition of the dupe offered in a *Moving Picture World* editorial, "Who is Pirating Films?" from July 6, 1907 was: "A 'dupe' film is a duplicated film; that is, one manufacturer copies a film made by another, thereby saving the expense of posing the original, and offers it to the public as his own, perhaps under a new title. The method adopted is that a film made in Europe, say, and not having been copyrighted is bought, placed in the printing machine with a negative film and exposed. The result is a 'dupe' negative, from which positives are now made and sold as original films" (275). A remake, according to an editorial from *Moving Picture World* (September 21, 1907) is a "pirated" film: "A 'pirated' film is one where the ideas of one manufacturer have been obtained by another, who, using other models, has reproduced the subject. The plots of, say, a trick film—a harlequinade, a burlesque, or a pathetic subject—have been obtained either by espionage, advance copies or purchase from a dishonest employe [*sic*], and reposed with identical settings and sent out as original to the detriment of the originator of the first production" (451).

9. Dupes, for example, were of two kinds; there was the dupe, say of an Edison film, that was distributed by another company as an original Edison film; many companies also bought and duped or distributed films to which they affixed either new titles and/or their own names.

10. It duped uncopyrighted domestic films as well (Musser, *Emergence* 278).

11. This case will hereafter be referred to as *Biograph v. Edison*.

12. Jeanne Thomas Allen, André Gaudreault, and David Levy's discussion of these two cases, respectively, in "Copyright and Early Theater, Vaudeville, and

Film Competition," "The Infringement of Copyright Laws and Its Effects (1900–1906)," and "Edison Sales Policy and the Continuous Action Film, 1904–1906" were instrumental to the construction of my argument.

13. In an instance of the pot calling the kettle black, it is ironic that Edison should seek an injunction against Lubin, since Edison had Vitagraph dupe "uncopyrighted Lubin and Amet films, which it then marketed" (Musser, *Emergence* 278). The difference between the practices of the two companies hinges on whether the material was copyrighted or not. Edison's films were copyrighted and therefore infringement was prosecutable. It would seem that the Edison Company took advantage of the legal definition of public domain, without suffering any pangs as to whether its activities could be morally justified.

14. According to Kemp Niver, "The practice of sending paper copies made from the original negative of a moving picture continued until about 1916, many years after the motion picture law went into effect" (258).

15. In patent rights procedure, which can involve a considerable delay, a patent is conferred on an applicant when the patent office determines that the patent claim "involves something novel and has not been anticipated" (Spring 119). But in copyright registration, the "Copyright Office issues its copyright certificate instantly and automatically on any and all material submitted, without examining such material or similar prior material to ascertain if there are similarities or anticipations" (Spring 119). Nor, for that matter, does the Copyright Office check if material is properly registered.

16. *Edison v. Lubin* had established proper registration procedure for a single-shot film.

17. Public domain applies to "material which may be freely copied and used by anyone at any time" (Spring 122). These works include "ideas, concepts, material, historical events, news, and action episodes arising in the past and present in the external world" (122–23). It also comprehends the "great mass of classic literary, dramatic, musical, and intellectual creations, written in the past" (123). And finally, it describes contemporary works in which the "creator has lost his common-law copyright by publication without obtaining a statutory copyright; and works as to which the author attempted to obtain a statutory copyright, but as to which the copyright is invalid by reason of technical flaws or failings" (123). Copyright protection, as we shall see, is intended, not to protect the integrity of the work so much as the author's right to profit from his or her work for the period permitted by the law.

18. Expression is the central consideration in piracy trials. As Samuel Spring notes, copyright protects original expression, not ideas: "The right granted under a copyright is against *copying* of the *expression* set down, not

against the use of the material and varied ideas created, or facts and information gathered by the author from the objective world of facts. The 'Idea alone, apart from the means of expressing it, is not protected' by a copyright" (Spring 116).

19. "By the summer of 1904 the tide had turned [against Edison]. In January, a mere month, that is, following the completion of *The Great Train Robbery*, Biograph had released *The Escaped Lunatic*, one of the earliest American 'chase' subjects. They followed it up with *Battle of the Yalu* in March, *Personal* in June, *The Moonshiner* in August, *The Hero of Liao Yang* in September and *The Lost Child* in October. The Edison Company suddenly found itself having to struggle to keep up with remakes. Porter completed *Maniac Chase*, the Edison version of *The Escaped Lunatic*, in October 1904 and *Stolen by Gypsies*, Edison's remake of *The Lost Child*, in July 1905. In April 1904, the company had Porter hurry out a static rehash of Biograph's *Yalu*, called *Skirmish Between Russian and Japanese Advance Guards*" (Levy 210).

20. Indeed, from 1896 to 1898, the Edison Company's profits came primarily from film sales (Musser, *Emergence* 166–67).

21. As in Edison's patent registrations, the company could be the copyright proprietor because the "person who takes out the copyright, need not be the author." On the contrary, the "author, as an employee or independent worker, may assign the created work to another who may take out the copyright on the actual author's creation and thereupon, instead of the author, become the copyright proprietor thereof" (Spring 166). Edwin S. Porter was one such worker, as was Billy Bitzer, but neither was treated as the creative source or author of their works, therefore, neither would expect to be asked to assign their work to their companies. As David Levy points out, Edwin S. Porter was not treated like a valuable auteur so much as "an employee whose job it was to follow instructions": "he was rarely consulted on business policy or on decisions that would affect motion picture production (211). Indeed, it would seem that he even had little say in the decision to remake the series of the aforementioned 1904 Biograph films.

22. In *One Reel a Week*, Fred Balshofer, who worked for a short time for Lubin, recounts one incident in which he screened films—both originals and dupes—for sale for a new Lubin client: "After showing a few of the pictures made by Lubin without a sale, he [Lubin] had me run some dupes. Among them was *A Trip to the Moon*, one of Méliès['s] best pictures. Practice had made me quite expert at blocking out the trademarks, and the job on this picture was so good it was hard for our customer to believe his eyes. Suddenly he jumped up from his chair, shot his arm out in front of the beam of light from the projector, and shouted, 'Stop the machine.' Startled, I stopped grinding and turned on the light. Lubin stared at him wondering what was wrong. We found out soon

enough when the prospective buyer shouted, 'You want me to buy that film?' Lubin wanted to know why not. 'I,' the man bellowed thumping his chest, 'I made that picture. I am Georges Méliès from Paris'" (8–9).

23. Charles Musser notes that exchanges even affixed their names to films that they purchased; "A few [exchanges] also created their own 'head titles' to place on films, a residual strategy for claiming authorship. Thus the main title on a surviving print of Vitagraph's *Automobile Thieves* (1906) reads 'Bold Bank Robbery' and displays the logo of J. W. Morgan, a film renter in Kansas City" (*Emergence* 439).

24. For example, to more thoroughly adapt them to American audiences, great liberties were taken with Shakespeare's plays on the popular stage during the nineteenth century. It was at the end of the century that the plays were appropriated by a more highbrow sector of society, which proceeded to make of Shakespeare a cultural icon, to include his plays in the classic literature repertoire, thereby restricting performance to that of the original plays alone (Levine 42). Not only was Shakespeare tampered with, but other works as well. In translations of English gothic literature into French at the beginning of the nineteenth century, for example, translators did not "hesitate to change titles, delete entire pages and introduce new elements with a view to pleasing the reader and conforming to sensibilities that were dominant at the time" (Gambier 212). The notion of authorship in these instances was so loose that "many booksellers' catalogues actually listed the translators as authors" (213).

25. Jacques Deslandes even notices striking similarities between Louis Lumière's "shooting angles" and his "centering of images" and the period's postcards (268).

26. Miriam Hansen reads the inclusion of clips from the cinema's early stages as making a pronounced contrast between a "primitive" and a more evolved mise-en-scène: "For one thing, *Uncle Josh* displays a sense of narrative progression and closure which, in the projected films, is rudimentary at best. Moreover, by juxtaposing diverse genres and representational styles, the film subsumes them into a larger whole, at once more comprehensive and more advanced than the fragments quoted. Thus, even at this early stage the cinema's sense of its own, albeit brief, history is inscribed with a tendency toward subsumption and integration characteristic of the later institution" (28).

27. Janet Staiger's remarks concerning early companies' ability to protect their patent rights pertain equally to copyrights; "Technically, patent law suggests that the value issuing from an invention should go to its originator. However, access to legal restitution is not equal. Unless the inventor has sufficient capital to pursue rights, they are unenforceable" (190).

28. In later cases, this problem was solved by having a marshal seize the pirated goods. See, for example, *Crown Feature Film Co. et al. v. Bettis Amusement Co. et al.* and *Universal Film Mfg. v. Bettis et al.* (February 28, 1913), in *Copyright Decisions, 1909–1914*, (Washington: United States Government Printing Office, 1928): 42–44 (206 Fed. Rep.362. Ohio District Court 1913). Compare this solution with *Biograph v. Edison*, in which Biograph requests that Edison "'be compelled by an order of this court to deliver up to your orator all the copies of the said copyrighted photograph and all negative films thereof in the possession of the defendant or its representatives'" (264). Because the case was decided against Biograph, Edison was not obliged to surrender any films.

29. The inclusion of film in the Copyright Statute in 1912 may have killed blatant domestic duping of films, but it was at pains to stop piracy on the international market. Duping persists to this day not only in the sale of illegal prints to markets in the Far East, but also through the copying and sale of videos prior to their official release abroad, much to the distress of their owners for whom overseas' sales represent a significant source of revenue (Thompson 7).

30. The legal difference between early cinematic duping and remaking practices is for the most part that between literal and treatment copying, a difference that was strictly applied in *Biograph v. Edison*. According to Samuel Spring, literal copying is the "slavish rephrasing" of the words or images used by another author. Treatment copying occupies a much grayer area involving the appropriation of the "ideas, plots, character portrayal and dramatic conflict, situation and surprise, narrative suspense and plot manipulation" of another's work (117–18). In the latter instance, states Spring, "the decision is a matter of judicial appraisal" (117).

31. Levine notes that it was only at the turn of the century that Alfred Stieglitz was able to make a strong case for photography's artistic merits when the "camera, lens, plate, developing-baths, printing process and the like" became tools like a painter's brush. Prior to this, the camera was a machine for copying, and the photographer merely the person running it (162).

32. Charles Musser, too, notes that in *Biograph v. Edison*, copyrighting a moving picture as a photograph "prevented duplication of the actual image," as in the dupe, but that it did not "protect the subject matter or story" (*Emergence* 386). It would perhaps be misguided to conclude from this that, had it equally submitted the "subject matter or story" of *Personal* for copyright protection, Biograph would have won its case. Film producers were not thinking of motion pictures in terms of story per se. It was only when films became significantly longer in format and producers had concentrated editorial control, and had recourse to literature, theater, and original screenplays that the story played an important role in copyright registration and decisions. As we shall see later in this essay,

emphasis on the photographic nature of the medium shifted to the issue of the dramatization of written works, which involved a different domaine of copyright law: licensing. Dramatizations would more or less be considered different (see, for example, *Bobbs-Merrill Co. v. Equitable Motion Pictures Corp, et al.*, 232 Fed. Rep. 791–796, NY District Ct., S.D., 1916); in *Kalem Co. v. Harper Bros.* the judge, in citing a list of previous test cases, ruled that a "photograph can not be an infringement of a copyrighted book," that a "'book' is distinct from 'musical composition,'" that a "'photograph' is not a 'print,'" that a "'translation' is not a 'copy,'" and that "'stone' does not include 'metal plate'" (149). What mattered after the 1911 *Kalem Co. v. Harper Bros.* appellate court decision was that one be legally licensed to do a particular dramatization. Only the writer could bestow these rights, and the licensee could do only one dramatization in one medium, the writer never abdicating his or her "bundle of rights" (Spring 171–72).

33. The exhibitor was also sometimes even a filmmaker, making up for the scarcity of film product by taking his or her own local views or actualities (Deslandes and Richard 218–19, 243). Live narration, sound effects, hand-painting, even the making of local views and actualities contributed to the exhibitor's sense of having the last word on what took place during a screening.

34. Copyright law addresses first the issue of the right to profit from one's "creation," the criterion of which is determining the degree of originality belonging to the infringed work. According to Copyright Statute, the copyright holder has the exclusive right to "print, reprint, publish, copy, and vend the copyrighted work" (1909 Amendment).

35. In 1898, the Edison Company began proceedings against Blackton and Smith's Vitagraph company for copyright infringement (duping Edison films) and for patent infringement. Blackton and Smith avoided going to court and became Edison licensees, one result of which was that Edison copyrighted as its own films produced by Vitagraph (Musser, "American Vitagraph" 34–35, 44).

36. In America, this included entertainments such as vaudeville, the "Wild West, minstrel and magic shows, the burlesque, the playlet, the dance number, pornographic displays, acrobatics, and animal acts" (Hansen 29). Before permanent movie theaters in Europe, the cinematic experience belonged primarily to the fairground showbooths and tents. The European fairground context puts early cinema in the same company as and competing with other fairground attractions such as "marionette shows, menageries, waxworks, bird shows, magic and illusion shows, aquatic shows, circuses, sharp-shooting and knife-throwing exhibitions, peep shows, ghost shows, theater booths, tableaux vivants, etc. . . ." (Swartz 103). Jeanne Thomas Allen explores the industrial cinema vs. the preindustrial vaudeville in "Copyright and Early Theater, Vaudeville, and Film Competition" (178–180).

37. In *Kalem Co. v. Harper Bros.* (1911), the judges stated emphatically that a film exhibition is not a performance; "There are no cases in which an exhibition has been declared to be a dramatic performance or representation *unless human actors are present* and either performing themselves or at least causing dummies or puppets to move and act" (150, emphasis added).

However, in seeking protection, vaudeville acts that attempted to register as dramatic compositions were considered by the courts to be "effervescent, non-literary, too close to personal style and modes of behavior belonging to public domain rather than to private property" (J. T. Allen 181). Because cinema shared subjects/acts with vaudeville and other amusements, it would be natural to assume that reproduction of a vaudeville format would raise serious questions concerning a film's "story" and the latter's status as "private property." In *Biograph v. Edison*, for example, Judge Lanning seems to consider moving picture registration for copyright only as it pertains to the photograph; he states that a photograph merits copyright protection when it expresses an idea; he concludes that a "series of pictures that may be thrown in rapid succession upon a screen telling a single connected story of a man fleeing from a crowd of women" can be registered as a single photograph (267); and, in his reference to *Edison v. Lubin*, he implies that it is illegal to duplicate photographs from a positive print, a crime of which Edison was not guilty in this case. Because his judgment turns on questions of the photographic, not the dramatic, nature of the medium, he refuses to comment on the "literary" value of the "original" story. Instead, he cites *Munro v. Smith* (267–68), reminding the complainants that an idea cannot be copyrighted, only its expression.

38. An individual artist like Loïe Fuller, the originator of the Butterfly and Serpentine Snake dances, was unable to get an injunction for unfair competition against her imitators in *Fuller v. Bemis* (June 18, 1892). Indeed, one of Edison's first films for the kinetoscope featured a Loïe Fuller imitator, Annabelle Whitford [Moore] in her *Annabelle Butterfly Dance* and *Annabelle Serpentine Dance*. Ironically, the relative permanence of the filmic medium has preserved the imitator but not the originator.

39. James Cagney's stage director in *Footlight Parade* (Bacon, 1933) attempts to counter the apparent demise of the variety show by mass-producing prologue "units." He acts like a business chain that buys aspirin in bulk in order to be able to sell it at a cheaper price to the public. But in the assembly-line manufacturing of the musical number, the individual talent, not to mention identity, falls by the wayside to be replaced by a standardized product indistinguishable from other prologue "units" performing the same act. Variety "units"—even by their name alone—were a belated attempt to industrialize along the same lines as cinema, with the production company controlling distribution when renting out their "product."

40. According to Fred Balshofer, duping continued as a practice well into 1912: "Some of our Bison pictures were being duped and run in small theaters out in the sticks" (76). But it was becoming increasingly difficult to sell duped films. As Balshofer notes, by 1912, they could only be shown "in the sticks." In addition, either out of fear of copyright prosecution (because the courts often turn a deaf ear to claims that one was not aware that a film was pirated) or because of greater industry organization, theaters would refuse to show prints not bearing a company's trademark. Even these efforts, however, "did not stop the duping operation entirely" (77).

41. Paul C. Spehr in "Influences françaises sur la production américaine d'avant 1914" suggests that Pathé's film may have been the original, and not a remake of Biograph's film: "The film [*Personal*] was so popular that in less than 3 months Edison made a scene for scene imitation of it, photographed by Porter and entitled *How a french* [*sic*] *Nobleman Got a Wife Through the New York Herald Personal Columns*. . . . There also exists a Pathé Frères production on the same subject entitled *Dix Femmes pour un mari* (production No. 1200). I was unable to establish if the Pathé film had been projected in the United States before the Bitzer film, but there is no doubt that companies had a tendancy to steal mutually from each other" (108).

42. Robert C. Allen points out that "The copyright records upon which [Richard Arlo] Sanderson bases his study are the most useful index of American production trends during this period. It should be kept in mind, however, that not all films were copyrighted at this time. Sanderson's population before 1902 consists almost entirely of Edison product; Biograph films were not deposited for copyright until 1902." Copyrighting did not become routine even after *Edison v. Lubin* and *Biograph v. Edison*, as Allen notes, "I can find no Pathé films represented among the copyright records—a potentially serious problem since between 1904 and 1907 Pathé's American distribution of films equalled or exceeded that of any American manufacturer" (183–84n6).

43. See, *Bobbs-Merrill Co. v Equitable Motion Pictures Corp. et al.*, 232 Fed. Rep. 791–96, NY District Ct., S.D., 1916; *Stodart v. Mutual Film corp. et al.*, 249 Fed. Rep. 507, NY District Ct., S. D., 1917; *International Film Service Co. (Inc.) et al. v. Affiliated Distributors (Inc.) et al.*, 283 Fed. Rep. 229, NY District Ct., S. D., 1922.

44. The opening titles credit the film as being "adapted from David Belasco's Famous Comedy by Roi Cooper Megrue," with the screen version as the work of frequent Keaton collaborators, Clyde Bruckman and Jean Havez (third screenwriting credit is given to Joseph Mitchell).

45. *Personal* was not the first American chase film. According to Musser, Biograph's *The Escaped Lunatic* (1903) was "the first American production to be

structured around the chase." Like *Personal*, this film's chase contains a "simple but effective narrative as well as a coherent spatial and temporal world" (*Emergence* 352). It was remade by Edison as *Maniac Chase* in 1904.

46. Even improvised films result in a postproduction script.

WORKS CITED

Abel, Richard. *The Ciné Goes to Town: French Cinema, 1896–1914*. Berkeley: U of California P, 1994.

Allen, Jeanne Thomas. "Copyright and Early Theater, Vaudeville, and Film Competition." Fell 176–87.

Allen, Robert C. *Horrible Prettiness: Burlesque and American Culture*. Chapel Hill: U of North Carolina P, 1991.

———. *Vaudeville and Film, 1895–1915: A Study in Media Interaction*. New York: Arno, 1980.

———. "Vitascope/Cinématographe: Initial Patterns of American Film Industrial Practice." Fell 144–52.

American Mutoscope & Biograph Co. v. Edison Mfg. Co. 137 Fed. Rep. 262–268. NJ Circuit Ct., D. 1905.

Balshofer, Fred, and Arthur C. Miller. *One Reel a Week*. Berkeley: U of California P, 1967.

Chanan, Michael. "Economic Conditions of Early Cinema." Elsaesser 174–88.

Delisle, Jean, and Judith Woodsworth. *Translation Through History*. Amsterdam: Benjamins, 1995.

Deslandes, Jacques, and Jacques Richard. *Du Cinématographe au cinéma, 1896–1906*. Tournai: Casterman, 1968. Vol. 2 of *Histoire comparée du cinéma*. 2 vols. 1966–68.

Edison v. Lubin. 119 Fed. Rep. 993–94. PA Circuit Ct., E. D. 1903.

Edison v. Lubin. 122 Fed. Rep. 240–43. PA Circuit Ct. of Appeals, 3rd. Circuit. 1903.

Elsaesser, Thomas, ed. *Early Cinema: Space, Frame, Narrative*. London: British Film Institute, 1990.

Fell, John L. "Cellulose Nitrate Roots: Popular Entertainments and the Birth of Film Narrative." Leyda and Musser 39–44.

———, ed. *Film Before Griffith*. Berkeley: U of California P, 1983.

"Films Pirated and Duped." Editorial. *Moving Picture World* 21 September 1907: 451.

Fuller v. Bemis. 50 Fed. Rep. 926–929. NY Circuit Ct., S.D. 1892.

Gambier, Yves et al. "Translators and the Transmission of Cultural Values." Delisle and Woodsworth 191–225.

Gaudreault, André. "The Infringement of Copyright Laws and Its Effects (1900–1906)." Elsaesser 114–22.

———. "Showing and Telling: Image and Word in Early Cinema." Elsaesser 274–81.

———. "Theatricality, Narrativity, and Trickality: Reevaluating the Cinema of Georges Méliès." *Journal of Popular Film and Television* 15.3 (1987): 110–19.

Gaumont Co. et al. v. Hatch. 208 Fed. Rep. 378. PA Circuit Ct. 1913.

Guibbert, Pierre, ed. *Les Premiers ans du cinéma français*. Perpignan: Institut Jean Vigo, 1985.

Gunning, Tom. "The Cinema of Attractions: Early Film, Its Spectator and the Avant-Garde." Elsaesser 56–62.

Hansen, Miriam. *Babel and Babylon: Spectatorship in American Silent Film*. Cambridge: Harvard UP, 1991.

Harper Bros. et al. v. Kalem Co. et al. 169 Fed. Rep. 61–65. NY Circuit Ct. of Appeals, 2nd. Circuit. 1909.

Harper Bros. et al. v. Klaw et al. 232 Fed. Rep. 609–613. NY District Ct., S. D. 1916.

Harris, Neil. "A Subversive Form." Leyda and Musser 45–49.

Izod, John. *Hollywood and the Box Office, 1985–1986*. New York: Columbia UP, 1988.

Kalem Co. v. Harper Bros. 222 Fed. Rep. 55. NY Circuit Ct. of Appeals, 2nd. Circuit. 1911.

Levine, Lawrence W. *Highbrow/Lowbrow: The Emergence of Cultural Hierarchy in America*. Cambridge: Harvard UP, 1988.

Levy, David. "Edison Sales Policy and the Continuous Action Film, 1904–1906." Fell 207–22.

Leyda, Jay, and Charles Musser, eds. *Before Hollywood: Turn-of-the-Century American Film.* New York: Hudson Hills, 1987.

Lowry, Edward. "Edwin J. Hadley: Traveling Film Exhibitor." Fell 131–43.

McCauley, Elizabeth Anne. *Industrial Madness: Commercial Photography in Paris, 1848–1871.* New Haven: Yale UP, 1994.

Musser, Charles. "The American Vitagraph, 1897–1901: Survival and Success in a Competitive Industry." Fell 22–66.

———. *The Emergence of Cinema: The American Screen to 1907.* Berkeley: U of California P, 1994. Vol. 1 of *History of the American Cinema.* 6 vols. 1990–99.

Nama, Charles Atangana, et al. "Translators and the Development of National Languages." Delisle and Woodsworth 25–63.

Niver, Kemp R. "Paper Prints of Early Motion Pictures." Fell 258–63.

Pearson, Roberta. "Cultivated Folks and the Better Classes: Class Conflict and Representation in Early American Film." *Journal of Popular Film and Television* 15.3 (1987): 120–28.

Reed, Joseph W. *American Scenarios: The Uses of Film Genre.* Middletown: Wesleyan UP, 1989.

Sadoul, Georges. *Lumière et Méliès.* Ed. Bernard Eisenschatz. Paris: LHerminier, 1985.

Shiff, Richard. "The Original, the Imitation, the Copy, and the Spontaneous Classic: Theory and Painting in Nineteenth-Century France." *Yale French Studies* 66 (1984): 27–54.

Spehr, Paul C. "Film Making at the American Mutoscope and Biograph Company, 1900–1906." *Quarterly Journal for the Library of Congress* 37 (1980): 413–21.

———. "Influences françaises sur la production américaine d'avant 1914." Guibbert 105–15.

Spring, Samuel. *Risks and Rights in Publishing, Television, Radio, Motion Pictures, Advertising, and the Theater.* New York: Norton, 1952.

Staiger, Janet. "Combination and Litigation: Structures of U.S. Film Distribution, 1896–1917." Elsaesser 189–210.

Swartz, Mark E. "An Overview of Cinema on the Fairgrounds." *Journal of Popular Film and Television* 15.3 (1987): 102–108.

Thompson, Kristin. "Report of the Ad Hoc Committee of the Society for Cinema Studies, 'Fair Usage Publication of Film Stills.'" *Cinema Journal* 32.2 (1993): 3–20.

Toulet, Emmanuelle. "Le Cinéma à l'Exposition universelle de 1900." *Revue d'histoire moderne et contemporaine* 13 (1986): 179–209.

Williams, Alan. "The Lumière Organization and 'Documentary Realism.'" Fell 153–61.

"Who is Pirating Films." Editorial. *Moving Picture World* 6 July 1907: 275–76; 13 July 1907: 291–92.

CHAPTER FIVE

Sound Strategies:
Lang's Rearticulation of Renoir

TRICIA WELSCH

When one innovative and well-respected director sets out to remake the work of another, and when those two talents disagree on practically every aesthetic and methodological issue that filmmaking presents, the result is likely to be a pair of films as disparate as Jean Renoir's *La Chienne* (1931) and Fritz Lang's *Scarlet Street* (1945).[1] What Thomas Leitch calls "the characteristic promise of the remake—that it's just like the earlier film, only better" is even more complicated when the film in question is an American re-presentation of a foreign film, since American audiences may not recognize and respond to the "improvement" (146). Leitch proposes that remakes typically rely on "a triangular notion of intertextuality," in which the three sides of the triangle are formed by a literary original, a film translation of that original, and another film that stands in relation to the first two (147).[2]

An increasingly intricate relation between "originals" and "remakes" ensues when an American remake of a foreign-language original (itself adapted from a literary source) also recapitulates its director's most recent work, a commercially successful picture familiar to American audiences. Lang remade Renoir's *La Chienne* only after he had directed a "pilot" version of *Scarlet Street*, *The Woman in the Window*, the year before. In addition to the sophisticated adaptation process between a foreign language original and an American remake, we must thus consider the dynamics of the same-director remake. The motivations behind a same-director remake—a desire to improve on a first version, reprise a happy relation with cast and crew members, achieve a second financial success, and replay favored scenarios—must also be factored into the equation. In short, *Scarlet Street* is a remake not only of *La Chienne*, but also of *The Woman in the Window*. The triangulated relation that results enriches all three films.[3]

It took more than a decade before Hollywood could find a way to capitalize on Renoir's success with *La Chienne*. Paramount optioned the property almost immediately after its French release, and Ernst Lubitsch worked on several versions of a script during the mid- and late 1930s. Renoir's film, which veered between farce and pathos, seemed ripe for "the Lubitsch touch," yet even Lubitsch could not finesse the deadly consequences of adultery in *La Chienne*. Renoir's film tells the story of a hen-pecked clerk (and amateur painter) who falls for a prostitute, is bilked by her and her pimp, and eventually kills her, leaving the pimp to be convicted and executed for the murder while the clerk hits the streets, *Boudu*-style, revelling in his newfound freedom. After several attempts to get the story past the Breen Office, Lubitsch abandoned his project—and, after Lubitsch dropped out, Paramount's plans to remake Renoir's film languished (Bernstein, "Tale" 47n20).

The project sat on the shelf until 1944, when Fritz Lang, looking for an inaugural project for his semi-independent production company, Diana Productions, rediscovered it.[4] Working in conjunction with producer Walter Wanger and actress Joan Bennett, Lang approached *La Chienne* eagerly; it followed on the heels of his successful collaboration with Bennett on *The Woman in the Window*, released earlier that year. The new film would again star Bennett opposite Edward G. Robinson and Dan Duryea, her leading men in *Woman*; Lang would produce himself, with Wanger as executive producer. They were hoping to make, said Lang, "a new film and not just a copy" (Eisner 257).[5]

What would have constituted a "copy" for Lang is unclear, but the film that resulted distinctly reprised the formal and narrative concerns of *Woman*, even as, with equal firmness, it reconfigured the style and tone of Renoir's original.[6] Lang's "new" film prioritizes his consistent thematic interest in narratives about desire and guilt. Where the Renoir film lets the murderer escape to a life gleefully unfettered by bourgeois cares,

Lang's remake shows the criminal's desperation and divided self, dramatizing the precept uttered by a minor character in the film: "No one gets away with murder." Whereas the French film depicts an "exotic, dangerously unregulated" culture, the remake asserts American values by establishing a punishment to fit the crime.[7] Finally, whereas Renoir sympathizes with the murderer's difficulties and creates a detailed social and economic milieu, Lang concentrates on the "intellectual horror" of the violent trap in which the killer finds himself (Lambert 97). Lang saw in Renoir's movie a situation and characters he could refashion according to his tastes and, partly in response to lingering dissatisfaction with his most recent film, concern about his reputation as a director. Irked by criticism of the "it-was-all-a-dream" ending of *The Woman in the Window*, yet eager to continue exploring the implications of that film's theme, structure, and style, Lang reconvened its cast for *Scarlet Street*.

Nowhere is Lang's revision of Renoir's work more pointed than in the sound design for his "new" film. If remaking foreign films in the States had the putative advantage of supplying a ready-made product to be imitated, Lang nonetheless minimized his reliance on Renoir in a way consistent with his aesthetic preferences and Hollywood studio practice at the time. *Scarlet Street* repudiates not only the laissez-faire perspective of *La Chienne*'s narrative but also its innovative sound techniques, for which Renoir was justly famous.

This essay will examine some of the differences in the soundtracks for the two films, in order to demonstrate the equivocal compliment Lang paid to Renoir in remaking *La Chienne*. Michel Chion has written, "Sound more than imagery has the ability to saturate and short-circuit our perception" (33). The soundtrack for *Scarlet Street* audibly contradicts Renoir's in *La Chienne*. Renoir provides audiovisual density, asking the listener to navigate a sea of accents, noises, musical interludes, and cleverly modulated gradations between loud and quiet sounds.

Conversely, Lang pares down the sound track, using few noises but carefully constructing the dialogue track so that it doubles back on itself, obsessively repeating certain lines and complicating their meaning. *Scarlet Street*'s dialogue conceals as much as it reveals, underscoring the deceptions of his characters. In repeating musical motifs, Lang also uses what Chion calls "on-the-air" music to trigger an increasingly interiorized narrative (77). The insistent repetition of verbal exchanges in *Scarlet Street*, so different from Renoir's inclusion of a wide variety of sounds, also reconfigures *The Woman in the Window*'s heavily mechanized sound

track. In that earlier project, noises made by objects are repeated to connote danger; thus, the control of objects (so that they make minimal
noise) can mean the difference between freedom and entrapment, life
and death.

JEAN RENOIR: KEEPING FAITH WITH CHAOS

Renoir once proclaimed, "One starts with the environment to arrive at
the self" (*My Life* 171). His use of sound in *La Chienne* demonstrates how
he applied this tenet even in his first important "talking picture." Renoir
enthusiastically embraced the new technology and made a low-budget
film—*On purge bébé* (1931)—in six days to prove that he could be
trusted with more expensive talkie projects (106–07).[8] He professed that
with the advent of sound he recognized his true interest in filmmaking:
"Only when the actors began to talk did I gradually realise the possibility
of getting to the truth of the character. It was when I began to make talking pictures that I had the revelation that what I was most deeply concerned about was character" (Bergan 113). He made films, he said, just to
hear certain dialogue spoken aloud.[9]

Renoir creates both densely textured sequences in which dialogue,
sound effects, and music compete for the viewer's—or even the players'—attention and simpler sequences that feature verbal exchanges
without much sonic layering. Although he preferred to record sound on
location, Renoir saved his energy for sequences that would benefit most
from clustered or overlapping sounds. These sequences often occur in
social settings and feature a number of performers; several scenes in *La
Chienne*, for instance, take place in a café frequented by Dédé, the working-class pimp. Although he is conversing with only one man, we hear
the scraping of chairs as other patrons enter and exit and the clinking of
glasses throughout. A dull murmur of talk comes from other tables, and
we can hear a waiter calling an order to a bartender. Occasionally Dédé
and his companion seem distracted by these noises, and their exchange
is visibly interrupted a few times by the incursion of extraneous sounds.
In another instance, a character deep in conversation glances back over
his shoulder as a mechanical piano suddenly begins to play. The sound
of the music temporarily inserts itself into the character's consciousness,
which in turn enhances the realistic rhythm, complete with pauses, of
their conversation.

Although such sound effects neither advance the narrative nor develop character directly, they do both indirectly, by enriching the overall texture of the scene. We learn much about Dédé from his environment, from the company he keeps, and from his jittery responsiveness to the start of the music. Renoir faithfully reproduces the café ambience without stripping it of details that might seem unnecessary or even distracting. He believed that close observation was a precursor to artistic creation and took care to recreate onscreen the details he had observed. Paraphrasing his father, Jean said, "'If you paint the leaf on a tree without using a model you risk becoming stereotyped, because your imagination will only supply you with a few leaves whereas Nature offers you millions, all on the same tree. No two leaves are exactly the same. The artist who paints only what is in his mind must very soon repeat himself.'" He noted approvingly that his father "mistrusted imagination," a practice his own sound strategies replicated by their inclusiveness (*My Life* 171).

Despite the relative primitivism of sound technology in France in the early 1930s, Renoir went to painstaking lengths in *La Chienne* to record sounds that represented the social and natural environments of his characters: "I wanted the realism of genuine buildings, streets and traffic. I remember a gutter whose waters rippled in front of a house which was to serve as background for an important scene. The microphone made it sound like a torrent. . . . In those days we did not possess directional microphones. I solved the problem by taking a close-up of the gutter and thereby justifying the noise it made" (*My Life* 106–07). This example suggests Renoir's commitment to sound and his willingness to commit an image to justify (or cover) it.

Even locations that seem private permit the incursion of complex sound effects that extend the world beyond the frame. When the clerk Legrand is at home, for example, he hears a girl playing a piano in the apartment opposite. We briefly see his neighbors across the way through the window, but Renoir carries the sound of the piano (or variously, a child's lisping voice) throughout the ensuing scenes between Legrand and his wife. The placidity of the people living opposite the unhappy couple is a powerful contrapuntal draw. Since we can hear the noises they make, Renoir suggests that they can hear Legrand and Adèle quarrel: the couple's private misery thus becomes a public—if offscreen—verbal performance for the neighbors. Although the music across the way is extraneous to *La Chienne*'s plot, it opens up and dynamizes the frame, suggesting that adjacent spaces are full of life, that there are stories to be told, and people to know. Renoir believed that dialogue was "only part" of the soundtrack: "a sigh, the creak of a door, the sound of footsteps on the pavement, things such as these can say as much as the spoken word" (*My Life* 104).

Renoir also uses offscreen sound effects to great advantage. For instance, the sound of Dédé's footsteps jogging down the steps from Lulu's flat when she has just entreated him to stay audibly articulates her loneliness and frustration. Similarly, the off-camera sound of Lulu's paper knife cutting the pages of her novel while Legrand pleads with her to love him shows how little she cares. Sometimes, Renoir uses noise (or its absence) to develop characterization. A tentative link is thereby created between personal freedom (even irresponsibility) and the ability to make noise. Dédé, for example, is associated with fairly raucous environments (like the café) and is responsible for a succession of loud or jarring noises: he drives an ostentatiously loud car; he slaps Lulu; he knocks a metal tin of candies from her hands to the floor, where they scatter noisily; and he slams doors. In contrast, Legrand seems to be trying to disappear, and when he makes noise it causes trouble: he sneaks into his apartment in the dark, accidentally knocking over a painting and drawing his wife's ire; he quietly removes money from her bureau and from the safe at work. He talks back to his wife, but only after she leaves the room and can't hear him.[10] It is only when he has devised a way out of his marriage that he comes home singing drunkenly; later that night he helps create the noisy free-for-all that will attract the neighbors and the police and secure his freedom.

The two men's speech reinforces this pattern of noisy liberation versus quiet servitude: Legrand's voice is quiet and low until the end of the film, when he is living on the streets, whereas Dédé's is loud, crude, and self-confident.[11] Assisting in his own disaster, Dédé jokes with the magistrate adjudicating his trial for murder, telling his lawyer to "shut up." Worse, he silences his attorney during the trial, and harangues the jurors with (unavailing) protestations of his innocence. Confident that he is verbally the master of every encounter, Dédé digs his own grave. Tellingly, Dédé is led from his cell to his execution in total silence. Further, it is because of Legrand's lies at the trial, presented in appropriately bourgeois language and cadences, that Dédé must endure this (ultimate) silence.[12]

The coming of sound offered a new way to explore class divisions between characters—that is, through characters' differing speech patterns.[13] Renoir paid careful attention to the accents of his characters in *La Chienne*; he coached Janie Marèse to rid her of convent-trained speech

FIGURE 5.1. Dédé (Georges Flamant) threatening Lulu (Janie Marèze) with a corrective slap in Legrand's (Michel Simon) pied-à-terre in Jean Renoir's *La Chienne* (1931). Courtesy of the Museum of Modern Art, Film Stills Archive.

inflections inappropriate to her character as a streetwalker, and spoke with pride of rendering "very authentic slang" in his presentation of Dédé.[14] Renoir clearly tried to characterize the female players by attention to the pitch and tempo of their voices; for instance, Adèle's shrill, grating voice gets on our nerves.[15] In fact, she is so thoroughly characterized by her unpleasant voice that Legrand exploits it to pull off his escape: he knows Adèle will scream hysterically on cue, which is exactly what he needs her to do. Equally, Lulu's whiny and petulant tones signal her frustrated inability to regulate Dédé's behavior; when she laughs uncontrollably at Legrand, believing she can at least control him, he kills her. André Bazin praised *La Chienne* by saying, "We have the impression that the dialogues were partially improvised to fit each actor's style" (28). In this film, in fact, voice is destiny.

Music also colors the social environment, most unforgettably in the climactic scene in which Legrand stabs Lulu to death, then exits her building unheard and unseen. Although a crowd has formed outside her door, the people are distracted by some street musicians, whose music also drowns out Lulu's last cries and her struggle with Legrand. Instead of showing the violent attack on-screen, the camera goes outside to listen to the music; the song competes for the viewer's attention even at this critical moment, forcing us to acknowledge its presence despite the compelling action occurring upstairs. Renoir lingers insistently over the music, then cuts back and forth between the interiors of the apartment and the street; the slow trickle of information enhances suspense and interest.

The results were dispiriting: early responses to *La Chienne* suggest that audiences were confused by the layered complexities of the sound track. Renoir's insistence on capturing street noises was outside their (limited) experience of film sound.[16] As Dudley Andrew observes, "The heralded naturalism of this film . . . comes less from the plot than from the way we must struggle to follow that plot while it competes with countless other voices, dramas, and inconsequential vibrations making up the chaotic chorus of social life" (104–05).[17] Renoir often spoke of the complete freedom he enjoyed while making *La Chienne*: "I was ruthless and unbearable. I made the film as I wanted, as I understood it, without the slightest regard for the wishes of the producer. I never showed him a single page of my shooting script or a word of the dialogue, and I arranged it so the rushes would remain unavailable until the film was completed" (Bazin 156–57).[18]

During the 1930s in France the number of films produced annually was twice what it had been during the previous decade, and with the demise of the two major French studios, "film making became an intensely speculative activity indulged in by a myriad of tiny, undercapitalized companies" (Armes 68). These (temporary) conditions allowed for (equally temporary) freedoms in France, so it is not surprising that Renoir had creative control. As Ginette Vincendeau says, "If Renoir is still the world's idea of a great auteur, able to pursue his own preoccupations while addressing a popular audience, it is important to see that this was due to the conditions in which he worked" (36). These conditions allowed Renoir to indulge his penchant for open mise-en-scène, his fondness for location shooting, his reluctance to cut too often, and his strong preference for layered and ambient sound. A combination of disarray and design delighted Renoir, who sympathized with a writer criticized for not designing his plays more carefully: "'It struck me at the time that I could have given them a shape,' [the writer] said, 'but it seemed like breaking faith with chaos'" (Gilliatt 25–26).

FRITZ LANG: REVERBERATION AND REPETITION

Although Lang shared Renoir's interest in the possibilities of early sound, his inaugural sound film, *M* (1931), made the same year as *La Chienne*, evinces a different artistic strategy. Consistent with his later practice, Lang used overlapping dialogue to provide economical transitions between scenes or to create connections among disparate groups of people (as when one person begins a sentence and another person in another location finishes it, thus dramatizing a city-wide concern for the lost child). Further, as Lotte Eisner notes, "One word, one sentence can be the trigger for a new scene, without necessarily overlapping directly" (121). In *M*, Lang used dialogue asynchronously, in one instance to withhold information about a speaker's identity from the audience, in another to illustrate a striking absence (a mother's voice calling for her lost child). He uses sound effects sparingly but with thrilling precision: a breathy, off-key whistle alerts a blind man that a murderer is nearby; the trapped man scratches at a door, trying to claw his way to freedom. As these examples demonstrate, Lang's use of sound is pointed, not atmospheric: every sound has a particular, specific, and limited function.

In fact, Lang derided the use of sound for its own sake. He rejected using ambient sound for purposes of realism because he believed the practice to be *un*realistic, adding that he had been "confused" by the inclusion of street noises in a New Wave film:

> When I shot *M* in 1930, I came to one conclusion about sound and it is still correct: if you are sitting alone at a sidewalk café and you have nothing to do, you watch the street and you are aware of a thousand noises—a car passing by, a woman's heel on the pavement, the sound of glasses on the neighbouring table, a little dialogue here and there. But if you are sitting with somebody you love, or you're having a business talk, you don't hear the noise anymore, you only hear your own conversation because you are only interested in the words of the person you love or the business or the things you have to say. (Bogdanovich 100–02)

The notion that the listener doesn't hear certain noises in effect liberates the filmmaker from the obligation to reproduce them. Lang's remarks about the proper use of sound techniques consistently reflect his tightly controlled approach to narrative, and his compatibility with the direction Hollywood sound cinema would take. The sound aesthetic he embraced in the early 1930s was not compromised by working conditions in Hollywood. Even when sound cinema was in its infancy and most open to experimentation and improvisation, Lang eschewed those practices that might have diminished his control over the finished product, such as on-location recording or ambient sound. However inventive his sound techniques became throughout his career, this principle remained firm.

Whereas Renoir strives in *La Chienne* to create densely textured sonic environments that reveal his characters' complexity, Lang adopts a more schematic approach for *Scarlet Street*. Here sound underscores a consistently focused, highly constructed narrative in which each element has a distinct function. Lang uses dialogue to advance the plot and displays little inclination to explore the casual twists and turns of a typical Renoir conversation. Moreover, *Scarlet Street* is a *film noir* that accents the fated hopelessness of its players through the jagged diagonal lines, harsh contrasts, and unnerving claustrophobia of its mise-en-scène. Therefore, Lang retains much of the passivity of Renoir's clerk without the anarchy that intrigues Renoir. The French director's cinematic strong suit—unpredictability—is not Lang's gift. Accordingly, the rearticulation of *La*

Chienne as *Scarlet Street*, a narrative of transgression and punishment, features a less digressive approach to sound. In paring Renoir's layered sound track to a minimum and insisting on what Raymond Durgnat called a "metallic . . . architectural fatalism," Lang remakes Renoir by overturning his accomplishments in *La Chienne* (74).

Specifically, sound effects in Lang's remake repeatedly serve to prompt conversations. There are few extraneous sounds, signalling that the most important environment for Lang is not the natural or the social but the interior, mental landscape. Noticeable sounds are carefully recorded to have an immediately observable impact on the diegesis, and if they do not signify immediately, they almost always pay off later. Nothing seems accidental, in keeping both with Lang's rigorous preplanning and with *film noir*'s emphasis on the inevitable. In fact, a single sound effect can set in motion a chain of elaborately connected events or speeches. One important example occurs in a conversation Chris Cross has with Kitty on a restaurant terrace. As the camera cranes down through the branches of a leafy tree toward their table, we hear a bird sing, and Chris observes contentedly, "That robin sings just like I feel." He whistles back, a liquid, trilling warble, then laughs and says that he hasn't whistled like that for forty years: but today he feels "like a kid" again.

A sound effect prompts dialogue and sets up the dynamics that direct the rest of the scene: while Chris analogizes himself to the natural and unfeigned—he is literally responsive to nature—Kitty presents herself artfully, arranging her face to hide her derisive laughter at his naiveté. Lang cuts back and forth between them as they begin to discuss his painting, extending the nature motif into this part of their conversation as well. Chris says that a painting has "to grow," as feelings grow from attraction toward love: "Every painting, if it's any good, is a love affair." In this brief exchange, prompted by a bird's song carefully placed in the sequence, Lang establishes that Chris's most "natural" feelings—those having to do with love and creativity—are antithetical to Kitty's calculated constructions of those same processes. For Renoir, a bird's song was one note in a grand symphony, but for Lang, the sound was a prelude to a (human) conversation about the bird, one that would signify the speakers' estrangement. Even better, for Lang, the sound has symbolic resonance: the feline "Kitty" is a bird's enemy, and she will prey on and destroy the weaker, more fragile Chris. In the felicitous economy of film sound and image typical of Lang, a birdcage also appears in Chris's home, suggesting his entrapment there as well.[19]

Having thus directed our attention away from sound effects in their own right and toward the interpretation of those sounds by his characters, Lang insures that we have heard the significance of this exchange by repeating it later in the film: when Kitty pretends to be the painter of Chris's acclaimed canvases, she parrots his words about the creative process. His verbal self-revelation becomes part of her deception. Ideas she once smirked at suddenly gain credibility: they have economic value (the only kind she understands), and through them she can speak the language that deceives art critics and dealers into believing that she is a talented painter. Kitty, who pretends to Chris that she is an actress, actually does her best acting for the art critics, recalling her lines perfectly and using Chris's words to seduce the powerful men where they failed to seduce her.

Lang expects the dialogue to carry a lot of weight in these scenes, and the carefully crafted conversations give far more attention to scripted remarks and the actors' vocal styles than to ambient sound. In fact, nothing—no details of set design or costuming, for example—distracts us from Kitty and Chris at their table. Of the forty-five shots in this sequence, only the first features a moving camera (which stops when it arrives at the couple); the remaining forty-four images are reverse angles, which make for a relentlessly compact, structured scene. This tight focus builds tension and interest primarily through the verbal patterns in the couple's conversation, which cue the viewer to register the visual discrepancy between Chris's innocent happiness and Kitty's coolly appraising response to him.

Scarlet Street's soundtrack highlights the film's similarities to *The Woman in the Window*, in which Lang also worked through issues of duplicity and thwarted desire. The earlier film also carefully constructs the dialogue track, as characters trap themselves through slips of the tongue and wishes spoken aloud that come all too true. Both films open with a colorless middle-aged man wistfully expressing his desire for a lovely young woman; in both, the wish quickly conjures her appearance. Both films feature dialogue spoken by one figure that gets repeated—with an unpleasant twist—by someone else, as well as dialogue that sounds accusatory to a guilty person ("I just caught you in time," spoken to a man as he leaves his office at the end of a day, has a nasty ring when that man has just been stealing from the company safe).

Lang's fascination with this type of ironic, reverberant dialogue is analogous to his reliance on the noises produced by machines, especially in *Woman*, in which ticking clocks, car horns, idling motors, police sirens, and the click of an apartment door's security entrance are repeated, each time threatening to reveal guilt by drawing someone's attention. *Woman*'s protagonist becomes morbidly aware of sounds beyond his control, extending the film's notion that destiny is mechanized and uncontrollable. Lang uses what Chion terms "null extension of the sound environment" by shrinking the sounds in the acoustic field to those heard by a single character: when the protagonist cannot hear a conversation in which he is vitally interested, the spectator becomes equally frustrated (87). Similarly, an excess of verbal detail deliberately delays a bit of information that the main character is anxiously awaiting and makes his tension palpable. Such examples demonstrate Lang's keen interest in manipulating the soundtracks of both films, as well as his determination that no effect would be—or seem—accidental.

In *The Woman in the Window*, Lang constructed a system of sounds in which every tone was meant to register a particular impression. *Scarlet Street* continues this scheme but puts even more emphasis on the protagonist's mental confusion by using subjective-internal sounds—to use Chion's definition, sound "which corresponds to the physical and mental interior of a character," including "mental voices, memories," and the like (76).

If Renoir decried sound dubbing as "equivalent to a belief in the duality of the soul," Lang seized on it to dramatize this split economically and strikingly.[20] In *Scarlet Street*'s most compelling use of sound, Chris hears over and over again in his head the sweet nothings that Kitty and her lover, Johnny, are whispering to each other when he discovers their affair. The tormenting sounds lead Chris to murder, but after the couple's death he hears a new, modified version of their conversation, one that now invites him to a ghostly debate.[21] The voices taunt him: "Now we're together," they say, and, "You brought us together forever." Words Kitty once said—"You're old and ugly"—have a new ending, "and you killed me." The spectral pair mock and hector Chris: sometimes their speech overlaps, becoming unintelligible; at other times it plays at a speeded-up or slowed-down pace, garbling the voices and rendering them even more unnatural. These distortions dramatize Chris's self-division and his slipping hold on reality.

Another sound motif, a record skipping on a turntable, begins in synch with the image (we see the needle missing its groove), but ends up incorporated into Chris's sound loop as well. On one occasion, the droning repetition of "in love . . . in love . . . in love . . ." from "Melancholy

140

FIGURE 5.2. Johnny (Dan Duryea) and Kitty (Joan Bennett) in Chris Cross's (Edward G. Robinson) pied-à-terre in Fritz Lang's *Scarlet Street* (1945). Courtesy of the Museum of Modern Art, Film Stills Archive.

Baby" is triggered in Chris's mind by the on-off buzz of a neon sign outside his flophouse room. This in turn trips another familiar soundtrack, Johnny and Kitty's cooing love talk, which repeats itself in an endless round. Variously overlaid with cackling laughter, or with a phantom organ eerily reprising the opening bars of "Melancholy Baby," the voices torment Chris, punishing him for his crime. Even as he is revived from a failed suicide attempt, the reassuring language his neighbor uses—"It's all right, old man"—is the very epithet Kitty used to dismiss Chris. As if on cue, we again hear her voice calling, "Johnny, Johnny"; again one sound trips off another in a nightmarish sequence.

Sound was dangerous in *Woman in the Window*, but by *Scarlet Street* it is contagious as well. Dialogue gets repeated as it passes from person to person; sound effects recur with disturbing familiarity; and both contribute to an economy of repetition that defines *Scarlet Street* decisively. This repetition serves a narrative function even as it underscores the double identity of *Scarlet Street* as a remake. A preoccupation with repetition is strangely fitting in a remake that itself replicates the director's prior film. Both a rejoinder to Renoir and a further development of Lang's work in *Woman, Scarlet Street* asserts its authority by overstating its case.

BAD DREAMS: REPETITION AND ANXIETY

Lang's work with repetition is further shored up by the congruence between his expressionist film heritage and *film noir*'s concern with the divided self. In both *Woman* and *Scarlet Street*, for example, repetition gets thematized as doubling. In *Woman*, an improbable number of surfaces are mirrored, replicating the images they display; in *Scarlet Street*, Chris's shadow is thrown on the wall, in a spectral projection of his body, doubling him the way the voices he hears reiterate what is in his head.

Both films feature characters who are divided against themselves, who disguise antisocial impulses and actions by their mild façades. *Film noir*'s voice-over narration, a radical doubling that constitutes the speaker as both an actor in the narrative and a figure who stands outside it (thus estranging him from both perspectives), might have been a natural choice for either *Woman* or *Scarlet Street*. The use of sound in both films recalls *noir*'s voice-over, which is often unreliable or futile, knowledge coming too late to do its speaker any good (as in *Sunset Boulevard* [Wilder, 1950], which is narrated entirely by a dead man). In fact, Lang's next picture, *The*

Secret Beyond the Door (1948), another Diana Production starring Joan Bennett, continues the trajectory begun in *Woman* and *Scarlet Street* by featuring misleading voice-over narration: we believe that a man describing his murderous fantasies has actually committed the crimes to which he is "confessing." In addition, in *Secret*, "Lang was interested in a new method of narration: the heroine's 'thought voice' in voice-over," which was meant to be read not by the leading lady but by another actress, thus multiplying the levels of duplicity (Bernstein, *Walter Wanger* 215).[22]

Likewise, in both films, the mental disorder of Lang's protagonists goes far beyond what Renoir envisioned in *La Chienne*. Locating *Scarlet Street* in Lang's expressionist tradition of whirling dreams and fantasies— an influence prominent in *Woman* as well—is therefore as necessary as thinking of the film in terms of its French ancestry. Lang's fascination with dreams may be connected to the repetition of sounds and scenarios as manifestations of a character's unconscious guilt and desire for punishment. Both *Woman* and *Scarlet Street* follow a dream-like call-and-response progression, as both protagonists find the wishes they utter disturbingly fulfilled.

The Woman in the Window reproduces Professor Wanley's nightmare in alarming detail: he responds to a sexy, alluring woman and is punished with the incapacitation of his intellect, becoming literally unable to imagine his escape. At the last moment, he wakes up, terrified but innocent of any crime except desire. More drastically, the protagonist of *Scarlet Street* ends up homeless, tormented by voices in his head that produce mental terror akin to that suffered (albeit temporarily) by the professor in *Woman*. Lang exhibits his characteristic interest in disturbed mental states by reconceiving *Woman*'s dream (an evanescent experience) as *Scarlet Street*'s insanity (a more permanent and less permeable condition). The radical freedom Renoir's main character chooses becomes powerlessness for Lang's protagonists—not once but twice, before *and* within the Renoir "remake."[23]

Scarlet Street concludes with a deranged, guilty Chris Cross wandering the streets; he is not dreaming, but his vacancy recalls that of a sleepwalker. Wish fulfillment and the mesmerizing illogic of dreams fascinated Lang throughout his career: he claimed that he had proposed the infamous frame in *The Cabinet of Dr. Caligari*, which suggests that the entire story is the raving of a lunatic held in an asylum. Strikingly, Lang acknowledged the similarity between this frame and the one in *Woman in the Window*, but claimed that the repetition was "unconscious—I didn't even *think* I was copying myself at the time" (Bog-danovich 64). Clearly, repeating himself did not bother Lang.[24] In fact, he likened his own creative process to dreaming, and made films, he claimed, "almost as if . . . sleepwalking" (401–02).[25] The films that resulted, however, are highly polished, not improvisational in any way. The perfect closure within the mise-en-scène, the lack of extraneous detail, the inescapable web of circumstance, and especially the employ-ment of mesmerizing, distorted sound all contribute to the claustro-phobic nightmares in both *The Woman in the Window* and *Scarlet Street* and draw attention to the striking differences between Renoir's "origi-nal" film and Lang's American work.

As Michel Chion writes, sounds and images "have tendencies, they indicate directions, they follow patterns of change and repetition that cre-ate in the spectator a sense of hope, expectation, and plenitude to be bro-ken or emptiness to be filled . . . an audiovisual sequence functions according to this dynamic of anticipation and outcome" (55). Both Renoir and Lang thoughtfully noted the tendencies expressed by the soundtrack; *La Chienne* and *Scarlet Street* offer the attentive listener a great deal of information about the shape and trajectory of their narratives and lead the viewer-auditor toward certain outcomes. Both directors adjusted their earliest practices as sound conventions became codified; yet Renoir maintained his early attachment to an extended sound environ-ment (that enlarged his playing field), just as Lang, with equal consis-tency, continued to limit the sound environment in his films (effectively tightening the focus on individual figures in the mise-en-scène). When he promised to make *Scarlet Street* "a new film and not a copy" of *La Chi-enne*, Lang renewed a commitment to his own sound strategies. Chief among the voices echoing in his ear was the siren call of *The Woman in the Window*.

NOTES

I am grateful to Thomas Leitch, who generously allowed me to quote from his revised essay on the remake; to Jennifer Forrest and Leonard Koos, whose thoughtful comments helped with drafts of this chapter, and to *Cinema Journal*'s anonymous but perceptive and gentle readers.

1. Leo Braudy has called Renoir's and Lang's styles "the two most dis-tinct cinematic methods of portraying the visual world," methods which he

characterizes as "open" and "closed." These classifications remain helpful and may be productively extended to a consideration of their sound strategies in this pair of films as well. See Braudy, *The World in a Frame* (44).

2. *La Chienne*, moreover, was never commercially released in the United States; it premiered at the Museum of Modern Art in an unsubtitled version in February 1954, and was finally shown with subtitles at the New York Film Festival in September 1975. See Christopher Faulkner's *Jean Renoir* and *The Social Cinema of Jean Renoir*.

3. *Scarlet Street* fits into a number of the categories of remakes found in Robert Eberwein's suggestive essay, "Remakes and Cultural Studies." Elsewhere in the volume, Leo Braudy speaks of the remake as concerned with "unfinished cultural business, unrefinable and perhaps finally unassimilable material that remains part of the cultural dialogue—not until it is finally given definitive form, but until it is no longer compelling or interesting" (331).

4. The 1940s saw the expansion of what Janet Staiger has called the "package unit" system of production, which coordinated labor and materials for individual film projects (Bordwell et al. 330–35). For a consideration of three atypical films Lang made at Twentieth Century–Fox just before this period, see Smedley.

5. Lang told Peter Bogdanovich, "The Renoir film is really a wonderful picture, but [screenwriter Dudley] Nichols and I purposely never looked at it. We had seen it years ago, but we wanted to be absolutely uninfluenced by it" (66). Matthew Bernstein disputes this, saying that Wanger's efforts to locate a print were unavailing (*Walter Wanger* 421).

6. Matthew Bernstein observes that at Diana Productions Lang used his power as a semi-independent filmmaker "to experiment with new formal concerns" (*Walter Wanger* 215). Lang biographer Patrick McGilligan concurs that *Scarlet Street* was Lang's "single most autonomous production" (317).

7. Leitch notes that this is a typical move: when an American filmmaker remakes a foreign film, the strategy of disavowing ancestry is reinforced by a process of "colonization" that insistently "textualiz[es] not only the predecessor films but the foreign culture . . . as romantic, exotic, dangerously unregulated, and . . . to be repudiated as uncompromising, difficult, and ultimately unresponsive to the demands of American consumers" (57 in this volume).

8. Roy Armes calls the filming of *On purge bébé* "cheap, literal, and totally conventional" (81).

9. A case in point was *La Bête humaine* (1938), which Renoir claimed he made in order to hear Severine tell Lantier: "'Don't look at me like that, you'll

wear out your eyes.' I find that so beautiful, and I said to myself that I had to make a movie in which you could put a phrase like that" (Ciment 17). See also Célia Bertin 81.

10. Alexander Sesonske finds the "most insistent aspect of the dialogue" in the film "Legrand's frequent failure to respond to the talk around him, his apparent obliviousness to much of what he must hear. . . . Renoir has used his dialogue to separate Legrand from others and display him as lost in the ordinary world" (90).

11. Donald Phelps calls Michel Simon's voice the "funky, insidious woodwind" that is "the central instrument of Renoir's vocal stylization" (69).

12. Dédé's failure to say "hello" to Lulu's concierge—another silence—incites that woman's suspicion; she investigates and finds Lulu dead. His uncharacteristic silence here makes Dédé vulnerable.

13. Alan Williams reads Renoir's attention to speech in *La Chienne* in terms of his political commitment to the Left: "The range of vocal styles in the film makes its sound track not merely interesting in texture (as aural montage), but implicitly redolent of class conflict" (227). See also Michel Marie. Such political engagement did not interest Lang, and he used accent, volume, and pitch less conspicuously than Renoir. This may also reflect the relative novelty of the English language for Lang.

14. Renoir instructed Janie Marèse to imitate Maurice Chevalier (*My Life* 110). In a letter to Dudley Nichols, Renoir specifically mentioned his pride in the film's dialogue: in Dédé, he said, he had "not an actor, but an authentic character who brought me his true way of speaking." In this letter (dated September 27, 1941), Renoir invited Nichols to consider remaking *La Chienne* with him in Hollywood. (Nichols eventually scripted the film for Lang.) (*Letters* 125).

15. Renoir believed the voices were crucial to characterization: "I heard Michel Simon interpret this character with a slightly monotonous voice, with the voice we hear in the film now, a voice that avoids outbursts, highs, and lows. . . . I didn't choose Madame Bérubet for the wife, Michel Simon brought her to me. He said to me, 'I see what you want, you want me to have a slightly somber, slightly dull voice, and opposite me you want a wife with a loud voice. In that case, I'm going to bring you Bérubet'" (*Renoir on Renoir* 173).

16. Renoir's recording strategies probably helped obscure the primacy of individual sounds. Rick Altman writes, "Whereas live sound provides an extraordinary number of variables, each permitting and promoting selective attention, recorded sound folds most of those variables into a single, undifferentiated source. In a live situation, we easily differentiate among the various sound sources surrounding us, but with recorded sound no such clear distinctions are possible" (29).

17. For a discussion of contemporary responses to the film, see Andrew 197. Andrew highlights Renoir's distinctiveness; by comparison, Ginette Vincendeau argues that Renoir's mise-en-scène was not anomalous in French cinema, but was "part of the French mainstream" (36).

18. Indeed, the producer expected a comedy and was dismayed to find on the film's completion that it was a grim tale.

19. See also E. Ann Kaplan's discussion of how Lang renders the division between public and private space in this film "natural" in "Ideology and Cinematic Practice in Lang's *Scarlet Street* and Renoir's *La Chienne*." Sylvia Harvey also reads the birdcage as a metaphor for the "impotence," "routinised boredom," and "sense of stifling entrapment" that characterize marriage in *film noir* (29).

20. Renoir regarded dubbing as "an outrage. If we were living in the twelfth century, a period of lofty civilization, the practitioners of dubbing would be burnt in the market-place for heresy. . . . There is not a yard of dubbed film in *La Chienne*" (*My Life* 106). Renoir repeated this concern frequently: "Accepting dubbing means refusing to believe in the kind of mysterious connection between the trembling of a voice, the expression . . . in short, it means we have ceased to believe in the unity of the individual" (Bergan 336). See also Renoir's letter to Pierre Blanchar of December 31, 1944, in Renoir, *Letters* 160–62; and *Renoir on Renoir* 173.

21. As Phelps observes, "The pursuit of the guilty by admonishing or razzing ghosts was not new to Lang." The footsteps that follow Spencer Tracy's character in *Fury* are another instance in which subjective-internal sound plays a crucial role (71).

22. For David Bordwell, these experiments with narration have a common trajectory: "Lang's American films frequently construct a 'paranoid' spectator through a narration that brutally and abruptly manipulates point-of-view in order to conceal gaps and force the viewer to false conclusions" (82).

23. Lang may have felt drawn to redo this scenario to address criticism he received for ending *The Woman in the Window* as a dream. As late as 1948, he was justifying his decision in print, saying the expected resolution would have been "defeatist . . . a tragedy for nothing, brought about by an implacable Fate," adding that the audience would certainly have rejected such an ending (Eisner 247). Screenwriter Nunnally Johnson recalled Lang's commitment to this ending: "I did not want this inner story to be a dream. . . . I wanted it to be a story told by someone. . . . But Fritz preferred the dream" (Eisner 255). Lang also claimed that *Woman*'s happy ending produced a lot more revenue than a "defeatist" one would have (McGilligan 313).

24. Jean-Pierre Coursodon notes that Lang repeated his own remake strategy by casting Dana Andrews in a pair of "strikingly similar" successive films

(*While the City Sleeps* [1955] and *Beyond a Reasonable Doubt* [1956]). Here, as in *Woman* and *Scarlet Street*, "the second of the two films introduces a shift for the worse, from innocence to guilt." Coursodon calls this recurrence a "habit" of Lang's (202). This habit apparently rubbed Renoir the wrong way: McGilligan quotes Lotte Eisner as saying that Renoir "didn't want to have anything to do with [Lang], because he resented Lang's remakes of *La Chienne* and *La Bête humaine*" (471).

25. Lang also spoke of his inspiration as "somehow dreamlike, situated between reality and unreality," and said that his decision to become a filmmaker "emerged with the same curious, almost somnolent certainty which I later felt with all my films" (Eisner 13).

WORKS CITED

Altman, Rick. "The Material Heterogeneity of Recorded Sound." *Sound Theory, Sound Practice.* Ed. Rick Altman. New York: Routledge, 1992. 15–31.

Andrew, Dudley. *Mists of Regret: Culture and Sensibility in Classic French Film.* Princeton: Princeton UP, 1995.

Armes, Roy. *French Cinema.* New York: Oxford UP, 1985.

Bazin, André. *Jean Renoir.* Ed. François Truffaut. Trans. W. W. Halsey II and William H. Simon. New York: Dell, 1974.

Bergan, Ronald. *Jean Renoir: Projections of Paradise.* Woodstock: Overlook, 1992.

Bernstein, Matthew. "A Tale of Three Cities: The Banning of Scarlet Street." *Cinema Journal* 35.1 (1995): 27–52.

———. *Walter Wanger, Hollywood Independent.* Berkeley: U of California P, 1994.

Bertin, Célia. *Jean Renoir: A Life in Pictures.* Trans. Mireille Muellner and Leonard Muellner. Baltimore: Johns Hopkins UP, 1981.

Bogdanovich, Peter. *Fritz Lang in America.* London: Studio Vista, 1967.

Bordwell, David, Janet Staiger, and Kristin Thompson. *The Classical Hollywood Cinema: Film Style and Mode of Production to 1960.* New York: Columbia UP, 1985.

Braudy, Leo. "Afterward: Rethinking Remakes." Horton and McDougal 327–34.

———. *The World in a Frame: What We See in Films*. Chicago: U of Chicago P, 1976.

Chion, Michel. *Audio-Vision: Sound on Screen*. Ed. and trans. Claudia Gorbman. New York: Columbia UP, 1994.

Ciment, Michel. "Entretien avec Jean Renoir (*sur La Bête humaine*)." *Positif* 173 (September 1975): 15–22.

Coursodon, Jean-Pierre, with Pierre Sauvage. *American Directors*. Vol. 1. New York: McGraw-Hill, 1983.

Durgnat, Raymond. *Jean Renoir*. Berkeley: U of California P, 1974.

Eberwein, Robert. "Remakes and Cultural Studies." Horton and McDougal 15–33.

Eisner, Lotte. *Fritz Lang*. London: Secker and Warburg, 1976; New York: Da Capo, 1986.

Faulkner, Christopher. *Jean Renoir: A Guide to References and Resources*. Boston: G. K. Hall, 1979.

———. *The Social Cinema of Jean Renoir*. Princeton: Princeton UP, 1986.

Gilliatt, Penelope. *Jean Renoir: Essays, Conversations, Reviews*. New York: McGraw-Hill, 1975.

Harvey, Sylvia. "Woman's Place: The Absent Family of Film Noir." *Women in Film Noir*. Ed. E. Ann Kaplan. London: BFI Publishing, 1980. 22–34.

Horton, Andrew, and Stuart Y. McDougal, eds. *Play It Again, Sam: Retakes on Remakes*. Berkeley: U of California P, 1998.

Kaplan, E. Ann. "Ideology and Cinematic Practice in Lang's *Scarlet Street* and Renoir's *La Chienne*." *Wide Angle* 5.3 (1983): 32–43.

Lambert, Gavin. "Fritz Lang's America." *Sight and Sound* 25.1 (1955): 15–21.

———. "Fritz Lang's America." *Sight and Sound* 25.2 (1955): 92–97.

Leitch, Thomas M. "Twice-Told Tales: The Rhetoric of the Remake." *Literature/Film Quarterly* 18.3 (1990): 138–49.

Marie, Michel. "The Poacher's Aged Mother: On Speech in *La Chienne* by Jean Renoir." *Yale French Studies* 60 (1980): 219–32.

McGilligan, Patrick. *Fritz Lang: The Nature of the Beast*. New York: St. Martin's P, 1997).

Phelps, Donald. "*La Chienne*: Legrand's Illusion." *Film Comment* 32.1 (1996): 67–71.

Renoir, Jean. *Letters.* Ed. Lorraine LoBianco and David Thompson. Trans. Craig Carlson, Natasha Arnold, and Michael Wells. London: Faber and Faber, 1994.

———. *My Life and My Films.* Trans. Norman Denny. New York: Atheneum, 1974.

———. *Renoir on Renoir: Interviews, Essays, and Remarks.* Trans. Carol Volk. New York: Cambridge UP, 1989.

Sesonske, Alexander. *Jean Renoir: The French Films, 1924–1939.* Cambridge: Harvard UP, 1980.

Smedley, Nick. "Fritz Lang Outfoxed: The German Genius as Contract Employee." *Film History* 4.4 (1990): 289–304.

Vincendeau, Ginette. "The Exception and the Rule." *Sight and Sound* 2.8 (1992): 36.

Williams, Alan. *Republic of Images: A History of French Filmmaking.* Cambridge: Harvard UP, 1992.

CHAPTER SIX

The Raven and the Nanny: The Remake as Crosscultural Encounter

ALAN WILLIAMS

At the end of World War II, American films flooded French movie theaters; this is well-known, and the consequences well-examined. At the
same time, however, a smaller wave of French (and other European) films
from the war years washed into U.S. "art houses" and also into the hands
of a recently enlarged group of Hollywood decision makers. These films
arrived at the very beginning of the decline and fall of the American "studio system" (the Paramount consent decree came in 1948, but weakness
in the system had already appeared when many major stars formed their
own production companies). Independent productions, or "indies," were
increasingly prominent, as were "semi-indies," or films technically made
by a major studio but in reality shaped largely by autonomous units
within it.

With this decentralization of production decisions, came an expansion of the range of possible responses to that eternal Hollywood problem: where to get the basic narratives for the huge number of films to be
made each year? The accumulated French production of four years of
German Occupation would have seemed a tempting source of ready-
made, pre-tested material. The most striking of these projects, alas, never
became a film (for reasons that are still not entirely clear): Max Ophuls

was slated to adapt and direct a remake of *La Duchesse de Langeais* as a comeback vehicle for Greta Garbo (in the part so brilliantly played by Edwige Feuillère in the Baroncelli/Giraudoux original).[1]

Two less striking projects did get made, one a semi-independent work by director-producer Otto Preminger, the other an "indie" star vehicle for Jane Wyman. These adapted Clouzot and Chavance's *Le Corbeau* (1943) and Stelli and Campaux's *Le Voile bleu* (1942), respectively, both important commercial successes of the Occupation years.[2] The resulting films, *The Thirteenth Letter* (Otto Preminger, 1951) and *The Blue Veil* (Curtis Bernhardt, 1951), can tell us much about the norms and typical cultural themes of the American cinema as opposed to the French, as well as suggesting more general lessons about the benefits and pitfalls of transcultural *bricolage*. However, we must also keep in mind that these are not merely cultural transpositions, but also (as it were) trans*historical* exercises. For the French originals come from a demoralized country under enemy occupation, whereas they are remade in peacetime in a country that was a "superpower" both in the world at large and in world cinema.

Le Corbeau is an essential work for world film history, if only because its meanings are still being debated. (Was it "anti-French"? "anti-Vichy"?) These debates can be largely avoided here (and we cannot recount in full the celebrated plot), but one must still pay attention to the film's very specific historical context. It opens with a characterless expository scene and then immediately shifts to its principal thematic material with the presentation of Dr. Germain, the character played by Pierre Fresnay. (Either begin with your big star, or delay his or her entrance to the point where the delay is noticeable—this is a norm of "classical" cinema everywhere. *The Thirteenth Letter* begins with a different character, the one played by Charles Boyer, because Boyer is a bigger star than Michael Rennie, even though Rennie takes the Fresnay role and therefore has the larger part.) In this first narrative unit, the film's major thematic concern is clearly voiced: Germain's hands are bloody after an attempted delivery of a baby. He tells the patient's mother (or grandmother? in any event the movie opens and closes with Germain looking at an elderly woman) that "the mother is saved." She replies, "Oh doctor, you didn't do that," and he says "Yes; and honestly." In other words, Germain has performed what in the 1990s America is called a "partial birth abortion" to save the mother's life.

The cluster of motifs begun here can be summed up with the question: which is more valuable, the mother or the child? Much later, Dr. Germain will overtly generalize this question: which is more important, the present or the future? Or to extend the question still further (which neither Germain nor the film is prepared to do, but certainly some audience members would have): should one risk one's own life (in wartime, under the Occupation) to insure a better life for others, at a later time? Surely this was a question on the minds of many spectators, who had to decide between feeding themselves or feeding their children, or between accepting the German Occupation or resisting it. None of this cluster of concerns makes its way into *The Thirteenth Letter*: its doctor Pearson has no particular problem with choosing the mother or the child—in fact, he has become a general practitioner and not an obstetrician. Nor is he accused by the town's unknown poison-pen letter writer, as is Germain, of being an abortionist. Preminger and Koch keep the anonymous letters, of course (though the thirteenth one has no particular significance in the plot), but make the accusation against the young doctor be simple adultery.[3]

If *The Thirteenth Letter* jettisons the sensitive issue of abortion, the film nonetheless reproduces much of *Le Corbeau*'s cinematographic style. In Clouzot's film, we are frequently aware of the fact that we are being told a story; we remain aware, periodically, of a narrator who knows more than we do, who takes us places and shows us things without letting us know why. Often, this is accomplished entirely or in part through camera movement, which is a dominant stylistic trait of the work. Most viewers probably don't notice the full extent to which Clouzot moves his camera, but *Le Corbeau* (like *The Thirteenth Letter*) has a truly remarkable number of tracks, pans, crane shots, tilts, and combinations thereof for a film of its period. It is difficult to characterize Clouzot's use of the moving camera. It is not exactly *expressive* (of a world, of an authorial gaze), as for example Renoir or Ophuls's movements would be. Nor is it purely *functional*, an efficient way of following the action with a minimum of fuss, as so often seems to be the case when Howard Hawks moves his camera. (Most of the movements in *The Thirteenth Letter* are, in the final analysis, of this sort.) Nor is it a marker of distance and objectivity, as a moving point of view seems to often connote in the films of Autant-Lara.

One reason for this litany of negatives is that camera movement is not formally dominant in *Le Corbeau*; it is, rather, one of two formal poles in the film. Movement almost always calls attention to the *look* of the camera, to the fact that it is an agent of our vision. But vision itself is an obsession in Clouzot's film, both at the level of narration—not just camera movement, but high and low angle shots, and other devices that render our act of seeing a conscious one—but also at the level of the story. In the fictional world, people are looking at other people, almost all of the time. There is a great deal of shot-reverse shot editing, and the edits are often not timed in response to dialogue (where we should look to best gauge the impact of a word, a tone of voice) but to the characters' glances. Some of these are literally (clinically) hysterical: bug-eyed expressions of disbelief or shock. There is also an unusually large number of subjective shots, including one apparently seen through a keyhole. It is as if there is a constant war going on to control the visual field, between the film's unseen narrator and its characters.

It is important to note, however, that the obsessive importance of the gaze in *Le Corbeau* does *not* make it, as many currents in recent film theory might have it, a film about voyeurism. The look, both within the film and *of* the film, is not one of sexual pleasure, or at least not primarily so. The characters' looks do not seek sexual release, but *knowledge*, for this is a film about paranoia and understanding more than it is a film about sex. The gaze here often has erotic possibilities, but they are rarely realized. And if the contest over control of the gaze is not an erotic one, but a paranoid tug-of-war with power as the prize, then it is all the more interesting that there are two characters in the film who correspond, functionally, to the positions of film viewer and film narrator. Germain is in the position of the viewer, while the psychiatrist, Dr. Vorzet is, as we learn at the very end of the film a narrator—a *writer* (of the anonymous letters, with the help of his wife), the one who controls the destinies of the other characters. Like the film's own storytelling agency, Vorzet knows what will happen before it happens, because he has planned it.

Along with dueling points of view—between the narrator and the characters, and between Vorzet and Germain—*Le Corbeau* sets in play what one might term *dueling world views*. This makes it, in a very French way, a thesis film (like *Le Voile bleu*, as we will see below)—with the notable caveat that Clouzot and Chavance have set two theses in opposition, both of which clearly refer to the film's historical context. The letter-writing campaign is implicitly compared to the Occupation: it is evil, it comes from the "outside" of normal society, it corrupts and causes mass hysteria. Vorzet and Germain have two, very different "lessons" to be drawn from the experience of the community under stress. Vorzet's thesis

is that evil is *always there*—all people are both good and evil, and it
depends on context to bring them out. His interpretive grid is properly
Manichaean (or more specifically he subscribes to the Albigensian heresy
which is the subject of another great Occupation film, *La Fiancée des
ténèbres*): God and the Devil are equally powerful, locked in perpetual
struggle; both are "divine." You cannot stop the struggle. Germain, on the
other hand, believes in moral absolutes. He says that going through the
experience of evil (= the Occupation) can make one stronger: "Le mal est
nécessaire," as he opines at one point. But evil is not necessary because it
is as powerful as good, but because it helps to *purify* and *clarify* good. The
experience of evil helps Germain to love a woman again, after the death
of his wife, and to give up the quasi-abortionist stance that he has at the
beginning of the film.

From this summary, it might be assumed that *Le Corbeau* is, in fact,
a fairly simple "thesis film," and that Germain is shown to be right, and
Vorzet wrong. But things are not at all that simple. Recall that Vorzet is
the narrator/director-figure; he is in a position of superior knowledge
throughout the film. Germain, standing in for the viewer, is constantly
duped. Are we really to identify with such a weak character? (And Vorzet,
on the other hand, is shown as having quasi-supernatural powers.) When
Howard Koch adapts *Le Corbeau* as *The Thirteenth Letter*, this is one of
the principal things he "fixes." The Germain equivalent (played by
Michael Rennie) is notably strengthened, and the Vorzet figure (Charles
Boyer) is (less obviously) weakened and marginalized. In perhaps the
major plot change, Pearson/Germain actually discovers the identity of the
letter writers before anyone else—while in *Le Corbeau*, Germain comes to
the wrong conclusion and has to be set right by his lover, only to arrive at
the criminal's house too late to be anything but an observer.

But this change mainly serves to indicate the great originality of *Le
Corbeau*, where the conflict of moral and cinematic points of view is not
so easily resolved. Contemporary critics on the political left clearly felt
that the film takes Vorzet's side, showing a France easily corrupted by the
evil which has arrived. More recent Anglo-American critics, also of the
left, such as Evelyn Ehrlich in her wonderful book *Cinema of Paradox*,
have defended the film against Clouzot's critics, seeing it as at least anti-
Vichy and probably anti-Nazi as well (177–87). Until recently, this had
become the standard academic interpretation, but now there is a counter
reaction to this. Noël Burch and Geneviève Sellier, for example, argue in
La Drôle de guerre des sexes du cinéma français for a right-wing reading of

the work (191–96).[4] Perhaps someone, in all of these debates, is "right." But it seems more likely that the film itself is constructed as a paradox, a logical conundrum, a riddle with no good solution.

Along with what I have called the conflict of points of view, many other things vanish when Howard Koch and Otto Preminger adapt Clouzot and Chavance's classic work. What one might call the original work's pretensions to universality are severely limited. The first symptom of this is to be seen in the opening title cards. *Le Corbeau* begins with a simple (later, much explicated) phrase: "A little village . . . here or elsewhere" (*un petit village . . . ici ou ailleurs*). *The Thirteenth Letter's* equivalent statement of location reads: "This picture was photographed in its entirety in a small French-Canadian community in the province of Quebec." In other words: "A little village . . . not here, but elsewhere." Significantly, the abortion issue vanishes utterly as well—presumably this would have been considered tasteless by American audiences in the 1950s, and by Koch, Preminger, and Fox studio head Darryl Zanuck. Another way of summarizing many of the changes brought by the American team would be to say that for a philosophical drama of basically social issues, has been substituted a drama of almost purely *individual* choices. All of this is hardly surprising, since what gave the conflict its electric impact in 1943, and continues to do so today to some extent, is something *The Thirteenth Letter* could never have had—the awful context of the German Occupation. What remains? In the finished film, not much except for the mystery plot and one moral issue from the original: can (should) a good man love a bad woman? In terms of body imagery in both films, this question might be better, if playfully, stated as: "can a *tight* man love a *loose* woman?" because both Germain and Pearson have the overcontrolled, repressed movements so characteristic of the classic French cinema's portrayal of the bourgeoisie.

Koch makes this the main question of the film by changing the "backstory" of Germain/Pearson. In Chavance's script, Germain has quit his practice as a celebrated, Parisian brain surgeon because an obstetrician misguidedly (or so Germain thinks at the film's beginning) put his wife's life in fatal jeopardy in order to deliver their baby. Then he flees to a small town, becomes an obstetrician, and always makes the other choice—in "doubtful" cases, to save the mother. Preminger and Koch's Dr. Pearson, on the other hand, has fled London because of his wife's suicide, for which he was partly responsible: she had been unfaithful to him, he could not forgive her and take her back, and so she killed herself. As in so many

Hollywood films, the hero gets a second chance to do things right. (In the classical period, this topos is much more typically American than French. Think, to take one example among hundreds, of the various second chances in Hawks and Furthman's 1939 work *Only Angels Have Wings*. In most classic French films, as various commentators have noted, there *are* no second chances at tough decisions.)[5] At first, Pearson assumes that Denise cannot love him, because she has had sexual relations with other men before him. Finally, he rejects this attitude, and accepts her love.

Perhaps this plot turn is one of the reasons why *The Thirteenth Letter* was set by Koch and Preminger in French Canada. For in a Hollywood film's utopian vision of an ideal America, one would expect Denise to be a "good bad girl," in Wolfenstein and Leites's formulation—a woman who seems "bad" but is later revealed to be "good," and thus worthy of the hero's love (as a "bad girl" would presumably not be) (*Movies* 25–47).[6] But in *Le Corbeau*, Denise is sexually "bad" (experienced), and Koch and Preminger do not change this state of affairs much (though they do play it down). In both films, the hero gains in wisdom and peace of mind by loosing his bourgeois prejudices against loose women, but in *Le Corbeau* this is a comparatively minor (almost comic) theme, while it becomes a major concern of *The Thirteenth Letter*. This is, arguably, not terribly promising moral/intellectual material for an ambitious fiction film, particularly compared to Clouzot and Chavance's original work. But Howard Koch had something else in mind to fill the relative intellectual vacuum of *The Thirteenth Letter*. He wanted (as Norman Corwin would also try to do in *The Blue Veil*) to explore the "human drama" of his story, by fleshing out the characters, making them not *types*—as they so clearly are in *Le Corbeau*—but "round" characters, "real people." He wanted to draw, as writers so often do, on an experience from his own life: he had once known a man who came to share his wife's extreme paranoid delusions, in a case of *folie à deux*. Koch and Preminger had to meet with Zanuck for approval of the project:

> What finally emerged was that [Zanuck] liked the script, except for the revelatory *folie à deux* scene, which he said should be cut. Since this was the scene that I felt most necessary and original, I objected.
>
> "But, Mr. Zanuck, this gives the basic motivation for the murder. Otherwise, the picture is just about any two psychopaths committing a crime."

158

FIGURE 6.1. "Bad" girl Denise (Ginette Leclerc) gets ready for Dr. Germain's (Pierre Fresnay) professional visit in Henri-Georges Clouzot's *Le Corbeau* (1943). Courtesy of the Museum of Modern Art, Film Stills Archive.

FIGURE 6.2. Denise (Linda Darnell) trys to seduce Dr. Pearson (Michael Rennie) in Otto Preminger's *The Thirteenth Letter* (1951). Courtesy of the Museum of Modern Art, Film Stills Archive.

"Well, that's what they are, aren't they?"

"Yes, but with a very special psychological problem connected with a man's love for his paranoiac wife. That's what makes it a *folie à deux*."

"The audience doesn't give a damn about *folie à deux*. They've come to see two crazy people committing murder."

"I don't agree. Without that particular relationship, the picture makes no sense. It's an obligatory scene."

Zanuck . . . gave me a hard look. "In this studio I decide what's obligatory." (Koch 176)

So Zanuck won the argument, and *The Thirteenth Letter* did not explain *folie à deux*. As far as American audiences were concerned, the studio head was probably right, but his decision left the film somewhat impoverished. When you cut the thesis out of a thesis film, what do you have left? In the case of the *The Thirteenth Letter*, the answer seems to be—despite handsome cinematography and reasonably good performances—rather little.

This first example demonstrates what during the classical period is a typical conflict between the flat-character, thesis-film orientation of so much of "classic" French cinema and the "human drama" approach favored by Hollywood, including writers who were essentially slumming there like Norman Corwin and members of the innermost writerly establishment like Howard Koch. It was Samuel Goldwyn who is reported to have said, "If you want to send a message, use Western Union." This is something that French filmmakers of the classical era would not have agreed with. A surprising number of the great works of French cinema are, to some degree, thesis films—though typically, exactly what the thesis is, is not completely clear. Renoir and Spaak's *La Grande Illusion* (1937) provides one example of this (productive) ambiguity, *Le Corbeau* another.

Scriptwriter Norman Corwin and Director Curtis Bernhardt arguably had better luck with *The Blue Veil* than Koch and Preminger had with their remake of *Le Corbeau*. In part this is clearly due to the fact that *Le Voile bleu* is certainly not a masterpiece but simply a very effective *mélo féminin*, or "woman's picture." *The Blue Veil*, in other words, has much less to live up to. Like *The Thirteenth Letter*, *The Blue Veil* is comparatively faithful to the narrative structure and even on occasion to the dialogue of the original work. (In this, international remakes are strikingly different from ordinary remakes—such as, in France, the various versions of *Le Bossu*. When a new version is made of an older film within the same film culture, obvious differences are typically introduced, often simply to justify the project.)

Le Voile bleu tells the story of Louise Jarraud. Other characters have a place only in relation to her; the film almost never leaves her. The time of the story is from mid-World War I to the time of the film's making, in mid-Occupation; Louise goes (somewhat improbably, in only thirty years or so) from young to very old (almost doddering) woman, as she acts as nursemaid for a series of children, none of them her own. The film is structured as a series of relatively discrete stories, of the various families Louise works for, and her relations with them. Generically it is, therefore, not merely a *mélo féminin* but a *film à sketches*, or "sketch film"—inspired by the great success of the similarly structured great success of 1938, Duvivier's *Un Carnet de bal*.[7]

The various children are all substitutes for Louise's own child, who dies in the first sequence (her husband has been killed in the Great War). She first cares for Frédéric, baby son of a middle-aged petit bourgeois widower, in a Parisian apartment house. She leaves when Monsieur Perrette proposes marriage, she refuses, and he marries a rather nasty middle-aged woman who lives in the same building. (This is notably a misogynist portrait; the character is played by Jeanne Fusier-Gyr, who plays the same sort of old harpy in *Le Corbeau*.) Then Louise takes care of Gérard, son of a well-to-do family, at their country estate. Here, she receives a second proposal, from the child's uncle. Louise accepts but does not go to the train that will take them to Algeria to be wed, because Gérard desperately begs her not to leave him.

In a toy store that is a recurrent location through most of the film, she gets a third, oblique proposal, from the ironically named Monsieur Lancelot, the clumsy proprietor. Louise does not pursue the matter. Instead, she takes charge of Charlotte, preadolescent daughter of a famous choreographer. She leaves that job when the girl starts calling her "mother" (at her first communion [!]—the choreographer is absent for professional reasons). Her next child is the sickly Daniel, who for health reasons cannot go with his parents to Indochina (the film's second reference to the French colonies). Louise offers to take care of the boy while they are gone, so he will not be placed in an institution. Daniel's parents do not send money for his care, and Louise moves with him to the country and struggles to make ends meet. After many years, the parents return, suddenly, and Louise flees with Daniel, whom she now considers her "real" son; the police find them and return the boy to his biological parents.

By this time Louise is in her sixties, and no longer considered vigorous enough to care for a small child. She takes a job as a scullery maid in a household with two children; she befriends the older one and helps him make peace with his lot in life. An accident takes her to a hospital where the doctor is—miracle of storytelling magic!—Gérard, the second child we saw her care for. He organizes a reunion of "Loulou" and her former "children," now grown up and successful. In one of the most emotionally excessive scenes in an excessive genre, this gathering takes place on Christmas eve, and Louise receives a final present: beside a beautifully trimmed tree are Gérard's two lovely children, who are now Louise's to care for. The group of former "children" present her with her blue veil, emblem of nanny-hood.[8]

Received (left-wing, academic) wisdom about *Le Voile bleu* is that it is "Pétainiste" through and through. Certainly it has things in it that the Maréchal and his associates would have approved of, most notably a critique of "family values" under the Third Republic. It is never stated overtly, but one quite logical reading of the text is that France suffered the *débâcle* of World War II (utter defeat in roughly six weeks, with massive desertions) because of bad family values—or rather, an almost complete *lack* of family values. But what *were* these "values"? Probably the best source for making sense of the cultural assumptions underlying the classic French *mélo féminin* is Rhoda Métraux and Margaret Mead's *Themes in French Culture*, all the more so in the case of *Le Voile bleu* since the work was based on interviews, psychological tests, and cultural objects (prominently including films) from the late 1930s to the early 1950s.[9] (Much of its analysis, therefore, is less relevant to the more Americanized France of today.) In her introductory monograph, Métraux concentrates, as good anthropologists of her day were wont to do, on the issue of kinship. Since France is not an exotic, "other" society, *structure* of kinship is not at issue; what was most salient was French *attitudes* toward kinship issues. For her, as for the other Mead disciples who studied European culture at this time, the central, typically unspoken cultural theme of French life was the *foyer*.

One translation of this term could be "nuclear family," since the minimum requirement for an intact *foyer* is a mother, a father, and one or more biological children. (Adopted or stepchildren could never be completely integrated into the *foyer*. For many years, only infertile couples had the legal right to adopt a child in France, a fact much discussed in *Themes in French Culture*.) But "family" misses the point, for the English word doesn't capture the "autonomous" nature of the *foyer*, which designates a biologically related group "who live together in a fixed place and form a closed circle" (Métraux 2). Now the *foyers* in *Le Voile bleu* get more and more disturbed as the film goes on. Louise's first job is to replace, temporarily, a mother who has died, and at the end of that story the *foyer* is reconstituted, as well as it can be, by the father's remarriage. The next *foyer* is biologically intact but emotionally dysfunctional: the parents leave the children at home and pursue a life of easy pleasure outside the home, neglecting their "heavy charge" to "*faire quelque chose de bien* for each child" (Métraux 5–6). The next *foyer* is worse: no father, and a mother who works! Finally, the worst of all: parents who abandon their child entirely because he is too weak, and too costly, for their ambitions (to prosper in Indochina—in *Le Voile bleu* family values are clearly more important than colonial expansion). This is the case where Louise loses control and raises the child as her own, until a *juge d'instruction* regretfully ("*c'est la loi, Madame*") returns him to his biological parents.

Louise, in this context, represents the supermother ideal needed to restore the country's moral health. Her excess of maternal nature helps her supplement and heal the damaged *foyers*. Part of the force of this reading comes from the "sketch film" structure: the same thing happens over, and over again—Louise comes into a dysfunctional family and supplies the missing maternal warmth it needs to produce good family members and therefore good citizens. We *only* see families corrupted by bad values (women's attempts to leave the home, parents' sacrificing their children to their love of money or social standing or adventure), and the corruption gets worse and worse as the film progresses (and time passes). Louise's "children," at the end, are the proof of her good influence, for they have turned out well (e.g., one is a doctor). But here is the contradiction: What do they do? They give her a blue veil and symbolically ask her to care for the *next* generation (they have not learned that they should do it themselves).

This brief discussion may seem to lean too heavily on a fragile vehicle, but not in a French cinematic context. *Le Voile bleu* clearly demonstrates the French cinema's love of the thesis film, and equally clearly shows how a successful film need not have a clear thesis. Clarity, in fact, is probably inimical to commercial success with this sort of work. *Le Voile bleu* and thesis films like it are not simple propaganda; they are like ideological Rorschach texts for film audiences—who can make of them almost what they will. (As, to take one of the most notable examples, the fascist critics Bardèche and Brasillach found in *La Grande Illusion* a film that promotes the love of war.) When Norman Corwin came to adapt *Le Voile bleu*, one of his major accomplishments was to conceal the work's sketch-film structure, a transformation which inevitably lessens the sense that what is offered is a depiction of the parenting practices of an entire society. This is entirely in keeping with the American cinema's emphasis on the individual and his or her problems. In the late 1940s and 1950s, this interest sometimes manifested itself in a specific subject matter: psychotherapy (typically, but not always, psychoanalysis). But even when no psychiatrists appear in the story, an emphasis on the *therapeutic* is often near the surface, as it is in *The Blue Veil*: in Corwin's script (and not in François Campaux's), Louise does not want to take care of children but is urged to do so because "it might be good for you, in view of your loss." Whether the job really *is* good for Louise is a question the film poses but does not answer; instead, another question comes to displace it: by what *methods* should one care for children? Louise is the major representative of one-half of a dichotomy: some characters, like her, believe that one should respect the child and let it dictate, to some extent, how one treats it. One could call this the Benjamin Spock approach. (Remember that there was, from its first appearance in 1946, heated debate about Spock's *Common Sense Book of Baby and Child Care*.) Other characters, such as a very bossy candidate to replace Louise as nursemaid to young Fred (child #1), have the more traditional, pre-Spock approach:

> I have definite rules about bringing up children; and from long experience, I don't believe in letting a child have its own way. I don't believe in picking them up every time they cry. That's the quickest way to spoil a child.

After we hear this little speech, early in the film, Louise is periodically seen picking up, or otherwise comforting, children when they cry. The man she almost marries, during story #2, is not the impoverished, younger-son adventurer figure that Campaux imagined but a teacher who shares Louise's "modern" ideas about how to treat children.

This crucial episode—when Louise rejects the chance to marry and have a family of her own, with a man who loves her and whom she loves—is the occasion for one of the most significant changes that Corwin brings to the original script. There, Louise does not go to meet the man she loves because she feels too obligated/attached to little Gérard. In *The Blue Veil*, she feels bad about leaving little Robbie, but does not give up her dreams for him. Instead, Jerry, the sympathetic tutor to Robbie's older brother, has a last-minute talk with the boys' mother, Mrs. Palfrey, just before the new couple is to leave for Beirut, where Jerry will teach. Mrs. Palfrey advises caution, saying, "I've seen a lot of mistakes made in moments of youthful rashness." She manages to make Jerry doubt his own impulses. In a beautifully written scene on the train (which she does not miss, in Corwin's version), he expresses his newfound misgivings and she replies, "I *like* being rushed." He says, "I just want you to be *sure*," and she answers "I *am* a little hesitant, now." And so it goes: Mrs. Palfrey's subtle poison does its work, and Louise does not board the boat for Beirut but stays in her role as surrogate mother.

Now, although Mrs. Palfrey does, effectively, close off the only pathway Louise will find that leads to marriage and a family of her own, this doesn't mean that she is an evil person. *The Blue Veil* differs markedly from *Le Voile bleu* in that the former does have a fair number of genuinely wicked, or at least dislikable characters, whereas Corwin's script has only one—the rejected nanny candidate who doesn't believe in spoiling children (and she is a figure of grim fun). No, Mrs. Palfrey isn't wicked, she's just a *grown-up*. She doubts "youthful" impulses; her talking Jerry out of acting on his feelings is the unconscious equivalent of not picking up a baby when it cries, in the film's scheme of things. The ruling binary opposition of *The Blue Veil*, finally, is between children and childlike adults on the one hand, and the grown-ups on the other. This allows Corwin to create the equivalent, in a way, of *Le Voile bleu*'s paradox: in the original work, only by *not* being a mother can Louise serve as the ideal of national motherhood (in a nation full of bad mothers). In the American version, the tragedy of Louise's life (for the film does aspire to a tragic dimension, however modest and implicit) is that the only way she can finally stay on the side of the children in a world of grown-ups is to renounce becoming a "real" mother herself. However, in *The Blue Veil* this paradox is worked out in entirely individual terms; the film refuses to become an argument for children's liberation, or to suggest a comparison between the oppression of children and the repressive structure of society as a whole (as happens in Vigo's *Zéro de conduite*, for example).

That Corwin was aware of this "danger" (if you want to send a message, use Western Union) is suggested by his transformation of the character of the toy shop owner. In Campaux's original script, this figure is a classic (for French cinema), gentle father figure.[10] Corwin makes him younger (old man–young woman romances being considerably rarer in Classic Hollywood cinema than in the French—where they are, effectively, the norm, in some periods) and turns him into a stereotypical Upper West Side Marxist, spouting workers' rights in Central Park (with a variation on the stereotype: the character is Irish). He is, at first, as much a figure of fun as the nasty nursemaid, before his love for Louise becomes the more important thing about him in the film. No, Louise's dilemma is "beyond" politics, "bigger" than class relations. From a classical Marxist perspective, this is the most important bit of false consciousness vehicled by the work. In the end, in *The Blue Veil* as in *Le Voile bleu*, Louise's consciousness completely takes over the film, and the overwhelming, entirely emotional fact is that she again has children to mother, regardless of what it all means. Get out your handkerchiefs, the films all but say in their closing minutes, now is the time to cry. Forget France, forget Dr. Spock, forget any misgivings you might have about the forces that gave Louise only these particular choices in life. Forget all this, and cry. And feel good, or feel bad, afterward; at least you have cried—though for what (beyond this one, fictional character), well, that is for you to figure out.

NOTES

[Jennifer Forrest's interview with Norman Corwin in Appendix A, and Corwin's letter to Jerry Wald, *The Blue Veil*'s coproducer, in Appendix B, show the types of stylistic and narrative decisions at issue in the remake of the Classic Hollywood period—*eds.*].

1. On this project, see Bacher 322–27. The project's independent producer, Walter Wanger, was also responsible for the best-known Franco-American remake of the prewar period, *Algiers* (from Duvivier and Spaak's *Pépé le Moko*).

2. *Le Voile bleu* was thought for many years to have been *the* top grossing film of the period; presumably *The Blue Veil*'s creators thought so, too. Today we know that the film's success was exaggerated by critics and historians such as Jacques Siclier. In fact, the top grossing film of the Occupation was, according to Colin Crisp's recent research, Delannoy and Cocteau's *L'Eternel Retour*; *Le*

Voile bleu was enormously successful in the provinces, but less so in the crucial Paris region. See Crisp, "What Did Occupation Audiences Want to Watch?" paper delivered for "French Films of the German Occupation," Rutgers University, 2 November 1996.

3. The only significance of the new title that I can find is that the thirteenth letter of the *alphabet* is "M," an allusion to Fritz Lang's famous proto–*film noir*.

4. Let us note, however, that Burch and Sellier argue that while *Le Corbeau* shares the "right anarchist" ideology of Clouzot's collaborationist associates, the film nonetheless condemns patriarchy and promotes a progressive, if idealized, view of women—attitudes it shares with the cinema of the Occupation in general.

5. The French cultural theme that contrasts with the Hollywood *topos* of the second chance is Disappointment, or Missed Opportunity. See Wolfenstein and Leites, "Plot" 103–06.

6. Wolfenstein and Leites note that "French films tend to concentrate on the bad girl. Where a conflict between a good girl and a bad girl arises, the man tends to prefer the bad one. However, a variety of devices are used to etherealize or ennoble her" (*Movies* 41).

7. In *Un Carnet de bal*, an older woman revisits the men whose names she finds on the dance program of her first ball. One has become a drunken abortionist, one a mobster, one a monk, and so on. She ends by adopting the child of the man, now dead, whom she really loved. Like *Le Voile bleu*, therefore, the film has a narrative progression of sorts. Perhaps one ought to call such works quasi-sketch films (to distinguish them from the films with entirely different, unlinked episodes), though French critics and historians make no such distinction.

8. This is the tearful, awful, affecting conclusion to a remarkably effective "weepie." It is impossible to speak honestly of it, as spectatorial experience, in anything but personal terms. When I, for one, see this sequence, I both cry unrestrainedly and hate the film for making me do so. Perhaps this double reaction is due to the fact that I disagree violently with what I take to be the film's ideological stance—women should be loving mothers, and not choreographers, etc.—but I cannot help myself from submitting to its highly manipulative assault on my emotions. I presume the film would have less impact on a spectator who has never been the primary caretaker of a child, though I wonder how *much* less.

9. Métraux's essay is invaluable for almost any study of classic French cinema.

10. Sexually active (or potentially so) father figures abound in classic French cinema, in the analysis of Noël Burch and Geneviève Sellier. See the classification system in ch. 1 (23–56) of this seminal work.

WORKS CITED

Bacher, Lutz. *Max Ophuls in the Hollywood Studios.* New Brunswick: Rutgers UP, 1966.

Burch, Noël, and Geneviève Sellier. *La Drôle de guerre des sexes du cinéma français.* Paris: Nathan Université, 1996.

Ehrlich, Evelyn. *Cinema of Paradox.* New York: Columbia UP, 1985.

Koch, Howard. *As Time Goes By: Memoirs of a Writer.* New York: Harcourt, Brace, Jovanovich, 1979.

Métraux, Rhoda. "Themes in French Culture." Métraux and Mead 1–68.

Métraux, Rhoda, and Margaret Mead. *Themes in French Culture: A Preface to a Study of French Community.* Palo Alto: Stanford UP, 1954.

Wolfenstein, Martha, and Nathan Leites. *Movies: A Psychological Study.* New York: Atheneum, 1970.

———. "Plot and Character in Selected French Films: An Analysis of Fantasy." *Themes in French Culture: A Preface to a Study of French Community.* Palo Alto: Stanford UP, 1954. 89–108.

CHAPTER SEVEN

Sadie Thompson Redux: Postwar Reintegration of the Wartime Wayward Woman

JENNIFER FORREST

The Unfaithful (Sherman, 1947), *Miss Sadie Thompson* (Bernhardt, 1953), *Mogambo* (Ford, 1953), and *Gaby* (Bernhardt, 1956) are films that seem related only by the sexual transgressions of their heroines. *The Unfaithful* is a *noir* melodrama with Ann Sheridan in the role of Chris Hunter, a housewife who has murdered a man in her own home, a man who turns out to have been her lover during her husband's wartime absence. *Miss Sadie Thompson* stars Rita Hayworth as a woman with a questionable past whose arrival on a South Pacific island incites a missionary to reform her, and at the end to rape her. *Mogambo* tells the tale of Victor Marswell/Clark Gable, a white hunter in Africa, and his affairs with two very different women: the wise-cracking, sexually casual companion to wealthy men (Eloise Y. Kelly/Ava Gardner) and the aristocratic, well-mannered wife of a British anthropologist (Linda Nordley/Grace Kelly). Kelly wins Marswell when the latter does the "noble" thing and leaves the decent married couple intact. *Gaby* stars Leslie Caron as a ballerina who, when she learns of her fiancé's reported death at the front, overreacts to her refusal to sleep with him on the eve of their one-day whirlwind romance by sleeping with other soldiers on the eve of their transfer to the front. When her fiancé miraculously returns, Gaby is no longer pure of body and feels that she cannot legitimately marry him.

However different their stories, all four films are also remakes. *The Unfaithful* is a remake of *The Letter* (Wyler, 1940), itself a remake of Jean de Limur's 1929 film of the same name. *Miss Sadie Thompson* is the second remake of *Sadie Thompson* (Walsh, 1928), the first being Lewis Milestone's *Rain* (1932).[1] *Mogambo* is directly related to the 1932 Victor Fleming film *Red Dust* in which Gable played the male lead opposite Jean Harlow, and for which John Lee Mahin reworked his original screenplay. The latter film, however, did spawn a 1940 contribution to the *Maisie* cycle with *Congo Maisie* (H. C. Potter), and *Torrid Zone* (Keighley, 1940); while these films neither recognized nor credited their filiations with *Red Dust*, each clearly reproduces its narrative structure.[2] Finally, *Gaby* is a remake of *Waterloo Bridge* (LeRoy, 1940), with the latter being a remake of James Whale's 1931 film of the same name. Not only, therefore, are these four films all remakes, they are second remakes as well.

Hollywood has always regularly recycled material in order to cut down on general production costs. It has also striven to cater to—and keep satisfied—its audiences with a steady menu of the same-but-different. In the 1950s, Hollywood refashioned successful and less successful films from the 1930s in what was either an attempt both to woo people away from their television sets and to recreate the "homogeneous" audience of the prewar, or a way to buy some time until filmmakers figured out what the postwar, "fragmented" audience[3] wanted (Ray 138).[4] And yet, one cannot adduce *The Unfaithful, Miss Sadie Thompson, Mogambo*, and *Gaby* as merely the result of sound industry economics or just recourse to previously tried and true production packages designed to stave off impending financial disaster. Since there was hardly a rotating shelf of films lined up in order to be reworked and updated, one must wonder why studios chose to remake some pictures not only once but twice, sometimes more.[5] One must also consider: (1) why the degree of remaking in which the studios engaged from the 1930s through the 1950s has never been duplicated since,[6] (2) if there is a relation between remaking and the production of the seamless Classic Hollywood picture, and (3) why many 1950s filmmakers fell back upon already "twice-told tales." The answer may reveal that the originals and remakes of the old Hollywood studio period differed very little in their social and cultural functions and, in light of the worldview disseminated by the studios, that they were anything but financially and aesthetically competitive with each other.

According to Robert Ray, Classic Hollywood filmmakers—major five and minor three studios—strove to dominate both the domestic and international markets through standardizing filmmaking such that "different ways of making movies would appear as aberrations from some 'intrinsic essence of cinema' rather than simply as alternatives to a particular form that had resulted from a unique coincidence of historical accidents—aesthetic, economic, technological, political, cultural, and even geographic" (26). Economic factors contributed a great deal to the aforementioned "naturalness" attained by Hollywood's productions: (1) standardization of the conditions of production and exhibition (standardization was essential to the industry's sustenance and growth), (2) consideration of a film's potential performance nationwide across America and in those countries that censored material, (3) control of new technologies in the hands of a few (for example, "RCA's and Western Electric's sole control of sound technology"), and (4) the fact that the "major studios had come under the financial control of either the Morgan or the Rockefeller interests." These factors, including production quotas, explain why Hollywood "work[ed] endless variations around a few basic patterns" (Ray 30).

When discussing the remake of the Classic Hollywood period, it is natural to consider overwhelmingly the pressure of economic factors, but such films from the era equally invite an examination of their historical and moral functions. The second remakes in this study take place in a world war and/or post–world war context, making dramatic social disruption and its consequences the site for reaffirming a traditional worldview. More specifically, they directly or indirectly comment on the popular reaction to and campaign against perceived threats to accepted social-sexual roles and to the American family, both casualties of the war climate. Social instability is figured through the sexually transgressive woman and the films focus on her behavior during a period of crisis (here represented by World War II). Each film works to enact a return to normality through the reintegration of this woman into the traditional American family and her traditional social-sexual role, a reintegration made possible by the tolerance and forgiveness, first, of an understanding man and, second, of a sympathetic society. The Classic Hollywood remake occupies a central position in this strategy.

THE CLASSIC HOLLYWOOD FILM:
ORIGINALS, REMAKES, GENRE, AND STAR PERSONAS

Films from the classic era also command evaluation of their aesthetic value, and it is the "classic" of the term *Classic Hollywood film*—a term under which the films studied in this chapter are classified—that holds the key to an understanding of the moral underpinning of the Classic Hollywood remake, highlighting a particular artistic and literary notion of the copy that is denied the remake of the new Hollywood. The art historian Richard Shiff states that, "Classic art, and indeed anything that is classic, serves as a model. The classic image that is proper is a commonplace and a common property" (171). That which is deemed "proper" implies conventionality, and therefore enjoys the status of appearing "true," "more acceptable," or natural to its culture's members (164). Classic film, like classical painting, promotes a concept of originality, not based on difference, but on sameness. Repetition is part and parcel of the classical system's way of presenting its products as natural. What appears as natural, true, and proper in a representation is so by virtue of a re-production that encourages the embracing of a similar worldview on all members of a community (169). A comparison of the terminology used by Robert Ray to describe the hegemony of the Classic Hollywood system ("different ways of making movies would appear as aberrations from some 'intrinsic essence of cinema'") with Shiff's description of the classical manner in painting suggests that the word "classic" is an appropriate definition of this cinematic period's productions. The Classic Hollywood film, Ray contends, "subordinat[ed] . . . every cinematic element [such as individual style] to the interests of a movie's narrative" in an effort to create the apparent seamlessness of its structure (Ray 32). Its privileging of the audience's perspective, along with the pervasiveness of a standardized notion of cinematic narrative construction, constituted the conventions of the cinematic illusion of reality. Shiff notes that Classical painting promotes a particular form of representation as "real" and "true" such that any deviations from the norm during the hegemony of Classical painting were rejected. In a like manner, any straying from the conventional narrative structure of the Classic Hollywood film—Orson Welles's privileging of style over narrative, for example—valorized an individual experience at the expense of the collective and, until the rise of the art-cinema audience, was doomed to marginalization, if not failure.

From a modernist perspective, Classical homogeneity points to a school's aesthetic poverty. Modernists distinguish themselves from Classicists by arguing that the Classical tradition's shared worldview relies upon resemblance rather than on "originality or selfhood" (Shiff 168). For the Classicist, however, precedence is hardly a determining factor in an evaluation of a work's merits. On the contrary, Shiff contends, "Raphael and Masaccio can share the same originality" (168), without undermining their worth as artists. Whether one approaches Classic Hollywood films from a commercial or an aesthetic perspective, it is clear that a similar worldview informs them. Films formally resembled each other such that those directors who excelled by working well within the Classic Hollywood "formal paradigm" are usually those who have been historically denied any authority by critics, Michael Curtiz's work being a notable example. Films also resembled each other thematically not only because the studios sought to replicate the success of their own and their competitors' films, but because the worldview espoused by Hollywood—its way of "indexing both a collective, traditional manner of vision and the external reality that falls under its gaze"—encouraged the establishment of recognizable generic conventions in which each masterly contribution, while recalling its model, would equally distinguish itself as an example of the dominant paradigm. Finally, the effort to give priority to those films that serve as the "first member of a repetitive series" is misguided because those films which best exemplify the Classic Hollywood "formal" and "thematic paradigms"[7] do not compete with each other. As Shiff explains, "Ingres'[s] style looks like Raphael's style," and both participate in the Classical style, which is accepted as the natural way to view the world (168–69). Similarly, as regards classic cinema, George Cukor's style looks like Victor Fleming's style, which looks like Classic Hollywood style, which looks like reality as we accept it. It would therefore be erroneous to subject both original and remake from this period to the same "modernist" aesthetic criteria used in evaluating films that belong to the post-studio system.

The Classic Hollywood remake would have been destined, however unconsciously on the part of its creators, to perform a specific function beyond just repeating financially successful formulas. The appearance of certain remakes at crucial moments of social-historical change—the Depression, World War II, postwar reintegration, the Cold War, moments that at worst threaten the self-evidence of the dominant thematic paradigm—may point to that paradigm's continued authority to restate its and its audience's link to a similar cinematic *and* moral tradition. On the one hand, those remakes that rewrite their endings, like *The Unfaithful* and *Gaby* where neither heroine is punished (by murder or suicide, respectively, as in their immediate predecessors), appear to break with the rigid censure of prewar society in absolving their heroines of their crimes and, in doing so, emphasize that times have changed: they draw attention to the historical specificity of both their theme and their audience. But all the remakes in this study, new endings and old, also claim with a more resounding voice that nothing has changed in the basic moral foundation of the American society of the "classical" period, especially with respect to women's place in that society. More specifically, as Susan Hartmann notes, while negative postwar images of women in popular culture "indicated ambivalence about or opposition to changes in women's activities and life-styles," the success of these images in promoting the "feminine mystique" to both men and women points even more strongly to the "*endurance of old attitudes* about what women should be and fears of what they might become" (204; emphasis added).[8] The films under question articulate a different historical context (manners, dress, social issues, etc.) than their originals only to reaffirm their affiliation with the originals' greater moral, social, and cultural agenda (a woman's social destiny is marriage and housewifery, her biological destiny is mothering; a man's social destiny is marriage and the economic support of the family[9]).

Like remakes from silent to sound in the Hollywood of the 1930s, Hollywood in the 1950s utilized the new techniques available (color, cinemascope, 3–D, etc.)—modifications of which these second remakes all took full advantage in one way or another—modernized the original story and created something new. In addition, filmmakers often shifted genres from the original's dominant mode into those of the remake period. Howard Hawks remade *Ball of Fire* (1941), for example, as a musical, *A Song is Born* (1948). Indeed, an inordinate amount of postwar remakes became musicals. *Miss Sadie Thompson*, too, is semimusicalized, capitalizing on Rita Hayworth's singing and dancing talents so as to recall the musical genre. Switching genres, extensive updating, changes in locale and in characters' professions and class, and technological advances are said to reflect a break both with the past and with an often formidable precursor. What motivates a filmmaker to remake an older, often "classic" film is the artistic and financial competition that is said to arise between original and remake. In financial terms, an original that was in circulation at the moment of the release of a remake was usually withdrawn so that the two films would not be in direct competition. But that remakes reenact the primal scene of attempting to overthrow and usurp (the authority of) their originals relates more directly to the post-1960s cinema than to the period which precedes it. Until the 1950s with the fall of the Hollywood studio system, the rise of the art-house audience, and the advent of the French *politique des auteurs* (popularized by Andrew Sarris in the United States), the relationship between a remake and its original was anything but antagonistic. First, as regards the studio system, film companies as a general rule remade their own, not other companies' properties. In addition, like actors and actresses under contract, directors were assigned to projects and often only saw the working scripts shortly before shooting was scheduled to begin. The same directors were often not even included in the final editing process.[10] There is little room here for struggle with powerful precursors. Second, as regards the art-house cinema and auteurist criticism, Robert Ray states that, although "our sense of the postwar era's films has been decisively, and perhaps permanently, shaped by auteurist critics," they were not the cause but a sign of the disappearance of the "homogeneous audience [that] had responded uniformly to the industry's products" (140–41). In other words, the recognition the French critics accorded some directors as authors with distinctive cinematic signatures/individual styles heralded in an aesthetic system headed by redoubtable author(itie)s/directors and their original, sometimes—in the case of a retrospective revaluation of old Hollywood directors—"classic" texts. But, while some post-1960s directors struggled to rival and free themselves from the influence of these daunting precursors, such was not the case for the pre-1960s director. Finally, while the illusion of reality created by films may depend greatly upon the current abilities of cinematic technology and the concurrence of audiences to the adequacy of that illusion, updated—but still "classic" period—versions of Classic Hollywood films remain faithful to the same narrative approach, seamless construction, and ideology of their originals, offering a much more enduring sense of the real than the technical illusion of reality is ever capable of producing.

The four remakes in this study—*The Unfaithful, Miss Sadie Thompson, Mogambo,* and *Gaby*—belong to the transitional postwar period in which Hollywood and its audience were beginning to realize that the "Classic Hollywood film was no more than a provisional model, created by a special set of circumstances, and capable of being challenged or replaced by alternative forms" (Ray 131). On unsteady legs, Ray informs us, Hollywood "turned more and more to the presold picture, a movie based on an already successful novel, story, Broadway play, fairy tale, or biblical legend" (131). But Hollywood had always turned to the presold property, and it continued to operate, therefore, according to business as usual. To the presold property group we can add the remake, a practice of which the filmmakers from the 1930s to the 1950s seemed particularly fond. But rather than disavow their originals, many (if not most) of the 1950s remakes bank, if not on the memory, then the example of their precursors in order to both create and manipulate the conditions for the remakes' reception: they openly refer to and exploit the familiar narrative and melodramatic structures as well as the signifying and allegorical authority of the originals with the aim of assuring social and ideological continuity.[11] If audiences didn't remember *the* Sadie Thompson of *Rain* or of its earlier version, then they would certainly be familiar with *a* Sadie Thompson type like Vantine in *Red Dust*.[12]

The remakes in this study also invoke not only their own filmic forerunners, but a whole gamut of contemporary cinematic conventions, from easily recognizable generic markers (women's film melodrama, *film noir*, the musical) to the powerful symbolic aura produced by previous performances informing a star's persona, elements which work both to overdetermine with a vengeance the film's signifying register *and* to highlight its affiliation with the dominant classic mode. Regarding genre, Peter Biskind notes that the "studio infrastructure, with its army of salaried writers, actors, and directors and its constant stream of films-by-formula, made genre possible; when it disintegrated, genre disappeared." Another, and perhaps more telling, factor in the death of studio-era generic production was the "collapse of the shared assumptions on which genre depends and which makes its conventions seem natural" (Biskind 337). Genre and the Classic Hollywood remake apparently both express classical ideology by the very principle of repetition that defines them. The kind of repetition that marks the Classic Hollywood film, then, as contends Robert Ray, may have far deeper implications than simply Hollywood's good business sense:

> Clearly, American movies drew on a store of motifs that had become coded, detachable units, capable of migrating from film to film. Their recurring appearances in widely dissimilar genres indicated

the extent to which each Hollywood movie, far from being created from scratch, was mediated through an inherited mythology and structured around a received thematic paradigm. (224)

Repetition, or intertextuality, was the operating principle behind Classic Hollywood ideology, and it is, as noted earlier, in perfect accordance with the prescriptions of classical art and literature. It functions to reproduce a widely accepted worldview, to which the creation of internal censoring within the industry had its hand in giving focus. Hollywood perceived itself not only as an entertainment industry but as performing an important service toward the preservation of the values of the community (and the world) at large, values based on "styles, rules, modes, conventions, themes and sensibilities" that are deemed "proper" to that community (Cuddon 149).[13] In other words, this is a worldview that is classical by definition.

The role of a star's persona in classic intertextuality is equally as important as, and perhaps inseparable from, that of genre in its contribution to a film's expression of Classic Hollywood's "inherited mythology" in that a star's image is an "already signifying complex of meaning and affect" (Dyer, "Resistance" 92). In "The Idea of Genre in the American Cinema," Edward Buscombe claims that certain films are successful *not* from any "distinctive directorial contribution" (he offers Michael Curtiz's *Casablanca* as an example) but "derive their power from the traditions of a genre." While this comment appears a trifle dismissive of Curtiz, he is alluding to an important source of narrative development within a film. He cites as instrumental to *Casablanca*'s success the significant contribution made by the Humphrey Bogart persona in its ability to recall Bogart's previous (*noir*) roles. It would seem that genre creates persona—the Western certainly did so with John Wayne—and that inversely persona is evidence of genre (19–20).[14] Indeed, persona can become quite generic in its encounter with prior characterizations of a role. Jeanne Eagels, who played the first Sadie on the stage, established early on the trajectory of further castings of Sadie. In her refusal to play a common prostitute ("I don't want to be a prostitute. . . . The play doesn't really call me one. . . . I can't feel myself a prostitute. I don't want me to be cheap, sordid, vulgar" [qtd. in Lawrence 190n3]), Eagels took the sting of irredeemable sin out of Maugham's Sadie and made her into a modern woman. Gloria Swanson's earlier roles as former flappers who marry, philander, divorce, but who are generally good eggs who deserve to escape moral retribution cinematically validates while expanding upon Eagels's characterization of good/bad girl Sadie Thompson. Joan Crawford's 1920s flapper intersects with Swanson's flapper, expands upon her through Crawford's early 30s independent woman who valiantly surmounts whatever trials befall her, and constructs a Sadie Thompson who has been down on her luck, who did what she could to survive, even prostitution, but who is at heart a good girl. But Rita Hayworth as Sadie Thompson goes even further than the others by breaking the confining barriers of the women's melodrama and contributing her persona as a dangerously sensual *film noir* femme fatale (*Gilda* [Vidor, 1946], *The Lady from Shanghai* [Welles, 1948], and *Affair in Trinidad* [Sherman, 1952]),[15] along with her currency as wartime pin-up (thus attracting both the male spectators of these films and men who returned from the war). As Richard Dyer notes, "Hayworth was primarily a 'love goddess,' and as such very much a star for heterosexual men" ("Resistance" 96). The appeal to male viewers is clear in an advertisement for the *Miss Sadie Thompson* in the *New York Times*, which boasts, "See Rita in 3D! She's the only dame with a kiss of flame!" As a singing, dancing Sadie Thompson, Hayworth draws upon the heritage of her seductive singing roles in *Gilda* and *Affair in Trinidad*—yet another boost for male audience attendance—as well as upon her singing and dancing in a fair number of early 1940s movie musicals, attracting the patrons of this genre, which during the early 1950s was still at the height of its popularity. Dyer points out as well that "her role as partner (rather than menace) in musicals" along with her real-life marriages and the birth of her daughter had also made her a highly sympathetic "identification figure for heterosexual women" ("Resistance" 96). There is another facet of persona that must be considered, however, in the presence of Rita Hayworth in this particular remake. Her absence from the screen for several years after 1948 was long enough to significantly damage her box-office draw upon her return. Like *Affair in Trinidad*'s unmistakeable narrative and visual links to the earlier *Gilda*, *Miss Sadie Thompson* called upon the entire subgenre of good/bad girl melodramas to replace temporal rupture with the illusion of continuity. Rather than attempt to eclipse or drive into obscurity the earlier versions of the Sadie Thompson story, Bernhardt's remake actively sought to recall them to the audience's mind.

While the three actresses—Swanson, Crawford, and Hayworth—are very different performers with very different personas, they all draw upon a related concept of the independent, sometimes socially and sexually transgressive woman. In each version, if Sadie Thompson is bad, it is

FIGURE 7.1. Sadie Thompson (Gloria Swanson) surrounded by military men (including the film's director as Sergeant Tim O'Hara) at Trader Horn's upon her arrival on Pago-Pago in Raoul Walsh's *Sadie Thompson* (1928). Courtesy of the Museum of Modern Art, Film Stills Archive.

FIGURE 7.2. Sadie Thompson (Joan Crawford) exchanges some banter with Trader Horn (Guy Kibbee) upon her arrival on Pago-Pago in Lewis Milestone's *Rain* (1932). Courtesy of the Museum of Modern Art, Film Stills Archive.

FIGURE 7.3. Sadie Thompson (Rita Hayworth) with Sergeant Phil O'Hara (Aldo Ray) upon her arrival on a South Pacific island in Curtis Bernhardt's *Miss Sadie Thompson* (1953). Courtesy of the Museum of Modern Art, Film Stills Archive.

by circumstance but certainly not by nature: she is at heart a good girl who just needs the right man to understand and guide (i.e., marry) her. Similarly, *Gaby* manipulates Leslie Caron's dancing as well as her youthful exuberance and naiveté in such musicals as *An American in Paris* (Minnelli, 1951), *Lili* (Walters, 1953), *The Glass Slipper* (Walters, 1955), and *Daddy Long Legs* (Negulesco, 1955) to invoke the musical as a genre of "integration," in which all conflicts are resolved at film's end (Schatz 29). The authority of her musical past is to promise the happy ending that the original melodramas—the category into which *Gaby* falls—did not deliver. The Leslie Caron persona from these films—gamine making the transition to or being initiated into sexual adulthood—solicits our sympathy for her actions and encodes them as essentially innocent. Her persona is not sullied by her reckless behavior in *Gaby.* Instead it withstands bombardment just as Gaby does the falling bombs in London. And Ann Sheridan's roles as a level-headed girl-next-door type in 1930s social-crime dramas, as well as her musical performances, disposes the viewer to withhold unremitting condemnation of Chris's indiscretion in *The Unfaithful.* The Ann Sheridan persona makes Chris a sympathetic character even despite her repeated lying. Chris Hunter's earlier incarnation as Leslie Crosbie in *The Letter*, on the other hand, is defined by the Bette Davis persona, which often involves a manipulative woman who may or may not be transformed by a picture's end (e.g., *Jezebel* [Wyler, 1938], *Dangerous* [Green, 1935]): Leslie/Davis has to work on the audience if she is going to win them over, whereas Chris/Sheridan has the spectator on her side from the outset. All the remakes discussed here bring their stars' personas to bear—sometimes in contradictory ways—on the reception of their themes and their power to reiterate classic ideals.

The Unfaithful, Miss Sadie Thompson, Mogambo, and *Gaby* incorporate their originals, not to pay homage to their precursors so much as to insist upon the validity of the model presented. They call upon the semantic system operating in the prewar originals so as to encode and enact the resolution of their postwar stories, just as would a genre film, or any Classic Hollywood picture for that matter. These four remakes are all unmistakably postwar films, and it is unlikely that the historical contextualization of the war/postwar periods in their productions is the result of chance. World War II did not just provide for new cinematic variations on old themes. It represented the harrowing passage from one way of life nostalgically viewed as unified to another perceived as marked by social dislocation, and many films from the ten-year period following the war promoted the romantic myth of a prewar utopian family/society to which they portrayed the possibility of a postwar return. Included in this effort to reestablish ties with an earlier period, these remakes exploit the power of the figure of woman to bear the burden of social instability, relying upon their originals, or, to be more precise, upon the Classic Hollywood thematic and formal paradigms, to fuel the fantasy of a stable, neatly compartmentalized life (marriage, sexual division of labor with the wife at home or in "women's" jobs, the man outside the home)—even, if not especially, for those relationships with the shakiest of foundations—as the allegorical remedy for perceived social disintegration.[16]

Studies of Cold War science-fiction films and their 1980s post-Vietnam versions have shown that comparisons between remakes and originals make evident the historical conditions of their production. The same is true for *Unfaithful, Sadie, Mogambo,* and *Gaby.* As mentioned earlier, the Sadie Thompson of the 1928 film is a not-so-virginal post–World War I, flapper exercising her sexual and expressive freedoms. Like other flappers she is "honest of heart and deserved the hero's love" (Banner 175) and can be reinserted into the traditional role of wife. The Sadie Thompson of *Rain* (1932) is a Depression-era working girl whose saint-like transformation under the hands of Reverend Davidson offers her as a symbol of self-sacrifice; she admirably resigns herself to and thereby transcends the trials ahead of her (i.e., she is an allegory for the economic adversity befalling most Americans). The Sadie Thompson of the 1953 film is a post–World War II good/bad girl who is forgiven her errors, and through that forgiveness domesticated according to 1950s standards by her understanding husband-to-be Sergeant Phil O'Hara.[17]

In light of the very different and historically relevant readings that the same basic story can elicit, we can infer that the cycle of remaking during the Classic Hollywood period was not always—or not only—a routine business operation, but one that appealed to the ideological agenda established by an original (as in genre films as well) and its appropriateness for grounding a related treatment of present-day concerns, a process that goes beyond mere updating.[18] For example, if certain post–World War II science-fiction films like *The Fly* (Neumann, 1958), *Invasion of the Body Snatchers* (Siegel, 1956), and *The Thing from Another World* (Nyby, 1951), addressed ideological preoccupations ranging from the Cold War threat of nuclear annihilation to that of a sinister and pervasive Communist infiltration, their quasi-generic precedence designates them as ideally suited for providing the narrative format for films destined to "juxtapose and associate film images with concerns and anxieties felt by American audiences in regard to perceptions of repressive problems" (Katovich and Kinkade 619, 621), as well as appealing to a familiarity with the resolutions furnished by the conventions of the original. While the remake cannot help but emphasize its differences from the original—differences that surface in the historical distance that has informed the social, historical, and cultural orientation of its creators and audience—it also underscores the relation that links both films together, working to erase the difference between past and present, and reassuring the remake's audience with a sense of continuity.

As early as *Rain* (1932), a reviewer from *Photoplay* seemed to anticipate that Sadie Thompson's tale would be retold again, noting that the film tells an "adult story that never seems to grow out of date" (qtd. in Quirk 102), a comment that would have been more appropriate for the 1953 version since the original had been made only four years earlier, and also considering that in 1932 there were other Sadie Thompson types appearing in films. The status of the tale as timeless is perhaps here another word for a film's remakability, indeed for the remakability of all classic Hollywood films that address core American values. The very fact that a given classic film is remade is testimony not only to its original's remakability, but as well to the original's position too as a remake of sorts, and not only because it serves as an example of the Classic Hollywood formal and thematic paradigms, but of America's Judeo-Christian moral tradition. The allegorical archetype that may inform all four groups of films in this study, for example, is that of Scripture's tale of Mary Magdalene, the prostitute who is reformed by the tolerance and love of Christ.[19] Each group of originals and remakes relate to environments marked by social upheaval or national crisis and threats to traditional roles—post–World War I social revaluation in the wake of women's suffrage, the popular misperception of the 1920s flapper as economically emancipated (by suffrage) and as sexually unconstrained, the Depression, World War II along with its temporary sexual role reversals, postwar readaptation (men leaving military for civilian life, women being fired from "men's" jobs and being encouraged to return to the home), reintegration (men returning home, some in one piece, others not, physically and/or mentally), and general reconstruction—and regardless of their endings, the image that emerges is that of the power of unconditional love to wash away all traces of transgression and summon in social/spiritual regeneration.[20] These films encourage compromise and coming togetherness, values which are not only representative of the 1950s pluralist agenda, but of the American dream that informs the Classic Hollywood paradigm.

SAVING THE SOUL OF THE
WARTIME WAYWARD WOMEN

An examination of *The Unfaithful, Miss Sadie Thompson, Mogambo,* and *Gaby* reveals direct references to the historical context of World War II, to the disruptions it effected both during and afterwards on the basic fabric of American society, and to the way that women were to a large extent held "responsible for society's ills—either because they were failures as mothers or because they had left the home for work," or because they were or had been unfaithful or less than perfect wives (Banner 231). And according to Betty Friedan's research on the effects of the successful 1950s "feminine mystique" campaign to domesticate women, we can even include in this list those women who felt guilty for not finding fulfillment or happiness in housewifery and childrearing. Enlisted in the effort to reassert traditional social-sexual roles were "certain sociologists, psychologists, anthropologists, educators, authors, and physicians" (French xvii). "Social welfare and child-care experts," states Susan Hartmann, "called upon women to pay more attention to their maternal duties. Psychologists and psychiatrists emphasized women's biological destiny and diagnosed feminists as neurotics or worse. And in articles, stories, and advertising, women's magazines glorified the housewife and mother" (213). The authoritative influence of these experts worked to rewrite the destinies of transgressive women—those who denied or strayed from their innate "femininity" (Friedan 43)—by no longer condemning them to social ostracization or punishment, presenting their errors, not as terminal, but as eminently curable.

Of particular importance in the conceptualization of the experts' propaganda, the historian Lois Banner notes, was the postwar fascination with psychology. Sociologists, anthropologists, and psychologists were primarily influenced by Freudian psychoanalysis's emphasis on the formative sexual and identity struggles of childhood as determining factors in adult mental health or dysfunction, and their prescriptions for the future located women—not just the good ones, but all women—as wives and mothers as central to social equilibrium. At stake was not only the health of the 1940s generation of children, potential victims of divorce and absentee working mothers, but women themselves who, as laborers or professionals, would perhaps irrevocably harm their own psychosexual well-being, a condition which apparently only flourished in marriage and the bearing of children:

> The Freudians argued that women could attain emotional stability only through domesticity and motherhood. Women who worked denied their deepest needs and risked being unable to experience love or sexual satisfaction. This, in turn, threatened the family, and, according to the most apocalyptic thinkers, the whole of Western civilization. (Banner 233)

The remakes in this study articulate the concerns of the postwar generation and invoke the familiar echo of their original films, as well as the classic aesthetic and morality of which they are an example, in order to effect women's return to the "normal" family unit, which would, in turn, save "Western civilization." But whereas in the originals the moral imperatives informing social conduct were taken for granted, their remakes seek to affirm their "transcendent moral truths in a secular, naturalistic world" by directly or indirectly appealing to the authority of secular guides (Cawelti 47). The shift from a religious to a secular model does not diminish the authority of the Classic Hollywood film, for the ends remain the same: to preserve the status quo. For example, Howard Joyce/James Stephenson's speech to the jury in *The Letter* (1940) rings empty both to himself and to a theater audience horrified by Leslie Crosbie/Bette Davis's manipulation of human lives; the only way to restore social (and spiritual) order is for the lover's Asian widow to murder Leslie. When western law obstructs justice (Stephenson), a greater moral law intervenes to exact just retribution (the lover's wife). Its remake, *The Unfaithful*, however, has Larry/Lew Ayres's summation to the jury address the legacy of the war in its devastation of the American couple, most notably through divorce. He speaks the language of authority and compassion to a jury that will acquit Chris/Ann Sheridan of her crime because the fate of the American couple/social order ultimately rests on the outcome of her trial:

> [B]ear in mind that she acted under unusual and powerful circumstances. Have we forgotten the war so quickly? Have we forgotten

how many lives were dislocated, how many personal casualties took place far from the battlefield? Christine Hunter would not have been unfaithful if her husband had not been taken from her. If there had been no war she would not be in this court today. Therefore, I beg of you, ladies and gentlemen, in arriving at your decision, do not allow the defendant's unfaithfulness to becloud the issue. Her punishment for that sin must be decided by her husband and society.[21]

At the closing of the film, both her husband and society will forgive her sin.

Similar shifts take place in the Sadie Thompson films. Dr. McPhail is dishearteningly impotent beside Mr. Davidson's moral strength in the two earlier versions; he cannot intervene in the melodramatic machine's way of righting wrongs. But Dr. McPhail becomes remarkably prescient and combative in the 1953 version by virtue of his background not only in surgery but in psychoanalysis as well. Early in the film he diagnoses Davidson's obsession with stamping out evil as a projection of the latter's own desires:

> DR. McPHAIL: Fanatics are often too obsessed by what they're fighting against to know why they're really fighting it.
>
> HORN: Oh, you mean, like the guy who's against drinking but what he really wants is to hit the bottle?
>
> DR. McPHAIL: Yes, yes. All of us have hidden desires which we disguise in one way or another.

In this way, Dr. McPhail's diagnosis not only foreshadows Davidson's rape of Sadie but also classifies his behavior as a mental illness, thereby demonstrating the amazing power of science to predict, explain, and even to heal. McPhail's knowledge, talent, and tolerance, however, is intended in no way to challenge religion's moral authority. On the contrary, science exists here to support religion's fundamental premises. So, for example, to Mrs. Davidson's statement that her husband "despises women of that kind, " McPhail counters that "The founder of our religion was not so squeamish." Neither is the tolerant Dr. McPhail, through whom science promises to tangibly perpetuate American society's traditions and values.

The post–World War II remake both rewrites the scripts of both earlier versions to fit the context of its audience (i.e., times have changed) *and* renews ties with a past homogeneous society where social roles, modes of conduct, and solutions to problems were well-defined (i.e., nothing has changed). Where pre–World War II social transgression— women giving birth to children out of wedlock, being sexually active (or operating as prostitutes or being unfaithful to their husbands), or choosing careers over housewifery and childrearing[22]—was often redeemed through sacrifice (of illegitimate children, of romantic love, of career),[23] postwar erring is answered with tolerance and forgiveness. The postwar woman whom psychotherapists and other experts told to realize her sexual potential in marriage was no longer to be punished (except by domestication and culturization)—times *had* changed. The vigorous encouragement for her to view housewifery and childrearing as woman's natural role in life, however, resembled strikingly the model offered by the 1930s. Female reporters and executives in 1930s comedies and dramas are constantly being told how unqualified they are for their jobs even though they seem to be acquitting themselves quite well (e.g., *Front Page Woman* [Curtiz, 1935]), and heavy emphasis is placed on how unfeminine (and hence, unnatural) women are in a man's world (e.g., *Female* [Curtiz, 1933]). In this light, nothing had really changed.

John Cawelti notes that, "a favorite feminine stereotype in the novels and films of the thirties and forties" was the "'good-bad girl,' a heroine who appears at the beginning of the story to be wild and even immoral but who is eventually revealed to be a truly chaste and loving woman" (43). It is not surprising that the "good-bad girl" was the heroine of these social melodramas because they represented an attempt to "resolve increasing anxieties and ambiguities about the moral nature and proper social role of women by creating an active and even aggressive heroine who discovered her rightful place in a passionate and deep attachment to a morally revitalized and loving man" (Cawelti 44). Like all social melodramas, the themes of the melodramas from the 1940s and 1950s offer "romantic love as an ultimate value," defend "monogamous, family-oriented relationships between men and women," and "attempt to define true and false conceptions of success and status" (Cawelti 47). So, it is not just because Americans demand happy endings of their films that the four remakes cited rewrite or recontextualize the conclusions of two of their originals; they are also performing a social function. They reconstitute the couple through the reintegration of the wayward woman specifically into the framework of the traditional family and into society in general because they articulate the postwar effort to effect social reconstruction according to a powerful preexisting model. As Peter Biskind notes,

"Happy endings . . . are not only a recompense for the life well lived but also a pat on the back for the society that makes it possible to live life well" (3). Hollywood sought support for its myth of the propriety of its paradigm just as much as it disseminated it.

The postwar *Unfaithful, Miss Sadie Thompson, Mogambo,* and *Gaby* abandon 1930s censure and prewar propaganda, promote nostalgia for a rosy-colored recent past, and stress that nothing has really changed; people—even wayward women—still want the same things as before, but unfortunate events have intervened to wound these women's characters. This is nothing, however, that a little psychoanalysis or understanding can't cure. We are given an earlier glimpse of the form that this understanding and forgiveness can take in *Since You Went Away* (Cromwell, 1944), where Danny Williams/Craig Stevens, the young soldier whose pain from physical burns is eclipsed by that of his emotional wounds, is cured so effectively by Dr. Sigmund [Freud?] Golden, that he returns to the front to resume duties rather than take the discharge available to him. In *Mogambo*, there are two scenes in which Kelly/Gardner and a sympathetic Brownie/Philip Stainton share their respective emotional and physical "scars"; while Kelly's scars may have set her on the wrong track, the solidity of her instinctual/biological and moral fiber remains unimpaired. For example, her fascination with kangaroo pouches and her interactions with all the baby animals at Marswell's African post identify her by nature as a mother, and her devout confessional with a priest reveals that she will uphold, not destroy, America's basic values. All she needs, the film implies, is to be purified by love and shunted onto the right track by the right man; from there she can proceed to fulfill her role as wife, and as the mother and caretaker of a future generation. In *Miss Sadie Thompson*, Davidson is blind to the natural mothering qualities to be found in Sadie, who sings sweetly "Hear No Evil" to Trader Horn's children. His inability to see anything but sin in Sadie and in the island natives, and his refusal to bend, invalidates him as a reliable authority and puts in question his methods and the type of social stability he promotes. Modern psychology and its compassion for human suffering and error is there to take up the baton.

HOMEFRONT HEROINES AND WAYWARD WOMEN

For postwar audiences, Davidson's neat division of the world into right and wrong, good and evil, would have been most reminiscent of wartime doctrine. During World War II, Hollywood cooperated with government directives and produced films designed to promote support for the war effort. Images of ideal soldiers overseas and ideal wartime conduct on the homefront figured in the propaganda of these films. Many films outlined the tasks required of the responsible American married woman/fiancée. Husbands in the service needed their wives to provide moral support in upholding the values for which they were fighting away from their families, support which amounted more or less to maintaining the home and the family structure, its reputation, and raising the family's children.[24] The government needed women to physically support the war effort with their labor in government and military offices, factories, hospitals, and canteens, in the sale of war bonds, in the rolling of bandages for the Red Cross, and in the significant sacrifices incurred by shortages of all kinds—food, housing, clothing—and through the raising of the children of the next generation. If, on the one hand, their wartime efforts bestowed on women a heretofore unparalleled economic equality with men and social respectability, they were nevertheless reminded through all public channels, not that their efforts represented an advance in their social status, but that they were designed to "bring their men home more quickly and to help make the world a more secure place for their children" (Hartmann 23).

Anne Hilton/Claudette Colbert fits the description of the ideal wife and mother in *Since You Went Away*; she lets out a room to two military men (retired Colonel Smollet/Monty Woolley and Lieutenant Tony Willet/Joseph Cotten) to help with the housing shortage; she resists with absolutely no wavering the attentions of family friend Tony/Cotten, remaining steadfast in her faithfulness to her husband, Tim, even long after he has been reported missing in action; she works as a welder in a factory after she realizes halfway through the film/war that she has not done enough for the defense effort—her daughter Jane/Jennifer Jones, however, has been dutifully working as a nurse's aid for the Red Cross, while the youngest, Brig/Shirley Temple, has been energetically rolling bandages, selling war stamps, and collecting salvage—and with the knowledge that her employment is only for the duration of the war; without much complaint she becomes frugal with or does without the things that prior to the war she took for granted—new clothes, cake, sleeping in her own room; and she is a perfect mother, providing sober and wise guidance and emotional support for her two teenage girls.

Emily Hawkins/Agnes Moorehead's divorcée, on the other hand, serves as a striking contrast to Anne/Colbert, behaving in ways that a "good" wartime woman should not. First, she is divorced, the implication being that her divorce is the result of her selfishness and her inability or unwillingness to curb her appetites. As regards her sexual desires, she is noticeably on the hunt for men—indeed, the only reason she attends or sponsors canteens is for her own pleasure—tinting her overt sexuality with the same lack of control that dominates her other actions. Second, she refuses to do without that which had become luxuries during the war: she continues to dress extravagantly and hoards blackmarket goods (she boasts, "I have a cold storage all to myself just filled with goodies!" while "good" women solicited "anti–black market pledges" [Hartmann 22]). And to add insult to injury, she not only does nothing for the war effort, she is downright unpatriotic, complaining to Anne about all the "flag-waving" in the preacher's sermon.

In another example from the period, *Tender Comrade* (Dmytryk, 1943) avails itself of similar oppositions between the "good" woman and the "bad" woman in its depiction of a group of women rooming together while their husbands are at war. In contrast to her other roommates, Barbara/Ruth Hussey, as Mary Ann Doane notes, is "excessive in the realm of sexuality," cheating on her husband while he is away by actively dating other men. Her excessive sexuality is aggravated by her "excessive desire for material goods," in her "tendency toward overconsumption" (292). The wartime "bad" woman commits transgressions that are depicted not only as jeopardizing her marriage/engagement, but in a cause-effect relation, threatening the war effort as well as the basic fabric of American society. The unfaithful/promiscuous and/or brazenly egotistical woman depicted in these films is morally reprehensible, and Hollywood's message is unambiguous about her social status; she is socially irredeemable.

The immediate postwar cinema had already shown the good wartime wives and mothers how to adjust their behavior to the end of the war, proposing Milly Stephenson/Myrna Loy in *The Best Years of Our Lives* (Wyler, 1946) as the postwar Anne Hilton of *Since You Went Away*, who responds appropriately to the needs of her husband, and contrasting her against the selfishly opportunistic Marie Derry/Virginia Mayo who worked in a night club and cheated on her husband, Fred Derry/Dana Andrews, during the war and after her husband's return. An extreme example of what happens to the unfaithful wife occurs in *The Blue Dahlia* (Marshall, 1946) in which Johnny Morrison/Alan Ladd's wife is murdered, the police assuming that Johnny/Ladd killed her because of her infidelity.[25] Although Helen Morrison is murdered by a blackmailer, she is also indirectly and implicitly punished for adultery, much like Leslie Crosbie/Bette Davis for both infidelity and murder in the 1940 version of *The Letter*.

With the end of the war, the opposing images of the self-sacrificing wife/fiancée and the self-absorbed, self-gratifying woman collapse in some films, creating in their place a new, more understanding approach to and redefinition of the previously shunned wartime wayward woman. In these postwar scenarios, the "bad" woman cannot even remotely resemble an Emily Hawkins or a Marie Derry if she is going to be redeemed. Emily Hawkins and Marie Derry are the bad women of the good/evil polarity who are juxtaposed with the good Anne Hiltons and Milly Stephensons at the other end. The postwar wayward woman, however, exists in a world of shades of gray, possessing traits that belong to both Emily Hawkins *and* Anne Hilton; she is portrayed more sympathetically as a "good" woman who made a terrible, but not utterly unpardonable mistake. So while *The Unfaithful*'s Chris Hunter, once her lie is discovered, is initially described by her friend/lawyer as "no different than all the other cheating, conniving women [seeking divorce] that parade through my office," her infidelity is tempered by her laudable wartime activities of working for the Red Cross and the U.S.O, and in her effort to make her letters to her serviceman husband "as cheerful as possible so as not to distress him." These films generally confront their heroines' missteps head-on, with each heroine's entourage ultimately evaluating the enormity of her transgression according to quite different standards than those employed before or during the war. These characters strive to enter into and understand the psychological motivations behind the heroine's act, motivations that, while they do not always justify her slips of conduct, place them firmly within the realm of the curable.

The 1950s good/bad girl's actions are initially judged according to the old rules of the good/evil dichotomy—Marswell/Gable enjoys the favors of Kelly/Gardner, but writes her off as nothing more than a girl of much too easy virtue; Sergeant O'Hara/Aldo Ray initially rejects Sadie/Rita Hayworth as "dirty" upon learning about her past, as does Gregory/John Kerr his fiancée Gaby/Leslie Caron and Bob Hunter/Zachary Scott his wife Chris/Ann Sheridan. Early in *Miss Sadie Thompson*, an ideological confrontation between Dr. McPhail and Mr. Davidson tests whether science or religion is best qualified to interpret, and ultimately to pass judgment on, human behavior; they buck heads over the question of evil and how one in a position of authority should deal with women like Sadie. Davidson believes evil exists as physical, almost scientific, evidence:

DAVIDSON: Evil is a fact, like right and wrong. I know what you think, Doctor, that there's no such thing as immorality, that everything's relative. I know what you and other men of science believe, what Freud, and Adler, and Jung have brought on the world, destroying values.

McPHAIL: Now just a minute . . .

DAVIDSON: Destroying moral values! Leading people to believe that they're not directly responsible for their actions. But we are responsible! Each one of us must choose between good and evil. We must isolate evil, stamp it out, the way you fight an infectious disease!

Miss Sadie Thompson effects a reordering of semantic registers that delegitimizes Davidson's authority, reversing those qualities normally associated with science and religion such that Davidson's religious practices assume the appearance of impersonal, fact-finding science ("We must isolate evil, stamp it out, the way you fight an infectious disease"), and McPhail's medical manners resemble those of the benevolent priest ("The founder of our religion was not so squeamish"). Through his diagnoses, McPhail uses the same Freud, Adler, and Jung decried by Davidson in support of those very values Davidson claims have been destroyed by modern psychology. The implacable rigidity of the old system—Davidson's system of censure and intolerance—gives way under the weight of an understanding which remarkably resembles Christian brotherly love. Davidson's god, as Sadie points out, is "nothing but a cop," adhering strictly to the letter of the law, while McPhail's works individual miracles through the all-seeing, all-knowing light of science. In pitting Davidson against McPhail, the film dramatizes the debate between conservative traditionalists who see the end of civilization in the experts' relativism and the climate of permissiveness, and the social scientists who claim that only they can assure a return to the social harmony of yore.

The films' narrative development strives to show that there are other factors beside free will that account for the choices one makes in life, extenuating psychological and social circumstances such as bad judgement, grief, emotional and/or financial stress, duress, or distress, or years of abuse; Kelly lost her husband in the war and fell apart as a result; Gaby thought she had lost her fiancée at the front; Chris was terribly lonely while her husband of two weeks was away for two years; Sadie had been dealt a bad hand of cards since childhood. These women were either not strong enough or the tests they underwent were too over-whelming. But these films also propose that responsibility for their fall lies just as much with their husbands and husbands-to-be. So while in *The Unfaithful*, Bob/Zachary Scott presents his actions as above reproach ("I married her because I loved her," "Is it my fault I was sent overseas?"), his cousin Paula/Eve Arden reveals how his ulterior motives were selfish and thoughtless:

> PAULA: What you wanted was a whirl and a memory. You wanted a beautiful woman waiting for you and you didn't want anyone mak-ing time with her while you were away. So you hung up a no-tres-passing sign like you'd stake a gold claim. You didn't marry her, you just took an option on her.
>
> BOB: She could've said no.
>
> PAULA: While the band was playing? Listen, I was there. I saw you making with that uniform, and that "today we live" routine. And then you were off.

Similarly, *Miss Sadie Thompson*, *Mogambo*, and *Gaby* advised American society not to be too quick to jump to superficial conclusions about some women's wartime conduct, and about where to lay blame. In a secular age, the penetrating gaze of social science comes to the aid of a faltering tradi-tion, not to supplant it, rather to ensure the latter's continuity.

SEX AND THE MARRIED WOMAN

While post-1950s comparisons between remakes and their originals tend to favor the latter,[26] offering the copy as parasitical and as conceptually and stylistically inferior, evaluating the Classic Hollywood remake accord-ing to the same modernist critical criteria obscures the rich, symbiotic relationship that it maintains with the Classic Hollywood model. The remake from the classic period formally and thematically references the original so as to reaffirm the hegemony of the dominant "classic" paradigm. The naturalness, the logic, and the balance of seamless Holly-wood narrative construction prevail, even where there appeared signs of change in morals and manners, which were the inevitable result of his-torical events and shifts in fashions. Differences emerge in the remake as a result of its need to "preserve the past without denying the present" (Shiff 167). Hovering in the wings of Hollywood's retelling of once-told tales was the dramatization of the conflicts facing American society in the postwar period: the specter of Nazism and the resurfacing of the Communist bugaboo, the latter a product of the Cold War. Compromise, not extremism, was advocated. Perhaps more important, however, the postwar remakes did not challenge the traditional "sexual division of labor where women assumed responsibility for the home and men went out into the world to earn a livelihood" (Chafe 96). Betty Friedan claimed in 1963 that after 1949, "Fulfillment as a woman had only one definition for American women . . .—the housewife-mother" (44). But women's fulfillment easily since suffrage had never been promoted in any other fashion. If the postwar woman was encouraged to explore her sexuality, partially a consequence of the influence of Freudianism in popular culture, it was not because women were on the road to sexual liberation, rather it was to create another avenue of release for those energies women might be tempted to apply to "masculine" jobs (Friedan 240). Feminine sexual satisfaction became equated with female identity, and both were put in the service of domestication by the era's experts. As Friedan points out, for the housewives-mothers of the 1950s, "there is no road to achievement, or status, or identity, except the sexual one" (266, 271).

Dejected spouses and lovers, angry male workers ill at ease with women on the workforce, indeed, the entire nation, could forgive the wayward woman's misplaced sexuality if she redirected her energies toward marriage and motherhood. The same was true for the 1920s flapper and the 1930s independent woman, each of whom could be permitted their sexual freedom as long as it did not "alter the basic distribution of roles between men and women" (Chafe 96). If the postwar period was marked by the instability of a society in transition, as most historians suggest, then the work of the postwar remake as a practice is to revert to the meaningful formulas of the Classic Hollywood production of reality in an effort to induce a climate of overall moral as well as historical continuity. This greatly informs our understanding of Hollywood's postwar remaking frenzy (an activity unequalled since then), its renewed interest in and vigorous production of genre films, and its insistent appeal to the star personas' "already signifying complex of meaning and affect" (Dyer, "Resistance" 92). Like Classical art that "seeks out first principles, original truths, and disseminates them through repetition" (Shiff 169), Hollywood in the postwar period repeated with a vengeance.

NOTES

1. All three versions of the Sadie Thompson story are based on W. Somerset Maugham's short story "Miss Thompson," with extensive borrowings taken from John Colton and Clemence Randolph's play "Rain" (1921). After the popular success of the play Maugham changed the title of his story to "Rain." *Dirtie Gertie From Harlem* (Spencer Williams, 1946) credits True T. Thompson with original story and screen adaptation, but the writer clearly lifted large bits of narrative from the earlier Sadie Thompson films in the exotic island locale, and the themes of the female protagonist's self-exile from the States and the tormented preacher and his efforts, first to reason with Gertie, and in his failure, to have the island governor deport her. Because this essay deals with the remake in the context of Classic Hollywood ideology, *Dirtie Gertie*, a film featuring an all black cast and possessing noticeably low production values, falls in the studio system's margins, thereby disqualifying it as an example of the Classic Hollywood remake.

2. Strangely enough, Leonard Maltin refers to *Torrid Zone* as a "variation on *The Front Page*."

3. The "fragmented" audience is composed of two audiences: those who go to art cinemas, and the "old-fashioned, entertainment-seeking moviegoers" (Ray 138).

4. In noting that cinema patronage dropped well before the advent of television, Robert Sklar cites as instrumental factors the rise in the birth rate following World War II ("young adults committed their time and money to home and family building"), and the rise in ticket prices that resulted from the entrance of small independent theaters in the competition for first-run movies. In the latter instance, the lower-income filmgoers, whom the industry considered its "faithful supporters," simply couldn't afford to go quite as often to the cinema (274).

5. Kenneth Macgowan notes that "producer Bryan Foy boasts that he used the plot of *Tiger Shark* (1932) successfully in ten other films by changing the title, the locale of the story, and the names of the characters" (344). In another example, Jeanine Basinger claims that *Our Blushing Brides* (Beaumont, 1930) is just one in a similar line of remakes: "This movie [*Our Blushing Brides*] is a reworking of a 1925 silent called *Sally, Irene, and Mary*, in which Crawford, Constance Bennett, and Sally O'Neill play three show girls in a Broadway revue who represent three different attitudes toward love and career. This idea was so popular with audiences that it turned up over and over again for the next three decades, in such movies as *Girls About Town* (1931), *Ladies in Love* (1936), *Three Blind Mice* (1938), *Moon Over Miami* (1941), *Three Little Girls in Blue* (1946), *How to Marry a Millionaire* (1953), *Three Coins in the Fountain* (1954), etc., etc." (110).

6. In "Conglomerates and Content: Remakes, Sequels and Series in the New Hollywood," Thomas Simonet shows that, contrary to contemporary film critics' claims that Hollywood today remakes films to a heretofore unparalleled degree, there were statistically more remakes made during the Classic Hollywood era than at any other period in film history.

7. I am using the terms offered by Robert Ray to denote the Classic Hollywood film's seeming "invisible style" (the formal paradigm) (32), and the American myth's promise to resolve "incompatible values" (the thematic paradigm) (55).

8. Betty Friedan defines the "feminine mystique" as the ideology that "says that the highest value and the only commitment for women is the fulfillment of their own femininity. . . . The mistake, says the mystique, the root of women's troubles in the past is that women envied men, women tried to be like men, instead of accepting their own nature, which can find fulfillment only in sexual passivity, male domination, and nurturing maternal love" (43). Although the "feminine mystique" promoted the image of woman as destined biologically to be a housewife and mother during the postwar period, Friedan comments that this "new" image is really no different than the old; while one can isolate certain cosmetic differences between these images, the effort to maintain the sexual division of labor (men working outside, women in the home) remains the same.

9. Peter Biskind notes that American popular mediums mobilized in order to get men as well as women back into the home: "The millions of American men who were coming back from Europe and the Pacific in 1945 found, to the surprise of many, that man's place was in the home. Home was more than a pipe, slippers, and a warm bed. For one thing, it was the seat of the family, the domestic version of the group so favored by pluralists. 'Whether you are a man or a woman,' as *The Woman's Guide to Better Living* put it, 'the family is the unit to which you most genuinely belong'" (250–51).

10. Tino Balio quotes David O. Selznick on production practices at Warner Brothers: "Selznick noted that at Warners, the director is 'purely a cog in the machine' for 'ninety per cent of the Warner films' and is 'handed a script, usually just a few days before he goes into production'" ("Feeding" 79).

11. These remakes are hardly isolated instances in cinematic history. For example, Amy Lawrence notes that, in the early sound years, "In order to maintain the necessary level of popular intelligibility, *Rain* and the many other remakes and adaptations of the era summon earlier forms to shore up their ability to signify and to stave off the fragmentation caused by attempts to incorporate sound" (72). And although the earliest cinema (the "cinema of attractions") did not adopt the format of fairground and vaudeville entertainment to deliber-

ately exploit their relationship with older traditions, a link with precinematic popular forms was nevertheless established by maintaining the familiar signifying conventions of those forms. (I am using the term coined by Tom Gunning.)

12. The November 2, 1932, *Variety* review of *Red Dust* describes Jean Harlow's Vantine as the "Sadie Thompson of the territory." Tino Balio remarks of Harlow's best pictures, *Red Dust* and *China Seas* (Garnett, 1935), that they "contain hot-love-in-the-isolated-tropics plots in which she plays Sadie Thompson types opposite Clark Gable" (242). It can even be said that Jeanne Eagels portrayal of Leslie Crosbie in the 1929 *The Letter* recalls however indirectly the Sadie Thompson from the preceding year; Eagels played Sadie in the theater and was perhaps chosen for the film role for her stage performance in "Rain."

13. Norman Corwin, the screenwriter for *The Blue Veil* (1951), *Scandal at Scourie* (Negulesco, 1953), and *Lust For Life* (Minnelli, 1956), echoes much of what has been said about Louis B. Mayer and his moral directorship at M-G-M: "One of the most prominent of all of the filmmakers in the history of Hollywood was Louis B. Mayer, who felt that every picture should deal with the sacredness of motherhood, with what we consider the values of home. His outlook on those matters was famously conservative and traditional, Norman Rockwell to the tenth power. I've been in Mayer's home, I had dinner there once, and he talked about the enduring value of family and motherhood and how wholesome the Mickey Rooney pictures were, and that sort of thing" (315 in this volume).

14. Richard Dyer also includes a star's public image as a contributing factor in a star's image: "A star's image is constructed both from her or his film appearances (typical roles, modes of presentation, performance and dress styles, etc.) and publicity (including promotion, advertising, fan magazines and gossip)" ("Resistance" 92).

15. Not only does *Affair in Trinidad* reteam Rita Hayworth and Glenn Ford from the cast of *Gilda*, it is a "virtual remake" of *Gilda* (Silver 387). Columbia produced both pictures, making *Affair*'s position as disguised remake likely.

16. If many filmgoers were unfamiliar with the originals upon which the remakes were based, they would nevertheless have learned from film reviews in the major newspapers about the earlier productions. Short of familiarity with the originals, the generic cues of the remakes were sufficient to direct a reading of them.

17. Not to be underestimated, *Miss Sadie Thompson* can also be read as a parable of the Communist purgings by the H.U.A.C, with the rigidly reform-minded Mr. Davidson/José Ferrer as representative of the narrow-minded intolerance and general hypocrisy of Senator Joseph McCarthy, J. Thomas Parnell, and the latter's committee henchmen.

18. After all, many of the directors and stars associated with these productions actively sought to bring them about. For example, Frank Sinatra wanted to reprise John Garfield's role in *Four Daughters*, and Fritz Lang wanted to do his version of Jean Renoir's *La Chienne* (1931).

19. Consider the following conversation between Mrs. Davidson and Dr. McPhail regarding Sadie in the 1953 film:

> MRS. DAVIDSON: Thank heaven she's gone. She disturbed Mr. Davidson horribly last night. He despises women of that kind.
>
> DR. MCPHAIL: The founder of our religion was not so squeamish.

20. Another example of a similar recourse to 1930s cinematic prototypes is provided by Douglas Sirk's remakes of John Stahl's *Imitation of Life* (1934) and *Magnificent Obsession* (1935) in 1959 and 1954 respectively. The 1959 *Imitation of Life* especially solicits the original's ability to resolve a family and social crisis to inform its own resolution, a resolution undermined only by Sirk's ironic visual stylization and Lana Turner's detached air. The threatened family depicted in this 1950s melodrama articulates the postwar climate of hostility toward the working woman and fears about the future stability of America and its family in her absence from housekeeping, wifely duties, and childrearing. Richard Dyer notes that Lana Turner's appearance of "being detached from events" is central to the characterization of Lora: "[S]he plays a character, Lora, who is, or becomes, a person on show, performing, presenting an image, to be thought of neither as an essence (i.e., an inner human being expressing her self through presentation) nor as interacting with others and circumstances" ("Lana" 424). He asserts that acting ends by being the "key metaphor for imitation in the film," highlighting the doubtful success of the reconstituted family at the film's end.

21. *Gaby's* Gaby uses a similar rationale when she says to her fiancé Gregg/John Kerr, "Oh Gregg, if I had only known you were still alive." At film's end, Gregg cites the war not as a standard test for the quality of human behavior but as an obstruction to its normal expression. He offers his forgiveness and his love: "Dearest Gaby, this [as he points to a bombed section of London] isn't us. None of this is. Gaby, we can't blame each other for what the war has done. Stay with me, please."

22. For example, in *Dangerous* (Green, 1935), Bette Davis plays a destructively egotistical and manipulative woman who is transformed through true love for another man; she fulfills her obligations both to her employer and to her permanently maimed husband with unmistakable devotion and self-sacrifice.

23. These films share a lot with the unwed mother scenarios of many melodramas from the 1930s. According to Christian Viviani in "Who is Without Sin: The Maternal Melodrama in American Film, 1930–1939," the Depression figures as the crisis informing the narratives of these films. The unwed mother who gives up her

child to have him or her raised in the more traditional family unit embraces anonymity as she watches his or her progress. This fallen woman "reconquer[s] her dignity while helping her child" to be able to "re-enter society thanks to her sacrifices," as in *Stella Dallas* (Vidor, 1937). For Viviani, the thematics of sacrifice serve as a "clear metaphor for an attitude America could adopt in facing its national crisis" (178). Everyone would have to abandon self-interest in order to ensure the welfare of the next generation. In a similar light, these post–World War II wayward women melodramas equally preach the abandon of self-interest to women working when there was no economic need, women putting children in child-care facilities instead of tending to them in the comfort and familiarity of the home, women getting an unprecedented number of divorces. Also the unwed mother of the 1930s maternal melodrama is never reinstated into the society of her prefall life; Viviani notes that, "morally she is still more or less rejected" (176). But she is not totally ostracized, as she participates in the rebuilding of Depression America through her work.

24. The role of wife as member of a family unit is evident in historian Susan M. Hartmann's description of a husband addressing the question of his wife's defense work in a 1943 *McCall's* article. While the husband is generally supportive, he concludes, however, by saying that "'there will be a better mutual understanding when women return to their homes,'" a statement which for Hartmann implies that husbands—like employers and public officials (23)—took for granted that wartime work was temporary and that they believed that "the greatest benefit of paid work was not to the woman but to the marital relationship" (200).

25. Regarding *The Blue Dahlia*, Carl Macek notes that the original screenplay by Raymond Chandler identified Buzz, Johnny's war buddy who suffers from blackouts, as Helen Morrison's murderer: "Originally, Chandler wanted Buzz to be the actual killer, blinded and desensitized by the brutalizing effects of the war. The studio met with objections from the Navy and forced Chandler to rewrite the film implicating Dad [the hotel detective] as the murderer" (Silver and Ward 37). In the postwar period the studios were still responsive to the needs of presenting the war effort with a good face.

26. Typical of this response to the remake is critic Molly Haskell, who is quoted as saying, "I don't think there was ever a case where the remake was better" (Young H17+).

WORKS CITED

Balio, Tino, ed. *Grand Design: Hollywood as a Modern Business Enterprise, 1930–1939.* Ed. Tino Balio. Berkeley: U of California P, 1995. Vol. 5 of *History of the American Cinema.* 6 vols. 1990–99.

––––––. "Feeding the Maw of Exhibition." Balio 73–107.

––––––. "Production Trends." Balio 179–312.

Banner, Lois W. *Women in Modern America: A Brief History.* 2nd edition. New York: Harcourt Brace Jovanovich, 1984.

Basinger, Jeanine. *A Woman's View: How Hollywood Spoke to Women, 1930–1960.* Hanover: Wesleyan UP, 1993.

Biskind, Peter. *Seeing is Believing: How Hollywood Taught Us to Stop Worrying and Love the Fifties.* New York: Pantheon, 1983.

Buscombe, Edward. "The Idea of Genre in the American Cinema." Grant 11–25.

Cawelti, John G. "The Evolution of Social Melodrama." Landy 33–49.

Chafe, William Henry. *The American Woman: Her Changing Social, Economic, and Political Roles, 1920–1970.* London: Oxford UP, 1972.

Cuddon, J. A. *The Penguin Dictionary of Literary Terms and Literary Theory.* 3rd edition. New York: Penguin, 1991.

Doane, Mary Ann. "The Moving Image: Pathos and the Maternal." Landy 283–306.

Dyer, Richard. "Lana: Four Films of Lana Turner." Landy 409–28.

––––––. "Resistance Through Charisma: Rita Hayworth and *Gilda.*" *Women in Film Noir.* Ed. E. Ann Kaplan. London: BFI Publishing, 1980. 91–99.

French, Brandon. *On the Verge of Revolt: Women in American Films of the Fifties.* New York: Frederick Ungar, 1978.

Friedan, Betty. *The Feminine Mystique.* New York: Norton, 1963.

Friedrich, Otto. *City of Nets: A Portrait of Hollywood in the 1940's.* New York: Perennial, 1986.

Grant, Barry. *Film Genre Reader II.* Austin: U of Texas P, 1995.

Gunning, Tom. "The Cinema of Attractions: Early Film, Its Spectator and the Avant-Garde." *Wide Angle* 8.3–4 (1986): 63–70.

Hartmann, Susan M. *The Home Front and Beyond: American Women in the 1940s.* Boston: Twayne, 1982.

Katovich, Michael A. and Patrick A. Kinkade. "The Stories Told in Science Fiction and Social Science: Reading *The Thing* and Other Remakes From Two Eras." *The Sociological Quarterly* 34.4 (1993): 619–37.

Landy, Marcia, ed. *Imitations of Life: A Reader on Film and Television.* Detroit: Wayne State UP, 1991.

Lawrence, Amy. *Echo and Narcissus: Women's Voices in Classical Hollywood Cinema.* Berkeley: U of California P, 1991.

Macgowan, Kenneth. *Behind the Screen: The History and Techniques of the Motion Picture.* New York: Dell, 1965.

Quirk, Lawrence J. *The Complete Films of Joan Crawford.* Secaucus: Citadel, 1968.

Ray, Robert B. *A Certain Tendency of the Hollywood Cinema, 1930–1980.* Princeton: Princeton UP, 1985.

Schatz, Thomas. *Hollywood Genres: Formulas, Filmmaking, and the Studio System.* Philadelphia: Temple UP, 1981.

Shiff, Richard. "Phototropism (Figuring the Proper)." *Retaining the Original: Multiple Originals, Copies, and Reproductions.* Ed. Center for Advanced Study in the Visual Arts: Symposium Papers VII. Washington: National Gallery of Art, 1989. 161–79.

Silver, Alain and Elizabeth Ward, eds. *Film Noir: An Encyclopedic Reference to the American Style.* 3rd edition. Woodstock: Overlook, 1992.

Simonet, Thomas. "Conglomerates and Content: Remakes, Sequels and Series in the New Hollywood." Ed. Bruce Austin. Norwood: Ablex, 1987. Vol. 3 of *Current Research in Film: Audiences, Economics, and Law.* 83–97.

Sklar, Robert. *Movie-Made America: A Cultural History of American Movies.* Rev. and updated ed. New York: Vintage, 1994.

Viviani, Christian. "Who is Without Sin: The Maternal Melodrama in American Film, 1930–1939." Landy 168–82.

Young, Josh. "The Best French Films You'll Never See." *New York Times* 30 Oct. 1994: H17+.

CHAPTER EIGHT

Hiring Practices:
Simenon/Duvivier/Leconte

LEONARD R. KOOS

JACQUES: Our story, sir, isn't the only thing that's been rewritten. Everything that's ever happened here below has been rewritten hundreds of times, and no one ever dreams of finding out what really happened. The history of mankind has been rewritten so often that people don't know who they are anymore.

MASTER: Why that's appalling! Then they *(indicating the audience)* will believe we haven't even got any horses and had to trudge through our story like tramps?

JACQUES *(indicating the audience):* They? They'll believe anything! (69)

—Milan Kundera, *Jacques and His Master* (1981)

In the recent "documentary" *Lumière et compagnie* (Moon, 1995), whose goal was to commemorate the centennial anniversary of the invention of cinema, an original Lumière cinematograph was made available to forty international directors who subsequently used the apparatus to create their own films by employing the mechanical conditions of production of the dawn of filmmaking. The French director Patrice Leconte's effort with the supposedly primitive machine serves as the prefatory offering. By way of introduction the iconographical moving images of Auguste and Louis Lumière's 1896 short film *Arrivée d'un train à la Ciotat* are shown. Then, period still photographs of La Ciotat's vigorous palm trees further establish the southern French locale as Leconte's voice-over commentary is heard in which he explains his motivation for participating in the project as well as what he hoped to convey in his film. He insists that his interest in the project revolved around the idea of "recording the differences."[1] In the film that Leconte does make with the cinematograph, the familiar yet different image of a contemporary La Ciotat railroad station appears on the screen. Despite the similarly diagonal axis of action along the railroad tracks with respect to the camera throughout the single, stationary shot, a camera position which invites immediate visual comparisons to the Lumière brothers' film, in Leconte's film the platform holds no waiting passengers. The train, shiny and modern, approaches the station from the right of the frame, does not slow down, and disappears off screen to the left, making no stop at La Ciotat.[2] So much for the differences.

And yet, Leconte's contribution to *Lumière et compagnie*, ostensibly a remake of the Lumière brothers' film, albeit brief, suggestively implicates the entire history of cinema in the process of remaking and exhibits fundamental characteristics and issues of that process, not least of which is the remake's problematic and potentially contradictory rhetoric of originality within the framework of an avowed repetition. Documenting differences would seem to inscribe and maintain the inescapable referential presence of the original in the remake. Moreover, Leconte's insistence on recording the differences while at the same time remaking the Lumière brothers' film—here historical, political, cultural, and economic, just as much as aesthetic—underscores, within the consistency of a continuation of sameness, a formidable anxiety of influence that emerges in the predatory oppositionality by which Leconte signs his film, particularly in the radically remade ending. The rhetorical and aesthetic statement made by Leconte in the prologue to *Lumière et compagnie* informs upon his film *Monsieur Hire* (1990), a remake of Julien Duvivier's postwar allegory of collaboration and conformism *Panique* (1946), itself a somewhat liberal adaptation of the 1933 novel *Les Fiançailles de M. Hire* by Georges Simenon.[3]

THIS GENRE FOR HIRE

NORMA DESMOND: Just a minute you. You're a writer, you said.

JOE GILLIS: Why?

NORMA DESMOND: Are you or aren't you?

JOE GILLIS: That's what it says on my guild card.

NORMA DESMOND: And, you have written pictures, haven't you?

JOE GILLIS: Sure have. Want a list of my credits?

NORMA DESMOND: I want to ask you something. Come in here.

JOE GILLIS: The last one I wrote was about Okies in the dust-bowl. You'd never know it because when it reached the screen, the whole thing played on a torpedo boat.

—Charles Brackett, Billy Wilder, *Sunset Boulevard* (1950)

Film remakes can provide the film critic or historian with a potentially rich opportunity to examine the aesthetic, economic, political, social, and cultural development of the medium. Moreover, when the remake is produced within a single cultural tradition, an additional level of commentary and interpretation opens up in which the evolution of an entire culture can be charted. Such is the case with the triad of works of Simenon's novel, Duvivier's film adaptation, and Leconte's remake, each produced at historically different if not pivotal moments in the history of twentieth-century France. These historical moments—the mid-1930s, the postwar era, and the contemporary period—in turn, inform on the differences in each version of the Hire story, not the least of which is its exceptional generic malleability as it passes from the crime novel to the *fait divers* in *Les Fiançailles de M. Hire*, to the social drama of *Panique*, ending up with the character study/love story of *Monsieur Hire*.

The major elements of the Hire story, from Simenon through Duvivier and on to Leconte, conform to a fairly consistent plot structure. In questionable circumstances, a woman is murdered in an empty lot and suspicion falls on Hire whose distance from his neighbors and expressed misanthropy make him a natural suspect for both the neighborhood and the police. Hire, from his apartment, watches the alluring Alice in her room across the courtyard, perceives her mistreatment at the hands of her lover, and offers her his protection. Alice and her lover, the actual murderer, put their own plot into motion in which Alice pretends to respond to Hire's advances as the two make plans for a romantic departure while the bloody purse of the murdered woman is planted in Hire's apartment. After its discovery, when Hire returns to the neighborhood, he is greeted by an angry mob. In an attempt to escape, he scrambles up through the stairways of his building and climbs onto the roof, a chase which, with varying details according to the version, proves to be fatal for Hire. While the basic elements of this story remain constant in the three articulations of the Hire story, it is in the divergence of the details amplifying this structure that the aesthetic dynamics of the remaking process become visible.

While avid readers of Georges Simenon would certainly recognize in his fourth ironically titled novel *Les Fiançailles de M. Hire* certain elements of plot and setting that return again and again in the author's novelistic universe, they would no doubt be surprised by a portrayal of "the Paris police force seen from the point of view of a suspect" (Marnham 173). Nowhere to be found in this novel is the methodical attention to detail and ethical rigor of an Inspector Maigret in the police department. Rather, the inspectors of *Les Fiançailles de M. Hire* drink heavily, freely consort with shop assistants in shadowy doorways, spy on the comings and goings in the neighborhood, have files complied on any number of the community's residents, fall asleep in Hire's apartment while awaiting his return, and decide, based on little more than gossip and neighborhood prejudice, to suspect Hire in the brutal robbery and murder of the streetwalker Léonide Pacha, known on the streets as Lulu. Appropriately enough, these designated representatives of the law operate in the suggestively named, seedy community of Villejuif on the outskirts of Paris, a setting that participates in a well-developed tradition in French literature and culture that figures the suburbs as sites of political, legal, and social transgression.[4]

As the novel opens, a fundamental figure of the story is presented: blood. The concierge, while delivering Hire's mail, spots a bloodied towel in his apartment. Although later verified to be the result of a razor cut from shaving—the police inspector without warning rips the bandage off Hire's face to reveal the wound and causes it to bleed again—the mechanism of suspicion has decisively and irrevocably been set into motion with Hire as the prime suspect in the sadistic murder and mutilation of the prostitute. Even Hire's physicality, despite and perhaps because of its banality, participates in his status as suspect in Simenon's novel: "He was not fat. He was flabby. His volume was no more than that of an entirely ordinary man, but you had no impression of bones and flesh, nothing but a smooth and soft matter, so smooth and soft that his gestures were ambiguous" (12). Later, when Hire voluntarily makes a visit to the police commissioner in an effort to reiterate his innocence in the face of what seems to be an arbitrarily malicious investigation, the commissioner opens their police file and traces Hire's checkered past. Hire's true family name is revealed to be Hirovitch despite his feeble assertion that "my father already called himself Hire" (110). Hire's father, a Polish Jew who made his living as a tailor in the *rue des Francs Bourgeois* in the *Marais* in Paris was known by the Paris police for having "indulged occasionally in usury." Hire, having renounced his father's profession and moved from the Jewish quarter where he grew up—ostensibly another step toward assimilation—and although a French citizen, was exempted from military service due to a weak heart that had never, Hire freely admits, manifested itself as a malady. After a series of quasi-honorable jobs, Hire, through an unnamed backer, ran a small publishing house which specialized in pornographic works on flagellation, one of which landed him in prison for six months. Also represented in Hire's dossier is a reference to his present occupation as a sort of con man who sells nearly worthless money-making kits to unsuspecting correspondents who answer his newspaper ad. Given the politically polarizing context of French society in the mid-1930s and the free circulation of anti-Semitic rhetoric therein, Hire's Jewish "blood" underscores his status as a foreigner and further marks him in the eyes of the police as a duplicitous criminal whose pleas of innocence cannot be believed.[5] Moreover, the narrative insistence on Hire's equivocal physicality further dissociates him from the so-called French community by denying him the depth and detail of what Jean-Paul Sartre called "the aristocracy of the body" in the anti-Semite's self-fashioning rhetoric (*Anti-Semite* 118). Hire's lack of definite physical dimensionality, added to his onomastic incompleteness in the story and in the narrative (he is known only as M. Hire throughout the novel), ultimately finds its counterpart in his ambiguous actions. As Maurice Piron has noted, Hire "is solely described by his outward behavior: a distancing effect results in which the apprehension of his personality is completely elusive" (Gauteur 5). Denied the depth of the intimate and the personal, Hire is an entirely public figure to be used as the public sees fit.

In the final scenes of the novel, the details of the theme of blood return as, upon the discovery of the bloodied purse of the dead prostitute that the creamery shop assistant Alice had planted in Hire's apartment, Hire is greeted by the angry neighborhood mob upon his return home. The unified hatred of Hire, a thinly veiled representation of the period's ambient anti-Semitic tendencies, leads to an intoxicating violence as their punches and blows "made a funny sound on Hire's flesh, such an exciting sound that they all wanted to hear it" (171). In his attempt to flee and escape the bloodthirsty crowd and the attendant policemen, Hire ends up clinging to an upper ledge of his building where he collapses, and while the rescue firemen carry him down, he dies of a heart attack far above the watching crowd. In the end, *Les Fiançailles de M. Hire* seems to be an indictment of the power of prejudice in which the tyranny of the crowd can absolutely victimize the individual and a denunciation of the designated structures of authority in society whose relative impotence not only fails to maintain social order but also willfully creates a perpetrator where there is none. However, the generic structures in which *Les Fiançailles de M. Hire* participates hinder an unequivocal reading of the novel as a statement of social commentary. Very nearly antithetical to the detective novel wherein the order of the law is reestablished with the solving of the crime and the discovery of the villain's identity, *Les Fiançailles de M. Hire* vacillates between the crime novel and the sordid *fait divers*, a staple of French journalism which, from the nineteenth century onward, and in the briefest of formats, narrated the sensationalistic details of horrific crimes and unexplained events. In the final analysis, the stereotyping of character and setting echoes the ultimately abject banality of the *fait divers*, a blood-chilling moment that passes. The social commentary of *Les Fiançailles de M. Hire*, however insightful or trenchant, is ultimately marginalized and quickly forgotten in the process, like the end of the protagonist as the final sentence of the novel conveys: "And they were in movement, in Villejuif, because a whole little world was two hours late" (180).

ENGAGEMENTS

> For collaboration, like suicide, like crime, is a normal phenomenon. Only, in times of peace or in wars that do not end with a disaster, these elements of the collectivity remain in a

latent state; since the determining factors are lacking, the "collaborator" neither reveals himself to others nor to himself, he goes on with his work, he is perhaps a patriot, because he does not know the nature that he carries within him and that will reveal itself one day in favorable circumstances. (43)

—Jean-Paul Sartre,
"Qu'est-ce qu'un collaborateur?" (1945)

The very title of Julien Duvivier's 1946 film *Panique* announces a significant modification of the Hire story as adapted from Simenon's novel. The erasing of the proper name of the story's main character from the film's title and its replacement by a simple common noun able to refer simultaneously to the main character and the community suggests an amplification of the Hire story that allegorically reverberates beyond the individual and the specific. Duvivier explained how he and coscript writer Charles Spaak conceived of *Panique*'s uniqueness with respect to Simenon's novel in the potential,

> absent from the novel—of reasonably enlarging in its consequences the most banal of *faits divers*. . . . If all of the action revolves around a crime, here the interest in the subject does not lie in the discovery of the assassin, nor in the twists and turns of the investigation: we wanted to make *Panique* a film of social atmosphere. (Beylie 4)

Panique, then, unlike *Les Fiançailles de M. Hire*, pursues fuller character development and generically alters the plot's potential for suspense with regard to the identity of the murderer or to Alice's ultimate decision to betray Hire, which is never in doubt. Any suspense that remains, significantly reduced by several scenes that unequivocally prefigure the dénouement, leads to only one possible, predictable ending: the victimization of Monsieur Hire by the community.

In the telling opening sequence of *Panique*, a policeman interrupts a bearded vagrant's nap and forces him to move along. While the theme of exclusion figured significantly in Simenon's novel as the quasi-arbitrary decision of the crowd that the police are only too happy to accept, as it provides them with a convenient termination of a criminal case, *Panique*'s beginning suggests a closer relationship between the will of the group and the supposed protectors of the law, the latter being subordinate to the former. In the following images, Monsieur Hire arrives on the tramway whose terminus indicates once again the peripheral community of Villejuif. An immediate analogy between the vagrant and Hire is established by their beards, a stereotypical metonym of Hire's Jewish origin. The link between the two is further reinforced as Hire takes a photograph of the bum rummaging through a garbage can. As he will later explain to the duplicitous Alice, he now only takes pictures that document human misery.

Along with Hire's arrival is that of a traveling carnival whose employees soon discover in an empty lot the cadaver of Mademoiselle Noblet, a wealthy old maid who, at least in death, is respected by the same community that seems to have paid her little attention while she was alive. Soon thereafter arrives Alice, just released from jail after serving a sentence to protect her lover Alfred, whom she has come to rejoin. This trio of main characters circulates among a supporting cast of neighborhood figures which includes the local prostitute, the hotel owner, a salesman, the butcher, his ailing wife, their numerous children, a police inspector, and so forth.

From the outset, Désiré Hire's character in *Panique* differentiates himself from his predecessor in Simenon's novel. Here, Hire is a willing participant, however misanthropic, in the daily life of the community. Personal opinions about Hire have been formed as the result of his actions. The hotel owner defends Hire because he is a good client who pays his bills on time. The neighborhood prostitute remains antagonistic and suspicious of Hire who has demonstrated himself indifferent to her advances. While Simenon's Hire made his living capitalizing on the naiveté and greed of humanity, Duvivier and Spaak's Hire is an astrologer and spiritual advisor of sorts. His business card, which he gives to Alice, reads: "If you are worried about the future, if you doubt yourself and others, if you have lost life's joy, consult Doctor Varga." This profession, of course, will provide Alfred, in the wake of being physically overpowered and humiliated by Hire in the latter's office, with damaging evidence against Hire; he reports back to the neighborhood of the many strange books with foreign titles and the strange machines used to hypnotize that Hire keeps there. The fabricated malevolent strangeness of a dark, mystical Hire, in turn, permits a fuller demonization of his character in the neighborhood, his very presence an explanation for unexplainable maladies and ultimately, unsolved crimes.[6] Still, Hire resists such a facile superficialization of himself. His present circumstances and philosophy on life, he explains to Alice (in the house on the island in the Seine where he resided when he was a prosperous lawyer), are the result of the double betrayal of his beloved wife with his best and only friend. Since then, emotionally unable to help others much less himself, he merely documents humanity's injustices with a camera (unbeknownst to Alice, the police inspector believes that Hire photographed Mademoiselle Noblet's murder). As he explains to Alice, he nostalgically wants to rejoin the human community: "How I have tried to explain to them who I am. They're in a rush and judge by appearances." Hire, the unwilling or incapable narrator of his own misfortunes, is thereby unable to access, except in its most marginal forms, the social.

The society figured in *Panique*, it must be noted, is not meant to represent daily life under normal conditions. The film's events, illustrating Jean Renoir's contention that Duvivier's films create "a simultaneously realist and unreal world" (Beylie and Pinturault 78), are predicated on the existence of exceptional circumstances: the arrival and presence of the fair. With the arrival of the convoy of trucks carrying tents, amusements, and rides at the film's outset, the fair invades not only the space of Villejuif, but also persistently asserts its presence with lights and sounds at all hours of the day and night. Given the allegorical dimensions of *Panique* and Duvivier's expressed desire, upon returning to France after a five year sojourn in the United States during the war, "to treat a subject more related to the present situation" (Beylie 4), the fair as an occupying force seems, on first consideration, a curious choice in relation to the recent political disposition of France. The idea of war and military occupation as mass spectacle and entertainment, however, can be easily related to early modernist aesthetizations of modern warfare, particularly in the works of the Italian futurists and in Guillaume Apollinaire's poetry collection *Calligrammes* (1918). As Hire watches Alice at night, for example, the fair's flashing lights and vaguely orientalist music offer a seductive mix of image and sensation that adds fantastic proportions to an otherwise banal daily life and space. The amusements that the fair offers, as well, comprise a contained violence which, under other circumstances, would border on the criminal. Whether vicariously watching female wrestlers or actually joining in on the figurative violence directed at Hire in the bumper-car arena, the community wholeheartedly participates in the spectacle that occupies its space, a relationship effectively christened by the extreme long shots of the funeral procession of Mademoiselle Noblet from the perspective of the empty carnival ride. Of note, as well, is the ease with which the crowd passes from the figurative violence of the fair to the real violence of the victimization of Hire at the film's dénouement. Not even Hire's very real and violent death, after falling from the roof's drainpipe to which he could no longer cling, can abstract the insistent seduction of this occupying force. The music starts up again and the crowds, including Alfred and a wobbly Alice, return to ride the roller coaster. The circular motion of the ride, clearly a figure for the repetitive nature of such lapses in human history, also underscores the disorienting and dizzying effect of the fair on the inhabitants of the emblematic Villejuif.[7]

Panique ends with the strolling singer once again singing a song that laments humanity's treatment of its own. In this way, *Panique* explicitly resurrects "the populism of the 1930s" (Baillard 461), a Popular Front cinematic phenomenon to which Duvivier contributed the notable, albeit pessimistic, examples of *La Bandera* (1935), *La Belle Équipe* (1936) and *Pépé le Moko* (1936).[8] The film of the late 1930s that *Panique* resembles the most and specifically references is undoubtedly Marcel Carné's *Le Jour se lève* (1939), so much so that Raymond Chirat noted that "*Panique* is in some ways the negative of *Le Jour se lève*, where the assembled friends and neighbors struggle to save Jean Gabin" (109). But the resemblances go much farther than that. First, the Villejuif of *Panique*, actually a large set that Duvivier had constructed at great expense at Victorine Studios in Nice, visually imitates the town square and the rooftops' outline of the set designed by Alexander Trauner and is meant to represent a working-class neighborhood of Amiens in *Le Jour se lève*. Just as Hire watches Alice's window in *Panique*, the entire neighborhood watches François's window in Carné's film, in particular François's two love-interests, Clara and Françoise, who have an effective vantage point from across the square. Expressing a working-class solidarity with François, who has just killed the malevolent Valentin, the crowd below urges him to give himself up to the authorities. The situation can be worked out, they claim. In *Panique*, the hostile mob watching from below has sent Hire on his flight to the rooftop and his eventual death.[9] Finally, just as *Panique*'s firemen hurry to save Hire as he holds on for his life at the end of a drainpipe, the authorities of *Le Jour se lève* ascend to throw teargas in François's room and apprehend a criminal. While these two films end in different kinds of death—Hire's fall and François's suicide[10]—they are immediately followed by a reestablishment of the preceding narrative conditions, the return to the carnival in the former and the beginning of a new workday in the latter.[11]

The startling number of oppositional analogies between the endings of the two films privilege this portion of *Panique* as a postwar, inverted remake of *Le Jour se lève*. The visual, thematic, and political remaking of *Le Jour se lève* localized in the conclusion of *Panique* plots the changing coordinates of leftist sensibilities from pre- and postwar France. The Hire story, radically revised from Simenon's novel, then projected through an inverted version of Carné's late Popular Front politics, casts a shadow on prewar scenarios of political engagement as well as on postwar attempts at collaborationist revisionism. Truth and meaning—ultimately represented by the potential photograph of Mademoiselle Noblet's murder that remains around his neck even in death—while liminally existent, comes too late and is irrevocably deferred to a perhaps irrelevant future.

DISENGAGEMENTS

> Depth isn't what it used to be. For if the nineteenth century witnessed the long process of the destruction of appearances and their supplanting by meaning, the twentieth, subsequently, saw an equally massive process of the destruction of meaning . . . and its replacement by what? We find pleasure neither in appearances nor meaning. (8)
>
> —Jean Baudrillard, *Cool Memories* (1980)

No other director in recent memory, with the possible exception of Gus Van Sant and his 1998 shot-by-shot remake of Alfred Hitchcock's *Psycho*, has drawn so much attention to the original in the practice of remaking than Patrice Leconte on the occasion of the 1989 release of *Monsieur Hire*. In a number of interviews and disparate remarks attributed to the director, Leconte indicated, the story goes, that "he had once admired the Duvivier work, and, not realizing it was based on a Simenon novel, dreamt of remaking it someday" (Haskell 24). After reading the novel, Leconte persuaded co-scriptwriter Patrick Dewolf to do the same. The latter's response was mixed with regards to an adaptation as he found Simenon's novel "very nervy, it's very brazen" (Raskin 3). Claiming to ignore the novel and ostensibly Duvivier's film, Leconte and Dewolf proceeded with their version of the Hire story.

One of the organizing principles in Leconte and Dewolf's version becomes evident from the opening credits. Faithful to its title which

FIGURE 8.1. Shot of top-floor in which François (Jean Gabin) is holed up in Marcel Carné's *Le Jour se lève* (1939). Courtesy of the Museum of Modern Art, Film Stills Archive.

FIGURE 8.2. Shot of Monsieur Hire (Michel Simon) on the roofs above Villejuif in Julien Duvivier's *Panique* (1947). Courtesy of the Museum of Modern Art, Film Stills Archive.

refuses the personal event as in Simenon's novel and the social phenomenon of Duvivier's film, *Monsieur Hire* privileges character over action. Hire, framed in nearly obsessive close-ups and medium shots throughout the film, occupies a central position around which the film's two other main characters, Alice and the police inspector, gravitate. Emile, Alice's lover who inexplicably has killed the strange young woman Pierrette Bourgeois (an accident, Alice tells Hire), recedes into the story's background, rendering the idea of framing Hire for Pierrette's murder entirely Alice's design and doing. The film's other characters—the girl with the hiccups, the brothel prostitute, the watchful neighbor, the bowling spectators—play no role in the story beyond their narrational marginality, which differs from the social marginality and personal idiosyncrasy of Hire, Alice, Pierrette, and the police inspector. In previous versions, the community's tyrannical suspicion of such behavior led to the ultimate condemnation of Hire. In *Monsieur Hire*, however, the world is populated by strange, solitary figures who arbitrarily come into contact with each other.

The construction of the main characters in *Monsieur Hire*—which Leconte himself described as "a minimalist film" (Fernandez 9)—undergoes a process of reduction in which diversified characterization gives way to repetition. The film reduces and repeats to such an extent that its plot largely consists of an accumulation of these structures. Hire, with a life based on daily routines, repeatedly watches Alice while listening to the same piece by Brahms. The police inspector repeatedly has Hire run back and forth to his apartment building in an unsuccessful attempt at a positive identification by a taxi driver who may have seen the murderer flee the scene of the crime. In a scene that is visually precursive of the film's ending, Hire follows behind Alice and Emile around a skating rink. The music to which they skate, a slowed-down version of the Brahms piece Hire listens to while watching Alice, is abruptly interrupted by Hire's fall which leaves a trickle of bright red blood on the ice. In a film with colors so self-consciously washed-out that *Monsieur Hire* verges on the black and white, this bright red is repeated three times in the film: Alice's tomatoes, Hire's blood on the ice in the skating rink, and Hire's blood on the pavement after his fall from the building. Such repetitions impede and ultimately overwhelm the narrative dynamism of the unique in *Monsieur Hire*, leaving a skeletal plot which resists generic classification. Mystery, thriller, detective story, love story, *Monsieur Hire* flirts with each of these possibilities without ever settling on generic continuity.

One of the most striking changes in Leconte's remake of the Hire story, particularly with respect to Duvivier's film, is the nearly total erasure of the social, and thereby, the political. As a setting, for example, the highly codified suburban site of Villejuif has become in Leconte's film an entirely generic urban space.[12] The film's location shots, actually filmed in Brussels, offer no specific establishment of place and community. As with Alice, who has come to the city from an unidentified elsewhere, or Hire himself who shows Alice through the telescope a building where he used to live, this space has no other signifying potential beyond its residents' act of inhabitation. Playing little or no role in the life of this Hire, the community is even further distanced from the protagonist in death as the onlookers mutely witness, in slow motion and with little reaction, Hire hanging on to, and subsequently falling from, the building's edge. The social, *Monsieur Hire* seems to convey, is an outdated concept no longer applicable or relevant. Significantly, this Hire, when asked about his real name Hirovitch, responds that his father *and* grandfather had already used his present name, ascribing to Simenon and Duvivier's generation any possible meaning for the social equation.

Looming behind and reverberating through *Monsieur Hire*'s reductions and repetitions is an actively constructed ambiguity which provides Leconte with his most powerful remaking tool. *Monsieur Hire* poses questions without providing answers to such an extent that one critic remarked that "Leconte takes a sophomoric pleasure in loose ends and red herrings" (Phillips 66). While the existence of these loose ends and red herrings cannot be denied, they do serve to underscore the legitimizing rhetoric of the film remake that attempts to assert its authenticity while avowedly repeating its model. In *Monsieur Hire*, moreover, this justificatory position is accomplished by an innocuous recharacterization of the protagonist whose new details differentiate this Monsieur Hire from his predecessors. Rather than completely remaking Hire into too strange a character, Leconte admitted that "it was little oddities that interested me" (Raskin 9). Hence, Hire keeps white mice as pets in his tailor shop, unceremoniously places a dead one in a little box and drops it in the river by way of funeral, and finally liberates the mice next to train tracks when it looks as though he might leave with or without Alice. After an initial encounter with Alice, Hire gets a tattoo whose form the viewer never sees. Hire tells the story of an old woman who used to poison pigeons, then himself is shown feeding the birds. The oddities of Monsieur Hire, rarely public, pile up.[13] Such details seemingly

attain their ultimate signification as a function of their capacity to perform differentiation in the process of remaking itself.

The resistant ambiguity on which *Monsieur Hire* is built reveals a
final shift in the triangulated relationship it maintains with its predecessors. While Simenon's novel verged on the political and Duvivier's film
wholly participated in the political landscape of postwar France, the political message of *Monsieur Hire* is found precisely in its absence. As Stanley
Kauffmann perceptively remarked "Leconte . . . puts before us plaque
after plaque of mystery, almost like evidence of the unknowable" (27).
Monsieur Hire's refusal to settle on a genre, to specifically establish setting,
to attempt to answer the questions it asks, or even to outline agency in
the death of the main character, justifies its classification as a post-mod-
ern remake in which a defiant indeterminacy provides the falsely indelible signatures of endlessly unresolved revisions.

NOTES

1. All translations, unless otherwise indicated, are the author's.

2. Another remake of this Lumière brothers' film, Al Razutis's experimental short *Lumière's Train* (1980) has an equally radical ending which cross-
cuts, in positive and negative prints, between a loop of the train arriving from the
Lumière brothers' film and scenes of a wreck from Abel Gance's *La Roue*
(1921–23). Both instances—with a train always in the process of but never arriving or in a destructively preempted arrival—economically subvert the closure of
the Lumière brothers' film.

3. Duvivier himself was no stranger to the remake. He sonorized his
1928 film *Au Bonheur des Dames* in 1930 and completed the sound remake of
his 1925 *Poil de carotte* in 1931. Duvivier was contracted in 1938 by M-G-M
to remake his internationally successful *Pépé le Moko* (1936). Becoming disillu-
sioned with Hollywood and the studio system after completing *The Great Waltz*
(1938), Duvivier returned to France while John Cromwell ultimately directed
the decidedly weak remake of *Pépé le Moko* (*Algiers*, 1938), with Charles Boyer
"who dreamed of playing screen heavies but was much too gentlemanly to fill
Gabin's shoes," remade again by John Berry in 1948 as the musical *Casbah* with
Yvonne De Carlo and Tony Martin who "carries Pépé's crooner tendencies to
ludicrous extremes" (Martin 59). Interestingly enough, the remaking strategies
behind *Algiers* and *Casbah* insist upon citing the fundamentally foreign nature
of the original by, in the first instance, casting Hollywood's most successful
French actor of the 1930s and, in the second instance, assembling a cast that

included the quintessentially "international" actor of 1940s American cinema, Peter Lorre, in the role of Slimane, the indigenous Algerian inspector. Duvivier's *Le Golem* (1936) referred to two previous film versions of the story, Paul Wegener and Henrik Galeen's *Die Golem* (1914) and Paul Wegener's expressionist remake of that film *Die Golem: Wie er in die Welt kam* (1920). His 1939 film *La Charrette fantôme* remade Victor Sjöström's silent classic *The Ghostly Carriage* (1920). His Hollywood film *Lydia* (1941) is a liberal remake of his own *Un Carnet de bal* (1937).

4. From the mid-nineteenth century to the present, the Parisian suburbs, in contradistinction to their American counterparts, have retained in the French popular imagination the reputation as dangerous, transgressive, and ultimately discursively indeterminate places inhabited by the working and marginal classes. In *Les Fiançailles de M. Hire*, the suburban landscape of Villejuif is punctuated by unfinished roads, empty lots, and work yards, all of which contribute to a popularly recognizable urban code of representation whose spatial discontinuity opposes itself to the ordered space of post-Haussmannian Paris. For more on the problematics of suburban imagery in French culture, see Forrest and Koos.

5. Lucille Frackman Becker sees in Simenon's use of the foreigner an attempt to "symbolize man's fundamental solitude and alienation" (62). The same sort of character, a falsely accused Jew who is implicated by neighborhood rumors and gossip, would again be the basis of Simenon's novel *Le Petit Homme d'Arkangelsk* (1956). For more on this novel as it relates to *Les Fiançailles de M. Hire* as well as other Jewish characters in Simenon's works, see Becker 62–64.

6. This image of Hire, it should be noted, participates in the Jewish subtext of the Hire character. However, beyond isolated moments that associate Hire with Jews (the opening images noted above, the setting of Villejuif, and his supposed dark powers), Duvivier and Spaak resist a further development of this point. Unlike Simenon's Hire, a simple mention without commentary is made at the outset to the police that Hire's name was originally Hirovitch and is never revisited.

7. It is not by chance that Alfred takes Alice, shaken and perhaps ready to divulge her secrets to the police inspector after witnessing the death of Hire, to ride the roller coaster. A dizzy, disoriented Alice will clearly remain in his power as a silent accomplice. The shot of the two in the roller coaster that goes around and around recalls the artists' party sequence of another film containing a troubled love triangle (including, coincidentally, the actor Michel Simon), Jean Renoir's *La Chienne* (1931). In that scene, Dédé successfully convinces Lulu to "paint" the portrait of a rich client after a similarly disorienting waltz, made that much more effective by Renoir's handheld camera shot.

8. Armes is correct in noting that Duvivier was "the chronicler of the anticipated failure of the Popular Front, not its committed celebrant" (99). For *La Belle Équipe*, Duvivier shot two different endings, an overtly pessimistic one in which Jean kills co-owner Charles out of jealousy over Gina and a more optimistic one in which the two friends resist Gina's ploy to separate them. *La Belle Équipe* was originally released in France with the first ending, the one that Duvivier preferred. Shortly after the release of the film to mediocre critical reception and a lukewarm box office reaction, the producers asked Duvivier and Spaak to reconsider the film's ending and insert the more optimistic one. The new version was shown to a group of movie theater owners who enthusiastically endorsed the new ending. Both endings were shown at a preview at the Le Dôme movie theater in the Parisian suburb of La Varenne. The Saturday night moviegoers overwhelmingly preferred the optimistic ending, and *La Belle Équipe* was re-released in France with that ending. The other ending was used for the international distribution of the film.

9. Another aspect of the inversion of the figure of a Popular Front collectivity in *Panique* is related to the casting of Viviane Romance in the role of Alice. Romance had gained stardom in the 1930s with a series of what were called "bitch" roles, the most notable being in Duvivier's own *La Belle Équipe* and Augusto Génia's *Naples au baiser du feu* (1937). During World War II and the German Occupation of France, however, her roles, with the notable exception of the main character in Christian-Jacque's *Carmen* (1943), departed greatly from the prewar years as she portrayed several sympathetic melodramatic heroines. Duvivier's casting of Romance as the duplicitous and seductive Alice in *Panique* ironically echoes his preferred ending to *La Belle Équipe* in which the collective effort is destroyed by the plottings of the "bitch" Gina who is an outsider and a threat to the social order. In *Panique*, however, the plottings of the seductress are not only successful, they are supported by the community as Hire is menaced by the mob. In this way, through the image of Viviane Romance whose prewar roles an audience of 1946 would most certainly remember, Duvivier adds another dimension to his remaking of mid-1930s Popular Front sensibilities.

10. The differing deaths in *Le Jour se lève* and *Panique* also have ramifications for the ultimate reception of each character. François, much like Pépé le Moko at the end of Duvivier's film, through his gesture of self-punishment or definitive escape, incarnates the nobility of the antihero. Hire, on the other hand, all too human, can no longer hold on to the drainpipe and falls to his somewhat unextraordinary death. Rooftops are important sites in Duvivier's films during this period and, unlike those in the films of René Clair which participate in an urban carnivalesque, are often associated with death. In *La Belle Équipe*, the main characters who have entered into a collective venture and are renovating a suburban *guinguette* with lottery winnings, must climb onto the roof and lay on the

loose tiles during a violent rainstorm in order to save their efforts from destruction. Later, shortly before the *guinguette* "Chez Nous" opens, Raymond plants a French flag on the roof proclaiming to those assembled below that it is the "workers' flag." The accordion music down below starts up again, and Raymond, losing his footing while dancing on the rooftop, falls to his death. The images in *Panique* of Hire on the rooftop are further overdetermined by the series of shots that lead to Georges's death in Duvivier's *La Charrette fantôme* (1939). In that film, Georges, who has led a less than exemplary adult life, hears the grinding wheels of the grim reaper's phantom chariot, climbs out onto the roof and, after having slipped down to the gutter pipes, waits in a horrified silence for death to carry him away.

11. The chase and ultimate death of Hire in *Panique*, with the seeming comic detail of Hire moving through the apartment of a surprised elderly couple, indirectly alludes to the similar hybridly generic sequence in Roberto Rossellini's neorealist classic *Rome, Open City*, wherein the nazis raid the apartment building while the priest, after having rescued the bomb-throwing youngster, has to knock out an old man with a frying pan so the gestapo will believe he is administering last rights when they arrive. This sequence ends much more abruptly as Pina, while chasing after the paddywagon carrying away her fiancé Francesco, is shot by the nazis in full view of the assembled residents of the building. Interestingly enough, the beginning of Rossellini's film, in the German commandant's speech on the policing of Rome while looking at a map of the city divided into sectors, is an explicit reference to the description of the Casbah at the beginning of Duvivier's *Pépé le Moko*.

12. The contemporary French suburb continues to be a powerful figure of transgressive potential in the French cultural imagination, yet the constituent elements of that figure have markedly changed since Duvivier and Simenon's works. As represented in a number of recent films like Mathieu Kassovitz's *La Haine* (1995), Thomas Gilou's *Raï* (1995), Medhi Charef's *Le Thé au harem d'Archimède* (1985), Malik Chibane's *Hexagone* (1994), and Jean-François Richet's *Etat des lieux* (1995) and *Ma 6-T va crack-er* (1997), the contemporary French suburb is perceived as a series of HLM complexes populated by an immigrant underclass whose disenfranchised youth are seen as instigators of the violence and riots that regularly break out there. Given this latest chapter in French suburban imagery, Leconte's decision to relocate Hire to a more innocuous urban setting corresponding to his obvious middle-class status seems entirely justified.

13. It should be noted that the other main characters of *Monsieur Hire* exhibit their own patterns of eccentricity, from Alice who attempts to seduce Hire with a bag of tomatoes to the police inspector whose interest in the murdered Pierrette perversely surpasses professional curiosity.

WORKS CITED

Armes, Roy. *French Cinema*. London: Secker & Warburg, 1985.

Baillard, Pierre. *L'Age classique du cinéma français; du cinéma parlant à la Nouvelle Vague*. Paris: Flammarion, 1995.

Baudrillard, Jean. *Cool Memories*. Trans. Chris Turner. London: Verso, 1990.

Becker, Lucille Frackman. *Georges Simenon*. Boston: Twayne, 1977.

Beylie, Claude. "Les Trois visages de Monsieur Hire." *L'Avant-Scène du Cinéma* 390–91 (1990): 4.

Beylie, Claude and Jacques Pinturault. "Julien Duvivier, un grand professionnel." *L'Avant-Scène du Cinéma* 390–91 (1990): 78–79.

Chirat, Raymond. *Julien Duvivier*. Paris: Premier Plan, n.d.

Fernandez, Carmen. "A propos du découpage." *L'Avant-Scène du Cinéma* 390–91 (1990): 9–10.

Forrest, Jennifer. "Paris *à Rebours*: Where Huysmans Put the *Faux* in *Faubourg*." *South Atlantic Review* 62 (1997): 10–28.

Gauteur, Claude. "Du côté de chez Simenon." *L'Avant-Scène du Cinéma* 390–91 (1990): 5.

Haskell, Molly. "Room With a View." *Film Comment* 26 (1990): 22–24.

Kauffmann, Stanley. "Monsieur Hire." *New Republic* 23 April 1990: 26–27.

Koos, Leonard R. "Terrains Vagues: Writing the Fin de Siècle Suburb." *Images of the City in Nineteenth-Century France*. Ed. John West-Sooby. Adelaide: Boombana Publications, 1998. 201–11.

Kundera, Milan. *Jacques and His Master*. Trans. Michael Henry Heim. New York: Harper & Row, 1985.

Marnham, Patrick. *The Man Who Wasn't Maigret: A Portrait of Georges Simenon*. New York: Farrar, Strauss and Giroux, 1992.

Martin, John W. *The Golden Age of French Cinema, 1929–1939*. Boston: Twayne, 1983.

Phillips, Julie. "Strange Bedfellows." *Village Voice* 24 April 1990: 66.

Raskin, Richard. "Sur *Monsieur Hire*; Un entretien avec Patrice Leconte." *(Pre)publications* 150 (1995): 3–18.

Sartre, Jean-Paul. *Anti-Semite and Jew*. Trans. Georges J. Becker. New York: Schocken Books, 1948.

———. "Qu'est-ce qu'un collaborateur?" *Situations III*. Paris: Gallimard, 1949: 43–61.

Simenon, Georges. *Les Fiançailles de M. Hire*. Paris: Arthème Fayard, 1960.

CHAPTER NINE

Twice Two:
The Fly *and* Invasion of
the Body Snatchers

MARTY ROTH

> If, then, artists currently labelled postmodernist have sought to
> challenge the modernist emphasis on originality by privileging
> the notion of the copy . . . it is not just because they come after
> modernism, but rather because they have sought to recover the
> repressed half of the binary opposition original/copy which has
> been behind modernist discourse all along.
>
> —Michael Messmer (41)

In postmodern aesthetics, the work of art has been recast as an item in a
series of endless remakes: the original and unique work of art has been
replaced by a tarnished and overwritten work of culture. Hollywood,
however, has always been a production company in the grip of a repetition compulsion: its work has generally been a copy of some previous
stage of film story. Although there may have been a literal starting point
to these sequences, an "original" would have had to exist outside the film
system, since it would have belonged to the province of Literature which

alone acknowledges originality. Opposition between the idea of an original and a copy is nicely played out by the four films that will be the subject of this chapter: *The Fly* ("Fly" [1958], *Fly* [1986]) and *Invasion of the Body Snatchers* ("Invasion" [1956], *Invasion* [1978]) either as earlier and later pairs or as paradigm sets.[1] This collection consists of a pair of 1950s science-fiction horror films remade in the "new wave" of horror film in the 1980s, one by a generically eclectic filmmaker, Philip Kaufman (who tries to make every film new, thus, original), and the other by a horror director, David Cronenberg (who repeats familiar stories and formulas). New wave horror film included literal recycling of films from the 1950s: not only *Fly* and *Invasion*, but also *The Thing* (John Carpenter, 1982) and *The Blob* (Chuck Russell, 1988). This movement also showed symptoms of an extremely infectious serial virus which led to five versions of *Halloween* and *Nightmare on Elm Street*, and nine *Friday the 13th*s.

This chapter is not so much taken up with a pair of originals and their remakes as with two horror paradigms which act out between them the logic of the original and the remake, singularity and repetition—one and two. The logic of the remake finds generic rather than chronological expression here. Both "Fly" and *Fly* are concerned with the construction of unique visual monstrosity; both "Invasion" and *Invasion* with endless duplication. In the second part of this chapter, I read only "Invasion," since part of the originality of *The Fly* is that it does not lend itself to allegory (a sinister form of duplication).[2] Don Siegel's "Invasion of the Body Snatchers," on the other hand, spawns allegorical translations just as the pods which it encloses infect ever-increasing terrain by duplication.

Horror fiction often begins by making a move from one to two (from the number of the human to the number of the uncanny or demonic). The opening of Poe's "William Wilson," for example, tells us how uniquely depraved the narrator is, but the first thing we discover when we get into the story is that there are two of him. Henry James's *Turn of the Screw* opens on Christmas eve with a story that holds its audience breathless. Afterward, there is a pause and finally someone says that it "was the only case he had met in which such a visitation had fallen on a child." The storyteller replies to this assertion of uniqueness and originality, by saying "two" twice: "it's not the first occurrence of its charming kind that I know to have involved a child. If the child gives the effect of another turn of the screw, what do you say to *two* children" (7).

The two filmic movements of horror films from the 1950s and 1980s are not easily differentiable, unlike the clear distinction between "classic" and "contemporary" that Robin Wood lays out in his "Introduction to the American Horror Film." Contemporary horror film is constituted by the following elements: "the 'double' motif (that is, the hero and monster are doubles), the definition of the 'monster' as the product of the normality it threatens (the return of what normality represses), and the location of horror at the heart of the bourgeois-capitalist family" (20). The science-fiction horror film of the 1950s operated more or less as a halfway stage in this schema. The two films considered here also divide that historical trajectory between them: "Fly" looks back to classic horror film—it starts up like one as we track in to dark factory grounds until the camera is startled by a howling cat—while "Invasion" looks forward to contemporary horror. In "Fly," the horror is still exotic, closer to the Frankenstein monster than to Norman Bates, while in "Invasion" the monstrous is all too ordinary.

Writing on Jean Baudrillard, Kate Linker has said that "central to postmodern productions . . . is the decline of *affect*, the passionate investment of anxiety that characterized the Modernist period, and its replacement by *effect*, the alternately jarring and fascinating lures of technological incandescence" (46). Another difference between classic and contemporary horror cycles (which films of the 1950s do share) is a difference in effect: in the history of special effects, of spectacle. Both of the later films initiate a move to the postmodern city as the place where technique is continuously on display. It is almost as if the second versions were made to index and display new potentials of the industry, as Steve Neale has written of the science-fiction film: "from a certain perspective, the narrative functions largely to motivate the production of special effects, climaxing either with the 'best' of those effects (*Close Encounters of the Third Kind*) or with the point at which they are multiplied with greatest intensity (*Star Wars*)" (31).[3] Spectacle is no small matter here since it is a constituting principle of the horror and science-fiction genres, so that contemporary horror film brings genre into the condition of musical comedy: for the first time, films divide themselves between a mode of voyeuristic narrative and one of specular fetishism; and like musical comedy, they directly display the two modes of cinema, diegesis and spectacle.

The technological sophistication that divides recent from earlier horror spectacle indexes an aesthetic opposition between, putting it simply, *looking away* and *looking at*, disgust and fascination.[4] In the earlier periods, horror belonged to what one was forbidden or unable to look at: the aesthetic of the horrible matched the inability of the films to exhibit

228

FIGURE 9.1. Hiding the horrible transformation under a hood in Kurt Neumann's *The Fly* (1958). Courtesy of the Museum of Modern Art, Film Stills Archive.

229

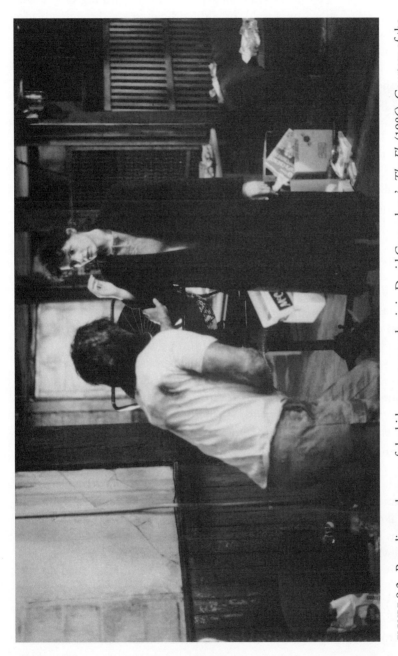

FIGURE 9.2. Revealing each stage of the hideous metamorphosis in David Cronenberg's *The Fly* (1986). Courtesy of the Museum of Modern Art, Film Stills Archive.

their horrors. The camera often looked away for us, turning to a substitute image (shadows on a wall), or eliding the moment through a blackout. In Vincente Minnelli's *The Bad and the Beautiful*, the young director and producer (Barry Sullivan and Kirk Douglas) have been assigned to direct a B movie, "The Doom of the Cat Men." The budget is inadequate and the costumes are ludicrous, but Douglas has an idea: "When an audience pays to see a picture like this, what do they pay for?" "To get the pants scared off them." "And what scares the human race more than any other thing?" Douglas walks over and turns off the lights. By contrast, in films like *Fly* or *Alien* (Ridley Scott, 1979) and *Aliens* (James Cameron, 1986), the horrified/fascinated gaze is compelled to pay attention; we are not allowed to look away. As Philip Brophy writes, "John Carpenter's graphically 'realistic' suspense horror [*The Thing*, 1982] is a world away from Howard Hawks's B-Grade classic, showing *everything* that the original only alluded to" (10). In "Fly," André (Al Hedison) wears a head mask and tells Helene (Patricia Owens) not to look at him; in *Fly*, almost all we seem to do is look at Seth Brundle (Jeff Goldblum).[5]

As paradigm sets, *The Fly* and *Invasion of the Body Snatchers* also contrast as looking at and looking away. The first set glories in extreme visual monstrosity while there is no visible monstrosity in the second: one set of films offers us everything (monstrosity, difference), the other nothing to see (sameness, ourselves).[6] In this way, these two stories recapitulate the original opposition between *Frankenstein* and *Dracula* (a repulsive monster and a seemly gentleman) that was put in place at the founding moment of horror film. The two dispositions of the gaze reprise conflicting versions of the cinematic connection, between a Barthean fascination (looking at) and a Metzian disavowal (looking at and looking away).[7]

Another difference between the two cycles is that the second is aware that it is looking again. The later films express their connection to earlier horror film as pastiche. If old discarded gods tend to return as buffoons, remakes of horror film often return as comedy. In *Fly*, Jeff Goldblum performs manic stand-up comedy: "He does broken-rhythm double-takes on his own dialogue," Pauline Kael reports (126). His character, Seth Brundle, is both manic and maniac, resembling the infantilized "mad doctor" type played by Christopher Lloyd in *Back to the Future* (Robert Zemeckis, 1985). In *Invasion*, the move is toward screwball comedy. Kaufman's film bears a remarkable resemblance to Howard Hawks's *His Girl Friday* (1940): the dialog is fast-paced and delivered in a soft but staccato screwball fashion. The party scene, for example, is directed at screwball pace, with characters placed so as to look cramped in the frame. The proliferation of telephone activity in the film may also be an homage to *His Girl Friday*. *Invasion* also engages the great screwball theme, confusion of identity, which unfolds in passages of scatterbrained incoherence.[8]

The four films considered here play out the patterns of original and copy, (of one and two), both as two sequences and as two paradigm sets. While the two sequences, "Fly"/*Fly* and "Invasion"/*Invasion*, consist of an original and a remake, the first set details the slow and careful production of uniqueness while the second is devoted to an an extensive process of duplication. As for the remakes themselves: *Fly* is an original film that has almost nothing in common with the 1958 film of that name, while *Invasion* is a very close copy of its original.

As a fiction, *The Fly* is exactly what it appears to be, while *Invasion of the Body Snatchers* is split as to mode, presenting itself either as a marvellous invasion from outer space or an uncanny paranoid delusion: these two alternatives are regularly debated across the face of the fiction in rapid shifts from absolute disbelief—"No one could possibly impersonate Ira without you and me seeing a million little differences, think about it, and then you'll know that the trouble is inside you"—to paranoid conviction—"Don't just sit there measuring me for a straitjacket, do something, get on the phone."

The relationship of one to two works the other way as well: the theme of *Invasion of the Body Snatchers* is identity, the theme of *The Fly* is otherness. In the first, horror is the ambiguity of identity—

> "Have you talked to him?" Miles asks a patient. "It's him, it's your uncle Ira."
>
> "He is not."
>
> "How's he different?"
>
> "That's just it, there is no difference you can actually see. He looks, sounds, acts and remembers like Ira."
>
> "Then he is your uncle Ira."

—while horror, in *The Fly*, is a function of inconceivable otherness. In *Invasion*, Elizabeth has the conviction that Jeffrey is not Jeffrey—"On the outside he's still Jeffrey, but on the inside, something is different. Something is missing, emotion, feeling. He's not the same person." Identity is so fragile here that to be separated from someone even for a moment is to run the risk of having them completely transformed.

Both the originals and remakes invest heavily in doubling, very often the doubling of an original and a remake. In *The Fly*, an object is disintegrated and reconstituted in another place; when Seth comes out of the teleportation process, he asks, "Is it live or is it Memorex?" At the scene of André's murder, the police see the dial of the factory press set at two: "It doesn't make sense. Whoever did this . . . did it twice!" Another scene of multiplication gives the viewer a shot of Helene fragmented into fifteen partial images in imitation of a fly's vision.

Invasion of the Body Snatchers is very much about doubling, about a human population taken over by vegetable simulacra. David Kibner (Leonard Nimoy), the leader of the pods, is first seen at a book-signing party where multiple copies of a smiling publicity poster cover the walls. In both films, everyone has an uncanny double, and it is not clear (on the upslope of a crisis) that it is possible to distinguish between them. The lack of distance between the original and the copy is scandalous and apocalyptic. Even if there is a difference between the two, humans learn to override it (for the pods, that is their destiny): "They can be fooled. Don't show emotions. Hide your feelings."

Invasion of the Body Snatchers and *The Fly* are not only concerned with doubling but also exchange. Pods exchange with their hosts. Teleportation is a mirror exchange (a choice theme of horror film since *The Student of Prague* in 1913). Objects are reconstituted as they travel from one pod to another, but in one instance the trademark on the "second" ashtray is written backward. In general, the movement from "Invasion" to *Invasion* is a movement from opposition to exchange, a double site where critics first talked about the difference between us and them and later pointed out the irony of how similar things were on either side of the human/pod divide (Sarris 43; Westerbeck 52).

André and the fly engage in a most literal exchange: he has the fly's head and left claw while the fly has his hand and head. The two brothers, André and François (Vincent Price) split the diegetic territory so that André is present only in flashback, François only in the present. In *Fly* Seth's opposite number has the same initials—Seth Brundle and Stathis Borans (John Getz)—and a wittily inverse relationship to him: the film opposes a hero in increasingly revolting deliquescence to an attractive villain who looks like a model for *GQ*. However, Ronnie (Geena Davis), the woman who is desired by both hero and villain, has no aversive reaction to Seth—she looks at him, hugs him, and treats him as if there were no visual or tactile disturbance, while recoiling from his handsome rival.

The paranoia of *Invasion of the Body Snatchers* invades and alienates the viewer as well. Once we accept the idea that pods take over people, we wait for "pod people" to appear, and any behavior that seems odd or sluggish becomes a confirmation of their presence. Everyone we meet and much that we see is mantled in this possibility, a shot of Matthew just staring, for example. Anyone who doesn't have the crisp edge of attention on his or her face might be a pod. To stare is to take the risk of being identified as one of those nonhuman things, but this is a story that should induce staring. At the autograph party, the allegations of alien takeover and Kibner's patter make many of the guests uncomfortably resemble pods.

The Fly, as Thomas Doherty writes, resists translation—"*Videodrome* is about watching TV and what it might do to you. We all watch the box. *The Brood* is about outer-limits therapy and child abuse and many of us have had experience of both. *The Fly* is about mutating into an insect and there's just no connection"—while *Invasion of the Body Snatchers* insistently reproduces allegorical readings that engage a wide variety of political and social contexts—the entire range of modernism, I am tempted to say (41; see Kael 127).[9]

The first and most engaging identification of this fiction of pod exchange was as a political allegory of the Cold War, and this originally promised to lend a seriousness to popular film, beyond even that of literature which had been estranged from politics since the turn of the century. The pods have been variously understood to refer to both the threat of international communism and the threat of nativist movements that attempt to contain international communism, as well as the threat of mass society and consumer capitalism. That is the short list; a full inventory is even more inclusive: "On deeper analysis, the film also had cogent things to say about the destructive nature of short-sighted, provincial, small-town life; about McCarthyism; about the kind of creeping paranoia induced in common man by inconceivables like the rampant power of the Atom and Hydrogen bombs . . . about the fear of communism . . . as an encroaching, fierce, godless, world villain . . . about the American doctor" (Bartholemew 52).

Ernesto Laura writes that it was "natural to see the pods as standing for the idea of communism which gradually takes possession of a normal person, leaving him outwardly unchanged but transformed within," or as Miles Bennell (Kevin McCarthy) cries, "They're taking us over cell by cell" (183–84). They work while America sleeps so that America will continue to sleep: Miles tells Becky (Dana Wynter), "We can't close our eyes all night. Or we may wake up changed." The pods promise their victims freedom from fear, anxiety, and desire. The pod community is another Cold War fantasy fleshed out in domestic imagery: fade in to a happy American town, friendly neighbors, homey activities; pan out to peripheries of barbed wire and signs in Russian.

The lobotomized behavior produced by the pod exchange could be referred not only to a communist takeover of the mind but, more specifically, to the brainwashing of American prisoners of war in Korea (Sayre 184). "Invasion" was set in August 1953, immediately after the Korean armistice, when American newspapers were full of incredulous reports about the "turncoats" who chose Communism over home (Johnson 6).

On the face of it, however, "Invasion" is far from an internationalist story. It tells of an American small town that turns on its only two cosmopolitan members (characters who are inflected by professionalism, college education, and divorce) and pursues them with pent-up hysteria. The film "allowed the local druggist, the PTA chairwoman, or the cop on the beat to become the enemy" (Biskind 140). To further confuse the identification between this and the McCarthy witch hunts the film's male lead had the same surname as the Wisconsin senator.

The pod invaders, then, have been identified both as essentially un-American and essentially American, but this opposition can easily turn into an exchange if we recognize "Communism" to be a production of McCarthyism (LaValley 200, Steffen-Fluhr 208). Such an equivalence is built into the construction of the fantasy: the film has to use the same actors for aliens and Americans; "we" and "they" look alike, total otherness is represented by absolute similarity.

Made twenty-one years after "Invasion," Don Siegel's *Telefon* can be read as his commentary on the earlier film and its crossed allegorical readings. It presents an America dotted with communist sleepers, but here the "sleeper" is the ordinary, "decent" American: "We drilled them in every detail of American life. They believed they were the

Americans they replaced." The "American" turns into the totalitarian zombie when a fixed signal is given; then he or she instantly moves to perform preassigned duties, ignoring what they had been doing the moment before—a household task or a family squabble. The signal, a line from a Robert Frost poem, "miles to go before I sleep," is a sly reference to "Invasion."

On the cultural front, the threat of alien takeover in "Invasion" also referred to familiar humanist fears of the 1950s, fears of mass culture and conformism that were emerging, so it was believed, from the predictable degeneration of social relations in a capitalist democracy. Morris Dickstein has written that the zombification in the film is "surely a warning about conformity and loss of identity in a monolithic society. The monsters are no more than our ordinary, timid, complacent selves. People 'turn' just by letting go, falling asleep—they can be caught napping as their freedom ebbs away" (74). The pod exchange, according to Michael Rogin, refers to the loss of the self to its manufactured double (262).

Mass culture posed the same threat to American virtue as communism did: mass culture was the homegrown equivalent of international communism. In 1952, *The Partisan Review* canvassed American intellectuals on the dangers posed by Stalin's Communist state, and most of those interviewed agreed with the editors that "democratic values" "represent the only immediate alternative as long as Russian totalitarianism threatens world domination." Unfortunately, America had by this time been taken over from within: it was now a "nation where at the same time cultural freedom is promised and mass culture produced" (Arvin 285). And the mass culture referred to was fictionalized as a (Communist) horde: a "mass culture which will overrun intellectual and aesthetic values traditional to Western civilization" (Arvin 286). Louis Kronenberger made the analogy explicit: "in the exact same way that we oppose regimentation of thought on political grounds, we must oppose regimentation of taste on cultural ones" (445).[10] From a humanist perspective, both communism and mass culture represented a drugging of the American mind.

References in "Invasion" like the following—"No pain. Suddenly; while you're asleep, they'll absorb your minds, your memories, and you're reborn into an untroubled world"—also connected easily with the more literal drugging of America in the 1950s via the mass marketing of tranquilizers: the third truck dispatched by the public address system is sent to Milltown. The numbing of American virtue in *Telefon* is more a function of drugs than ideology, and two years after "Invasion" Don Siegel made one of the first "drug epidemic" films, *The Lineup*, which evokes the paranoid fiction of a ubiquitous criminal conspiracy that smuggles drugs into America inside curios bought by unsuspecting travellers in the Far East. The specter that is raised by this scenario, a totally turned-on America, is a replication of the pod conspiracy.

"Invasion" is set in small-town America, and it evokes the myth of the American heartland in continuity with a bucolic past. Returning from a convention in the big city, Miles says, "At first glance everything looked the same. It wasn't. Something had taken over the town"—a labyrinthine statement since that "something" reproduces a new and horrifying form of sameness. In the culture of the 1950s, the small town was reinterpreted as the place where everyone is ruthlessly the same, where we discover that sameness is not the same—not continuity or tradition but a form of mechanized death.

Invasion has also been the site of sociological reading, stimulated to some extent by the need to differentiate the second film from the first. It has been read as a fable about contemporary bureacracy, law and order conservatism, and the apathy of the 1980s. The pod spokesman tries to connect it with the breakdown of the nuclear family—"Don't you see, it's people stepping in and out of relationships too fast because they don't want the responsibility. The whole family unit is shot to hell"—the concerns about environmental contamination, homosexuality, and right-to-life activity (Sarris 46).

If *Invasion of the Body Snatchers* released an epidemic of interpretation and allegorization, *The Fly* was relatively dormant symbolically, but it too hinted of extensions. If the first paradigm set proliferated politically and socially, the second (particularly *Fly*) was sexually resonant. In his "virginal" state, Seth is at an impasse with his project of teleportation because, as the script carefully tells us, he is unable to understand "flesh." After making love with Ronnie, however, he finds that he can transport living matter. The darker side of sexual entanglement changes him even more radically: in a fit of jealousy, he drunkenly transports himself one night and fails to notice a fly in the machine. His transmuted self has enormous reserves of energy: he becomes sexually aggressive and wants to fuck all the time—"Oh God," Ronnie cries, "how can you keep going, you can't have any fluid left in your body." Critics have read *Fly* as an allegory of both the sexual revolution—"These transporting chambers bear an intriguing resemblance to Reich's orgone boxes; and indeed a Reichian sense of the energizing properties of sex echoes throughout the film" (Williamson 25)—and its aftermath, the AIDS epidemic.[11]

If the foregoing variations on story and meaning have any contributions to make or remake to a general theory of film practice, it is primarily that the relationship of the original and copy, the first and second, is a dialectical one. I may have begun by saying that the original is the province of literature, the remake of popular culture, but I meant that not as a statement of fact but of imaginary self-constitution, one of those wilful definitions that ignore the similarity between the high and low end of cultural production. The painterly tradition is much more given over to remake than film could ever sustain. In Nathaniel Hawthorne's *Marble Faun*, for example, the "Mephistopheles" of "Picture-Galleries" visits an American copyist residing in Rome and whispers in her ear how specious is the art of the "mighty Italian Masters," What "a terrible lack of variety in their subjects!"

> A quarter-part, probably, of any large collection of pictures, consists of Virgins and Infant Christs, repeated over and over again, in pretty much an identical spirit. . . . Half of the other pictures are Magdelens, Flights into Egypt, Crucifixions, Depositions from the Cross, Pietàs, Noli-me-tangeres, or the Sacrifice of Abraham . . . [while] the remainder of the gallery comprises mythological subjects, such as nude Venuses, Ledas, Graces, and, in short, a general apotheosis of nudity. (336–37)

NOTES

This is a reprint of an article originally published in *Discourse* 22.1 (2000): 103–16.

1. The four films consist of two pairs ("Fly"/"Invasion" and *Fly*/*Invasion*) and two paradigm sets ("Fly"/*Fly* and "Invasion"/*Invasion*).

2. A distinction that Leo Braudy makes in *Play It Again, Sam* is close to the one I make here (so perhaps this binary is common to the horror genre):

the various versions of *Dracula* . . . flirt with the question of fidelity to the original text, while the remaking of *Dr. Jekyll and Mr. Hyde* is less significant than its revision into so many different formats: the sharing of identities between a white man and a black man, an older woman and a younger woman, a human and an alien, to mention only a few. (331–32)

3. "The special effects [in *Invasion*]," Paul Petlowski wrote, "are remarkable. The scene when Elizabeth begins to crumble in Matthew's arms is a technical marvel, arguably the most convincing disintegration ever put on film" (71).

4. This may be putting it too simply. William Paul sees the aesthetic of disgust as a necessary condition for the genre to function at all:

Full vision of the monster is often anticlimactic to the extent that the horrible requires obliqueness in order to defy our powers of conceptualization. . . . *Alien* represents the most extreme version of this method since its monster keeps changing with every partial view we have of it, finally becoming both smaller and more humanoid as we achieve unobstructed vision. (370–71)

5. Even from the beginning, however, there had to be a "horror" payoff in these films. In "Fly" the image of the monster is displayed for a scandalous moment, and that "glimpse" was common to other 1950s films (such as *It Came From Outer Space* [Jack Arnold, 1953]). James Whale's *Frankenstein* (1931) presents a theatrically attractive monster to our sustained glance. At the beginning of the film, however, the unveiling of the monster is slow and involved. The assistant, Fritz, cringes from the monster's hand sticking out under the cover, and Henry tells him that there is "nothing to fear, no blood, no decay, just a few stitches" (referring to the principle of suture which stitches us into the film as well). Henry then pulls the cloth away, but the face underneath is bandaged. Shortly after, a knocking at the door interrupts the experiment, and they must again cover the body before they let anybody in, but they do it behind posts and equipment, so that we can't even see the cover-up.

6. This is not strictly true of *Invasion*. Kaufman borrows from George Romero to introduce a "living dead" quality into the culminating chase, and from Joe Dante to invest the pod people with a "howling" aura, but the point of the second film is still the undetectible substitution of monstrosity for humanity.

7. Writing on Robert Wise's *The Body Snatcher* (1985), J. P. Telotte makes the opposition between looking away and looking at a difference between literature and film, whereby literature withholds and film shows:

that almost tangible literary quality for which the Lewton films are justly esteemed has often made for a strangely *uncinematic* evaluation of them.

They have been praised as 'ambitiously literary,' and 'poetic,' and have been lauded *for what they did not show*, as if their success were largely due to Lewton's prizing literary techniques over established film practices. Knowing too that grotesque visions, given their initial shock effect, cannot stand sustained scrutiny—by the camera or the human eye—that they tend to become "something to laugh at," Lewton altered that final horrific scene as well. (26–27)

8. Self-reflexivity is also expressed by condensation—if horror films are split among scientist, monster and woman (i.e., *Frankenstein*), in *Fly* the first two are clearly merged. According to Judith Williamson, *Fly* tells the

> Frankenstein story with a twist, for Brundle is both inventor and monster; the two roles are elided, neatly bringing back together the two sides of "human nature" that gothic literature split. Where Mary Shelley had the scientist recoiling in horror from his invention, Brundle becomes remarkably exhilarated, flinging himself into his disease with great humor, bottling the parts that fall off, video-taping his eating habits for future science lessons. (25).

9. This is another way of indexing the humanism of *The Invasion of the Body Snatchers* and the postmodernism of *The Fly*

10. See also Arvin, 287 and Niebuhr, 302–03.

11. Nothing in *Invasion of the Body Snatchers* deforms or threatens the integrity of the body; the threat is a perfectly formed human being. In *The Fly*, there is not only the mutation of the surface and structure of the body but also the loss of individual body parts. When Seth bites absentmindedly at a fingernail, it comes off in his mouth. He presses his finger and it squirts fluid. Toward the end, Ronnie pushes at the lower half of Seth's face as he pulls her into the pod— and it falls off. In his bathroom cabinet, he preserves his lost parts in jars: "artifacts of a bygone era. Brindle Museum of Natural History."

WORKS CITED

Appelbaum, Ralph. "Are we pods . . . yet?" *Films and Filming* 25 (1979): 10–16.

Arvin, Newton. "Our Country and Our Culture." 186–288.

Bartholemew, David. "*Invasion of the Body Snatchers.*" *Cineaste* 10.1 (1979–80): 52–54.

Biskind, Peter. *Seeing Is Believing.* New York: Pantheon, 1983.

Braudy, Leo. "Afterword: Rethinking Remakes." *Play It Again, Sam: Retakes on Remakes.* Ed. Andrew Horton and Stuart Y. McDougal. Berkeley: U of California P, 1998. 327–34.

Brophy, Philip. "Horrality—The Textuality of Contemporary Horror Films." *Screen* 27.1 (1986): 2–13.

Dickstein, Morris. "The Aesthetics of Fright." *Planks of Reason: Essays on the Horror Film.* Ed. Barry Grant. Metuchen: Scarecrow P, 1984. 65–80.

Doherty, Thomas. "The Fly." *Film Quarterly* 40.3 (1987): 38–41.

Hawthorne, Nathaniel. *The Marble Faun.* New York: Penguin, 1990.

Herrmann, Claudine, and Nicholas Kostis. "'The Fall of the House of Usher' or The Art of Duplication." *Substance* 26 (1980): 36–42.

James, Henry. *The Turn of the Screw and Other Stories.* New York: Penguin, 1983.

Johnson, Glen M. "'We'd fight . . . we had to': 'The Body Snatchers' as Novel and Film." *The Journal of Popular Culture* 13.1 (1979): 5–16.

Kael, Pauline. "The Current Cinema: Bodies." *New Yorker* 6 Oct. 1986: 126–30.

Kaminsky, Stuart M. "Don Siegel on the Pod Society." LaValley 153–57.

Kronenberger, Louis. "Our Country and Our Culture." 439–45.

Laura, Ernesto G. *"Invasion of the Body Snatchers."* LaValley 182–83.

LaValley, Al, ed. *Invasion of the Body Snatchers: Don Siegel, director.* New Brunswick: Rutgers UP, 1989.

Linker, Kate. "From Imitation to the Copy to Just Effect: On Reading Jean Baudrillard." *Artforum* 22.8 (1984): 41–53.

Messmer, Michael. "Making Sense of/with Postmodernism." *Soundings* 68.3 (1985): 404–26.

Neale, Steven. *Genre.* London: British Film Institute, 1980.

Niebuhr, Reinhold. "Our Country and Our Culture." 301–03.

"Our Country and Our Culture." *Partisan Review* 19.3–4 (1952).

Paul, William. *Laughing Screaming: Modern Hollywood Horror and Comedy.* New York: Columbia UP, 1994.

Petlowski, Paul. *"Invasion of the Body Snatchers."* *Cinefantastique* 8.2–3 (1979): 71.

Rogin, Michael Paul. "Kiss Me Deadly: Communism, Motherhood and Cold War Movies." *Ronald Reagan, the Movie and Other Episodes in Political Demonology*. Berkeley: U of California P, 1987. 236–57.

Sarris, Andrew. "Peas in a Pod." *Village Voice* 25 Dec. 1978: 46.

Sayre, Nora. *Running Time: Films of the Cold War*. New York: Dial, 1982.

Steffen-Fluhr, Nancy. "Women and the Inner Game of Don Siegel's *Invasion of the Body Snatchers*." LaValley 206–21.

Telotte, J. P. "A Photogenic Horror: Lewton Does Robert Louis Stevenson." *Literature/Film Quarterly* 10.1 (1982): 25–37.

Westerbeck. Colin L., Jr. "Screen: Cloning Around." *Commonweal* 2 Feb. 1979: 52–4.

Williamson, Judith. "Cinema: In Dreams." *New Statesman* 11 Dec. 1987: 24–25.

Wood, Robin. "Introduction to the American Horror Film." *American Nightmare: Essays on the Horror Film*. Toronto: Festival of Festivals, 1979. 1–36.

CHAPTER TEN

Three Takes On Motherhood, Masculinity, and Marriage: Serreau's Trois Hommes et un couffin, Nimoy's Remake, and Ardolino's Sequel

CAROLYN A. DURHAM

Although *Three Men and a Baby*, Leonard Nimoy's 1987 re-vision of Coline Serreau's *Trois Hommes et un couffin* (1985), clearly did not inaugurate the current trend of American remakes of French comedies, it did serve to focus the attention of film critics of both nationalities on the phenomenon. That the recurrent reflections of different reviewers (see, for example, Boujet, Canby, Mordore, and Pertié) all typically center on questions of cultural difference and specificity is hardly surprising; such concerns would appear to be inherent in the very concept of the "remake" as indicated by the bilingualism of the word itself. Moreover, despite parallel—and often contradictory—claims to the originary and original nature of their own cultural product, reviewers on both sides of the Atlantic reveal a similar awareness that one particularly key difference and/or specificity is at issue. Though each film had comparable commercial success in its country of conception, neither film was fully able to duplicate this audience appeal in the country of its model or copy.

However paradoxically, this situation would seem to reflect the simultaneous presence and absence of significant cross-cultural interests.

Yet, at the same time, Nimoy's and Serreau's films can also lay claim to another potentially important source of distinction that has remained persistently invisible in the popular press. Alone among contemporary Franco-American intercultural repetitions (cf. *L'Homme qui aimait les femmes/ The Man Who Loved Women; Cousin, Cousine/ Cousins; Les Fugitifs/ Three Fugitives; La Femme Nikita/ Point of No Return*), this one involved a directorial substitution that altered not only nationality but sex as well.[1] *Substitution* is indeed the appropriate term in this context, since Touchstone Studios initially hired Serreau, who both wrote and directed *Trois Hommes et un couffin*, to remake her own film as well. Subsequent to her withdrawal for "health reasons" shortly before shooting was scheduled to begin (Mancini 33), she was replaced by Nimoy, who directed *Three Men and a Baby* from a script that James Orr and Jim Cruickshank "based on" Serreau's original screenplay.[2] Thus, the failure to consider simultaneously the possible significance of gender and culture seems a somewhat curious oversight in this case, particularly since the importance of the former is also clearly encoded in the very titles of the two films.

Within the realm of academic criticism, however, I am neither the first nor the only person to view *Trois Hommes* and its remake as fertile ground on which to explore gender and culture. In contemporaneous issues of *Contemporary French Civilization* and *Camera Obscura*, Raymonde Carroll and Tania Modleski use the respective insights of cultural anthropology and feminist theory to inform readings of Serreau's and Nimoy's films. Their discussions reflect and reconfirm—as does my own at present—the potential value of the "remake"; indeed, given the filmic texts under consideration, such a critical repetition seems highly appropriate, if not inevitable. Moreover, although I frequently concur in Carroll's and Modleski's contextual assumptions and often agree with their specific textual interpretations, I also find their conclusions limited by methodological approaches that are both exclusive—and mutually so. The tendency they share to privilege one film over the other and, more importantly, to focus exclusively on *either* gender *or* culture in many ways duplicates the critical approach that characterizes the popular press.

Thus, as Carroll engages in a careful comparative analysis of *Trois Hommes* and *Three Men* that serves to accentuate cultural difference and specificity, she inevitably brings to light distinctions between the two directors' conceptualizations of sexual identity and gender roles. Her very narrow understanding of "gender," however, as both separate from and subordinate to "culture," means that Carroll's exposure of what she calls the "invisible verities" of culture effectively renders the evidence of gender invisible in its turn. For example, not only does her stated focus on "cultural presuppositions" explicitly preclude any attention to such issues as cinematic specificity or narrative structure (347), but in a cross-cultural discussion of interpersonal relations that includes the categories of friends, the couple, parents and children, adults and babies, and men and women, she regards gender as irrelevant to all but the very last (358).

Yet, when gender is finally seen to *be* at issue, as in the case of Modleski's feminist analysis, it tends in its own turn to become the *only* issue, now blocking out any parallel attention to cultural or linguistic difference. If Modleski's strongly psychoanalytical approach leads almost inevitably toward an important privileging of issues of gender, it tends just as inevitably to repeat the cultural blindness that characterizes traditional Freudian psychoanalysis. Carroll and Modleski might each be said to practice a particular form of imperialism characteristic of her own cultural origins. Where Carroll reiterates the dominance of national identity *à la française*, Modleski reinscribes a typically American belief that our relationship to others is one of fundamental resemblance. Her assumption that Serreau's and Nimoy's films are essentially indistinguishable leads her to reduce the French film to an infrequent reference point in an analysis that in fact focuses almost exclusively on the American remake and within which *Trois Hommes* is always "more" or "less," "better" or "worse" than *Three Men*—but never significantly "different from" it. To the extent that Modleski's analysis still depends upon a comparative context, it too is determined on the basis of gender, not culture: she briefly contrasts Nimoy's *Three Men* with another American film, John Ford's *Three Godfathers* (1946), whose plot substitutes a male for a female baby.[3]

By focusing respectively on context and text, on a cultural "container" and a textual "contained," Carroll and Modleski reenact the very transformation encoded in the titles of *Trois Hommes et un couffin* and *Three Men and a Baby*. The shift from basket to baby, from container to contained, identifies a linguistic reversal that recurs frequently in the translation of French into English. J. P. Vinay and J. Darbelnet, in their comprehensive study of the comparative stylistics of French and English, argue that this practice, called "modulation," reflects the coexistence of two distinctive worldviews: one prone to abstraction and generalization, the other to concrete pragmatism. Importantly, such differences have no independent or absolute existence; they both surface and take on meaning only in a comparative context. Thus, the "Frenchness" of Serreau's film cannot be fully understood without paying equally close attention to the "Americanness" of Nimoy's. Similarly, my particular theoretical interest in the remake lies in what it may allow us to discover not only about culture and/or gender but about the nature of the relationship *between* the two. From this perspective, the parallel versions of *Three Men* offer us a particularly appropriate context for exploration—not, of course, because of a fortuitous change in the sex of the director (which, at most, serves only, and only after the fact, as an opportune sign of the gender differences that lie elsewhere)[4] but because of the narrative incoherence that each film reveals independently and which their comparison serves to make particularly evident.

Serreau posits and Nimoy retains—but with a significant difference—two incompatible plot structures that are respectively en-gendered as male and female. An initial confusion of two "packages," of the heroin and the heroine, introduces narrative rivalry between a male story of action and adventure, of opposition to law and order, and a female plot of domesticity, of compliance with societal norms and values. (In French, of course, *heroin* and *heroine*—*l'héroïne* in both cases—are exact homonyms—same sound, same spelling, same etymology, same *feminine* gender.). Moreover, in the course of confirming narratives of different genders, the two films reveal an alteration of genre as well. The transformation of "feminine" French realism into "masculine" American comedy simultaneously exposes narrative structure as a reflection of worldview and makes visible the significance of gender for an understanding of each, both independently and interdependently.[5]

Trois Hommes openly announces its structural incoherence and explicitly identifies it as a problem of narration. Indeed, since the plot of the heroin has reached full closure early in the film, long before Jacques (André Dussollier) returns, it is in fact the narrative process itself, the *telling* of the story, that simultaneously reveals (and, in part, creates) a confusion that was not previously apparent. Thus, Jacques's initial inability to comprehend the discourse of "drugs, diapers, babies, and cops," which Michel (Michel Boujenah) and Pierre (Roland Giraud) shout out in chorus, reflects *en abîme* the viewer's first conscious encounter with incompatible plots and genres. Toward the end of the film, an explicit act of internal repetition serves as reminder and reconfirmation that the question of coherence centers on issues of narrative and narrativity. In one of the many scenes of diegetic "remake" that characterize Serreau's narrative structure, Jacques's own attempt to explain the drug plot to the narcotics agent who was himself an eyewitness dissolves once again into verbal chaos.

In the American version of *Three Men*, in contrast, past events are related to Jack (Ted Danson) quickly and clearly. Both the efficiency of the discursive function, now the responsibility of Peter (Tom Selleck) alone, and his respect for traditional dramatic structure support a narrative that is perfectly coherent in content and immediately comprehensible in meaning. In opposition to the French film, where narration serves to introduce confusion into a previously cohesive plot, the American telling of the tale functions inversely to conceal the absence of any preexistent unity of action. Indeed, the very possibility of narrative closure, which allows both Jack and the spectator a reassuring impression of understanding and significance, may well depend on its very artifice, since, in fact, Nimoy's film narratizes the drug story long before it reaches actual resolution. The continuity of the narrative process thus functions strategically and metaphorically to represent the false integration of two plots that remain essentially separate and distinct.

As feminist film theory has evolved from the germinal work of Laura Mulvey, Pam Cook, and Claire Johnston (see Penley), one recurrent method of interpretation has centered on the identification of moments of textual conflict or incoherence at which mainstream cinema invites a reading of its ideological contra-dictions, of what, like Michel and Pierre, it cannot, will not, or dare not express clearly. Seen from this perspective, the "separate but equal" incoherence of narrative structure that characterizes *Trois Hommes* and its remake reveals that the sociohistorical assumptions and desires of a given culture, on the one hand, and a particular inscription of the discourse of gender, on the other, are both closely related and strongly and mutually interdependent. Yet such a reading also suggests that regardless of the cultural specificity of any single "remake" of the story of gender, the misogyny of the message recurs repeatedly: "separate" is not "equal."

The "container" privileged in the title of *Trois Hommes et un couffin* reflects a narrative structure that repeatedly and doubly "contains"—that both "includes" and "confines"—a number of scenes and/or women (the two terms are here synonymous). The absence of these passages from the American remake provides a contextual contrast that increases their visibility and underscores their potential significance in the original. These scenes, internally recurrent, constitute the locus of the discourse of misogyny contained within Serreau's film. According to Lucy Fischer, most films, in keeping with the codes of classic realism, use the device of narrative closure to represent women's containment within patriarchy (245). Here each episode provides the film's three male heroes with a renewed opportunity both to act on their theoretical determination to exclude women from every aspect of their lives and to justify that position by exposing or denouncing female incompetence or both.

Two exemplary scenes should suffice as illustration, particularly since the first might initially seem to contradict the argument above. Pierre and Michel resolve their initial ignorance of childcare by consulting a female pharmacist (Annik Alane) whose very language—characterized by objectivity, categorization, enumeration, hypothesis, and logical consequence—confirms that the source of her authority derives from science and not from gender. But any temptation to read this passage as an argument for shared parenting, grounded in an assumption of equal access to acquired knowledge, seems hasty in light of its subsequent textual "revision." For the scene in which the men drive off the professional "Second Mommy" (Dominique Lavanant), who defines her own competence in terms of her diplomas and her knowledge of pediatrics, functions to undermine at one and the same time the authority of both women and science. Indeed, Pierre's response to the woman's assertion that "medicine is a serious business" (i.e., mothering cannot be left to men) makes explicit both the relationship between the two parallel episodes and their parallel relationship to narrative itself: "Have you ever heard the story that goes like this—medicine [la médecine] is a whore and the female pharmacist [la pharmacienne] her pimp?"

Why, we must obviously ask, might a film "made in France" not only seek—actively and on principle—to exclude women from childcare and to prove them to be either indifferent or incompetent mothers; but why would it also appear to reject everything connected to women, including the very associations posited within its own text and which seem most clearly advantageous to its male heroes' desire to parent? One possible explanation originates in the relationship between gender and culture. In France, the contemporary feminist movement has been most visibly defined by a theoretical discourse of "difference" in which female sexuality has been reclaimed and revalorized but not necessarily redefined. The female language of "écriture féminine" relies on metaphors derived from such "natural" aspects of the maternal experience as pregnancy, birth, and breast-feeding to celebrate the specificity of the female body. This theory has emerged, moreover, within a sociohistorical context in which the official voices of the dominant culture have been once again actively promoting pro-natalism.[6] I would propose that in such conditions the central ideological task of men who wish to parent consists in providing evidence of both their right and their ability to "mother."

Serreau's film logically inscribes this project as a two-part process. Given the pervasive cultural belief in women's biological "right" to mother, presumably internalized by men at least as completely as by women, the first stage requires the exclusion and the condemnation of all "real" women as a necessary prerequisite to any convincing assertion of men's own rights. Significantly, the men's principled commitment to an all-male household is initially expressed not as a general philosophy of misogyny but in terms of the very particularized rejection, both literal and metaphoric, of mothers, including their own: "We'll leave mothers [les mères] wherever they are." Moreover, this first necessity is reinforced by a further consequence of the initial cultural premise. For if the maternal role is "naturally" female, then men can prove themselves to be "women" and (therefore) "mothers" only through a process of direct substitution. In Serreau's film, this textual "remake" of men takes place through the feminization of the male narrative or, perhaps more accurately, through the incorporation of the men into a narrative already predefined as "feminine."[7]

Despite the inability of the men to *tell* their story coherently, the action itself, as I noted above, is perfectly cohesive. In direct contrast to the American film in which the drug deal becomes the dominant narrative, Serreau brings this male plot to rapid resolution in the absence of Jacques, baby Marie's biological father; his return appropriately coincides with the assertion, henceforth unchallenged, of the primacy of the female narrative of mothering. Indeed, the moment at which the narrators themselves begin to make sense is marked by the transition from what "isn't the problem" (the drugs) to what *is* ("the problem is the baby bottles, the diapers, the shit, and the laundry"). Moreover, in this context, the confusion that initially characterizes the narrative process can now be read as an inevitable result and an accurate reflection of the inseparability of the heroin and the heroine that guarantees the centrality of the female plot in Serreau's film. From the time of their delivery until they are returned to the dealers, the drugs are constantly concealed on the baby's body (in the American remake, they are quickly relegated to the diaper pail); thus

250

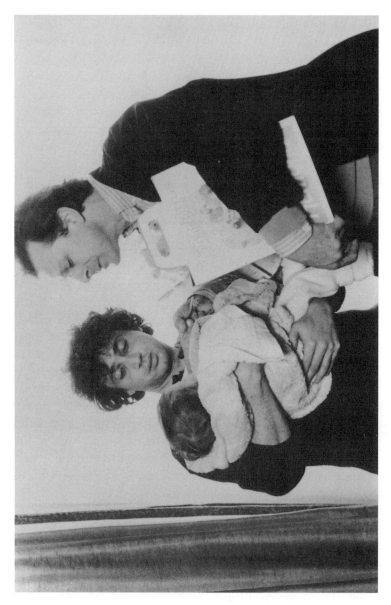

FIGURE 10.1. Substitute mothering in Coline Serreau's *Trois Hommes et un couffin* (1985). Courtesy of the Museum of Modern Art, Film Stills Archive.

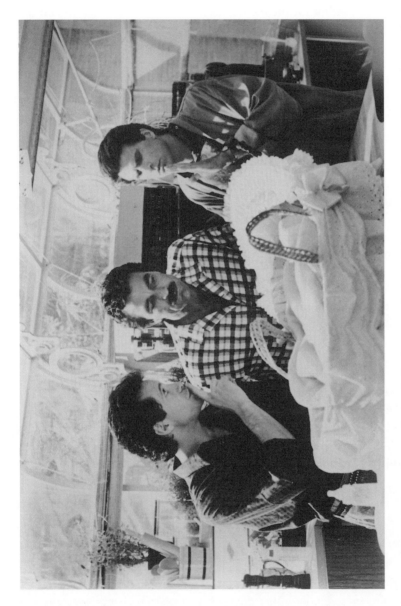

FIGURE 10.2. Three urban professionals singing a convincing lullaby to the bundle of joy of Leonard Nimoy's *Three Men and a Baby* (1987). Courtesy of the Museum of Modern Art, Film Stills Archive.

every episode of the drug plot unfolds in the context of childcare and in the presence of the baby. Indeed, concern for the heroine provides both the sole motivation for the heroes' decision to return the heroin and the only guarantee they offer the drug dealers that they can be trusted. At the moment of repetition, when Jacques himself attempts to explain the structure of the plot, his simulation of pregnancy offers visual support for the explicit identification of biological difference as the source not only of male anxiety but also of narrative confusion. No *male* narrative, argues Jacques, can ever pretend to coherence—short, that is, of undertaking the ultimate "remake" of the original story, of the story of our origins:

> If I could somehow remake the world, if I were God, this is what I would do. I would fashion Adam from Eve's rib rather than the other way around. At least that way things would have been clear from the beginning. We wouldn't have been led to believe that someone could be created from our rib. Because nothing is created from our rib. Not ever.

Jacques's subsequent lament about the inferiority of male creativity—"the only things that we can make are buildings, planes, cars"—is echoed much earlier and in a very different context in Nimoy's remake of *Three Men.* Peter's similar analogy—"I'm an architect for Christ sake. I build cities of the future. I put up skyscrapers. I can certainly put a goddamm diaper together"—no longer functions to establish a contrast between the inherent capabilities of men and women; it now serves to justify the extension of men's professional competence to include the realm of childcare. Moreover, Mary's biological father expresses his own right and ability to parent in precisely the same terms. Whereas Jacques's potential superiority over Michel and Pierre "naturally" surfaces as a frequent source of anxiety in Serreau's film, the American remake logically (indeed, literally) "reconceives" fatherhood as a question of "performance" rather than procreation. The alteration of Jack's original career as flight attendant aptly serves to emphasize his redefinition of fatherhood as a social "role": "I'm an actor; I can do a father."

Such a significant textual change reflects the dominant ideology of American feminism, which has consistently emphasized equality rather than difference, gender rather than sex, and societal change over biological destiny.[8] In this cultural context, the transformation of traditional roles that would result in men's active involvement in childcare does not require that they discredit and replace women; it depends rather on women's own denial of any inherent female ability to mother and their subsequent refusal to continue to substitute for fathers. Thus, although Nimoy essentially retains Serreau's structural model of recurrent scenes that focus on different women, agency now lies with the female characters who repeatedly reject motherhood and decline to help the men. As Rebecca (Margaret Colin), for example, denies Peter her assistance in the scene that establishes the pattern, she also dismisses his need ("You're very capable; you'll get through this just fine") and deconstructs his argument, challenging both its premise ("because [she's] a woman") and its conclusions (*she* "automatically know[s] what to do with babies" and *men* "don't know anything about babies"). The explicit repetition of this scene confirms its ideological importance. Jack's own mother (Celeste Holm) counters his pretense that "there's like a biological thing, an instant connection" between her and *his* baby with a similar strategy of simultaneous attack (an injunction to "cut the crap") and support (an assertion that he will make a "fine" father). Since the women's willing abandonment of childcare to men so clearly includes their parallel acknowledgement of male competence, it is not surprising that Nimoy's recurrent scenes gradually shift focus to replace reluctant mothers with examples of committed and adoring fathers (including not only the police detective and the taxi driver, but even, to some extent, the drug dealers themselves). Thus, traditional gender associations are broken down and new ones established at one and the same time.

But the American film's reflection of different cultural assumptions about gender merely displaces conflict, without in any way eliminating it. Nimoy's narrative structure confirms that men who "mother" need not prove their right and ability to do so; on the contrary, they must now demonstrate not that they are women but rather that they are still *men*. Thus, Nimoy quickly separates the heroin from the heroine and reverses the relative importance of the two plots. The male tale of action and adventure, designed to prove all three men's virility, now structures the film as a whole. That the significance of the story of the drugs lies not in its content but in its form is confirmed by the addition at the end of the remake of a chase scene; the race to and through the airport, totally gratuitous in terms of both plot and character development, serves only to confirm the status of Nimoy's three heroes as virile "men of action."

Moreover, if divergent cultural attitudes toward authority no doubt provide a partial explanation for the different ways in which Serreau and

Nimoy position their protagonists *within* the narrative of law and order, especially since cinematic representation has played a particularly significant role in shaping such attitudes, here too gender influences how the conventions of genre and ideology take on specific meaning. In aligning themselves with drug dealers, the heroes of *Trois Hommes* may well act in keeping with French film's fondness for the moral ambiguity of the *hors la loi*, but narrative analogy (reinforced yet again by the constant visual and verbal associations of "heroin" and "heroine") primarily functions in an ironic reversal to identify trafficking in "illegitimate" drugs and the usurpation of motherhood as parallel criminal activities and as equally subversive alternatives to the pharmacists and the police officers whose "legitimate" drug activity identifies them as the cultural representatives of conventional law and order. In general, the protagonists of *Three Men*, who now side with the police, show similar respect for Hollywood's very different ethical code, where the triumph of good over evil often makes the cop the hero. But Nimoy's men also practice their own culturally specific form of usurpation. As their passive support evolves into active participation, they take over the function of the police and solve the crime in their place. Not only do the American fathers receive authorization to parent from the defenders of normative social structures, but they replace the traditional representatives of author/-ity in order to rewrite the conventional narrative of law and order so that it will incorporate new roles for men.

Still, *Three Men's* insistent need to prove masculinity does not lead to the disappearance of the discourse of misogyny but only to its relocation. The titular removal of the baby from the basket metaphorically identifies an all too literal act of "robbing the cradle." The hostility to women that Serreau's Frenchmen direct at the mother resurfaces in Nimoy's film in the representation of the child, suggesting a shift in cultural conceptions of women's "natural" role from the maternal to the sexual; in the American context, misogyny appears to find its best expression in sexual objectification rather than biological destiny. (At the same time, of course, this particular "difference" also reflects a common cross-cultural pattern of the denial of the mother's sexuality.)

In a variety of ways, Nimoy's "baby" realizes the full metaphorical potential of the word itself; explicitly and repeatedly en-gendered as a female, this "baby" simultaneously represents and replaces the woman as sexual object. The concern that Michael (Steve Guttenberg) voices during the initial diaper change—"This is a girl; should we be doing this?"—immediately substitutes an illicit male/female relationship for normal parental/child interaction. Subsequently, in a direct inversion of the structure of the original film, the female narrative of childcare is masculinized and incorporated into a male "tail" of virility and sexual conquest. Peter reads *Sports Illustrated* to Mary; Jack showers with his baby daughter; and throughout Nimoy's film, male "mothering" functions primarily as a sexual turn-on, a highly successful strategy for attracting women. In one exemplary scene, Peter's identical rendition of "Goodnight, Sweetheart, Goodnight" serves in quick succession to calm Mary and to arouse Rebecca; and, in general, Nimoy's substitution of such conventional romantic lyrics as "I wanna be Daddy's Girl" and "The moment I met you baby" for the classical score of the French film provides a subtle and suggestive accompaniment for his story of the sexualization of a female infant (see also Modleski).

Feminist film theory, however, also posits that textual examples of conflict and incoherence can serve not only to expose mainstream cinema's hidden ideological assumptions but also to uncover the source of a potentially subversive discourse. Might it then be possible to reread the films' double message of misogyny from this perspective? One might argue, for example, that the commitment of Serreau's men to conventional female narrative no doubt results in a certain visual confirmation of the rhythms of domesticity, notably, its episodic, interruptible, and repetitive nature. The film is organized around a series of vignettes, each devoted to some aspect of childcare, and this structural representation of fragmentation and repetition seems to respect certain realities of many women's daily labor. Similarly, textual patterns of recurrence create a sense of internal rhyming that recalls narrative structures common in many contemporary female texts of "domestic realism" (see, for example, Aptheker and Juhasz).

On the other hand, change predicated on a simple reversal of gender roles, or on the substitution of one sex for the other in an otherwise unaltered script, seems more likely to confirm than to challenge traditional models of gender. Not surprisingly, then, Serreau's film also uses its male characters to reinscribe some of the most potentially harmful of societal assumptions about appropriate lifestyles for those whose responsibilities include childcare. Notably, *Trois Hommes* reinforces cultural expectations that childcare will be of necessity an exclusive occupation, incompatible with any other work and requiring a maternal presence in the home; the film further suggests that the couple remains the preferred model for the structure of the family. Indeed, the first third of Serreau's film focuses almost exclusively on the illustration of these beliefs. Caring for Marie constitutes a fulltime job for both Pierre and Michel; each totally abandons his regular paid work to take what Pierre explicitly identifies as "maternal leave." While their further mutual rejection of both physical separation and any division of labor might be read as an ironic admission that it takes two men to do the job of one woman, in context it also serves to support the ideology of the couple; for what links all the caretakers (female or male, natural or surrogate) who are denounced in the course of the film as incompetent is their common effort, always unsuccessful, to provide adequate childcare alone.[9]

In contrast, it is precisely the ability to rethink traditional childcare that could open up the possibility of a more optimistic reading of Nimoy's discourse of gender. Each of the three American men takes his turn at assuming full responsibility for Mary, and each integrates childcare with a continuing commitment to his usual professional responsibilities. Thus, whereas Serreau's film, whatever its intentions, inevitably encourages us to identify Michel as primary caretaker, precisely because of his proven domestic competence and his metaphorical ability to "work at home," Nimoy gives parallel visual importance to Peter as he visits construction sites with Mary in tow and to Jack at rehearsals with the baby in a back-pack. Such an integration of one's personal and professional life might lead us beyond traditional "mothering," whether masculine or feminine, toward a new definition not only of fathers but of parents, including female ones, as well.

This hypothesis would seem to find support in the contrasting ways in which the two films reach narrative closure. Serreau requires the mother (Philippine Leroy Beaulieu) to acknowledge her own incompetence and to restore the baby to the sole care (however temporary) of the men, whose confident assurance—"pour nous, ce n'est rien"—confirms their new alignment with the realm of the "natural." Although the association between narrative closure and the "containment" of women is usually a metaphoric one, *Trois Hommes et un couffin* literalizes this relationship in particularly revealing ways. In the final episode of a dramatic structure that has repeatedly confined women, Serreau's film ends not only with the visual imprisonment of both mother and daughter but with their permanent infantilization as well. In the last two shots of the film, we first see Sylvie (whose makeup, meant to suggest fatigue, in fact gives her the troubling appearance of a battered woman), curled up asleep in Marie's crib, sucking her thumb, and then Marie herself, who is caught in freeze frame just as she begins to take her first steps alone. Nimoy, in contrast, has his fathers alter family structure once again to make room (however marginal) for the mother (Nancy Travis). At the same time, however, the American film's persistent metamorphosis of French realism into comedy (and often farce), visually reinforced by the heroes' self-referential depiction as lifesize comic-strip characters, also consistently calls into question the seriousness with which we can take any appearance of a real commitment to change.[10]

"The manner in which words are strung together expresses a mode of thought that is as important as the thought itself," notes Vincent Canby, in the course of explicating Marin Karmitz's characterization of the current predilection of French directors for making films in English as "not a crisis of cinema but a crisis of culture" ("Ici se habla" 2: 1+). Implicitly, if not intentionally, Canby's words also permit a reading that suggests the important influence that narrative structure ("the manner in which words are strung together") has on worldview ("a mode of thought") during the process of reconstruction and reconceptualization that results in the cross-cultural remake. The films of Serreau and Nimoy provide a comparative example that highlights the further complication that gender brings to the contemporary cinematic narrative of "a crisis of culture." By telling the same story differently—to the paradoxical point of both relating two different stories and repeating the same story—*Trois Hommes* and its American remake help reveal the particularly complex ways in which culture and gender interact, in which narrative is simultaneously en-gendered by culture and acculturated by gender. Although the attempt to understand the interaction of those textual characteristics, if any, that might be respectively attributed to gender and to culture, is clearly a longterm project, cross-cultural comparison of narratives of gender already seems to offer a promising methodology and context for such an exploration. In the short run, such an approach has the immediate benefit of challenging western ideology's favorite story of identity by insisting on the fact and the richness of cultural diversity. Such attention to difference similarly addresses contemporary feminism's urgent need to renarratize the traditional tale of gender dichotomization as an internally pluralistic discourse.

The introduction to a special issue of *CinémAction*, devoted to remakes and adaptations, includes the useful reminder that "a theory of

the remake should not be constructed too hastily" (Serceau 9). Thus, it is
no doubt fitting that I initially completed an earlier version of this analysis (Durham, "Taking") only to discover that its subject matter had
already been "remade" by the subsequent release of Emile Ardolino's
Three Men and a Little Lady in December of 1990. Even the credits
announce this latest version of "repetition with a difference" as a particularly curious example of cross-cultural collaboration. Although Touchstone Pictures has clearly marketed *Little Lady* as a sequel to its own (and
Nimoy's) *Three Men and a Baby* (promoted, as a result, to the status of
"the original"), the film actually reintroduces itself as yet another remake
of Serreau's *Trois Hommes et un couffin*. Moreover, this Franco-American
coproduction (for which Jean-François Lepetit, for example, repeats the
role of executive producer that he originally created with *Couffin*) also
emerges from a particularly complex process of mediation among a number of contributors who differ by either nationality or sex—or both. Were
we to reconstruct the credits in the form of a synopsis, we would uncover
the rather awkward story of genesis that follows: *Little Lady* was "directed
by" Ardolino from a "screenplay by" Charlie Peters, which he developed
from a "story by" Sara Parriott and Josann McGibbon, which they "based
on" the film that was "written by" Serreau. Moreover, although international copyright agreements and/or multinational financial arrangements
may well provide a partial explanation for the unusually complicated
authorship of *Three Men and a Little Lady*, the contradictory nature of
this bicultural (and bigendered) hybrid—the "sequel-remake"—is also
reproduced within the narrative structure of the film where its very complexity significantly furthers our exploration of the interrelationship of
gender and culture.

   Little Lady begins as a realistic domestic comedy that borrows conventions of both gender and genre from Serreau's *Trois Hommes*. The
unexpected phenomenon of a sequel that returns to its own prequel's origins affords an unusual opportunity to reconsider the context in which we
initially compared French and American versions of the discourse of gender. In particular, *Little Lady* immediately raises new questions about the
relative progressiveness that potentially seemed to distinguish Nimoy's
understanding of parental roles and familial structure from their more traditional conceptualization in Serreau's film. Ardolino's sequel suggests
that the mere presence of the mother (Nancy Travis) may be sufficient in
and of itself to reestablish the "natural" primacy of her role; not only do
all three men (also played by the original American actors) significantly

alter their earlier behavior by now deferring to Sylvia's authority in any decision that involves Mary (Robin Weisman) but no comparable change occurs in the status of the biological father.

Moreover, in what would appear to be a second direct consequence of the mother's return, her new importance also provokes the same systematic attempt to undermine her as a woman that we originally encountered only in *Trois Hommes*. Although Jack, Peter, and Michael continue to share some responsibility for childcare, the only domestic chore still in sight is now performed by Sylvia alone, and it specifically serves to define her difference as one of incompetence: she is a rotten cook and *therefore*— we can only assume—she cooks relentlessly. Not even Mary will eat what her mother prepares; and the men have developed carefully choreographed movements that allow them to discard Sylvia's food efficiently the moment her back is turned. By positioning Sylvia as the unconscious butt of a repetitious joke that all the men in the film take turns sharing with the audience, Ardolino suggests that women's stupidity is rivaled only by their vulnerability and so succeeds in simultaneously justifying male hypocrisy and the mockery of women as a necessary and thoughtful act of protectiveness.

The move from margin to center that Sylvia effects in the gap that separates the final visual image of Nimoy's *Three Men* from the opening dialogue of Ardolino's *Little Lady* also heralds the return of the heterosexual couple and the traditional nuclear family. Indeed, our only real glimpse of the four adults' original (in every sense of the word) experiment in cooperative parenting comes in the form of the silent coda with which the sequel begins, and even this series of successively dissolving parallel images serves primarily as a rapid visual transition that takes Mary from infancy to preschool age. Still, what the sequel appears to introduce as an inevitable change in the child (in any child) more accurately reflects a significant revision of the specific discourse of gender, in keeping with the transformation of Nimoy's "baby" into Ardolino's "lady." Indeed, the particular semantic richness of these two terms empowers them alone to tell the whole story.

Just as the space between the metaphoric and the literal "baby" leaves room for Nimoy to write his contradictory tale of three men who continue to view women as sexual objects even as they become the responsible fathers of an infant daughter, the multiple meanings of the word *lady* function similarly to structure Ardolino's narrative.[11] As the relationship between the titles of the two films suggests, the heroes' lives now revolve around the mother rather than the baby. As a polite synonym for "woman" as well as a term whose references include "a female head of household," *lady* simultaneously names both Sylvia's new stature and its primary cause. At the same time, of course, the titular modifier "little" continues to recall both the masculine tendency to associate grown women with young girls (particularly evident in the closing images of Serreau's film) and Sylvia's actual domestic subordination. (Even the culinary tasks that act as the primary means of Sylvia's humiliation may be embedded in *lady*, which derives from the Old English *hlaefdige*, "kneader of bread.") Since the word *lady* further denotes "a woman to whom a man is romantically attached" and also serves as an informal equivalent for "wife," it similarly identifies the essential plot mechanism of *Little Lady*, which has now shifted from the story of parenting to the narrative of romance. Ardolino's already competent fathers must at present learn to be satisfactory husbands; as a result, they have begun to view women more as potential wives than as temporary sexual partners. Finally, if we interpret the lady of Ardolino's "title" as a reference to the one generally bestowed upon a British woman of rank, it even announces the particular event that precipitates the central dramatic crisis of the film: Sylvia's decision to return to England to marry Edward (Christopher Cazenove), a wealthy British director and landowner.

Regardless of who is assigned to play the central female part, however, the role itself remains primarily "titular" in both *Three Men and a Little Lady* and *Three Men and a Baby*. As one might well deduce from the exact repetition of the first words of the title(s), the sequel to Nimoy's picture essentially affords Ardolino a renewed opportunity to explore the changing nature of masculinity. In fact, not only are the two American versions of *Three Men* initially indistinguishable by name, but the identical strategy (Sylvia and Mary's imminent departure for England) serves in both films to reveal character and to motivate action. Ardolino's sequel now has as its central thematic and dramatic focus the selection of a suitable husband for Sylvia. His identity, however, remains closely associated with Nimoy's earlier concerns about parenting, since whomever Sylvia marries will automatically become Mary's "real" father at the same time. Although paternal love is not in and of itself a sufficient criterion to determine the appropriate spouse, its absence does constitute adequate grounds on which to eliminate any potential husband. Curiously, in this context too, *Little Lady* seems more reminiscent of the French original than of its American remake, for Sylvia's initial choice serves primarily, if indirectly, to suggest her own incompetence as a mother. To the extent that she ever takes seriously Edward's professed commitment to fatherhood, Sylvia voluntarily elects to believe in the self-directed performance of a fellow professional in the theater, despite its inability to convince Mary, its intended audience.

Subsequently, Sylvia is not only totally oblivious to Edward's plan to put his new daughter in an English boarding school immediately after the wedding, but she refuses to believe Peter and Michael when they expose his scheme; indeed, she goes through with a wedding ceremony that she believes to be authentic. Moreover, when she is finally faced with irrefutable proof, Sylvia's anger expresses the personal insult she feels as a result of Edward's willingness to lie to her more than maternal outrage at his treatment of her daughter. Thus Ardolino's Sylvia metaphorically repeats Sylvie's original abandonment of baby Marie in Serreau's film— but this time without the benefit of either necessity or extenuating circumstances. Indeed, in the pivotal scene at the very center of *Little Lady* in which Peter and Sylvia quarrel violently, his attack on Edward as the wrong father for Mary quickly evolves into the condemnation of Sylvia as an irresponsible mother. For the first and only time in either of the two American films, she is explicitly charged with her "original" crime of child abandonment: "I'm selfish? Well, I didn't leave my baby on a doorstep when she was six months old."

In another example of the Franco-American rapprochement that Nimoy's film seems to mediate between its original model and its own sequel, it is only with *Little Lady* that biological fatherhood becomes in any sense problematic in the American films. Ardolino now systematically sets out to discredit Jack, Mary's natural father, presumably in order to justify his eventual replacement by Peter. In a total reversal of the strategy introduced in Nimoy's film, where Jack's profession serves as the principal means for transforming fatherhood from a biological fact into a social "role" that can be "performed" equally well by all men, his acting career now identifies him as an unsuitable father. Moreover, it also serves to establish a clear link between Jack, Sylvia, and Edward: the three theatrical professionals are all to some degree denounced as parents. If those who have some "natural" claim on Mary—her biological parents and the man her mother selects as spouse and future father—are, in fact, defined as fundamentally "artificial," then one can logically assume that the opposing premise must also hold true, that is, the "real" father will by definition be an "unnatural" one.

In this context, the fact that Jack's career is less successful and respectable than Sylvia's or Edward's—he acts badly in laxative commercials and B movies while they direct and perform Shaw and Shakespeare—is clearly to his credit. Unlike Edward, Jack, according to Sylvia, can't "fool" anyone. Still, he periodically reveals a similar tendency to let his work take precedence over his child. That Jack is a fundamentally irresponsible, if entertaining, father is carefully and insistently pointed out to us early in the film. Despite persistent pleas and reminders and the predetermined importance of the event, Jack nonetheless arrives late for the family's interview with the directors of the primary school to which Mary has applied. More importantly, when he finally does show up to participate in what has clearly been established as the family's first attempt to gain public acceptance for its highly unusual parenting arrangements, lest they harm Mary, Jack is not only still costumed and made up as Count Dracula but he continues to play the role. The particular choice of disguise seems specifically designed to undermine the potential privilege of Jack's biological paternity by suggesting that this "blood" relation(ship) is a highly unhealthy one.

At the same time, Jack's portrayal as someone who preys on women is consistent with the reputation he established as a womanizer in *Three Men and a Baby* and could therefore serve the parallel function of exposing his unsuitability as husband as well as father—or rather, in the context of the sequel, his unsuitability as husband and *therefore* as father (the former is now a prerequisite for the latter). In general, however, the discourse of masculinity and sexuality is constructed quite differently in *Little Lady*. In yet another, and even more fascinating, reversal of Nimoy's emplotment of masculinity, in which nurturing fathers had to prove they were still men, in Ardolino's sequel, Jack is further disqualified as a potential husband and father precisely by his discrediting as a "man." The challenge to Jack's virility takes the specific form of an attack on his heterosexuality, the very locus in Nimoy's film of the proof of his heroes' manhood, particularly in the case of Jack whose exceptional powers of seduction distinguish him from Peter and Michael. At present, however, not only does Jack, unlike Peter and Michael, clearly *not* wish to marry, but he no longer appears to be involved, even casually, with any woman. More importantly, Jack's appearance is consistently coded as effeminate; another negative consequence of his profession means that we most often see him framed in mirrors, in costume, and heavily made up. In the single most telling sequence, Jack cross-dresses as Chiquita Banana; in the unlikely event that someone might actually miss the visual allusion to a gay man, the stage manager makes it explicit: "Hey, Fruit of the Loom—you're on."

In direct opposition to Jack, Peter is identified as the right father for Mary and the appropriate husband for Sylvia by both his success in those areas where Jack fails and his failures in those areas where Jack succeeds. Thus, in the love scene he attempts to rehearse with Sylvia in Jack's absence, Peter proves himself an awkward and unwilling actor, precisely because he is not acting: "Jack should be doing this. He's the actor. That was terrible. I was totally unbelievable." In contrast to Nimoy's film, not only has Peter now largely displaced Jack and Michael as primary parent, but the paternal role has been expanded in ways that begin to conflate the role of Mary's father with that of Sylvia's husband. Indeed, Peter's dependability—as Sylvia says, "I can always count on you"—would initially seem to make him as promising a husband as he is a successful father. Consistent, moreover, with the logic of the first film, in which Peter is involved in a serious, longterm relationship, we now learn that he was once briefly married. This revelation serves simultaneously to prove that Peter, unlike Jack, is not a confirmed bachelor and to justify his apparent unwillingness to marry again. Indeed, his very reluctance confirms the importance he attaches to such a commitment.

Yet, however paradoxically, the roles of father and husband actually turn out to be in competition and even contradiction in *Little Lady*. Jack describes both the stability of the newly patriarchal family Peter has constructed and the dilemma that it creates: "These last five years, with Mary and Sylvia and Michael and me, you have been the glue that kept us together. We depended on you. We made you the father and it worked. It's kept you from admitting how you feel about Sylvia. You love her, don't you?" (Or, as Jack goes on to conclude, more briefly and no doubt more characteristically, "It's tough being Papa Bear, isn't it?") Just as Jack and Peter can together legitimately claim to be "Mary's real father," the two men, defined retroactively as "best friends" in Ardolino's sequel, similarly embody different but closely related dimensions of contemporary masculinity. Appropriately, then, Peter and Jack, the latter disguised as a vicar, will both "marry" Sylvia in the concluding scene of *Three Men and A Little Lady*.

Not surprisingly, Jack's version of manhood is the more dated and conventional of the two. Jack epitomizes the phenomenon of male "commitmentphobia," which Barbara Ehrenreich characterizes as "one of the most striking changes of the seventies" in *The Hearts of Men*, her feminist analysis of the evolution of masculinity from the fifties to the eighties (121). Peter, on the other hand, is, if anything, *too* committed and not only to a conception of the role of the head of the family that would seem to preclude any personal attachments on his part. Peter also believes that he represents precisely what women seek in marriage (and in men): "You'd be surprised how practical women are about these things. . . . I think women want security." It seems particularly appropriate in this context to have just cited a female scholar's work on masculinity, since both American films emphasize the active role that women have played in redefining societal expectations for men. Thus Sylvia immediately and directly contradicts Peter's assertions about women's desires: "You know what I want? I want a man who'll make a fool of himself over me." In this case, to behave like a "fool" means quite literally that Peter must begin to *talk* (fool, from Late Latin *follis*, windbag, i.e., a talkative person), to express himself. As Jack urges, "Just say how you feel," and as Sylvia's mother confirms, Peter must learn to "open up," to become "comfortable with [his] feelings." He must come to understand and to articulate his own emotional needs as a *man* as well as a father and to recognize those of Sylvia as a *woman* as well as a mother. In other words, Peter must grow into the role of the "New Male" (Ehrenreich 127–28). That, by his own admission, it takes Peter five years even "to realize" his "true feelings" for Sylvia and until the final moments of the film to ask her to marry him for his own sake rather than "for Mary's"—"If there were no Mary, I'd still love you. . . . Am I making a big enough fool of myself?"—suggests the difficulty of such a transformation.

Still, in keeping with a (remade) fairytale tradition, the prince immediately sets out to prove himself worthy of the princess by the successful completion of the designated task. The second half of Ardolino's film, entirely devoted to Peter's efforts to "make a fool of himself," returns to the action plot that dominates Nimoy's American remake, even as the action itself is now relocated to the Europe of the French original. Narrative structures, however, continue to reflect changes in the construction of gender. Unlike *Three Men and a Baby*, where the heroes prove their virility by their success in attracting women, Peter is now the unwilling target of the lust of a would-be female seducer. The attempt by Miss Lomax (Fiona Shaw) to get Peter to declare and act upon his feelings for her illustrates once again the use of internal plot repetition to establish patterns of gendered behavior. More importantly, it supports Ehrenreich's argument about the centrality that sexuality plays in defining—and redefining—masculinity:

> The qualities now claimed for the authentic male self—sensitivity, emotional lability, a capacity for self-indulgence, even unpredictability—are still, and despite the feminist campaign to the contrary, recognizably "feminine." How much could a man transform himself, in the name of androgynous progress, without ceasing to be . . . "all male," or visibly heterosexual? Sanctions against homosexuality had always defined the outer limit of male rebellion. (128)

Although Ehrenreich suggests that such sanctions eased somewhat in the 1970s, the period to which she here refers, Ardolino's film would also seem to confirm her fear that the New Right's subsequent backlash against male conformity would restore a moral climate in which accusations of homosexuality could once again be used to control male "rebels" (161). Certainly, Ardolino is as eager to emphasize Peter's heterosexuality as he is to undermine Jack's. The inverse relationship between the two men is further reinforced by the use of the same strategy. Whereas Jack's career consistently serves to feminize him, Peter's profession, used by Nimoy as a metaphor for his competence as a father, is now repeatedly linked to his (hetero)sexual prowess. Early in the film, for example, when Mary suddenly asks Michael and Peter both *if* they have a penis and what it is, Sylvia replies: "Peter, you're the architect. Why don't you explain it to her?" Similarly, when Miss Lomax comes upon Peter gazing out the window at the tent set up for Sylvia's wedding, she suggestively murmurs: "Not so splendid as your mighty erections, I imagine." Peter's very name, of course, is a slang term for "penis," which may be why he can risk asserting that he is "impotent" in order to escape Miss Lomax; alternatively, Peter's "confession" may also reflect some residual male ambivalence about the "softening" effects of a newly emotional and sensitive masculinity. In addition, it confirms Peter's ability to "save" himself for marriage, in keeping with the conclusion to *Little Lady*, which also celebrates the redemption of the unwed mother of *Three Men and a Baby*. By virtue of marrying the father with whom, unlike Jack and Edward, she has *not* had sexual intercourse, Sylvia's "lost" virginity is metaphorically restored to her.

Three Men and a Little Lady confirms the importance, the complexity, and the ambivalence of the multiple ways in which gender and culture can interact in contemporary cinematic narrative. Ardolino's sequel recombines the bicultural concerns of its two filmic antecedents within the context of American society in the 1990s. Perhaps the most significant way in which *Little Lady* identifies itself as the sequel to *Three Men and a Baby* stems from a further realization of the potential inherent in Nimoy's film to alter traditional gender roles. Sylvia's refusal to be only a mother challenges the fundamental division between maternity, on the one hand, and the sexuality and autonomy of the adult woman, on the other. Since Peter has incorporated this denial of one's own needs, traditionally imposed only on mothers, into his own conception of fatherhood, the fact that he is forced (or allowed) to express his emotions and to act upon his feelings continues to undermine conventional expectations for parents as well as to revise stereotypical notions of American manhood.

At the same time, *Little Lady* also lends itself to a far more conservative cultural interpretation, whose realization, if not its justification, at times recalls *Trois Hommes et un couffin*. No doubt very real concerns about sexually transmitted diseases and the effects of divorce on children would be quite sufficient to provoke the return of marriage and of the two-parent family in a narrative remade in 1991. Yet the reemergence of particular themes and patterns first encountered in Serreau's film—e.g., the potential privilege of biological parenthood and its expression in a plot of exclusion and substitution—is also evident. Since this example might seem to suggest the existence of a link between gender and narrative that transcends cultural difference, let me take up in conclusion a counterexample, the one significant aspect of narrative incoherence in *Little Lady* that I have willfully ignored until now.

The action sequence designed to let Peter "make a fool of himself" takes the particular form of the stereotypical plot of the unhappy American tourist who endures, in rapid succession and in a highly exaggerated form, the greatest possible number of a foreign culture's most characteristic pitfalls. That Ardolino should film his version of what is surely an almost universal story is in and of itself neither surprising nor in any way inconsistent with the current political climate of the United States. What does, however, initially seem somewhat more difficult to explain is the specific choice of *British* culture as the focus of *American* dislike. Peter (and Ardolino) would have us believe, for example, that the British manufacture tiny, mechanically unreliable cars, which they then drive on the wrong side of the road; live in a country in which the harshness of the weather is rivaled only by that of the toilet paper; put their children in boarding schools whose barbaric conditions date back to Dickens; and, in general, are sexually repressed, class-obsessed snobs who deliberately mispronounce the English language for the sole purpose of provoking Americans.

I want to propose that this particular narrative of cultural clichés serves as a diegetic marker that reminds us that *Three Men and a Little Lady* is a Franco-American coproduction. Coincidentally, at about the same time that Ardolino's film was released, Jean Dondelinger, European Community Commissioner for Audiovisual and Cultural Affairs, asserted that "film is not, is no longer, a national product. Film today is by definition a transnational product" (87). Although coproductions have been a largely European phenomenon to date and one specifically designed, moreover, to counter Hollywood's ability to dominate the international film market, American remakes of French originals offer another illustration of the growing internationalization of cinema. Although the increasing fluidity of national and cultural boundaries may well produce such interesting new hybrids as *Little Lady*, clearly we can also expect changes of such historical and societal significance to be accompanied by considerable anxiety.[12] Hence, the displacements at work here. The cross-cultural animosity that American travelers traditionally reserve for the French is deflected onto the British, the historic focus of French cultural disdain. (Such national confusion might help explain the idiosyncratic presence of the Vicar, whose obsession with food seems more characteristically Gallic than Anglo-Saxon.) At the same time, this revolt against our own cultural ancestors, particularly within a context en-gendered by the "return of the mother," may well also serve as an apt metaphor for the traumatic interrelationship of a Franco-American sequel to a Hollywood remake of a French original.[13]

NOTES

Carolyn A. Durham, "Three Takes on Motherhood, Masculinity and Marriage," chapter 3 from *Double Takes*, © 1998 by the Trustees of Dartmouth College, reprinted by permission of University Press of New England.

1. Since 1987, the situation has twice recurred, albeit in reverse. Mary Agnes Donoghue directed *Paradise* (1991), the remake of Jean-Loup Hubert's *Le Grand Chemin* (1987); and Nadia Tass directed *Pure Luck* (1991), the remake of Francis Veber's *La Chèvre* (1982).

2. Of the many reviewers or critics who note the change in directors, Mancini is, to my knowledge, the only one to hazard any explanation. Carroll maintains that Serreau continued to act as "production consultant" throughout the filming of the Hollywood remake (346).

3. Several critics mention Ford's *Three Godfathers*, a Western in which three outlaws sacrifice themselves to save an infant found in the desert, in relation to Serreau's *Trois Hommes et un couffin*. Notably, in the course of reviewing Nimoy's remake, French reviewers tend to cite Ford as the real model for Serreau's film and thus as evidence of America's ignorance of its own cinematic heritage, especially since *Three Godfathers*, based on a novel by Peter B. Kyne, was also the title of the fourth film adaptation (Boleslawski, 1936). Certainly the two films, both Christmas parables, reveal potentially fascinating differences within American culture. In Richard Boleslawski's version, for example, the baby is clearly perceived to need a mother; and a murderer buys redemption by "delivering" the child to the "virgin" mother whose fiancé he has killed earlier in the film. In Ford's remake, in contrast, the dying mother delegates her maternal authority to the three outlaws collectively, and the film subsequently becomes a kind of "paternity" battle among the three godfathers and eventually the sheriff. On the other hand, neither film has much direct relevance to *Trois Hommes* or *Three Men*, although it is of interest to note that all three American films—Boleslawski's, Ford's, and Nimoy's—resemble each other and differ from Serreau's in one particularly significant way: fatherhood is not limited to the biological and both the right and the ability of men to "mother" is unproblematically assumed.

4. That the French should sometimes disagree about the significance of Serreau's sex, as evident in the discussion in *L'Avant-Scène*, is not necessarily inconsistent with some of the cultural beliefs we will see reflected in the film. In the opinion of André Dussollier, who plays the role of Jacques, "this film can only be written by a woman" ("Serreau" 101), although the only explanation he offers in support of this conviction—the fact that Serreau had recently given birth to a baby girl and therefore had to take care of her (104)—seems, if anything, directly contradicted as a specifically female issue by the very subject matter of *Trois Hommes et un couffin*. More generally, Serreau's reputation as a "feminist filmmaker"—mostly as a result of her 1975 documentary, *Mais qu'est-ce qu'elles veulent?*—tends to cause French reviewers to confuse her ideological positions with her sex. In relation to *Trois Hommes* specifically, Serreau has said "I'm not a professional feminist. I'm a filmmaker. I don't have any advice to give to spectators" (105). All translations from the French are my own, unless otherwise indicated.

5. Richard Corliss begins a review of John Sayles's *Passion Fish* with what he (no doubt appropriately) characterizes: "Humongous generalization of the week: Hollywood movies are masculine; foreign and independent films are feminine" (69).

6. Irma Garcia offers a particularly comprehensive overview of French feminist theory; see also the essays anthologized in Duchen, Eisenstein and Jardine, and Marks and Courtivron. On the pro-natalist campaign waged by the French government in the summer of 1985, see, for example, Zeldin (94) and Dudovitz (161). Although pro-natalist propaganda resurfaces periodically throughout modern French history, the billboard campaign of 1985 nonetheless stands out, not only for its intensity and visual appeal but as the first example of such a politics since the election of a socialist president in 1981.

7. In January of 1987, at a time when Serreau was still working for Walt Disney Studios, *L'Avant-Scène* published an excerpt from her projected screenplay for the American remake. Despite the editors' assertion that Serreau has entirely rewritten and reconceived her original film to adapt it to an American public and that the pharmacy sequence, in particular, is "totally different," the changes seem relatively superficial. The pharmacy is replaced by a Safeway, but Peter is questioned and advised not only by a female employee, as in Nimoy's version, but by two female customers as well. Thus, women as a group retain their authority as "natural" experts on motherhood; indeed, the scene ends with their sudden realization of the only plausible explanation for Peter's "fatherhood": "You know what? It's a kidnapping" (87–88).

8. As with French feminism, the sources are many and diverse. See, for example, Durham, *Contexture*; Moi; Showalter, who explicitly contrasts French and American feminist theory; and Chodorow, who reworks traditional Freudian psychoanalysis into a "sociology of gender."

9. To the extent that Serreau reconstructs the couple on an explicitly *heterosexual* model, it also serves one of the same functions as Nimoy's narrative of virility. Both directors appear equally homophobic in their desire to diffuse any suggestion of homosexuality, although once again, they adopt revealingly different strategies to achieve a common end.

10. Michael is a cartoonist, and the comic strip character he draws, "Johnny Cool," implicitly serves as something of a male role model. Although Michel, Michael's counterpart in Serreau's film, is also described as a *dessinateur*, his drawings play no comparable visual function in the French original. Indeed, the contrast between the opening credit sequences of the two films is emblematic of a Franco-American cross-cultural distinction between art and popular culture. At the beginning of *Trois Hommes et un couffin*, as the camera tracks through the men's apartment, we encounter a series of paintings of women and children, whose artificially somber and warm coloring and lighting determines that of the contemporary scene as well. *Three Men and a Baby*, in contrast, is framed by sequences in which Michael completes the cartoon murals, which depict scenes from his and his roommates' life, that cover the walls of the entryway to their penthouse.

11. Definitions are cited from the third edition (1992) of the *American Heritage Dictionary of the English Language.*

12. I am reminded of Vincent Canby's witty column satirizing French assertions that the poor reception reserved for *Trois Hommes et un couffin* by New York film critics was politically motivated in protest of France's refusal to allow U.S. planes to fly over French territory during the 1986 raid on Libya ("How France's 'Cradle'").

13. Only in the American films does the mother's nationality differ from that of the three fathers. The choice of a British identity for Sylvia serves simultaneously to represent the initial "foreignness" of the mother and of maternity and the possibility of their cultural recuperation, precisely through a return to our origins, at once gendered, cultural, and cinematic.

WORKS CITED

Aptheker, Bettina. *Tapestries of Life: Women's Work, Women's Consciousness, and the Meaning of Daily Experience.* Amherst: U of Massachusetts P, 1989.

Boujet, Michel. "Le Cinéma cocooning." *Evénement du Jeudi* 23–28 Nov. 1989: 110.

Canby, Vincent. "Bachelor Fathers." *New York Times* 25 April 1986: C8.

———. "How France's 'Cradle' Was Rocked." *New York Times* 11 May 1986, 2: 1+.

———. "Ici se habla Euro-English." *New York Times* 4 June 1989, 2: 1+.

———. "Movies Lost in Translation." *New York Times* 12 Feb. 1989, 2: 1+.

Carroll, Raymonde. "Film et Analyse culturelle: Le Remake." *Contemporary French Civilization* (1989): 346–59.

Chodorow, Nancy. *The Reproduction of Mothering: Psychoanalysis and the Sociology of Gender.* Berkeley: U of California P, 1978.

Corliss, Richard. "What Dreams Come To." *Time* 25 January 1993: 69.

Dondelinger, Jean. *Les Rencontres cinématographiques de Beaune* (17–21 October 1991). Unpublished proceedings.

Duchen, Claire, ed. and trans. *French Connections: Voices from the Women's Movement in France.* Amherst: U of Massachusetts P, 1987.

Dudovitz, Resa L. *The Myth of Superwoman.* London: Routledge, 1990.

Durham, Carolyn A. *The Contexture of Feminism: Marie Cardinal and Multicultural Literacy.* Urbana: U of Illinois P, 1992.

———. "Taking the Baby Out of the Basket and/or Robbing the Cradle: 'Remaking' Gender and Culture in Franco-American Film." *French Review* 65 (1992): 774–84.

Ehrenreich, Barbara. *The Hearts of Men: American Dreams and the Flight from Commitment.* New York: Anchor, 1983.

Eisenstein, Hester, and Alice Jardine, eds. *The Future of Difference.* Boston: Hall, 1980.

Fischer, Lucy. *Shot/Countershot: Film Tradition and Women's Cinema.* Princeton: Princeton UP, 1989.

Garcia, Irma. *Promenade femmelière: Recherches sur l'écriture féminine.* 2 vols. Paris: des femmes, 1981.

Juhasz, Suzanne. "Toward a Theory of Form in Feminist Autobiography: Kate Millet's *Flying* and *Sita;* Maxine Hong Kingston's *The Woman Warrior.*" *Women's Autobiography.* Ed. Estelle C. Jelinek. Bloomington: Indiana UP, 1980. 221–37.

Mancini, Marc. "French Film Remakes." *Contemporary French Civilization* 13 (1989): 32–46.

Marks, Elaine, and Isabelle de Courtivron, eds. *New French Feminisms.* New York: Schocken Books, 1981.

Modleski, Tania. "Three Men and Baby M." *Camera Obscura* 17 (1988): 69–81. Reprinted in *Feminism Without Women: Culture and Criticism in a "Postfeminist" Age.* New York: Routledge, 1991. 76–89.

Moi, Toril. *Sexual/Textual Politics: Feminist Literary Theory.* London: Methuen, 1985.

Mordore, Michel. "Portrait de star en bébé." *Nouvel Observateur* 22–28 Nov. 1985: 106.

Penley, Constance, ed. *Feminism and Film Theory.* New York: Routledge, 1988.

Pertié, Olivier. "Un Couffin pour cent millions de dollars." *Nouvel Observateur* 29 Jan.–4 Feb. 1988: 80–81.

Serceau, Michel. "Un Phénomène spécifiquement cinématographique." *Le Remake et l'adaptation.* Ed. Michel Serceau and Daniel Protopopoff. Paris: CinémAction, 1989. 6–11.

Serreau, Coline. *Trois Hommes et un couffin*. *L'Avant-Scène* 356 (1987).

Showalter, Elaine. "Feminist Criticism in the Wilderness." *Critical Inquiry* 8 (1981): 179–205.

Vinay, J. P., and J. Darbelnet. *Stylistique comparée du français et de l'anglais*. Paris: Didier, 1973.

Zeldin, Theodore. *The French*. New York: Vintage, 1984.

CHAPTER ELEVEN

Pretty Woman with a Gun:
La Femme Nikita *and*
the Textual Politics of "The Remake"

LAURA GRINDSTAFF

I was falsely accused of a hideous crime and sentenced to life in prison. One night I was taken from my cell to a place called "Section One," the most covert anti-terrorist group on the planet. Their ends are just but their means are ruthless. If I don't play by their rules, I die.

—Opening voice-over to
La Femme Nikita, the television series

One of USA network's most popular television shows of the 1990s, *La Femme Nikita* has an interesting textual pedigree. It was based on Luc Besson's 1990 French film of the same name, which was remade a year later as the Hong Kong action movie *Black Cat* (Shin, 1991, and immediately followed by the sequel *Black Cat II* [Shin, 1992]), then remade again by Hollywood in 1993 as *Point of No Return* (Badham, 1993). Significantly, the story told in all four versions itself points self-reflexively to the process of remaking, since *La Femme Nikita* is a tech-*noir* Pygmalion tale about a woman who is "rescued" from her original circumstances and made-over into something "better."

The remake is one of the most undertheorized yet longstanding of cinematic conventions, only lately emerging as an object of scholarly interest and debate (see Serceau and Protopopoff [*Le Remake*], Leitch, Horton and McDougal, Durham). Loosely defined as new versions of existing films, remakes appear to occupy a place in American consumer culture much like that of Barbie dolls or Beanie Babies: if it worked once, do it again. Why mess with a good thing? As Brashinsky puts it, "the remake is the most explicit gesture of a culture that . . . cannot express itself through anything but a quote" (163). Yet as Brashinsky and others also point out, the remake is simultaneously a rich site for critical analysis precisely because its derivative status—its very secondariness and duplicity—forces a certain theoretical stock-taking of conventional notions of authorship, authenticity, and originality.

Even at first glance we can see that "original" and "copy" stand in a somewhat different relation to one another depending on the particular circuit of exchange. For example, classic films can be remade by contemporary directors (as with *Father of the Bride* or *Cape Fear*), the same director can remake an earlier version of his or her own film (as with Hitchcock's *The Man Who Knew Too Much*), foreign language films can be remade for an English-speaking audience (as with *Breathless*, the 1983 Hollywood remake of Godard's 1959 original), or the new film can borrow so loosely from an older one it is not officially acknowledged to be a remake at all (as with *Body Heat*, based on *Double Indemnity*, or *Dressed to Kill*, based on *Psycho*). It should also be noted that the concept of the remake can extend beyond the immediate cinematic context, since films remake popular television shows (*The Brady Bunch, Mission Impossible, The X-Files, South Park*), while television shows remake popular films (*M*A*S*H, The Odd Couple, La Femme Nikita*), and both films and television shows remake or adapt comic book stories (*Superman, Batman, X-Men* and the like).

These various relations are complicated by the fact that many, if not most, "original" films are themselves adapted from plays, novels, or other literary source material—which in turn borrow liberally from, or are directly based upon, other literary sources. Moreover, the existence of generic conventions in literature, cinema, and television ensures that all narratives within a given genre can be considered in the broadest sense "copies" of one another insofar as genre texts recapitulate an established (though by no means static) set of thematic and iconographic codes. Yet the film remake is not itself a genre, nor is it a separate category of narrative, exactly; like its cousins, the adaptation and the sequel, the remake is a species of intertextual interpretation and translation, one that, because it typically retells a work of the same medium, foregrounds more obviously than does the adaptation or sequel its own indebtedness to another originary text (see Braudy and Brashinsky).

The case of "La Femme Nikita"[1] is an ideal vehicle through which to examine the complexities of the remake and its structural relations of indebtedness, since it cuts across mediums and across cultures, and since the "origin story" in this case is itself so clearly enmeshed in a web of intertextual operations. My main focus will be the circuit of exchange between France and the United States, not because the Hong Kong version is any less interesting or worthy of analysis (quite the contrary), but because France and the United States stand in a particular historical relation to one another regarding the matter of "original" and "copy." This historical relation looms large in the condemnation of Hollywood remakes by certain French critics, who see in Hollywood's appropriation of foreign films not only economic exploitation and cultural imperialism but confirmation of the United States' derivative cultural status. Thus *Point of No Return* and the later television series are to *La Femme Nikita* what the United States is to France and Western Europe—their "remake."

Yet, as I shall argue, the lines of cultural influence here are no *aller simple* but rather more complicated than the above cartography might suggest. In the case of "La Femme Nikita" specifically (and of the film remake more generally), original and copy must be seen as mutually constitutive concepts. Like the relation between self and other, they are implicated in ways that cannot adequately be described as a simple mirroring or reflection. That the U.S. media are exploitative and hegemonic is not in question; however, the fact that U.S. remakes of French films produce a hostile critical response in which the existence of the remake is framed as evidence of the United States' "natural" cultural inferiority also raises important psychoanalytic questions about the role of narcissism and aggressivity in self/other relations. My aim is not to establish which country makes better films, nor to deny the importance of economic explanations (after all, one does not remake a film expecting to lose money). Rather, I hope to use "La Femme Nikita" to address some general issues central to any discussion of the film remake—those of intertextuality, authorship, and genre—as well as explore from a psychoanalytic perspective how certain critiques of the

France-to-Hollywood remake are structured by self/other relations that, interestingly, closely parallel those of the Nikita storyline itself. A psycho-analytically informed framework allows me to avoid the problematic distinctions made routinely by media critics between "high" art and "low" culture, "good" original and "bad" copy—distinctions which, when applied to *La Femme Nikita* and *Point of No Return* in particular, also reproduce cultural stereotypes linking France (and Western Europe generally) with art and authenticity and the United States with commodification and mass production. As we shall see, the producers of the U.S. television series unwittingly reinforced this association by seeking to emulate the "international, European quality" of the French original rather than the (by implication) pedestrian quality of the American remake.

THEORIZING THE REMAKE AS TRANSLATION

In an essay titled "Twice-Told Tales," Thomas Leitch argues that implicit in the phenomenon of the remake is the suggestion that the original film was outstanding (otherwise, why bother to remake it at all?), and yet the remake will be better still (otherwise why not simply watch the original, or watch it again?) (142). Leitch suggests that remakes seek to mediate between the contradictory claims of being "just like their originals only better" in several ways, depending on, among other things, whether their main points of reference are the films they remake or the material on which both films are based; the first instance necessitates a certain attitude of fidelity or homage toward the original film, while the latter suggests a more revisionary stance. He outlines four different categories of Hollywood remake—the readaptation, the update, the homage, and the "true remake"—each with its own characteristic means of resolving the contradictory claims between sameness and superiority (142–45).

Andrew Horton and Stuart Y. McDougal's more recent and comprehensive edited volume on the film remake is less invested in developing a typology of the remake than in examining its limits and boundaries, and in extending the concept of remake beyond its narrow Hollywood context to encompass diverse cultures and different media. Most of the essays in this volume agree in one way or another that the remake is but a special and precise institutional form of the "structure of iterability" that exists within and between all films, one that has a particular affinity with genre at large (Wills 148). Like genre films, remakes are presumably attractive partly because they translate a favored narrative into new terms: a new cinematic language, a new era, a new social and political context. As such, and as Leo Braudy points out in his afterward to the volume, remakes, like genre films, are always at some level concerned with unfinished cultural (or psychological or economic) business.

Remakes are also fundamentally concerned with the issue of originality. Like adaptations, they are rereadings that both secure the status of some prior text as originary while at the same time challenging the fixity of its meaning. They thus intensify basic critical tensions pitting artistic or authorial vision against mediation and re-vision. Yet the distinction between vision and re-vision, reading and rereading, is not always obvious or neatly separable. For example, Hitchcock is considered one of cinema's greatest original auteurs, yet as McDougal points out, 70 percent of Hitchcock's films were adaptations of novels, stories, or plays, and even many of his films can be seen as "remakes" of earlier ones (the same claim has been made about the films of Jean Cocteau). Likewise, how far back should one go to uncover the founding narrative that has inspired a film or series of texts? As Braudy asks, "are James Whale's *Frankenstein* and Tod Browning's *Dracula* originary texts for the many versions that follow, or are they themselves remakes of the preceding plays, which are in turn remakes of the original novels of Mary Shelley and Bram Stoker?" (331). Or, he asks, why stop with *The Jazz Singer* as the inspiration for *The Benny Goodman Story* or *St. Louis Blues* when one could trace the line back to John Locke's argument for a paternal authority to replace the power of the monarch? Why stop at *Double Indemnity* (or the novel upon which it is based) as the progenitor text for *Body Heat* when one can go back to *Oedipus Rex*? Instances like this reveal how, the closer one looks, the blurrier the edges of what constitutes "the remake" become.

But the remake is not simply an extreme version of similarity, the point beyond which similarity becomes something more than a question of general influence. The remake involves structural repetition of a peculiar sort, one that I think can be explored fruitfully by the concept of translation. While remakes are not translations in any conventional sense, U.S. adaptations of foreign films certainly raise many of the same concerns about fidelity, superiority, and appropriation as do literary translations of foreign texts. Moreover, the status and fate of the original text is a central concern of translation theory, insofar as the term "translation" tends to invoke simultaneously the twin concepts of fidelity and betrayal. As Thomas Jackson notes, translation enacts an inevitable paradox, for to translate something is by definition to change it (81). Most obviously, what a Hollywood remake of a foreign film seeks to change is the status of the subtitles, replacing them with a new, second-order structure of iterability that neutralizes the "otherness" of the original film. To quote David Wills, "the translation that is the subtitles renders explicit the particular form of transposition that the Hollywood remake of a foreign film involves, namely, its removal to a more familiar place—a tramp falls into a Beverly Hills swimming pool instead of the Seine, a Las Vegas petty criminal falls for a French architecture student instead of a French existentialist hero falling for an American student and would-be journalist" (149).

How is this transposition to be accomplished, then? What is the task of the translator? What does it mean to render a "faithful" or "accurate" translation? Robin Lakeoff posits that one ought to be able to understand a translation "in the same spirit in which it was intelligible in the original," while Rosemary Waldrop insists the translator must "find the genetic code of the work" and "get from the surface to the seed" (qtd. in Jackson 83, 86). But "in the same spirit" and "genetic code of the work" still frame the discussion of translation as a question of intention or meaning, and whether meaning has been adequately conveyed. As Walter Benjamin points out, however, the seed or nucleus of a text is often best defined as the very element that does not lend itself to translation (75). Thus the most frequent point of discussion in translation theory concerns the faithful reproduction across linguistic barriers of something essential about an original text, which, paradoxically, might very well be impossible to convey since it is here that the specificity of the two signifying systems are at stake (see Andrew). It should also be noted that a concern with faithfulness or accuracy is not simply a static feature of the translation process but varies according to the status of the originary text, and it is far more pressing when the original is canonized or sacralized within cultural tradition than when it derives from popular culture. The "integrity" of popular sources is always less of an issue, since part of what distinguishes elite from popular culture in the first place is the latter's "openness" to appropriation and intervention. "High" culture texts, on the other hand, demand a more respectful, worshipful attitude. As Lawrence Levine has documented, the "sacralization" of certain forms of theater, art, opera, and music in the United States during the late nineteenth century necessitated, among other things, endowing these forms with unique, aesthetic properties that rendered them sacred, exclusive, and inviolable.

Translation involves more than the mechanical reproduction of meaning or the transfer of information from one language to another. Benjamin, for example, suggests that translation ultimately serves the purpose of expressing the central reciprocal relationship *between languages*, rather than any specific relationship between meaning/content and language. In translation, he writes, "the great motif of integrating many tongues into one true language is at work" (77). Translation reveals the unifying force that underlies all languages and makes each the necessary complement or supplement of the other; in so doing it "catches fire on the eternal life of the works and the perpetual renewal of language" (74). In other words, translations both express the concept of "pure language" by enabling communication across linguistic barriers and constitute the "afterlife" of original texts. Dudley Andrew suggests something similar in his discussion of cinematic adaptations; he argues that the dialectical interplay between the literary forms of one period with the cinematic forms of another can preserve the distinctiveness of the original text while allowing it a new life within the cinema. The concept of adaptation or translation here depends less on *fidelity to* the original than on the *fertility of* the original to inspire or stimulate continued cultural production.

According to Eve Bannet, this last point is important because it means, ideally, that the translator is not necessarily another writer's rival for fidelity to the truth but can be seen as his or her collaborator and ally, for if the translator is indebted to another writer (or filmmaker) for source material, the other writer (filmmaker) is indebted to the translator for prolonging the life of the work (175). On this point Bannet quotes Derrida: "the original is not a plenitude which would come to be translated by accident. The original is in the situation of demand, that is, of a lack or exile. The original is indebted *a priori* to the translation. It's survival is a demand and a desire for translation" (175). Yet if a translation ensures the longevity of a text, it is important to ask, particularly in light of the Hollywood remake: *What* gets translated and therefore "perpetually renewed?" Why are some works translated and not others, and to what uses are these translations put? Bannet notes that some scholars see translation playing a significant role in the struggle between rival ideologies both within and across national cultures, since *what* gets translated is often a function of a work's centrality or marginality in the culture of origin, and *how* it gets translated often depends on the political economy of textual production and reception in the target culture. For those working within a Marxist paradigm, she writes, "translation is a way one culture appropriates and/or naturalizes what properly belongs to another; translation is a way one culture depropriates another by depriving it of its own proper meaning(s) and values and turning it into an indeterminate, exotic or inferior 'Other'" (181).

While this is an important insight, it seems to take for granted that the appropriation of cultural texts is unidirectional and top-down, with more powerful or hegemonic national cultures targeting less powerful ones. Consequently, it is of limited relevance in explaining, for example, the Hong Kong remake (and its sequel) of *La Femme Nikita* or even Hong Kong cinema in general, which, as Patricia Aufderheide has noted, is highly imitative and unabashedly opportunistic in its appropriation of any film that has had international commercial success, especially Hollywood blockbusters. According to Aufderheide, the brazen imitation that characterizes Hong Kong cinema ironically permits a certain cultural autonomy over the reworked material: "like genre work generally, imitation emphasizes treatment, style, and selection rather than originality of raw material, and it positively values entrepreneurial opportunism. The attitude mirrors and even plays with prevailing stereotypes of Hong Kong commercial culture" (193). This observation is consistent with my own reading of the Hong Kong remake of *Nikita*, and even more so of its sequel, which plays up the intertextual references of the original film to the point of parody.

The notion that translation is a mechanism whereby one culture improperly appropriates what properly belongs to another does, however, perfectly describe the position taken by French critics Michel Serceau and Daniel Protopopoff, whose series of essays on contemporary American remakes of French films appears in a special issue of the French-language journal *CinémAction* devoted exclusively to the film remake. They note that while American releases play routinely in France, very few French films are viewed by U.S. audiences; instead, Hollywood executives typically buy the rights to these films and remake them for a domestic market at a substantial profit. However, Serceau and Protopopoff seem less concerned by issues of economic exploitation than by what they believe to be the inherent failure of American remakes to respect the aesthetic and moral content of the original films, films which are not canonized per se but are part of France's overall "superior" artistic culture. Their critique draws largely on André Bazin, who calls for a remake that would "start over at the 'source,' and follow a natural course in a new historical and social space" ("Les Remakes américains" 101). In other words, the remake must allow for changes motivated by cultural and historical differences between it and the original text, while not denying the basic integrity of the original source.

But as we have seen with regard to literary translation, this matter of difference between remake and original poses a dilemma, for concepts such as "basic integrity"—like "in the same spirit" and "genetic code"— are not easily defined, nor is it clear which changes might preserve it and which might violate it. Nevertheless, Serceau denounces *Three Men and a Baby* and *Down and Out in Beverly Hills* as "superficial traces" and "mere shells" of what were once psychological masterpieces because they stray too far from the original films, while at the same time lacking any social or cultural significance of their own ("Hollywood à l'heure de Paris" 114). A recent *Daily Variety* report on the Hollywood remake came to a similar conclusion, noting that "studios overlook key cultural differences in their rush for a quick translation," and that even when the original director is hired for the new film, "you lose the magic the second time around" (Williams and Mork 20). This was certainly the verdict for *Point of No Return*, characterized in the press as a slavish imitation and unabashed rip-off, and it was also the initial verdict for the *Nikita* television series before the show garnered something of a cult following among the crucial 30–something demographic, at which point the critical response grew decidedly more favorable.

To explain the aesthetic gap between copy and source considered characteristic of American remakes, Serceau and Protopopoff position Hollywood as an industry driven by crass materialism and tailored to the production of mass culture, in contrast to French cinema, which carries on the "higher" tradition of Classical art and literature. Consequently, not only is Hollywood looking to Europe for source material with greater frequency than ever before, the time lapse between the release of original and remake has grown shorter and shorter—in effect, American filmmakers do not even respect a proper mourning period before lining their pockets ("Les Remakes américains" 100). *Daily Variety* again confirms this observation, noting that between 1987 and 1993, Hollywood remade seventeen contemporary French films, all of them released in the 1970s, 1980s, and 1990s. Moreover, studio executives sometimes remake a film without showing the original at all—as when Disney remade the 1986 French film *Les Fugitifs* in 1989 and put the original on the shelf, effectively killing its chances for a U.S. market (Williams and Mork 8). Industry sources agreee that it is easier for Hollywood producers to approve and finance a project that has already achieved box-office success elsewhere than take risks with an entirely new one, despite the fact that remakes of foreign films are far from a sure thing in Hollywood. Yet the *Variety* report also suggests that the current American penchant for French films is partly the result of remake deals initiated by French filmmakers themselves, since French films often make more money for their directors as a U.S. prototype than they do as original films in France. As one critic observed, "Gallic directors are wringing their hands—sometimes all the way to the bank—over Hollywood's latest colonization and its effect on the French film industry" (Williams and Mork 5).

Interestingly, the association of France (and Europe generally) with an ideology of "high" art and the United States with the ideology of "low" culture gets reproduced in the discussion and promotion of *La Femme Nikita* the series. Self-described devotee of Besson's film, producer and executive consultant Joel Surnow has repeatedly stated in interviews that the series is explicitly modeled after the French original and not the U.S. remake—in fact, he admits never having seen *Point of No Return*. Apparently by very definition, the American version lacked the particular sensibility he was looking to reproduce, one that could only come from a non-American source. As Surnow put it: "Once we started [the series], I made it a point not to [see *Point of No Return*]. When I was casting the role, I found that American actresses didn't capture the right spirit. They came off almost shrill when they would try to play the anger and the belligerence. There's a real European quality to this, and [Peta Wilson's] slight Australian accent gives her sort of an exotic, international quality that I think the show needs" (Bobbin 20). Media critics likewise distanced the show from the American remake, never failing to name the French film as the progenitor text ("the show is based on the 1991 film of the same name, not the American version, thankfully. It has a lot of style going for it, which is something you don't see on network television" [Goodman C3]). None of this has endeared Besson himself to the series, however. He is reportedly "not keen" on the whole idea and although Surnow has connections to the same French studio for which Besson occasionally works, Besson has refused any involvement.

While the Hollywood remake phenomenon (both in film and television) may well be exploitative, and while forms of "high" (read "Western European") culture were developed in France before the United States, when it comes to filmmaking the artistic relationship between France and the United States is no *aller simple*, that is, one-way ticket. A subsection of *CinémAction*'s special issue on the remake is aptly titled "Aller-Retour" (round-trip ticket), which implies an awareness, however veiled, of the reciprocal relation between the two countries. This reciprocity is made explicit both when Serceau and Protopopoff credit Classic Hollywood films of the 1930s for having created the "fundamental narrative myths of the screen" which informed virtually all subsequent filmmaking worldwide, and admit that "the paternity of the remake is difficult to know" because even "original" films are predicated upon preexisting narratives whose roots are not accessible ("Les Remakes américains" 103). One might note here, for example, the influence of Russian formalism and German expressionism on American filmmaking in the 1930s or the influence of German Expressionism and Italian neorealism on *film noir* a decade later. Serceau and Protopopoff argue that both the United States and France have at one time or another been at the forefront of cinematic history; each has also experienced at some point a "lack" of identity, turning to the other for artistic inspiration. Interestingly, this account of their relationship places each country in alternating paternal and maternal roles. The result is a kind of androgyny where France is both the masculine "self" (author and creator) and the feminine "other" (the mirror image, victim of U.S. cultural imperialism), and where the "killing" of the French original by the American remake is framed as a kind of patricide.

In the end, however, the *CinémAction* critique is quick to conclude that this shifting and sliding has come to a halt—progressed, in effect, to the point of no return—and that France has replaced the United States as cinematic mythmaker. For Serceau, the increasing dependence of Hollywood on foreign cinema signals a "lack" within the U.S. film industry which he interprets as a profound crisis of inspiration, one that has apparently stymied film production everywhere but in France: "Given the current inspirational crisis that has affected cinema all over the world, we must state that French cinema is perhaps the only one to have retained its capacity for innovation and originality" ("Hollywood à l'heure de Paris" 114). This framing allows both authors to characterize the contemporary remake trend as Hollywood's "search for it's own shadow" ("Hollywood à la recherche de son ombre" 97), and proclaim the "death" of U.S. hegemony: the French have assumed the paternal role once and for all.

Rather than discount *Point of No Return* because it is a "bad" translation unable to reproduce the magic of the original or because it appropriates for U.S. commercial gain what properly belongs to France, it seems more productive to ask how this particular appropriation can challenge and advance our theorizing about the film remake. In *Reading Lacan*, Jane Gallop uses a psychoanalytic framework to address several implications of the failure of translation, an analysis that has relevance for some of the issues raised by Serceau and Protopopoff. As Gallop observes, "any translator, any person who devotes great time and effort to conveying someone else's words, is already operating with a strong identification, already wishing to operate as a double" (66). In other words, a translator may be drawn to a work because it mirrors himself or herself in some way. Lawrence Venuti makes a similar argument in his essay "Sympatico," suggesting that the translator becomes aware of his intimate sympathy with the foreign writer only when he recognizes his own voice in the foreign text.

It is perhaps no surprise, then, that Hollywood chose to remake *La Femme Nikita*, a film that many critics agree was highly Americanized from its inception. From this perspective, financial gain is only one of a series of potential attractions involved in the decision-making process: Hollywood executives and filmmakers are drawn to *La Femme Nikita* by a kind of primary narcissism because it provides them with a flattering image of themselves. At the same time, recognition is always simultaneously misrecognition as well. Translation is "prey to distortion" because it is "unwittingly deformed" by the translator's individual and collective imaginary (Gallop 66), and this opens up a site of difference which generates hostility. Hence, the negative critical response to film remakes. What this framework allows is a concept of "other" that is relational as well as oppositional: the other is always part of the self, and the very experience of self depends on the existence of other. Gallop suggests that the confrontation between original and copy provokes aggressive behavior in the original (or, more accurately, in its defenders) because of unconscious mechanisms operating in the constructon of the self/other relationship. According to Gallop, translations provide key sites or moments in literature (and, by extension, film) where the machinations of the mirror phase—the moment of recognition and misrecognition of self as separate from other—are staged and revealed.

ORIGIN STORIES: AMERICAN INFLUENCES

To summarize, the relationship between *La Femme Nikita* and *Point of No Return* is only one of a series of identificatory or mirroring processes, for both the attraction of American filmmakers to Americanized French films and the hostility on the part of French critics to Hollywood remakes are symptomatic of the Imaginary[2] relationship between copy and original. To complicate matters further, *Nikita* is a Pygmalion adaptation about a character who is literally "remade" against her will, creating a *mise-en-abîme* of remakes and attractions.

Evidence of *Nikita*'s "Americanization" exists on multiple levels, and U.S. media critics were quick to point out such influences, calling it "an ultraviolent mutation of the James Bond genre" (Alleva 373), "a Frenchified version of that notorious American genre, the political paranoia picture" (Simon 56), and "the latest prototype in France's search for the ultimate femme fatale" (Johnson 47). This last critic also compares *Nikita* to *Pretty Woman.* "In the guise of an action movie," he writes, "it unfolds as a thinly veiled sexual fantasy about a seductive slave—a punk Pretty Woman with a license to kill" (47). An *LA Weekly* article apprising the television series remarked that while none of the various remakes compared favorably to the original, "lack of originality" was hardly a credible critique since even the original wasn't all that original: "A lawless punkette, facing the gas chamber on a murder charge, agrees to save her own skin by becoming a polished assassin for a shadowy government agency. The crooked heroic element recalls Hitchcock's *To Catch a Thief,* the gleaming gunplay is straight out of *James Bond,* and the strong woman holding her own in a hyperbolic, comic-book universe is visibly the goddaughter of *Barbarella*" (82).

While I believe the most compelling and sustained intertextual references are to *film noir,* there are other aesthetic and generic links. Among them is indeed the James Bond espionage-thriller, the penultimate genre of the Cold War. Nikita is, after all, a Russian name; in fact, it is Khrushchev's first name, premier of the former Soviet Union from 1958 to 1964. Nikita Khrushchev was a force for change within the communist block: he instigated a policy of de-Stalinization and peaceful coexistence with foreign—especially capitalist—countries, negotiated for nuclear testing controls with the United States, and encouraged other eastern block countries to find their own paths to socialism, which, arguably, led to their growing independence. Khrushchev thus played a major role in thawing Cold War hostilities, adopting a more "feminized," permissive approach to both national and international relations. *La Femme Nikita* references the Russia-U.S. connection both through the Bond-ish narrative of political intrigue, and, more literally, through the naming of the two main characters: besides Nikita there is also her mentor/trainer, "Bob," whose quintessentially American name is never lengthened in the film to the more French-compatible "Robert." Nikita herself is linked to Khrushchev in yet another way: the Russian premier was well-known for certain personal eccentricities, particularly his boisterous vulgarity in public settings, and in the first half of the film, Nikita is nothing if not boisterous and vulgar in public—indeed, these qualities prove to be almost insurmountable barriers to her "reform." Interestingly, while the U.S. and Hong Kong remakes downplay the James Bond references to some degree, changing the Russian names of both the film and title character, the Hong Kong sequel plays them up. Indeed, *Black Cat II* could easily be read as a parody of the Bond genre. Much of the film is set in Russia, and involves the search for a stolen roll of microfilm that contains highly classified government information. At one point, we witness the attempted assassination of Russian president Boris Yeltsin, while the opening ski-chase scene following the murder of an unnamed Russian operative is an extended citation from *A View to a Kill* starring Roger Moore.

La Femme Nikita also recalls the recent emergence of strong-women action narratives such as the *Alien* trilogy and the *Terminator* films. In the original film, Nikita runs with a gang of thuggish drug addicts and kills a police officer in the course of a heist; she is caught and sentenced to die but so impressed are the authorities with her ruthless attitude that her death is faked so that she might be retrained as a government assassin. Like Sarah Conner of *Terminator 2* and Sergeant Ripley of *Alien(s)*, Nikita is a tough woman who packs a gun and knows how to use it—a lean, mean, fighting machine who moves easily within the traditionally masculine sphere of covert military-industrial operations. A central feature of all three characters is their hardbody androgyny, which not only minimizes the surface cues of gender difference (thus subverting their presumed naturalness), but poses a challenge to the narrative logic of classical film which, as many film scholars have argued, is powered largely by the oedipal desire to establish the nature of masculinity and femininity, and the difference between the two (see Bellour, Heath, and Mulvey). Although these films do ultimately tend to reassert traditional assumptions of gender specificity—Ripley and Conner are driven to heroism by "maternal instinct," while Nikita's femininity is reestablished through her rejection of violence—they do so only after the heroine in each case has considerably troubled its binary construction. Interestingly, in *La Femme Nikita* even the physical space of the heroine's transformation from hoodlum outlaw to government assassin carries an androgynous valence, for the underground complex that serves as her training ground is both the womb-like site of Nikita's "gestation" and "rebirth," as well as the phallic site of her induction to power.[3]

Thus the "Nikita" narrative places a (post)modern, strong-woman character at the center of what is essentially a classic Pygmalion tale. Performing the role of Henry Higgins are Nikita's two "midwives," one male and one female: spymaster Bob is in charge of her physical and intellectual training, while the sophisticated Amande schools her in the "feminine graces" of deportment and beauty. In the television series, Nikita is trained by fellow operative (and future lover) Michael, aided by the agency's chief strategist, Madeleine. As Madeleine tells Nikita in the pilot episode, "you can shoot, you can fight, but there is no weapon as powerful as your femininity." Overseeing the whole process is Operations, the steely-eyed, white-haired patriarch of Section One; together he and Madeleine function as the disciplinary "parents" of all the Section One operatives. This splitting of the Henry Higgins function into multiple characters emphasizes Nikita's task of embodying seemingly incompatible masculine and feminine qualities: aggressivity, ruthlessness, and physical strength with patience, grace, and beauty.

In the staging of these relations, the various "Nikita" texts share with certain other contemporary American films an iconography and visual style Constance Penley has called "tech-*noir*," in which machines and technology provide the texture and substance of the narrative.[4] Although Penley uses the term in reference to *The Terminator*, perhaps the prototypical tech-*noir* film is Ridley Scott's *Blade Runner*, which *La Femme Nikita* "quotes" in key ways. First, there is the similar iconography of the cavernous, subterranean government compound with its high-tech computers and an elaborate surveillance system where the heroine is remade, remolded, and reprogrammed in the image of her makers, given a new identity and a new past—a fate similar to that of the replicants in *Blade Runner*. Second, just as the most "human" of the replicants (Rachel) is implanted with the memories of her inventor's niece, Nikita is "implanted" with the memories of "Uncle Bob" during a key scene when Bob pays Nikita a surprise visit "on the outside." These memories function as any other: they are constructed representations that serve as "proof" of her identity. Photographs bear a similar burden in each film. Rachel shows Deckard a picture of herself as a little girl to prove she is human; in Besson's film, Bob shows Nikita photographs of her own funeral to prove precisely the opposite point: that she has no past, no humanity, no official existence, and is therefore easily "retired" should she step out of line or refuse to cooperate. All of the subsequent Nikita texts reproduce these scenes with remarkable consistency.

Elissa Marder suggests that in *Blade Runner* both replicants and photographs are supposed to function "as nonhuman receptacles for human image and memory. They are designed to reflect the human figure perfectly—to cast back an image of humanity in order to confirm our own" (97). The fact that both objects "fail" reveals that the relationship between subject and object, self and other, is never simply a mirroring; it is also a projection. Thus Nikita's *inability* to be a machine—specifically a killing machine—emerges as the central tension of all three film versions, and even more so of the later television series. Like Deckard, Nikita is a highly unwilling government assassin whose job causes her considerable psychic conflict. Like the replicants, she is "more human than human," in fact, too human for her own good, her remaking, in a sense, too successful. For while the rebellious Nikita of the film's opening scene kills without conscience, the very qualities that eventually "civilize" her, and allow her reintegration into civil society as a government operative, have made her vulnerable to human feeling and emotion—particularly love.

Thus the conflict between masculine and feminine mentioned above gets developed and transposed into a more fundamental conflict between human and machine, between emotion, passion, and compassion on the one hand, and the subordination of these qualities to a passionless, technocratic ideal on the other. This tension is experienced most excruciatingly by Nikita herself, but in the television series finds its echo in Michael and some of the other operatives as well—even, on occasion, parental authority figures Madeleine and Operations. Indeed, the relationship between the older couple mirrors that of Nikita and Michael in that it is fraught with a sexual attraction that can never be freely expressed lest the emotional fallout compromise their professional goals. The television series thus has the luxury of repeatedly dramatizing and developing the basic conflict between human and machine, love and duty, that the films must illustrate with greater economy. Notable in this regard is *Black Cat*, the Hong Kong remake, in which Erica (the Nikita character) is "implanted" not only with the memories of her death but also a computerized brain chip. As her mentor/trainer explains, the chip is a prototype, part of a government experiment, and will help her reach her "full potential" as an assassin. Not coincidentally, it also doubles as a surveillance device that enables the government to track her every move. Thus she is more obviously rendered a type of cyborg or robot under male control—but an emotional being nevertheless who experiences forbidden love. At the end of the film while Erica and her boyfriend are attempting a getaway, her trainer intercepts them and demands that she kill the boyfriend. So she shoots him point blank in the chest. He falls dead—or so the trainer thinks. But the boyfriend survives because she aimed for the left side of his chest and we know from an earlier scene in the film that, due to a unique genetic anomaly, his heart—ultimate signifier of love—lies on the right.[5]

The point of all this is not to celebrate *Blade Runner* or any other American film as the origin story for *La Femme Nikita*. The point is to reiterate that "the paternity of the remake is difficult to know," and that all creations involve re-creations, all presentations re-presentations. As Leitch and others have argued, remakes simply provide an unusually clear example of the operations of every genre: "Every film genre," he writes, "however modest its aims, positions its audience to expect the conventions of the genre but then withholds any explicit acknowledgment that it is borrowing those conventions." In other words, films constantly quote from one another but fail to properly cite their sources, performing what Leitch calls a "ritual invocation/denial" of discursive features (148). Taken to its logical conclusion, the ritual of invocation/denial implies there is no such thing as a truly original or authentic text, since the conventions of narrative and language itself preexist any individual author. This is, in fact, one of the fundamental premises of *Blade Runner*. As Kaja Silverman observes, "Deckard is an extended citation from *film noir*, and hence himself a copy, as is Bryant, the corrupt and unfeeling policeman. Tyrell is also a replicant of sorts; he reprises a whole history of imaginary scientists who give rise to unconventional life forms, from Frankenstein to Metropolis's Dr. Rotwang" (124). But the more profound sense in which the humans in the film might be said to be copies stems from Silverman's observation that subjectivity is relational, dependent upon others for its very existence. Thus Deckard is as much a replicant as Rachel because "his identity, like hers, is a composite of images that come to him from elsewhere, a representation of pre-existing representations" (Silverman 129).

Ironically, the distinction between original and copy seems easiest to make precisely when the original and its remake(s) are most closely aligned. That is, the more faithful the remake to the film remade, the less doubt there seems to be about questions of authorship, genre, and inter-textuality, because authorship and ownership are automatically attached to the "original" film. Thus, *Point of No Return* emerges as an unabashed commercial rip-off of *La Femme Nikita*, but the relationship of *Body Heat* to *Double Indemnity* is considerably more ambiguous, and the debt owed *Citizen Kane* by Alan Resnais's *Providence* or Todd Haynes's *Velvet Gold-mine* is more tenuous still. While I would not deny that *Nikita* is "supe-rior" to *Point of No Return* according to the aesthetic criteria film critics typically employ, or that Luc Besson—who both wrote and directed *Nikita* and was slated to direct the American counterpart before John Badham replaced him at the last minute—is a key authorial presence, our thinking about the remake must acknowledge the ways in which inter-textuality and generic conventions operate in the cinema, and in discourse more generally. The introduction of the television series—"a TV rip-off of a French movie rip-off of the last 30 years of American/English spy movies" (Simon 2)—complicates the "Nikita" lineage further still.

Significantly, *La Femme Nikita* already embodied a theory of the remake (and its failures) long before the *Black Cat* films or *Point of No Return* appeared on the scene. As a tech-*noir* adaptation of the Pygmalion myth in which a woman is subjected to a dramatic make-over, the "Nikita" narrative stands as a synecdoche for the relation between the original film and its copies. Moreover, just as the storyline within each text explores the power of one person or entity (Bob, Operations/Madeleine, the state) to remake the other (Nikita/Erica/Maggie) in its own image, the metanarra-tive told by Serceau and Protopopoff about the relationship *between* Hol-lywood remakes and their French originals is likewise about the power of one country (the United States) to remake the other (France) in its own image. If we consider that self/other relations are frequently gendered, this power relationship draws additional force from the metaphor of prostitu-tion contained both in the films themselves and, less directly, in the argu-ments of French critics disturbed by Hollywood's appropriation of French work. Nikita is pimped out for violence rather than sex by a patriarchal fig-ure; similarly, French sources quoted in *Daily Variety* are concerned about the increasing tendency of French directors, driven by financial considera-tions, to, in effect, "prostitute" themselves to powerful Hollywood moguls.

At some level, then, the Nikita narrative can be read as the story of a woman's struggle not to be "othered," that is, not to be subsumed by the (masculine) Self and destroyed, just as our French critics protest the era-sure of French originals by their American counterparts. In this regard, the films are playing upon what could be considered the base syntax of all *film noir*. The femme fatale of the classic *noir* films is invariably the hero's double or alter-ego at the same time she is his other. The femme fatale serves as the screen through which the male protagonist both sees himself and projects his deepest anxieties; he is simultaneously attracted and repelled by her, forced to realize through the figure of the woman the terms of his own narcissistic and aggressive subjectivity. *Film noir* thus represents a particularly clear example of the ideological project that characterizes much classic narrative cinema: the fetishistic construction of "Woman" (white, heterosexual) as the cultural repository of difference, rooted in castration anxiety (see Mulvey, Place, Harvey). In this sense, narrative cinema generally and *film noir* particularly perform a kind of textual remaking of their own: the remaking of white, heterosexual woman as an image "cut to the measure of desire" (Mulvey 67). This project, too, depends on the ritual of invocation/denial. *Noir* films invoke sexual difference (otherness), while simultaneously denying that this difference is a fiction and a function of the masculine subject's own psychic instability.

La Femme Nikita and its offspring are not mere replications of classic *noir* films, however. Most significantly, the Nikita character is the central protagonist as well as the "other." She is both hero, caught in a dangerous web of mystery and intrigue over which she has little control, and femme fatale, a mysterious woman with multiple and changing identities (signified by her three different names: Nikita/Marie/Joséphine in the French film, Maggie/Claudia/Nina in the American one).[6] Thus the films stand in a complicated relationship both to the *noir* tradition and to the oedipal tale which *noir* films enact—an origin story if there ever was one—because they ask the heroine to assume a masculinized and feminized relation to the phallus simultaneously. Many scholars have interpreted *noir* films as remakes of *Oedipus Rex*, a myth of destiny in which the son learns to know and accept his place under the law. The drama is concerned specifically with the primacy of male identity and male inheritance; the oedipal complex described by Freud articulates how men come to align themselves with patriarchal power by identifying with the obligations of heterosexual masculinity, while femininity signifies little more than lack and impotence. The "Nikita" narratives reconceptualize the classic oedipal tale around the figure of a woman/daughter, asking "what happens when a woman tries to assume the phallus for herself?"

In the original film and its U.S. remake, the bottom line is that things fall apart, just as they did for poor Oedipus. Our protagonist struggles for power in a gendered social space, subject to constant surveillance and male control. Like the oedipal son, she can gain access to cultural authority only through male kinship structures. Although she tests the laws of the patriarch (symbolized by the state) and attempts to circumvent its power, she must renounce her transgressive desires and identify with the masculine regime in order to assume her place as heir. This assumption is figured in Lacanian terms as the movement from the Imaginary to the Symbolic marked by the acquisition of language, the computers and cameras of the government compound serving as the screens or mirrors through which this acquisition takes place. At the same time, as a woman she is defined by a certain absence and lack, without a language or discourse of her own, the vehicle through which patriarchal violence literally reproduces itself. As prostitute for the state, she can never be the rightful heir to cultural authority, no matter how hard she tries. In some ways the television series makes this point more forcefully than any of the films because its serial structure allows a repeated staging of the confrontation between Nikita and the law while at the same time delaying indefinitely any final resolution. She wins strategic battles, but the larger war goes on.

The impossibility of our protagonist's situation is signified by the "perverted" family relations in which she becomes enmeshed, as is often the case in classic *noir*. As Sylvia Harvey notes, many *noir* films of the 1940s are structured around the destruction or absence of romantic love and familial stability. In the *noir* world, men and women seek sexual satisfaction outside the conventional bonds of marriage, a transgression that both leads to the destruction of these bonds and suggests that the expression of sexuality is at odds with marriage—emphasized by the presence of husbands on crutches or in wheelchairs, clear signifiers of impotence and castration (Harvey 29). The male protagonist, too, is typically "castrated" (feminized) in that he is subjected to the authority of a more powerful man and cannot control either his desire for the woman or the events that she sets into motion. The woman, of course, is the pivot around which the circulation of male desire plays itself out, the one responsible for male impotence and the ultimate dissolution of the family unit.

Familial relations in *Nikita* and *Point of No Return* are similarly perverted. In the beginning of the original film, the heroine's "family" is a gang of criminal drug addicts. She is sentenced to die for committing a kind of patricide: she kills a police officer, not only a father figure and representative of the law but a man who looks remarkably like her future mentor, Bob. When her death is faked so that she can be adopted by Bob and

Amande and retrained, they prove to be surrogate parents to a family of thugs not so different from the one she left behind. Indeed, in the French original, when Nikita arrives at her first assignment, each of her fellow operatives assembled in the basement of the hotel bears a striking resemblance to a parallel member of her old gang. In both films, her first impulse after her release from the training center is to start nesting: she chooses a mate and converts a dilapidated apartment into cozy living quarters. But her attempts to build a normal life with her partner are continually thwarted by the *ab*normal intrusion of the father and state into the home, and this intrusion is figured in decidedly sexual terms: inevitably the phone call from Bob announcing her next assignment interrupts an embrace or follows a moment of postcoital tenderness. Not only is she on 24-hour call, but the very conditions of her servitude emphasize the complex enmeshment of sexuality and danger so common in *film noir* and make a mockery of her attempts to live as other "normal" women do.

In true oedipal fashion, the father-daughter relationship between Nikita and Bob is fraught with sexual tension and is positioned simultaneously as a relationship between lovers. Although they kiss only once, he is clearly in love with her, and her childlike demeanor throughout the film suggests a certain innocence and impetuousness that he gradually corrupts. His incestuous desire is underscored midway through the film when "Uncle Bob" meets Nikita's fiancé and the two men are immediately positioned as sexual rivals. The perverse familial relations in the two films which signify the impossibility of the heroine's situation ultimately break down when she initiates a "divorce" from Bob by running away. Like the two title characters in the film *Thelma and Louise*, the protagonist solves the dilemma of being female in a patriarchal society by disappearing, disengaging from the system altogether, literally embodying the absence and lack assumed to characterize femininity from the outset. In articulating this withdrawal, however, an interesting difference emerges between the American and French versions of the film, a difference that is significant in light of the previous discussion of the remake as translation.

POINTS OF DIFFERENCE:
THE "FAILURES" OF TRANSLATION

Recall that Gallop considers the study of translations to be significant because they provide a kind of lens through which to investigate the

294

FIGURE 11.1. Pretty woman with a gun (Anne Parillaud) in the vein of the James Bond subgenre in Luc Besson's *La Femme Nikita* (1990). Courtesy of the Museum of Modern Art, Film Stills Archive.

machinations of the Lacanian mirror stage. Translations expose the self/other relationship as one that is about both a narcissistic overidentification with one's image (the failure to distinguish self from other—as in *Point of No Return*) and the misrecognition of the self as wholly separate from the other (a misrecognition which produces aggression—as in the French critical response to American remakes). Recall also that all translations are in a sense failures or betrayals; they can never faithfully mirror the other because the self always gets in the way. However, it may be possible, as Gallop puts it, "to catch the functioning distortions of the translation as translation" (67). In other words, it may be possible to uncover important aesthetic and sociocultural differences between original and copy by focusing precisely on those moments in the text when the differences between original and copy are most obvious and deliberate—those moments Philip Lewis calls "abuses of translation." The vast majority of *Point of No Return* follows *Nikita* faithfully, almost to the shot. Why doesn't the entire film do so? Why are certain scenes altered? Presumably the differences speak partly to assumptions Hollywood producers make about the preferences and tastes of American audiences. But what else do the cracks in the mirror reveal?

One of the key differences is that Maggie, Nikita's American counterpart, is physically a more feminine character than Nikita. Maggie wears shorter dresses and higher heels, has longer hair, and masquerades as the ditzy blonde girlfriend of an ambassador during her most important mission, instead of posing as the ambassador, as in the French version. In keeping with her feminine persona, Maggie is also more frequently imaged and photographed than Nikita. During her political and physical make-over underground, we see computerized "before" and "after" images of her face. The man she falls in love with on the outside is a professional photographer, and photographs of the two of them and of Maggie alone adorn the apartment they share in Los Angeles, a significant location since Hollywood is recognized worldwide as a cultural center of image production (the photographer's role is perhaps lifted from the Hong Kong remake, in which Erica poses as a professional photographer). These markers of femininity can be read either as emphasizing the gender fluidity of Maggie's character in that they contrast starkly with her more "masculine" qualities, as Jeffrey Brown argues,[7] or as heightening the to-be-looked-at quality of Maggie as object of the male gaze. This latter reading is supported by Pauline MacRory's analysis of the musical scores of both films. MacRory notes that whereas Nikita's

FIGURE 11.2. A more feminine hit-woman (Bridget Fonda) with an even bigger gun acquits herself competently in her unexpected first postindoctrination job in John Badham's *Point of No Return* (1993). Courtesy of the Museum of Modern Art, Film Stills Archive.

character develops from childishness to maturity, Maggie's central transformation is from masculine to feminine, a transformation underscored less by the narrative itself than the music, which works consistently and repeatedly to "excuse" Maggie's violence in ways that the French score does not.

Perhaps the most telling difference between the two films is the ending, which turns clearly on the subject of the female image, and more specifically male control over that image. In the French version, the final scene shows Bob confronting the boyfriend, Marco, about Nikita's disappearance after her third and final assignment. Bob demands to know where she is, and accuses Marco of withholding information to protect her. Marco in turn accuses Bob of *failing* to protect her. Each knows the other is in love with Nikita. We never see Nikita again, however; she is simply gone, and we are left with the two men seated opposite one another, staring blankly out the window. All they see are their own reflections, as if to suggest that the woman they knew (or thought they knew) is little more than a projection of themselves. The ending is thus somewhat ambiguous: we don't know what happens to Nikita. The U.S. ending is less so, perhaps a comment on the assumption of Hollywood producers about the inability of U.S. audiences to tolerate ambiguity in their action films. In *Point of No Return*, Maggie tries to bargain with Bob: a final mission in return for her freedom. She nearly dies when the mission backfires, and after a confrontation between Bob and the boyfriend the next morning at Maggie's apartment regarding her whereabouts, we cut to a shot of Maggie herself walking down the street through heavy fog, her face bloodied and bruised. Bob sees her as he is driving away. He gazes after her a long while before using his car phone to tell his superiors that Maggie is dead, killed in a car crash. With this one simple phrase, the film grants him the power to "free" her, to return her to the dead—the very place he "saved" her from in the beginning. As Maggie continues to walk, her image dissolves into a close-up of her face, which is gradually revealed to be a photograph that we have seen before; it was taken by her boyfriend-fiancé and hangs above the fireplace in their apartment. As the credits roll, the camera tracks forward until only her eyes are visible in the frame.

La Femme Nikita and *Point of No Return* both seem to suggest that the options for women in a phallic regime are limited. They suggest that women's bodies, like men's, can be drafted and used for the reproduction of state violence. In order to gain cultural authority, women, like men, must identify with the law of the father and at the same time accept their own subjugation to that law. Like men, women are subjected to, as well as subjects of, discourses of surveillance and social control. Unlike men, however, and in particular, white men, women are not the primary authors of these discourses, thus their perception of themselves as "free" agents is doubly fraught with contradiction—and becomes a rich site for cinematic investigation into the bounds and limits of patriarchal power.

Given this, the ending of the French film in some ways makes a more powerful and critical statement about patriarchy, not because it is more "original," but because if white male privilege is predicated upon female subjugation, it is significant that Nikita disappears of her own accord, needing no one's help or permission. In contrast, the more feminine Maggie has to make a deal with Bob, who then retains control over the terms of her freedom. Her life is still his to grant or deny, and she only lives in the end because, paradoxically, he pronounces her dead. The fact that her two-dimensional image remains, haunting the final shot with a gaze neither seductive nor defiant, is a fitting allegory for the position of women in Western societies and a reminder of the film industry's role— as well as our own spectatorial complicity—in the construction of women, even white heterosexual women, on the margins of cultural authority. As merely a copy or trace of Maggie's former self, this image might also speak to us of the inability of remakes to capture the "essence" or "genetic code" of their originals. On the other hand, perhaps the image is cause for guarded optimism, for it also suggests that even Maggie's absence is marked by a presence. The inscription of Maggie through the photograph can be read as a refusal to go away, a refusal to disappear, from either the film or patriarchal culture more generally. In Benjamin's terms, the photograph-as-translation constitutes the afterlife and afterimage of the original work, thereby prolonging its power and influence.

In a far more direct fashion, the *Nikita* television series carries on this function, making possible the afterlife of the original text a different medium as well as a different culture. And interestingly, despite the "low" status of American television, the series has been deemed far more successful than either the U.S. or Hong Kong remakes in reproducing the tech-*noir* aesthetic critics so prized about the original film. Ironically, the most mass of mass mediums seems to realize most fully Bazin's vision of the adaptation as capturing, not the "letter" of the original text, which can be emulated in mechanical fashion (as in *Point of No Return*), but the "spirit" of the original text, its tones, values, and rhythms. As Andrew reminds us, this is a more intuitive enterprise, since finding stylistic equivalents for such intangible qualities is precisely the *opposite* of a mechanical process (423). That a USA-network television series could "start over at the source and follow a natural course in a new historical and social space" ("Les Remakes américains" 101) is notable given the failure of Hollywood films, generally speaking, to do the same. The show's success may even have surprised its producers, for when the series debuted in January of 1977, critics were less than enthusiastic: "all style, no substance, a typical TV compromise" (Kelleher 3); "more annoying than entertaining" (Hall B5); "an exercise in hopped-up mayhem. . . . Xena gone Eurotrash" (Roush D3). Audiences seemed to disagree, however, and the show, which was recently renewed for a limited fifth season, proved to be one of USA's most popular series.

As Elizabeth Weiss observes in her essay on the 1970s TV show *M*A*S*H*, a television series itself can be viewed as a kind of ongoing remake. Also based on a popular film, *M*A*S*H* was constantly revising itself, and as it became a hit with audiences, the producers gained more creative freedom from both the network and the audience. *La Femme Nikita* seems to have followed a similar trajectory. Like *M*A*S*H*, which retained but "toned down" certain elements from the original film for livingroom reception (most notably the operating room gore and the irreverence toward authority), *La Femme Nikita* on TV differs from *La Femme Nikita* on film in ways that speak to both the possibilities and constraints of the new medium. It too was "toned down" for the small screen; in fact, USA executives rejected the original pilot script (which closely followed the films) in which Nikita was a drug-addicted cop killer given a second chance by becoming a government assassin. On television there is no reference to drugs, Nikita was wrongfully accused as the killer (she accidentally stumbles upon the back-alley knifing of a policeman and is left holding the murder weapon), and she is not really an assassin—she is part of a "covert, anti-terrorist organization." If she kills it is either out of self-defense or because the target is evil and "deserves" it. According to producers, her guiltlessness makes her more of an underdog, and hence more accessible to audiences, since people can understand being in the wrong place at the wrong time, but not intentionally killing a cop while high on drugs. Peta Wilson, the actress who plays Nikita, describes her character as "an anti-hero, an angel in wolf's clothing" (Deggans F1; Endrst E4).

The fact that TV's Nikita is innocent of the crime that landed her in Section One also heightens the basic narrative conflict—her ambivalence at being a trained killer and her constant struggle to reconcile personal morals with professional duty, suppressing all emotion in the process. While the original pilot episode tells the story of the film up to the point where Nikita "graduates" and assumes her new life as secret operative, subsequent episodes "remake" this basic tension over and over in different guises, radiating out to encompass a wide variety of circumstances and other characters as well. In all of this Nikita remains the chief signifier of humanity in a world grown increasingly inhumane. As she tells an unsympathetic Madeleine in the first season finale just before attempting an escape from Section One, "I don't know if I can do this anymore . . . where you see targets and security risks, I see flesh and blood, someone's son, someone's friend. . . . I can't live like this, I can't take it."[8]

Cheesy, yes, but effective on screen because both characters and story have developed and become more nuanced over time and because Nikita's compassion and moral uprightness do not prevent her from kicking butt at least once or twice an episode—a penchant she shares with strong-woman counterparts Xena, the Warrior Princess, and Buffy, the Vampire Slayer. Indeed, despite the blatant advertising embedded in the show itself (as one critic put it, "Nikita is dressed and re-dressed so often, she should have a runway"); despite the vacuousness of its "anti-terrorist" politics (the show operates in political nowheresville and has been described as *The Prisoner* meets *Mission: Impossible* for the Melrose set); and despite the fact that the protagonist, again like Xena and Buffy, is a beautiful, svelt, white woman, the show is compelling in no small measure because Nikita is strong, aggressive, and independent while at the same time caring and compassionate. Given our culture's conflation of femininity with passivity, *La Femme Nikita* thus has the potential to empower female viewers in ways that male viewers have been privileged to take for granted. As Judith Halberstam observes in another context, "the depiction of women committing acts of violence does not simply use 'male' tactics of aggression for other ends; [rather] female violence transforms the symbolic function of the feminine within popular narratives and it simultaneously challenges the hegemonic insistence upon the linking of might and right under the sign of masculinity" (191).

Moreover, because Nikita's home life is sterile and lonely compared to its film counterpart (in the TV series Nikita has no Marco character to mate and nest with), and because her relationship with Michael (the Marco substitute) is presented as off-limits, their smoldering sexual attraction continually thwarted and delayed, Nikita the TV character is more amenable to a queer reading than Nikita the film character. Less obviously coded as lesbian or potentially lesbian than Xena, Nikita is nevertheless not a typical femme fatale, either on- or off-camera. Over six feet tall with a lean, muscular frame and a husky voice, Peta Wilson—or "Pete," as she is nicknamed—played championship basketball in high school and is reputed to be an outstanding athlete. She was apparently so tomboyish as a child that her mother, in an odd instance of life foreshadowing art, sent her to modeling school to "feminize" her (Rubin D1).

CONCLUSION

As David Wills observes in his essay on the Hollywood remake of *Breathless*, "there can never be a faithful remake, and not just because Hollywood demands compromises or because things get lost in translation or mistakes occur, but because there can never be a simple original uncomplicated by the structure of the remake, by the effects of such self-division" (157). No cultural text is a simple or direct representation or translation of social life. Like all translations, cinematic and televisual translations of stories and events—whether written, imaged, or lived—are prey to distortion, unwittingly formed, and de-formed, by the translator/filmmaker's imaginary, not to mention the structural and institutional constraints of the medium itself. I have used "La Femme Nikita" to say something about the desire of filmmakers, scholars, and critics for authenticity, originality, and faithful reproduction, as well as the more general psychoanalytic desire for the wholeness and plenitude of an autonomous self unmarked by traces of the other. I have argued that the relationship between *La Femme Nikita* and its U.S. remakes is only one of a series of identificatory or mirroring processes, for both the attraction of American filmmakers and television producers to Americanized French films and that the hostility on the part of French artists and critics toward these remakes are symptomatic of the Imaginary relationship between copy and original described by Lacan. The metanarrative told by Serceau and Protopopoff about the relationship between French and American films is about the power of one country (the United States) to remake the "other" (France) in its own image, but at the same time, these French critics are struggling to do some othering of their own.

Drawing on literary scholars from Central and Eastern Europe who critique translation theories that side automatically with the "weak and dispossessed," Bannet writes: "at some formative point in its history, every

national culture has borrowed heavily from others by appropriative translations, and that this fact deconstructs all nationalistic claims to linguis-
tic-cultural supremacy. The existence of appropriative translations in all
cultures only goes to show that there is a fundamental lack of self-identity
in national cultures, as well as a fundamental interdependence" (182). For
Bannet, translation is always an implicit agreement between two parties
that "I will change you and you will change me" (176). The television version of the "Nikita" narrative is an extreme illustration, undermining any
semblance of either narrative or cultural "purity": as a U.S. television
show filmed in Canada, starring an Australian woman (who grew up in
Papua New Guinea) and a French-Canadian man, and based on an Amer-
ican-influenced French film that was remade twice, first in Hong Kong
and then the United States, the show is a veritable pastiche of intercultural referents.

Of course, the principal beneficiary of this postmodern text, like the
principal beneficiary of Hollywood remakes, is a U.S.-based media conglomerate. Thus film and television remakes are unlike literary translations in that the greater reach and profitability of the newer mass media
pave the way for greater potential cultural and economic exploitation. But
while the most obvious reason to remake a film is financial, this is not the
end of the story, for in order to turn a profit the remaker must also believe
that the particular narrative in question is still compelling and thus worth
retelling. In some cases, the remake might be another attempt to "get it
right" (as in Hitchcock's *The Man Who Knew Too Much*) or it might be
an attempt to rack focus on a story, pulling peripheral or background elements to the fore. In this sense, Braudy notes "similar stories are not so
much retold for a new period, but [rather] the new period allows another
step in what is otherwise an internal evolution of the story" (330). In
other words, the source film can be seen as an individual expression of a
myth to be retold, rather than as coterminous with the myth itself. Ultimately, such conceptions of the remake emphasize the fertility of the original text, rather than the fidelity of the remake, and posits both as participating in a larger cultural enterprise whose value is outside their specific
relationship altogether (see Andrew). As Braudy observes, "the remake
resides at the intersection of the genetic and the generic codes. In even the
most debased version, it is a meditation on the continuing historical (economic, cultural, psychological) relevance of a particular narrative. A
remake is thus always concerned with what its makers and (they hope) its
audiences consider to be unfinished cultural business" (331).

Just as classic *film noir* may express white male anxieties about a postwar economy and working women's newfound independence and power (see Harvey and Place), tech-*noir* action narratives like *La Femme Nikita* may reflect collective fears and desires about the nature of self and identity, the options for "phallic" women and their relation to patriarchal law, as well as the intrusion of state authority into one's personal life, especially the so-called "private" sphere of family and home. The various "Nikita" texts also explore the dilemma of remaining human in an increasingly dehumanized, technocratic world, and of the struggle not to be made-over in the image of an/other. As long as these themes remain compelling, as long as they have cultural resonance, they will be taken up and retold, transposed onto new terrain. Yet the landscape of the remake-as-translation is no *aller simple*, not only because the concepts of authorship, authenticity, and originality are themselves complex cultural constructs, but because the relationship between subject and object, self and other, original and copy is never simply a mirroring; it is also—quite literally in the case of *La Femme Nikita*—a projection.

NOTES

This is a modified version of an article originally published in *Camera Obscura* 47 (2001). Copyright 2001, Camera Obscura. All rights reserved. Reprinted by Duke University Press. This chapter is a "remake" of sorts, for it grew out of a Society for Cinema Studies conference presentation given in collaboration with friend and colleague, Julie Palsmeier. Many thanks to Julie both for her translation of the article by Serceau and Protopopoff and for the lively discussions we had about *La Femme Nikita* and its American remake.

1. I use quotes when indicating the overall story-phenomenon not limited to any particular version.

2. [In Lacanian psychoanalytical theory, Imaginary relations occur during the mirror-stage of child development. In this stage, the child has an illusory sense of his/her integration as an autonomous subject. True integration comes only with the Symbolic order and the entry into language. *Eds.*]

3. To complete the birthing trope, our heroine is finally expelled from the womb and allowed to live in the outside world after successfully completing her first assassination assignment in a high-priced restaurant—fittingly, on her birthday. The job is tough, and her escape narrow: she dives down a long garbage

chute leading from the kitchen to the street, propelled along by a giant fireball of explosives, then emerges from the dumpster covered with an "afterbirth" of food, blood, and muck.

4. The tech-*noir* quality Penley discusses is also related to an iconography and style Janet Bergstrom has described as an "advertising aesthetic" (see pages 33–37). There is something in such films, she insists, that speaks directly to the world of advertising. The connection is conceptual and perceptual rather than product-oriented, however, in that "an integrated, all-over design projects ambiance and doesn't necessarily focus on specific characters, objects, or actions" (33). Like certain kinds of innovative television advertising or music videos (which are, after all, extended commercials for musicians and their songs), this type of film exhibits "a compelling visual/aural design that is perceptually insistent, but semantically uncertain or in suspension" (34). In some cases, the relationship between advertising and film is direct; as Bergstrom notes, Ridley Scott had already made a name for himself with his unusual television commercials before directing *Blade Runner* and *Alien*, and his ads exhibit the same kind of dense, perceptual involvement and ambiguity of meaning as his films. Interestingly, Luc Besson has a similar career trajectory, having made commercials for French television before turning to feature films. In a review of *Nikita*, Stanley Kauffmann refers indirectly to the advertising aesthetic that Bergstrom identifies: "Besson is, in a good sense, an exploitative director. He knows how to get the most out of everything. With his cinematographer Thiery Arbogast, he pitches each sequence in a plaque of light that makes it look like a smart spread for *Vanity Fair*" (26). Brian Johnson of *Maclean's* concurs: "it's hard not to be dazzled by Besson's technique. The action scenes are riveting. The director's visual flair makes *Nikita* the most stylish French thriller since *Diva*" (47). Besson's background in commercial television is noteworthy not only because it links his visual style with Ridley Scott's (and hence links *Nikita* with *Blade Runner*), but because, coupled with Besson's reputation as one of France's hottest young directors, this background helps to muddy the French critics' separation of high and low culture along national lines (France = high art, the U.S. = commodity culture).

5. In the sequel, *Black Cat II*, Erica is literally a cyborg with full-blown bionic powers, the chip in her brain accessed by a remote control device much like those used for television sets or videogames. Whoever has the remote can literally turn her on and off. Consequently, she is little developed as a character, has almost no emotional affect, and barely contributes to the film's dialogue. The central tension between human and machine is thus replaced by the classic Frankenstein dilemma of how the government agency will control the monster it has created. As one fellow operative explains to another, her brain chip has not been wholly accepted by her body—she's a "sophisticated instrument" but "still in an experimental stage."

6. Note the two names Nikita is given when her training is complete and she leaves the underground compound to live in the outside world: Marie (Mary, her civilian name) and Joséphine (derivative of Joseph, her code name). Mary and Joseph are very apt, given the earlier metaphor of death and resurrection (rebirth). "Mary" could also be a reference to another biblical figure, the prostitute Mary Magdalene.

7. For Brown this fluidity or ambivalence is clearly illustrated by the widely circulated promotional still showing Maggie in her sleeveless black dress brandishing an oversized pistol, an image that neatly condenses the opposing signifiers of feminine and masculine identity and thus challenges traditional assumptions about gender specificity. As Brown notes, "while other action heroines symbolically garb themselves exclusively in masculine accoutrements, thus allowing their characters to be read as predominantly male, the use of obvious signs of femininity and masculinity in one image confounds the strict categorization of gender absolutism" (64).

8. The end of this season finale is much like the end of the film: Nikita fakes her own death and flees the country, hoping to elude Section One forever. The second season opener finds her waiting tables in a greasy-spoon restaurant in Singapore, fending off the boorish advances of male customers. This situation appears to be lifted directly from *Black Cat*, in which we are first introduced to the Nikita character not robbing a pharmacy, as in the French and U.S. versions, but waiting tables at a truck stop.

WORKS CITED

Alleva, Richard. "La Femme Nikita." *Commonweal* 1 June 1991: 372–73.

Andrew, Dudley. "Adaptation." *Film Theory and Criticism: Introductory Readings*. Ed. Gerald Mast, Marshall Cohen, and Leo Braudy. 4th ed. New York: Oxford UP, 1992.

Aufderheide, Patricia. "Made in Hong Kong: Translation and Transmutation." Horton and McDougal 191–99.

Bannet, Eve Tavor. "The Critic as Translator." *Postcultural Theory: Critical Theory after the Marxist Paradigm*. New York: MacMillan, 1993. 158–94.

Bazin, André. *What is Cinema?* Trans. Hugh Gray. Berkeley: U of California P, 1968.

Bellour, Raymond. "Hitchcock the Enunciator." *Camera Obscura* 2 (1977): 67–91.

Benjamin, Walter. "The Task of the Translator." *Illuminations*. Trans. Harry Zohn. New York: Schocken, 1969. 69–82.

Berenstein, Rhona. "Mommy Dearest: *Aliens, Rosemary's Baby*, and Mothering." *Journal of Popular Culture* 24.2 (1990): 55–73.

Bergstrom, Janet. "Androids and Androgyny." *Close Encounters: Film, Feminism, and Science Fiction*. Ed. Constance Penley, Elisabeth Lyon, Lynn Spigel, and Janet Bergstrom. Minneapolis: U of Minnesota P, 1991. 33–61.

Bobbin, Jay. "French Thriller 'La Femme Nikita' Becomes New USA Series." *Buffalo News* 12 Jan. 1997: 20.

Brashinsky, Michael. "The Spring, Defiled: Ingmar Bergman's *Virgin Spring* and Wes Craven's *Last House on the Left*." Horton and McDougal 162–71.

Braudy, Leo. "Afterward: Rethinking Remakes." Horton and McDougal 327–34.

Brown, Jeffrey. "Gender and the Action Heroine: Hardbodies and *Point of No Return*." *Cinema Journal* 35.3 (1996): 52–71.

Deggans, Eric. "Peta Wilson Finds Soft Side of 'Nikita.'" *St. Petersburg Times* 11 Jan. 1998: F1.

Durham, Carolyn Ann. *Double Takes: Culture and Gender in French Films and Their American Remakes*. Hanover: UP of New England, 1998.

Dyer, Richard. "Resistance Through Charisma: Rita Hayworth and *Gilda*." Kaplan 91–99.

Endrst, James. "Nikita Shoots From Down Under." *Toronto Star* 19 Aug. 1997: E4.

Gallop, Jane. *Reading Lacan*. Ithaca: Cornell UP, 1985.

Goodman, Tim. "This Nikita Sure Packs Heat." *Bergen Record* 19 Feb. 1997: C3.

Halberstam, Judith. "Imagined Violence/Queer Violence: Representation, Rage, and Resistance." *Social Text* 37 (1993): 187–201.

Hall, Steve. "TV Nikita Lacks Depth of Original." *Indianapolis Star* 10 Jan. 1997: B5.

Harvey, Sylvia. "Woman's Place: The Absent Family of Film Noir." Kaplan 22–34.

Heath, Stephen. "Film and System: Terms of Analysis, Part 1." *Screen* 16.1 (1975): 7–78.

Horkheimer, Max, and Theodor Adorno. "The Culture Industry: Enlightenment as Mass Deception." *Dialectic of Enlightenment.* Trans. John Cumming. New York: Continuum, 1993 [1944]. 120–67.

Horton, Andrew, and Stuart Y. McDougal. *Play It Again, Sam: Retakes on Remakes.* Berkeley: U of California P, 1998.

Jackson, Thomas. "Theorizing Translation." *Substance* 65 (1991): 79–90.

Johnson, Brian. "La Femme Nikita." *Maclean's* 8 April 1991: 47.

Kaplan, E. Ann. *Women in Film Noir.* London: BFI Publishing, 1980.

Kauffmann, Stanley. "Contradictions." *New Republic* 6 May 1991: 26.

Kelleher, Terry. "Nikita, All Style No Substance." *Newsday* 12 Jan. 1997: 3.

Kronisberg, Ira. "How Many Draculas Does It Take to Change a Lightbulb?" Horton and McDougal 250–75.

L.A. Weekly 5 June 1998: 82.

Leitch, Thomas. "Twice-Told Tales: The Rhetoric of the Remake." *Literature/Film Quarterly* 18.3 (1990): 138–49.

Levine, Lawrence. *Highbrow/Lowbrow: The Emergence of Cultural Hierarchy in America.* Cambridge: Harvard UP, 1988.

Lewis, Philip. "The Measure of Translation Effects." *Difference in Translation.* Ed. Joseph Graham. Ithaca: Cornell UP, 1985. 31–62.

MacRory, Pauline. "Excusing the Violence of Hollywood Women: Music in *Nikita* and *Point of No Return.*" *Screen* 40.1 (1999): 51–65.

Marder, Elissa. "*Blade Runner's* Moving Still." *Camera Obscura* 27 (1991): 88–107.

Mulvey, Laura. "Visual Pleasure and Narrative Cinema." *Feminism and Film Theory.* Ed. Constance Penley. New York: Routledge, 1988. 57–68.

Penley, Constance. "Time Travel, Primal Scene, and the Critical Dystopia (on *The Terminator* and *La Jetée*)." *The Future of an Illusion: Film, Feminism, and Psychoanalysis.* Minneapolis: U of Minnesota P, 1989. 121–97

Place, Janey. "Woman in Film Noir." Kaplan 35–67.

Roush, Matt. "Killing Time With Nikita Remake." *USA Today* 13 Jan. 1997: D3.

Rubin, Sylvia. "USA's Popular 'Nikita' An Assassin With Sizzle." *San Francisco Chronicle* 17 Sept. 1997: D1.

Serceau, Michel. "Hollywood à l'heure de Paris." Serceau and Protopopoff 113–23.

Serceau, Michel and Daniel Protopopoff, eds. *Le Remake et l'adaption.* Paris: CinémAction, 1989.

———. "Hollywood à la recherche de son ombre." Serceau and Protopopoff 95–97.

———. "Les Remakes américains de films européens: une greffe stérile." Serceau and Protopopoff 98–112.

Silverman, Kaja. "Back to the Future." *Camera Obscura* 27 (1991): 108–33.

Simon, Jeff. "La La La Femme Nikita is a Jolly Great Spy." *Buffalo News* 19 April 1998: 2.

Simon, John. "La Femme Nikita." *National Review* 27 May 1991: 56–7.

Venuti, Lawrence. "Simpatico: Translation as a Process of Interpretation." *Substance* 65 (1991): 3–20.

Weiss, Elizabeth. "M*A*S*H Notes." Horton and McDougal 310–26.

Williams, Michael and Christian Mork. "Remake Stakes Are Up: H[olly]wood Hastens Pursuit of French Pic[ture] Properties." *Daily Variety* 19 April 1993: 5+.

Wills, David. "The French Remark: 'Breathless' and Cinematic Citationality." Horton and McDougal 147–61.

APPENDIX A

Remaking Le Voile bleu: *An Interview with Norman Corwin, Screenwriter for* The Blue Veil

JENNIFER FORREST

FORREST: How did you get involved with the *Blue Veil* project? Who approached you?

CORWIN: I was approached by Norman Krasna.[1]

FORREST: Was his decision based on your previous radio work?

CORWIN: It had to be based on my radio work.

FORREST: Why did they pick that film and not any other? Do you think it could have been some unconscious program to try and get women to accept going back to their homes, to give up the jobs that they had assumed during the war?

CORWIN: I doubt that. I don't think there was any large philosophical concept or even a small one. I think it was more likely to have been that Krasna and Wald[2] found the rights were available, that they had an opportunity to use Jane Wyman, and that she may have been familiar with it, and wanted to do it. She seemed quite happy with that role.

FORREST: Well, she resembles strikingly the actress in the French version.

CORWIN: Is that right?

FORREST: I wondered how she got chosen for it. I mean, did they see the film and say, "Jane Wyman could play that role."

CORWIN: By the time I was approached, all that was in place, the casting, the rights and all that. They were looking around for a writer who could handle it. I think it was a gamble on their part because my career was in radio, and I had not proven myself in film. They may have had an American screenplay version before I got on it. I may not have been their first choice. Maybe they tried to get somebody else and A didn't like it, and for B, there wasn't enough money in it, and C had a better offer elsewhere.

FORREST: But do you think their choices would have been, say, "Let's pick A because s/he's been in the business, knows how to patch up a script, or to do an adaptation," as opposed to somebody who has a background in another medium, and who also writes. I mean, this was a big project. It had Charles Laughton, Joan Blondell, and Jane Wyman.

CORWIN: I'm pretty sure they must have spent a tidy sum on salaries for Wyman and Laughton. Those are the two, I think, most expensive items in the production. But Bernhardt was not Oliver North. The salaries then were not greatly inflated. I've forgotten what I was paid for it, but it was modest. The most I ever got on working for a film was on *Lust for Life*. And that's because it went on for a long time. I spent three, four months researching for it, not just the letters of Vincent, but the journals of Gauguin and Bernard. The history of the Impressionists entered into it, too, and the whole pre-Paris life of Vincent.

FORREST: *Lust for Life* was based on the letters?

CORWIN: That was my choice. That wasn't originally the plan. It was to have been based on the Irving Stone novel. But I was disenchanted by the book, and felt that nobody was a better source than Van Gogh himself, and his letters became my source.

FORREST: Do you feel that you used a lot more creativity in drawing from a source like the letters as opposed to working from someone's script?

CORWIN: In the adaptations I have made, I never felt comfortable simply taking the fabric and dying it a different color, or bringing to it merely a change of medium. That even goes for reusing my own material. I applaud modernizations when they're not arty, when they're not smart-ass. My policy is to honor the intent of the source. To me it's a form of desecration to write a poor man's version of the Bible, or a dumbbell's version of Hamlet.

FORREST: Are you making a distinction between the Romantic notion of the artist as inspired versus that of the artist as a craftsperson?

CORWIN: "Leda and the Swan" by Leonardo is going to be radically different from the "Leda and the Swan" of Picasso. The source is the same, it's the legend, it's mythology, but the execution is completely different. A different approach, philosophy, materials.

FORREST: But you wouldn't say that Picasso's interpretation is a poor man's version of Leonardo?

CORWIN: No, I wouldn't. I have the feeling that Picasso was original enough and forceful enough, so that you could not attach to his oeuvre the term "smart-ass." But we have an instinct about what is and what isn't kosher. It's a quality of honesty; it's a quality of integrity; it's a quality of respect. There are remakes, versions that are brilliant, that are wonderful. I thought *Carmen Jones* was a marvelous version of the Bizet opera. And when somebody had the enterprise to take themes from Borodin and work them up into a musical called *Kismet*, which ran successfully on Broadway, I say three cheers. There was no disrespect to Borodin. It was making very good use of valuable material.

FORREST: There are critics who make the distinction between the adaptation and the remake, and others who see no difference between them, they're all remakes, such that *Carmen Jones* is a remake, not an adaptation of Bizet's opera. Do you feel in your writing of the screenplay of *The Blue Veil*, that you were merely adapting? Did you feel any artistic weight carrying over from the original film?

CORWIN: No, there was not. My only source was a bad literal translation. I did not see the film. If I had, it wouldn't have helped me. It might have disenchanted me with the whole thing. But I entered this engagement with the attitude that I usually bring to anything that's proffered, [that] of challenge. The question was, "What can you do with this?" And I did the best I could. A very good example of my approach was a film not remade but based on [other] material—an insignificant film, but I think quite well done, which got respectful attention from a number of quarters—called *Scandal at Scourie*. I had great deal of pleasure working over material that had in a previous version been so ugly in its attitude of intrareligious feuding, Protestant versus Catholic, that it was rejected out of hand by the studio. It was grim. I saw an opportunity for a kind of sweetness in it. I'm afraid this sounds as though I'm giving myself points for a film you haven't seen, but it was another of the examples where I had adapted material, and brought what you so generously describe as "nuancing" to it. Most of the nuances of *Scandal at Scourie* were on the side of mere decency, a warmth and generosity of spirit that softened what in the original version had been sharp and acidulous. And done without losing the premise, the protagonism and antagonism that are the basis of all stories.

FORREST: We can perhaps compare the experiences. Did you ever do any original film work, writing your own script as opposed to doing a treatment on another's script?

CORWIN: I did.

FORREST: How did you feel about the process separating the two?

CORWIN: I would much prefer to do original material, which is ninety-five percent of my work. Very few adaptations. I would have liked that ratio to have been followed in films. But film was not my major preoccupation. When radio was abandoned by the networks, and the kind of radio I did no longer was in existence, my concentration was not on films, but on stage productions. And there I did original work. I also wrote a number of books. I did some television. . . .

FORREST: How long did it take you to do the screenplay for *The Blue Veil*?

CORWIN: Not long. It was not anything I toiled and toiled and toiled over. It came pretty smoothly.

FORREST: Do or did you know who did the translation of the French screenplay?

CORWIN: No. I remember not being very happy with the translation. I didn't get any help in the dialogue, which I thought pedestrian. I can't ascribe that to the lacks of the author, because it went through the hands of a translator.

FORREST: It's interesting to note that, like *The Blue Veil,* which is a remake, you again worked from another person's script in *Lust For Life,* which, as you say, was initially based on Irving Stone's novel.

CORWIN: On neither script did I go back to sources. For the French film I think I read the French synopsis, which was a poor translation as I recall. I make use of building blocks and avoid the antic. It happened with *Lust For Life.* I read Stone's book, and was not terribly impressed by it. And I then went to John Houseman, the producer. I said, "I don't think much of the book." The best things in it are quotes that I have of Vincent without attribution. I believe he [Irving Stone] quoted material from the letters without distinguishing between what he was quoting and what he was writing. I felt that nobody knew Vincent Van Gogh better than Vincent Van Gogh, and I proposed that we base the picture on his letters. Plus the journals of Gauguin, and of Emile Bernard. So I never went back to the book. I never consulted it.

FORREST: So were you basically given liberty more or less in adapting *The Blue Veil*?

CORWIN: Pretty much so. The producers, Wald and Krasna, had an association that did not last very long—two or three years. They made two or three pictures, of which this was perhaps their best. Jerry was much more conventional in his approach to the film than Krasna, who was himself a playwright, a good playwright. Krasna liked this script, and was very happy with it. Wald waited until the votes came in before he knew whether he liked it or not, and then decided that he liked it, because it got a nomination for Jane Wyman and got an award in some other category. The New York Film Critics gave her the award for best actress. And it had some distinguished people in it. Laughton was known all over the world. He did a beautiful job. One of his best. In a small role.

FORREST: Small, but very warm, human. It's a touching, but hardly maudlin, portrait. The other portraits aim for this same depth of character, whereas the French film is concerned with the sequence of situation, and therefore plays more for the tears.

CORWIN: Well, I hated that. To me, good Christ, there are so many legitimate tears in life. You can feel terribly upset for all kinds of people every day, in every news dispatch. So given this canvas, I certainly did my best to soak up as a blotter would all the excess tears. I wanted to make it honest, as honest as I could.

FORREST: The French version paints the portrait of a woman who basically sacrifices her whole life for children. Each episode adds to the scope of her sacrifice. Your version doesn't elaborate on this myth of maternal self-sacrifice. The Jerry Kean episode couldn't be further from this. Louise does have this last fling with love, and she almost does it, she's ready to be impulsive, and she's sure of herself. In the French film, Louise does seriously consider the Moroccan offer, but it is always in conflict with her surrogate mother duties. What initially decides her in favor of leaving for Morocco is Gérald's nastiness. Her life wins briefly, but only by default. But when Gérald recants his nasty words, it is as if there was never a contest between personal happiness and self-sacrifice. In the end it is as if she says, "It would have been wrong to leave," to think of herself, and that this was the last temptation with which normal life could test her. Your version is more the portrait of a woman's life. You did, however, keep the same general scene sequencing, the same families, with some modification, obviously.

CORWIN: Sure. I had respect for the basic premise of the thing. I don't mean to be condescending about the French version. I'm sure that if I had your knowledge of French, and could read it as comfortably as I read English, I probably would have respected and picked up on the circumstances in France, in its culture and the society at that time.

FORREST: Given the political climate surrounding the French *Blue Veil*, I was wondering why, of all the films that Krasna and Wald, or Bernhardt, could have picked, why they would have picked this particular film, and then why they would have picked somebody who has such an obvious liberal perspective to write the screenplay.

CORWIN: Let me try to answer that for you. All of this is speculation because there is nothing on paper, nor did we have conversations about the origins and provenance of the French film—Jerry Wald was apolitical.[3] I never knew him to come out strongly on any issue that absorbed or attracted the attention of liberals, or the left. Krasna, I suspect, was more liberal, but still not a name to be found in the ranks of the Committee for the First Amendment or in any of that. I don't mean to say that he was illiberal. But he was probably inactive as far as the political complexion of Hollywood's political intelligentsia was concerned.

FORREST: Do you think that he was just playing it safe or was it just indifference?

CORWIN: I don't think that they were attracted to, I don't think that they were even aware of, any political agenda in the original picture. Certainly it was never mentioned. When it was presented to me, it was, I believe, after an aborted script by another writer. Also, at that time, I do not think that Curt Bernhardt had any political inclination toward the left because in some transcript or other, an interview with him, he considered me pretty pink, a deep shade of pink. That came later. We were good friends. But never in connection with the film. The issue was never raised. I perceived it as a picture about motherhood, surrogate motherhood. Neither motherhood nor surrogate motherhood was considered material for the arena, the political arena. One of the most prominent of all of the filmmakers in the history of Hollywood was Louis B. Mayer, who felt that every picture should deal with the sacredness of motherhood, with what we consider the values of home. His outlook on those matters was famously conservative and traditional, Norman Rockwell to the tenth power. I've been in Mayer's home, I had dinner there once, and he talked about the enduring value of family and motherhood and how wholesome the Mickey Rooney pictures were, and that sort of thing. To him Dore Schary[4] was anathema. You know the history of Schary and Mayer. It finally came down to an issue whether they wanted to keep Schary or Mayer, and oddly enough M-G-M at that time opted to keep Schary. But Schary was definitely on the liberal side. He was constantly a target of recriminations and abuse by the Hollywood right. So I, who acknowledge being a political creature, was certainly sensitive to any political current flowing past or through this whole enterprise, and I was not aware of it.

FORREST: But of all the people they could have picked, they picked you. This was your first film, your first screenplay, they could have picked any old hand to do the job.

CORWIN: I had a high profile then. I was front and center. What was the year?

FORREST: '51.

CORWIN: Well, I had been a fixture in the media for some time, and had done commercial network broadcasting. Although I was never sponsored, I did full network programs, and big commemorative programs.[5] So I was known in this city.

FORREST: But was there at that period of time this crossing-over between mediums? Like going from radio to film to television?

CORWIN: Yes, it happened significantly with actors. Dick Widmark, Frank Lovejoy, Agnes Moorehead, all of them came out of radio. I was surprised and fascinated by your disclosure that there had been a political spin to the French version in the attitude toward motherhood. We know that the Nazis were infamously interested in getting production of new Nazis. Therefore they underscored the value of woman as a breeder. But that's not the emphasis of the French film and certainly not of the American version. I think it's simply a matter that they got the rights for peanuts, and they thought the product would be attractive. It's a woman's picture, a three-handkerchief woman's picture, and they bought it, just as they bought a lot of product that was a good buy. It may have been a kind of garage sale of movie material.

FORREST: So, you think that it boils down to the rights being available?

CORWIN: Yes.

FORREST: Obviously the woman's film had its market, so you think that they exploited it?

CORWIN: Right.

FORREST: Did you work very closely with Mr. Bernhardt?

CORWIN: I was on the set a good deal. We got along very well. We liked each other, and remained friends after the picture. But the working relationship was not close in the sense that I consulted him daily, or anything of the kind. He had valuable input. We respected each other. I recall there having been harmony on that film, much abetted by the fact that Krasna served as insulation between Wald and me. I seldom consulted or talked to Wald. I think, had Wald been the sole producer, it would not have turned out . . . I might not have even stayed with it.

FORREST: Bernhardt was one of many émigré, not only directors, but film people who had come over from Germany either long prior to or because of the Second World War. And I just wondered if you were aware of that community, and the contributions they were bringing to the development of cinema.

CORWIN: No, I never really entered that equation. He was a cosmopolitan type. I think he considered me to the left of him politically. He was a man of considerable charm. And skill. I thought he was talented. I liked him. It's nice when you have a rapport with your director.

What particularly interests me in going over ground discussed earlier, is that the original film, if it bore any of the mark of Vichy or Nazi influence, would not have included the thrust against militarism that I invented for the character of the storekeeper.

FORREST: Did you have any difficulty inserting that anti-militarism element in your screenplay?

CORWIN: No. Wald was practically a wall fixture. He had little to do with it. But Bernhardt welcomed it. And so did Norman Krasna. They enjoyed that. There was no wrangling. None of the usual *Sturm und Drang* of drafts and redrafts, and pink, yellow, blue, and green pages. It went along pretty smoothly.

FORREST: What are pink, yellow, blue, and green pages?

CORWIN: In the compilation of a screenplay of many drafts, they color code certain pages so that you know what draft that represents, thus you can easily spot it. You don't keep track of the page numbers; you keep track of the colors. That's when you're in a long labor of a film that will run three or four hours, and many versions. You can imagine with a film like *Cleopatra*, they must have had every color of the rainbow.

FORREST: There were a lot of significant changes that you made; one was the role of the toyshop man in that, in the original, he is a constant presence throughout. Every time Louise moves to a new family, he makes an appearance. Every time Louise goes to his toyshop, the scene usually ends with him proposing to her in some manner. And it's very charming. And that is why he doesn't like kids. He wants them out of the store whenever she's there. So it's not a general dislike for kids, it's just the circumstances. He just wants to be with Louise.

CORWIN: Right. A gallant form of pragmatism.

FORREST: In the American version, the change you made is that this man's role in Louise's life is not initially romantic. It only becomes romantic at the end when they're elderly. But he is a cynical voice, the voice of reason to a great extent, and a lot of that reason has to do with the antiweapons mentality, which did not exist in the original film. You say Bernhardt was for this antiweapon's angle?

CORWIN: Bernhardt was no Nazi. As Germans go, he was pretty liberal. But I was surprised and disappointed when I came across the transcript of some interview with him in which he thought I was to the left of Castro. He didn't say that, but he was sure that I was much farther to the left than I ever really was.

FORREST: I heard that when you were director of the Writer's Guild, one of the members made a comment that there wasn't anyone nicer than Norman Corwin, but that you had definite ideas about things. When you had your mind on something, and you had your passion behind it, you didn't let up. Even in the letter that you wrote to Krasna and Wald regarding the Palfrey scene, you were very intent on having your way because you saw it as the only logical solution. Was there any of that in your inserting the antimilitaristic discourse in your screenplay?

CORWIN: No. As I recall, there was very little attrition. The tone of it was not imperious, not argumentative. I was not attacking it as a lawyer would in a strenuously fought case. And if I did prevail, it was another measure of the general sense of agreeableness, amity, that existed in the writing of this film, and in the shooting of it. Because I was around [on the set], I would be consulted or make a suggestion.

FORREST: Do you remember any particular instance?

CORWIN: The instances were matters of degree, when I thought that there should be a little bit more or a little less of a particular emotion expressed. Things like that. Minor things. No big things. Whereas on some other pictures there were pitched battles.

FORREST: For example?

CORWIN: *Lust for Life.* There were no fist battles, but when the production went abroad, I didn't go with it, and when I saw some of the rushes come back, and I was distressed by the relationship with Theo. I thought Theo was being played like a cold mackerel. I brought this to the attention of Schary, and he agreed with me. So messages, cables went out. But I don't want to class myself in the role of the protector of Truth or a Galahad in any way. I was just a screenwriter. I was protective, let's put it that way.

FORREST: Well the Writer's Guild story about you seems to corroborate that there were certain instances where you had your own ideas about things

CORWIN: I think any artist who has conscience or pride in his work, finds himself called upon to defend it. I don't go by the standard that I can do no wrong. I have always been eager to be corrected or to listen to another point of view. And very often I've accommodated that point of view and been grateful for it. But when I see something obviously wrong that's going to hurt or damage the effect, or dilute a moment, a scene, an emphasis on storypoint, characterization, I think it is derelict not to speak up.

FORREST: But you say that that didn't happen on this particular film?

CORWIN: No. That is not to say that there was no input from Bernhardt. He was a good director. And sometimes, particularly in sensitive areas, such as the scene between Louise and Richard Carlson, the elopement scene. That was gone over very carefully and I discussed it with Curt. I cannot begin to recall the play by play of that, or of the interstices in considerations of the scene itself. I don't even know if that scene is in the original film. Was it? Was there, for example, the man who played the tutor? Was he in the original?

FORREST: Yes, there is an elopement scene. Dominique isn't a tutor but the brother of your Mrs. Palfrey. Dominique falls in love with Louise and, because of his disgust with his sister's nouveau riche life, decides to go off to Morocco, inviting Louise to join him. And he says to her more or less, "I'm going off tonight. If you'll come with me, be at the train station at 10:45." Louise is tempted and prepares to leave, but the little boy, Gérald, is particularly nasty to her the night she is expected at the train station, because he believes that she is leaving because she doesn't love him. His behavior decides hers, and she says to herself, "O.K., I'm going." And as she is about to go, the little boy cries, "Don't go Loulou, don't go!" After all, he is a neglected child and his need for love is so great. And she stays to assume her role again as surrogate mother.

CORWIN: I invented the train sequence in that whole thing, where he gets cold feet?

FORREST: Yes.

CORWIN: The woman says to him, "Are you sure you're doing the right thing?" And possibly this is impulse that you're acting on, and you might regret it. That plants a seed in his mind and he begins to back away. And she's sensitive enough to realize that he may be regretting his impulse. So that was my invention? You see, I have no recollection whatever of the source material, and of even the characters in the plot, so you have to remind me what it was, and . . . I can only speak from an imperfect memory.

FORREST: Another difference is that, in addition to the young Gérald, there are also two older children.

CORWIN: That wasn't in my film, was it?

FORREST: No.

CORWIN: Is mine a kinder, gentler version?

FORREST: It is much less stereotypical, much more nuanced, much richer in human emotion. For example, the train scene where Louise realizes that doubt has entered into Kean's mind. As regards Kean's proposed elopement with Louise, he seems pretty sure of what he's doing. But there is the preceding scene with Agnes Moorehead/Mrs. Palfrey where she seems to instil a doubt that wasn't previously there. She is the voice of rationality when she says more or less, "You know, these types of impulsive actions usually turn out badly, but I wish you the best of luck."

CORWIN: That's the way it happens. We are prone, those of us who are vulnerable, those of us who are not dogmatic and who say, "This decision is my decision" . . . for those of us who are flexible and have respect for another point of view, sometimes all it takes is that little caution, "Bear in mind, that if you are going to climb that mountain, there could be an avalanche."

FORREST: In the French version, Louise decides not to leave because Gérald, the little boy, desperately needs her. According to the French film's logic, in the struggle between personal gratification and self-sacrifice, she opts for the latter, and makes the morally "right" choice. In your film, there is no such conflict between Kean and Robbie. If she goes back to Robbie, it is not because choosing Kean would have been morally wrong. Kean's doubts destroy the viability of their impulsive departure.

CORWIN: [But there is] also the poignancy of somebody returning, who didn't walk out. And we've all been there.

FORREST: During the Occupation, La Centrale Catholique du Cinéma assumed the responsibilities of upholding certain social morals and standards. They had a ratings system which ranged from 1 to 6, 1 to 3 denoting the most morally appropriate films, 4 to 6 those morally reprehensible films. *Le Voile bleu* would have ranked really high on their moral scale. It is interesting that such a film became a Hollywood property, especially considering the types of modifications that you made to the tenor of the script. Let's take for example your toyshop man, Frank. In the French version, he dislikes children, but his dislike for them is based on the fact that, because of his love for Louise, he is jealous of the brief moments he gets to spend with her. But your version is completely different. From the very beginning, it is clear that he doesn't like children.

CORWIN: Well, you want to know my rationale behind that? I felt that the picture was dangerously exposed to the prospect of becoming sentimental and soupy. Therefore, wherever I could, I introduced a note of astringency. And I felt that that would take away some of the potentially cloying elements, or at least neutralize them. That was one of them. But you have to educate me as to what was in the original.

FORREST: Well, there is a scene, which obviously does not and could not exist in the French version, where the toyshop man, Frank, is with a woman client. Here is their conversation:

> FEMALE CLIENT: Do you have any toy bombing planes?
>
> FRANK: Yes, any particular model?
>
> FEMALE CLIENT: Four motor. Also, have you any tanks and guns?

FRANK: Is your boy expecting to be attacked?

FEMALE CLIENT: No, he just likes to play with those things. He has a little submarine that sinks when you let the air out. Have you seen that?

FRANK: No, but we have a nice toy guillotine that cuts the heads off sardines.

FEMALE CLIENT: Really?

FRANK: Yes, and we have a cute electric chair that operates on a battery.

FEMALE CLIENT: Oh?

FRANK: And a little gallows just about so high that you can hang dolls on.

FEMALE CLIENT: I think you're pulling my leg.

FRANK: I have a toy leg-pulling machine, too.

FEMALE CLIENT: I can trade elsewhere.

CORWIN: And that was not an expression of pacifism, although, you know, I am antiwar, antiwar, antiwar. But my contempt for manufacturers of toys, going for military hardware, the whole concept of this I find so sickening. And so, I was having my fun with that.

FORREST: But, at the same time, these toy weapons are not entirely without a context. You did situate them within the greater historical framework of the film. For example, Louise's husband dies in France during World War I, and the British husband is killed in England during World War II. His wife works in the Ambulance Corps. There's a telling conversation between this latter couple and Louise. The husband and wife are outside on the porch one summer evening. The baby can't sleep and Louise brings him outside saying that he wanted to ask about the world situation.

LOUISE: It's very warm and we couldn't sleep and he wants to talk over the world situation with you.

HUSBAND: Louise, you listen a lot to short wave. Don't you prefer British announcers?"

LOUISE: Well, in these times, yes.

WIFE: Why?

LOUISE: Oh, they're always so calm. They make you feel some-how that it isn't quite as bad as all that.

HUSBAND: The world may come to an end one of these days.

So, there is a certain, not necessarily fatalistic element to it, but a great consciousness of the events of World War II and the effects it had on people's lives. This couple refers to Hitler playing around with people's lives, and acting up in Munich. They refer to the attacks on Poland.

CORWIN: Every writer brings to his talent certain colors that he has used before, and that he keeps using. My work is pretty much informed by the state of the world.

FORREST: Does that go back to your radio work?

CORWIN: Oh yes, and even my comedies have a matrix of some social consideration. So that does not surprise me that that element is in it. . . . Actually, in terms of things I have written over the long range, this has perhaps the least of it, because it concentrates on the woman, on her plight, on her fate, and the fate of her children.

FORREST: Were you making a commentary about women after the war, encouraging them to go back to the home? Or were you just following the script more or less?

CORWIN: I was following the script more or less, because I was locked into that situation. After all, it's about a nanny. But never-theless, I don't know how much of this was a carry-over from the original concept of the script. But I'm a feminist. Since I was a kid, I've been for equal rights.

FORREST: Nevertheless, one can infer the message that women should return to their homes. For example, while the future Mrs. Hall is in London, and Louise is caring for her son, Tony, the toyshop man comments to Louise, "Don't you wonder why they've been there so long?" And Louise says, "She's doing her part, and I'm doing mine." On the one hand, there is an equal balance given to both of their jobs; they are both valid forms of service. But then, Mrs. Hall's postwar activities find her operating once again as a wife, hence her effort to recover her son. This message becomes clearer when Louise is around sixty, and she goes to an agency to get another job. The agency woman, of course, is very nasty and condescending to her, saying that the prospective employers want somebody who's a little bit stronger. Louise answers, "I was looking for a job in a home, not a steel mill." That's an interesting comment. It distinguishes between two types of feminine activities, one related to wartime efforts, the other related to the traditional feminine space, a space to which women's physical abilities, the film tells us, are best qualified. But while both original and remake share the theme of motherhood and womanhood, the social framework of the remake is distinctly American. In addition, in your screenplay, you have one mother, the starlet played by Joan Blondell, who is a bad mother not only because she is selfish, but because she is a working mother. The wife of the British man doesn't clean house well; she doesn't handle childcare well; she offers a cigarette to Louise; she and her husband have parties where a lot of liquor is consumed. When her husband is wounded, she goes to join him in England, and after his death, she joins the Ambulance Corps, leaving Tony with Louise for many years.

CORWIN: When she meets another man, an American. Does that happen in the original?

FORREST: No, no. It's the same tableau, only they literally do abandon the child. They are stereotypically bad parents. The family is experiencing severe financial difficulties. The husband has an opportunity in Indochina, but the child is too fragile for the climate. The wife, who probably should have stayed in France with her son, leaves him with Loulou to be with her husband. The message is clearly that the mother-child relation should come even before that between husband and wife.

CORWIN: Ah! I think what I did . . . I looked over the script last night in preparation for this meeting. I had forgotten what came next. You know, it's been so long since I was exposed to that. And I realized that there are no heavies in the picture. The people that are the closest to being heavy are the man and his wife. They are the closest we come to heavy people. But the others are pretty decent people, all of them. And though the tutor is weak, he's not a bad guy.

FORREST: They are all human characters.

CORWIN: Yeah. Was my version a warmer mix?

FORREST: In one sense, yes. It was less stereotypical. The French film had stereotypes. Not so in your version. For example, in the first tableau, Frederick Begley, Sr., marries his secretary, but a much longer period of time elapses between the initial hiring of Louise and his marriage. The child does grow up a little bit. There is time for Mr. Begley to realize that he is lonely, leading up to his proposal to Louise. In the French film, this is one of the shortest sections. The woman that he will marry lives in an apartment on the same floor as him. She's a seamstress who is very shrill, very domineering, and very catty. The widower wants someone to take care of his child. He sees that Louise is a wonderful woman and caretaker, and proposes. She refuses. And immediately after, on the rebound, he goes and asks the seamstress for her hand.

CORWIN: I made the Vivian Vance character somebody working close to him.

FORREST: And because she works so closely for him, it makes a lot of sense that she cares for him. She isn't a bad, scheming, or vindictive woman.

CORWIN: No, no. And even though—because we are rooting for Louise—even though she's moving in and wants to claim the territory, she's not a bad egg. She says, "Well, will two weeks notice be enough?" And you feel badly for Louise; it is a little crass on the part of this woman. But still, I think it's credible. In going over it last night, of course, I was looking at it from a vantage point of many years, and my own judgments, tastes, and proclivities change as everybody's does, or they become refined, or become diluted, or whatever. And I felt that the characters still ring pretty true, that they are recognizable, that they are not caricatured. And I was wondering about the French film.

FORREST: The widower episode is very caricaturized; the second family is nouveau riche, with typical nouveau riche behavior in their ridiculous efforts to hobnob with the real aristocracy. The third family is composed of the starlet and her daughter. It is perhaps this episode in the French film that is the least stereotypical of all. She is a performer at the height of her career, who also genuinely loves her daughter, Charlotte. Not to say that the Joan Blondell character doesn't love her daughter, but her motivations for missing her daughter's confirmation are based on an attempt to stop her career from falling. In the French film, it is a scheming agent and a producer who make her lose track of time, and hence miss her daughter's confirmation.

CORWIN: The Joan Blondell character redeems herself. She turns down the job. You know, she gets straightened out by this. And I thought that was an improvement, from what you tell me.

FORREST: It's interesting to compare the way each film deals with Louise's departure from the actress's family. In the French version, Louise leaves in a much more abrupt fashion. Charlotte runs after the departing Louise, and Louise, following the dictates of tough love, says to her, "You have to go back. I've got a better job. They're offering me more money." She's lying obviously, but she turns the child away from her to break the maternal bond. In your version, you give the child, Stephanie, the opportunity to make the final decision.

CORWIN: I did a better thing than that. I mean, I did a humane thing. She says to the kid, "You wouldn't deny, you know, that child needs me." She's lying. She invents a story that she's leaving. But she appeals to the generous spirit of Stephanie. And Stephanie accepts that, whereas it would be crass if she said, "It pays more," "It's a better job."

FORREST: That's perhaps something that reflects the cultural differences between the two films. That's something I thought we might also discuss. There are cultural differences in the original, things that would be acceptable in French culture that wouldn't be acceptable in ours. Like, for example, in the opening scene in the French version, the baby is taken away from the mother immediately after the birth. The nurses do not let her feed the baby for the first twenty-four hours, and the baby dies within those first twenty-four hours. The reason is, they say, "You have to get your strength up so that you can start nursing this child properly." The French would and did accept it. In your version, you have the nurses saying, "We're going to be coming in every four hours." This is a different version of motherhood and society's role in maternity. I don't think an American audience would have accepted the baby being taken away. I don't know if you made that decision consciously. It shows, however, that you were paying attention to what American audiences would credibly accept or react against.

CORWIN: These are considerations—the difference in milieux, in the circumstances, political and social—that I completely was unaware of, or I lost sight of the fact that this was made in Occupied France.

FORREST: This may not have been entirely your fault. The original French film, in a sense, dehistoricizes itself, which would add to this cult of motherhood because it would therefore not be locked into any specific period of time. The rare historical references in the French film revolve around such things as the time framework of the two World Wars. Louise's husband dies in Belgium during World War I. There are references to the colonial situation in Morocco and Indochina. Dominique sets off to settle in Morocco, and the negligent parents relocate to Indochina. Morocco and Indochina could be replaced easily with probably any other place name. In your version, the effort to situate the story appeals to a distinct historical context. History, here, reveals a lot about the story and about the characters' motivations. So despite the passing references to Indochina and to Morocco—obvious references to the French colonial situation—the French film does not even remotely achieve the same level of historicization as yours, where there's Hitler, where you mention the invasion of Poland, where there is a sense of historical actuality that acts as a subtext to Louise's story.

CORWIN: You have a big advantage over me in that you not only saw this picture more than once, but you saw it this very day. I haven't looked at it in years, you have a much fresher awareness of it.

FORREST: In the French version, the blue veil is actually only mentioned right at the end of the film, and this is because Louise is becoming a nanny again, this time to take care of Gérald's children. The film ends framing her putting it on. But you, much more richly, bring in the play of veils from the very beginning. For example, there's a reference to a nun's habit, and when Stephanie has on her confirmation gown, she talks about wedding veils. There is this play on veils all throughout, possibly referring to the different roles women play in society.

CORWIN: Let me ask you this, since you bring up the confirmation scene. In the original, was there an alternation between the audition and the confirmation exercise?

FORREST: Yes, I think there was. It wasn't an audition. It was her agent and a producer trying to get her to agree to a tour.

CORWIN: But was there intercutting in real time?

FORREST: Yes, I think there was intercutting in real time. This is how you knew that the mother wasn't going to make it in time for the confirmation. In your version, Stephanie calls Louise "mother" to have an attentive mother to show to her friends. In the French version, and I guess in French confirmation ceremonies, the children are supposed to go up to their parents at the beginning and ask their forgiveness for the pains that they've caused them. To participate in this part of the ritual, Charlotte has no choice but to go up to Louise as a surrogate mother.

CORWIN: That's an interesting . . . I like what the French did with that. And I think perhaps, if I was aware of that model, I felt that it would not be understood, because . . .

FORREST: We're a Protestant country?

CORWIN: That's right.

FORREST: Not Catholic?

CORWIN: That's right. That's a rather poignant concept to go up to your mother and ask for forgiveness. Of course, I reject that, because I think that in some cases, it might be the mother who asks the forgiveness of the child.

FORREST: Especially in this particular instance. Well, that's why I was wondering about your references to veils—wedding, confirmation, blue veils—in the preconfirmation scene.

CORWIN: I think perhaps you're giving me a little too much credit. I'm not sure that was a planned metaphor.

FORREST: But why did you keep the same title for the film? It seems to me that an American audience would not have understood what the blue veil means, since we're talking about a primarily Protestant audience. In the French version, I assume it would have been obvious to everybody what Louise was wearing.

CORWIN: It was not my choice. I had nothing to do with it. Whether it came with that title or not. Religion enters only in the confirmation scene.

FORREST: I wonder if nannies even wore blue veils in this country?

CORWIN: I don't think so. I never heard of it. Before or since.

FORREST: If there was no change in the use of the blue veil, there were, however, other changes necessitated by the different cultural contexts. Let's take for an example how Louise gets into her line of work. In the remake, Louise becomes a nanny because she goes to an agency to get a job. It is offered as a temporary remedy for her situation. In the French version—and this is definitely something that I think American audiences would not have accepted—upon her being released, maybe it was even part of the releasing process, the nurse at the hospital says to Louise, "Well, what are you going to do?" This represents the intervention of a social authority figure, like a doctor or a judge, into her life. The nurse is the one who rather forcefully says, "You should get into nursing," gives her the name of a family, and veritably sets her on her path. Given our highly developed sense of individuality and personal agency, this is not something that would or could have happened in the American film.

CORWIN: I agree. And I kind of like the idea that one gets into a career accidentally. In many cases, serendipity as it were, simple accident, actors become actors out of just a fluke; Rod Steiger was one. Somebody doesn't show up, and they're looking around, and they see somebody in the wings, and they say, "Hey, have you ever acted?" I like the fact that she doesn't start out with the resolve, "My career is going to be that of nursing."

FORREST: Especially since, in the French film, once Louise takes up her first ward, every proposal that's made to her by a man afterward is rejected with, "I have decided to dedicate my life to children" It's as if the role she has assumed divests her of her will and makes her submit to a vow of chastity of sorts.

CORWIN: That certainly conforms to the fascist concept of duty. Yes, that would be deadly. You know, one always has second, third, and fiftieth thoughts, long after something is done, and if I were ruminating about what I would have done differently were it done today, I would give long thought to whether I would make changes. What is your thinking? The American film, does it hold up?

FORREST: It comes off as a very American film. It is American in many respects. In French films there will sometimes be abrupt transitions between scenes or episodes, leaving the spectator to fill in a lot of information. You fill in those blanks, while also creating a greater sense of time, like in the Begley case, where Louise has the opportunity to develop a strong rapport with him over time. And therefore, Mr. Begley's proposal to Louise, far from being impulsive, represents a way to almost naturally fill the gap that was created in his life with the death of his wife. He recognizes this woman's extraordinary qualities. She rejects him, explaining, not as in the French film that she had lost both her husband and her child, but that she understands what loneliness is. She verbalizes something that he has not consciously admitted to himself, and that makes him start thinking. So when the secretary calls, it's as if Louise has put him back on track. It's a wonderful scene.

CORWIN: Also, it's a rebound, somewhat of a disappointment. At least he's attractive to somebody. It pulls him out of that despondency and the sense of rejection.

FORREST: There's a big difference in the last episodes of the two films. In your version, Louise works as a janitor in a schoolhouse. In the French version she ends up in a very nasty household with a caustic, autocratic, elderly woman, her bed-ridden daughter, and the latter's rotten boy and an infant. The grandmother causes Louise to fall down the stairs. It is thanks to this fall that Louise meets the doctor, Gérald, who was once her ward.

CORWIN: He's not an eye doctor in the French version?

FORREST: No, he's a regular doctor.

CORWIN: I have to give myself a good grade for making him an eye doctor because he's looking into the eyes of the woman and he says, "Have I seen you before?" Many, many years have gone by. And that's just what would happen. We always see a lot of people who have gone to medical school and have 500 patients, . . . and she's aged, and so he doesn't get it right away. But looking in her eyes, what better way?

FORREST: This brings me back to the types of changes that are and are not made to the original. There are parallel scenes/shots that exist in both films. There is also sometimes similar dialogue. So your script is often very faithful to the original. Then there will be distinct changes, especially in the aforementioned last episode. As I have said, in *Le Voile bleu*, it is as a result of an accident that Louise meets the doctor, who was once her ward. You rewrite that entire story and remove the Dickensian nastiness of the French episode. How do you account for, on the one hand being very faithful to the original, and then, on the other, totally reconceptualizing and rewriting entire scenes?

CORWIN: What dictated this was my admiration of the good things in the original and my rejection of what I considered improvable, unworkable, or unworthy of the characters. You suggest that what brings her to the doctor is an injury. [But] how much sweeter to look into one's eyes and to recognize something eye to eye. It's the greatest contact there is, you know, eye to eye, beyond touch, beyond God and man, than feeling contact. I brought them face to face, which is what happens when an optician or an optometrist looks in your eyes. The value of that commended itself to me, as well as the logic of "Haven't I seen you before somewhere?" That's happened to you and me in life, and will happen increasingly as we get older. I don't have much leeway, but you do. What was the treatment again of the meeting with the doctor in the French film? He was not an eye man?

FORREST: No. In falling down a flight of stairs, Louise either breaks her shoulder or her arm. She is an elderly woman at this point, so it is a serious accident. She is in a hospital, and when she hears the name of the examining doctor she realizes that he was her old ward, Gérald. If there is any looking into each other's eyes, it is only to facilitate or confirm recognition. But it is not the source of recognition.

CORWIN: Well, you see, there were all kinds of influences, I'm sure, directing me to do what I did. Because there are certain juxtapositions, certain contiguous situations, which are more personal than others, even what might be considered . . . even when the area of examination or exploration are the private parts, there's the need for objectivity in whatever the procedure may be. But looking into one's eyes is different. Let me give you a nice little example of that. It doesn't involve the eyes, but I found myself at the head table of an event in New York City. I was one of the speakers and—I've forgotten what the occasion was—but a woman came over to me, who was also sitting at the head table with her husband. And she rose from her seat and came over to me and introduced herself, and she said, "Do you remember me?" You know, that's an awkward question. You don't want to be rude and say, "No, I don't. Who are you?" But I expressed the proper hesitation. And she said, "We had a somewhat intimate relationship." And I realized that that was leading to some kind of joke, because I knew that there had never been. . . . And she said, "I was your dental hygienist." I mean, she was working on my mouth! And she was in my face! And so, as an eye doctor, of course, there's always a scientific objectivity there—there has to be. As this doctor is looking at Louise's eye, he's seeing its condition, but still, an eye is an eye. It's the window of our emotions, the window of recognition, of identification, and all of that.

FORREST: And both elements work at the same time.

CORWIN: Exactly.

FORREST: Might you have changed the venue in terms of the differing hospital experiences? I mean, the French film has a hospital scene in a large ward. I can't remember offhand how American hospital scenes were depicted in the late forties. Would there have been a big common ward?

CORWIN: It depends on the hospital and the situation. There are many different kinds of hospitals. But a doctor's office is much better. The tendency in a private office is to be more personal. In a ward, there is somebody listening to you in the next bed.

FORREST: You obviously gave a lot of thought to your adaptation of the script, and what you felt would be logical or human, all these qualities that we have been discussing. Do you feel that your version is rather a rewriting?

CORWIN: Yes.

FORREST: It's not the same film?

CORWIN: That's right.

FORREST: As I said earlier, there are a lot of things which are left unexplained in the French film. You, however, fill in the gaps. For example, we never learn in the French film how Louise gets by when she's raising the child whose parents have abandoned him. In the scene where Louise and Daniel move to the country because of his health, they move into a lovely little house, and I wondered where she got the money. In your film, we do; she does piece work, she takes in laundry . . .

CORWIN: One thing I don't understand in the traditional movie, or in many traditional movies, is how people live. Where do they get their money? At least in the whodunits, I mean in the sleuth pictures, we know that the private eye is a private eye.

FORREST: My question relates perhaps to the remake of most French films. In French cinema, there is a tendency to suggest rather than to fully develop certain ideas, to assume that the viewer is going to fill in a lot of the information. So, as in *Le Voile bleu*, a year can go by in which a relationship can develop, and yet we don't see that development. We have to fill in the gaps ourselves. In American films there is a tendency to clearly, if not meticulously, develop a narrative. This is the case in your screenplay. Was this a conscious effort on your part?

CORWIN: I can say, in making a general answer to that, that I am anti-obscurantist. I do not believe in spelling everything out. I believe in enlisting the collaboration of the audience. Not to have to indicate everything to them. But at the same time, I don't respect fancy technical dazzle for the sake of dazzle. My schooling there was my own experience, because I was once guilty of doing dazzle for the sake of dazzle in the early days [of radio]; I was experimenting with a new medium. And there were some capers that I initiated, and enjoyed. But my general approach is to be straightforward, not simplistic. You see, I am at a disadvantage in that I'm still not familiar with the French film, and even if I had the time to go through the whole thing, I would be at a great disadvantage in not understanding much French.

FORREST: I'm sure you've seen other French films, ones that are subtitled, that would allow you to notice the narrational differences between French films and those made in Hollywood.

CORWIN: I don't believe in a standardized structural approach. I don't believe that laws are made to be inflexible. I believe that part of the truly creative process is to learn the law and then break it creatively. And so, to me, each subject has its own demands, and since the content can vary greatly, so can the style. You manufacture a vehicle for a certain need. An automobile has no resemblance to a steamship, which has no resemblance to a space rocket. They have different purposes and missions.

FORREST: I was talking more in terms of cultural expectations and the influence of that culture that makes us Americans and the French French.

CORWIN: We are an amalgamation of all cultures. We, particularly Americans, are like that. Our language is a polyglot language. It draws from every language, thanks to the multiethnic structure and elements of our society, and that's enriching. We have influences that are popular, that are so much with us that we aren't even aware of them, we aren't even conscious of them. Jewish George Gershwin writing *Porgy and Bess*, which has wonderful African-American strands in it. Still notwithstanding the attrition, notwithstanding the downgrading and all the things that can be discouraging to a race or culture, notwithstanding the presence of Gingrich and Dole as important political figures, we're still a puissant, very colorful country, and our culture reflects that.

FORREST: But don't you think that we like to tell stories and hear stories in a certain way? The way we make movies or the way we make television stories, or the way we make any kind of story; there's a certain way of telling a story, for example, how you begin it, how you give information, how you end it. When you watch a French film, the strangeness you feel is not only that of the language, but of the way the French tell a story, too. You recognize that it's not the way that you tell a story, or that it's not the way that you normally hear stories told. In an American remake of a foreign film, that strangeness disappears.

CORWIN: Remaking is a form of acculturation, and this is organically true and natural, as it should be. The one thing I think I am, or would like to be, or hope I am, is a citizen of the world. And I think that's the hope of us all, to be citizens of the world. Parochialism and nationalism are responsible for the insularity that has caused so much bloodshed and agony. "My religion's better than your religion." And, "you're an infidel, I know the truth." And, "we've got to cleanse Bosnia of Bosnians, or of Serbs," or of whatever.

Wendell Willkie had a wonderful idea in his concept of One World. An obvious idea; it goes back to Confucius and other early philosophers. Willkie came back from the trip that he made for F.D.R. during the war.[6] He wrote a book, *One World*, that sold a couple million copies. That struggle undoubtedly will continue. But I do think that there is a great deal to be said for the individuality of the thumb print. There are six billion people and not two of them have the same thumb print. We are unique. And the axis of the world runs right through you, and me. The world revolves around us.

NOTES

[Norman Corwin is best known for his work in radio which began in 1934 with his show "Rhymes and Cadences." Corwin received national and critical attention for his "Plot to Overthrow Christmas" in the series *Words Without Music* at CBS in 1938. His most important radio work, of which he was usually writer, director, and producer, took place during the 1940s. It was the quality of his writing that brought him to the attention of the film industry. His first screenplay was for Curtis Bernhardt's *The Blue Veil*. He also wrote the screenplays for *Scandal at Scourie* (Negulesco, 1953) and *Lust For Life* (Minnelli, 1956), the latter for which he received an Academy Award Nomination. He is a multiple Peabody award winner, as well as a recipient of the Wendell Wilkie Association Award. He was a longtime head of the Documentary Film Committee for the Academy of Motion Picture Arts and Sciences. He currently teaches writing at the Annenburg School of Communications at the University of Southern California.

Le Voile bleu (Stelli, 1942), of which *The Blue Veil* is a remake, was made during the German Occupation of France, and was never distributed in the United States. Norman Corwin's drafts for *The Blue Veil*, therefore, drew solely upon a translation of François Campaux's original screenplay. As Corwin was equally unfamiliar with the historical context of the original's production, the interviewer linked the film's cult of motherhood with the pro-natalist program of the Vichy government, whose National Revolution policies resembled Hitler's. But as Alan Williams proposes in "The Raven and the Nanny: The Remake as Crosscultural Encounter," the film just as easily lends itself to another reading in which the film's moral stance finds the causes for French inability to prevent the Occupation in the absence of family values. While the questions often reflect the former position and determine to some degree the direction of Corwin's responses, it is also evident that, while Corwin's treatment participates in Dr. Spock-era considerations, his preoccupations in developing his characters concerned above all questions of narrative coherence—*eds.*].

This text represents the combining of two interviews that took place on May 15 and September 26, 1995, at Norman Corwin's home in Los Angeles.

1. Norman Krasna was a playwright, screenwriter, producer, and director of the Classic Hollywood period.

2. Jerry Wald was a producer and screenwriter who, in 1950, formed a production company with Norman Krasna.

3. Jerry Wald was not entirely apolitcal. The Committee for the First Amendment was organized by John Huston, William Wyler, and Philip Dunne to support the nineteen writers who had been subpoenaed by the House Un-American Activities Committee: "The committee gathered an impressive collection of supporters: Humphrey Bogart, Rita Hayworth, Katherine Hepburn, Myrna Loy, Groucho Marx, Judy Garland, Frank Sinatra, Gene Kelly, Paulette Goddard, Frederic March, plus a few literary figures like George S. Kaufman and Archibald MacLeish, and even a few of the big producers: Walter Wanger, William Goetz, Jerry Wald" (Friedrich 306). Wald did participate, however reluctantly, in the unofficial blacklisting practices of the late 1940s (Friedrich 382).

4. Dore Schary, producer, screenwriter, playwright, and director, was chief of production at M-G-M from 1948 to 1956.

5. For example, in 1941, Corwin did the Bill of Rights special to commemorate the 150th anniversary of the Bill of Rights. In 1943, he did "America Salutes the President's Birthday Party." And in 1945, his "On a Note of Triumph" celebrated V-J Day.

6. Wendell Willkie Award recipients flew around the world. Corwin's trip resulted in his radio show "One World Flight" (1947).

WORK CITED

Friedrich, Otto. *City of Nets: A Portrait of Hollywood in the 1940s*. New York: Perennial Library, 1986.

APPENDIX B

Norman Corwin Letter to Jerry Wald

Dear Jerry:

I have read your note of April 23rd, and Kurt's of the 24th, and here is mine of the 25th [1951].

I think you are both slightly possessed. We have talked out and fought over and rehashed and plowed under and reconstituted every page of this script, and you both keep coming back to assumptions that were dismissed weeks ago.

First: it is altogether false to say that in the Palfrey episode "we are trying to tell the story of . . . a family so involved with outside activities that they actually fail to spend any time with their own children and allow them to become brats." That is only a PART of the story and NOT the focal point. The focal point is *Louise,* not Robbie, not Harrison, not the Palfreys, not even Kean.

The story we are trying to tell is Louise's last fling at romance—of the tragedy of a near-miss, of a thing that didn't quite come off between her and a young man—of a door which shuts on her life, and confirms her in the way of the Blue Veil. THAT is the story—not one of parental neglect. If you emphasize the aspect of neglect, you are paving the way for one of the most boring yawns ever put on a screen, for you will be repeating yourselves. Don't forget that in the subsequent episodes, the Actress *neglects* her child, (the point of the episode); that in the Tony

---

Material provided by Norman Corwin, from his letters.

337

episode, the parents criminally *neglect* their child (the point of the episode). I think that it is risky enough that we even SUGGEST such neglect in the Palfrey episode.

It is all very easy to say that "left to their own devices, Harrison and Robbie would grow up to be real bums." I am not at all sure. They might grow up to be corporation presidents, because neglect would make them rugged individualists. Robbie, long after Louise goes out of his life, grows up to be an important eye specialist. Harrison died from Anthrax after a galant charge at Bastogne. I see no reason why, with the mild and benign neglect of the Palfreys toward their children, they should grow up to be psychotics or wastrels. I must point out to you that the Palfreys, inspite of Mrs. Palfrey's concern for the dog in the opening scene, DO NEVERTHELESS devote that scene to the discussion of the welfare of their children! I am against the caricature of rich, neglectful people. I am against *all* caricature. These are civilized people, and I reject the notion that when Louise leaves Robbie, the roof falls in and the child is started on the road to the Bowery Mission or the electric chair.

It is the corniest possible construction, and vastly dangerous, to suggest that we dramatize "the need Robbie has for Louise." The better we do that, the more certainly we alienate the sympathy of our audience from Louise. Because, ABOVE ALL LOUISE MUST NOT BE CONSIDERED A SAP FOR COMING BACK TO A ROBBIE WHO, HOWEVER CHARMING AND WINNING, IS LIKE ANY OTHER KID. Far better that she come back because she has nowhere else to go, PLUS her concern for Robbie, than that she cut herself down to soap-opera size by returning to a ward whom the audience KNOWS will be well taken care of no matter what happens within that household. This juncture of the script is potentially highly explosive, because we have something working here that never appears elsewhere; to wit, Louise's free choice as to her destiny. If she gets off that train because of a vision, clear to the audience, that Kean is a weakie, or because she's too great a romantic to want to marry under a cloud of doubt and second-thinking, then she has exercised a mature and understandable judgment, and is strong about it. If she gets off because Robbie means more to her than her own happiness and future, the audience will have every reason to feel, as it did in the French film, that Louise was weak and an *ass* to make the choice she did, that she deserves what happened to her later.

I don't know what is meant by "fuzziness" at the end of the Palfrey episode. To me honesty is never fuzzy, and when Louise comes into that room in the dawn hours, everything is crystal clear, including the prospect before her. Don't forget that we show Robbie on the screen about 1% of the time—less than we do with Stephanie or Tony, and not much more than we do with the Begley infant—and in this time we cannot get a big fire going under our audience about this kid. For Louise to make what will turn out to be the pivotal decision of her life, merely to spend another year or so with this boy, is asking the audience to accept more than I believe the situation justifies.

THE ACTRESS EPISODE: There was, as you may recall, a vast amount of flapdoodle about the reasons for the Actress leaving the company. It was decided, after the most searching consideration of all possible approaches, that the true course lay somewhere in between the old stereotype situations of this sort. In order to make Annie's problem "in trying to fight for her career in the theater" (as Jerry says) sharper than it is, you must go back into the very first treatment I came up with. There are only two reasons a girl fights for such a career—necessity, and vanity. We dismissed the first because you didn't want an economic basis, and we more or less adopted the second, since it had to be established that Annie was not a punk, but had some stature. If we dramatize this any more, it will require not just a few lines but additional pages, and I thought the idea at this point was to cut.

I see there is sentiment afoot for ending the Actress episode in the ice-cream parlor. That is my original treatment, plus a slight modification. Why fight me so hard on these things if you are going to come back to them all the time?

THE LAST EPISODE: I agree that Tony's mother can tell a good deal more about the reasons for her neglect for Tony, than she does at present—but only at the expense of dullness. Nobody really wants a full explanation from this dame, at a moment when so much electricity is generated inside the D.A.'s office. We are not interested in her memoirs or her excuses. We are interested in whether Louise is going to be frustrated again—whether she gets that boy back, or doesn't. You can have the mother try to justify herself if you want, but it will take a nice fat, dull speech at a moment when an express train of emotion should be thundering down the track. Besides, is this not entirely covered, or nearly so, in the scenes between Frank and Louise? That's what those scenes are mainly FOR.

I have no objection to reshaping and rewriting and reconstituting lines, scenes or pages—you have certainly found me cooperative all the way through on this score—but I object to anything which, in my view, tends to water-down, weaken, or follow a gravitational pull toward the cliché. I have too much respect for the combined judgments of us all to believe that you started cameras turning on this script before we were pretty well satisfied in our minds that the main points of character, motivation and logic had been settled. I believe that the experience on the stages so far, and the excellent results on the screen, indicate no flaw in these departments. The only time we seem to have got into trouble has been in fragmentary, minor departures from the script. Like the "Ready for breakfast" line.

Also, I feel I should point out that an arbitrary shift in a specified time relationship in the hospital scene, has opened us up to possible grave criticism, and even maybe laughs from mothers in our audience—the vast majority of whom have had babies in hospitals under these very circumstances. The point is that mothers are washed and fed in the morning before their babies are brought to them for feeding. We skip this. I understand why Kurt made the change—for the sake of brisk activity in the morning—but in doing so we have run smack into a big technical inaccuracy in the first moments of our film. Without claiming the slightest sanctity or privilege for anything I've written, I think one should approach the change of words or details in a thoughtfully-written script with the same kind of caution and care that one should approach altering notes or phrases in a thoughtfully-written piece of music. I mean this in no way to modify my feeling that Kurt is translating the script into film with a skill and artistry that transcends my highest hopes and expectations. Such is the case, and I feel lucky he is at the helm. I simply rise to suggest caution for safety's sake on all changes.

I will be glad to hear any and all rebuttal. The defense rests.

N.C.

CONTRIBUTORS

CAROLYN A. DURHAM is Inez K. Gaylord Professor of French at the College of Wooster in Ohio, where she also teaches in the Comparative Literature and Women's Studies Programs. She is the author of *The Contexture of Feminism: Marie Cardinal and Multicultural Literacy, Double Takes: Culture and Gender in French Films and Their American Remakes*, and of numerous articles on the modern novel and on film.

JENNIFER FORREST is associate professor of French at Southwest Texas State University, where she also teaches film in the Honors Program. She is the author of articles on late-nineteenth-century French literature and popular culture. She is currently working on a book-length study of the late-nineteenth-century circus in French literature, art, and popular culture.

LAURA GRINDSTAFF is assistant professor of Sociology and a member of the Graduate Group in Cultural Studies at the University of California, Davis. Her areas of expertise are media and popular culture, feminist theory, film theory, and ethnography and fieldwork. She has a book forthcoming with the University of Chicago Press on daytime television talk shows, and is currently coauthoring a book on cheerleading.

MICHAEL HARNEY is associate professor of Spanish and Portuguese and director of the Comparative Literature program at the University of Texas at Austin. He is the author of *Kinship and Polity in the "Poema de mio Cid," Kinship and Marriage in Medieval Spanish Chivalry*, a film article "Mythogenesis of the Superhero," and other articles on the social and cultural history of literature.

LEONARD R. KOOS is associate professor of French at Mary Washington College. He has most recently published on decadence, French colonial literature, postmodern detective fiction, and contemporary French immigrant fiction and film. His articles have appeared in journals including *Studies in Twentieth-Century Literature, LIT: Literature, Interpretation, Theory,* and *French Literature Series,* and in the essay collections *Images of the City in Nineteenth-Century France, Perennial Decay: On the Aesthetics and Politics of Decadence,* and *Forty Years of the French Republic: Actions, Dialogues, and Discourses.* He is currently writing a book on French colonial literature in nineteenth-century North Africa.

THOMAS LEITCH is professor of English and director of the Film Studies Program at the University of Delaware. His most recent books are *The Alfred Hitchcock Encyclopedia* and the forthcoming *Crime Films.*

MARTY ROTH is a professor of American literature at the University of Minnesota. He has published regularly in the areas of American literature, Hollywood film, and cultural studies in intoxication and addiction. He is just completing a cultural history of intoxication.

TRICIA WELSCH is associate professor and chair of Film Studies at Bowdoin College. Her work has appeared in numerous journals, including *Film Quarterly, Journal of Film and Video, Griffithiana, Film Criticism,* and *Cinema Journal.* She is currently writing a book on Fox Films before the company's merger with Twentieth Century in 1935. She is a passionate devotee of the silent cinema.

ALAN WILLIAMS is a professor of French and Cinema Studies at Rutgers University. He is the author of *Republic of Images: A History of French Filmmaking,* and has edited an anthology, *Film and Nationalism,* which is forthcoming. He is also the author of a series of influential articles on film sound.

FILM TITLE INDEX

NAME AND SUBJECT
INDEX

genre *(continued)*
101, 169, 176, 178, 182, 188,
199nn. 20, 23, 220n. 9;
melodrama, good-bad girl, 157,
167n. 6, 178, 182, 183, 192–93
(*see also* women; "good" wartime;
"bad" wartime); musical, 3, 4, 5, 9,
21, 57, 101, 174, 176, 178, 182,
227, 316; political paranoia film,
285; romance, 9, 57–58, 64, 216;
romance, family, 56, 260;
romance, international, 56;
science-fiction, 77, 79, 183,
226–27; screwball comedy,
230–31; tech-*noir*, 274, 287, 290,
298, 303, 304n. 5; thriller, 64, 67,
216; Western, 2, 3, 4, 7, 9, 46, 57,
71, 77, 101, 177, 268n. 5;
woman's film, 160, 161, 162, 163.
See also early cinema genres
Gere, Richard, 80
German expressionist cinema, 49,
141, 142, 219n. 3, 283
Gershwin, George, 334
Getaway, The (book), 65
Getz, John, 232
Gilou, Thomas, 221n. 12
Giraud, Roland, 246
Giraudoux, Jean, 59n. 1, 152
Godard, Jean-Luc, 27, 48, 56, 274
Goldblum, Jeff, 230
Goldwyn, Samuel, 160
Gone with the Wind (book), 65
Green, Alfred E., 182, 199n. 22
Griffith, David Wark, 17, 19, 109
Grundrisse, Die (book), 69
Gunning, Tom, 90, 107, 113, 198n.
11
Guttenberg, Steve, 245

Hadley, Edwin J., 104
Halberstam, Judith, 300

Hamlet (play), 45
Hammett, Dashiell, 3
Hansen, Miriam, 98, 118n. 26
Harlow, Jean, 170, 198n. 12
Harper Brothers, 108–10
Harper Bros. et al. v. Kalem Co. et al.
(1909), 108–10
Harper Bros. et al. v. Klaw et al.
(1916), 109, 112
Hartmann, Susan, 174, 185, 200n. 24
Harvey, Sylvia, 146n. 19, 292
Haskell, Molly, 200n. 26
Havez, Jean, 122n. 44
Hawks, Howard, 5, 6, 9, 21, 22, 31n.
6, 39–40, 42, 49, 157, 174, 230
Hawthorne, Nathaniel, 237
Haydn, Richard, 4
Haynes, Todd, 290
Hayworth, Rita, 4, 169, 174, 178,
192, 198n. 15
Hedison, Al, 230
Hemingway, Ernest, 68
Hepworth, Cecil, 111
Herzog, Werner, 29, 47
Hirsch, E. D., 58
Hitchcock, Alfred, 21, 22, 39, 42, 48,
49, 59n. 3, 65, 213, 274, 277,
285, 302
Hitler, Adolph, 323, 327, 335
Hollywood Production Code. *See*
censorship
Holm, Celeste, 253
homage. *See* remakes
Hong Kong cinema, 26, 273, 280,
286, 288, 295, 298
Hooper, Tobe, 42
horror film. *See* genre
Horton, Andrew, 30, 270
House of the Seven Gables, The (book),
49, 56
House Un-American Activities
Committee, 198n. 17, 336n. 3

Ladd, Alan, 4, 191
Lakeoff, Robin, 278
Landers, Lew, 32n. 6
Lane, Edward, 5
Lang, Fritz, 3, 4, 9, 21, 127–30,
    135–43, 143n. 1, 144nn. 4, 5, 6,
    145n. 13, 146nn. 19, 21, 22, 23,
    24, 147n. 25, 166n. 3, 199n. 18;
    Diana Productions, 128, 142,
    144n. 6
Lang, Walter, 4
Lange, Jessica, 51
Langlois, Henri, 22
Laughton, Charles, 5, 310, 313
Laura, Ernesto, 234
Lauzier, Gérard, 7
Lawrence, Amy, 197n. 11
Le Bargy, Charles, 33n. 15
Leconte, Patrice, 204, 205, 213,
    216–18, 221n. 12
Leder, Mimi, 33n. 20
Léger, Charles, 38
Leitch, Thomas, 127, 144n. 7, 276,
    289
Leites, Nathan, 157, 167n. 6
Lepetit, Jean-François, 258
Leroy, Mervyn, 5, 170
Lester, Richard, 47
Levine, Lawrence, 119n. 31, 278
Levy, David, 97, 111, 115n. 12,
    117n. 21
Lewis, Philip, 295
Lewton, Val, 238n. 7
Limbacher, James L., 30
Linker, Kate, 227
literary works. *See* adaptation;
    remakes
Litvak, Anatole, 8, 9
Lloyd, Christopher, 230
Locke, John, 277
Lorre, Peter, 219n. 3
Lovejoy, Frank, 316

Loy, Myrna, 191
Lubin, Sigmund, 94, 96, 111, 116n.
    13, 117n. 22
Lubitsch, Ernst, 31n. 3, 128
Lumière, Auguste and Louis, 89, 90,
    95, 98, 111, 114n. 2, 118n. 25,
    203–4, 218n. 2; cinematographe
    (camera), 90, 203, 204

MacDonald, David, 60n. 5
Macek, Carl, 200n. 25
Macgowan, Kenneth, 31n. 2, 196n. 5
MacMurray, Fred, 51, 52
MacRory, Pauline, 295, 297
Mahin, John Lee, 170
Maisie (film series), 170
Mallarmé, Stéphane, 68
Malory, Sir Thomas, 68
Maltby, Richard, 11
Maltese Falcon, The (book), 39
Mamet, David, 51
Mancini, Marc, 268n. 2
"Manifeste des sept arts, Le," 33n. 15
Mann, Michael, 38, 60n. 9
Mann, Thomas, 68
Mannoni, Octave, 53
Marble Faun, The (book), 237
Marder, Elissa, 288
Marèse, Janie, 132, 145n. 14
Marshall, George, 191
Marion, Frank J., 99
Martin, Tony, 218n. 3
Marx, Karl, 69
Marxism, 15, 71, 166, 279–80
M*A*S*H (television series), 299
Maslin, Janet, 33n. 19
Masson, Alain, 65
Maugham, W. Somerset, 177, 196n.
    1
Mayer, Louis B., 198n. 13, 315
Mayo, Virginia, 191
Mazursky, Paul, 2

184, 185, 190, 196n. 1, 200n. 25,
317, 322, 323, 327
Writer's Guild, The, 318, 319
Wuthering Heights (book), 49, 56
Wyatt Earp legend, 80
Wyler, William, 170, 182, 336n. 3
Wyman, Jane, 152, 309–10, 313
Wynter, Dana, 234

X-Files, The (television series), 274
X Men (comic book series), 274

Yeltsin, Boris, 286
Young, Josh, 27
Youngson, Robert, 48
Youthful Deeds of the Cid, The (book),
77
Yugoslavian cinema, 26

Zanuck, Darryl, 156, 157, 160
Zeferelli, Franco, 45
Zemeckis, Robert, 230
Zidi, Claude, 64